THE
FINELY FITTED YACHT

Ferenc Maté

ILLUSTRATED BY

Candace Maté

ALBATROSS PUBLISHING HOUSE

vancouver bc canada

Other Books
By

Ferenc Maté

"FROM A BARE HULL"
An Encyclopedia of Boatbuilding

"WATERHOUSES"
Houseboats and Floating Homes

THE
FINELY FITTED YACHT

BY

Ferenc Maté

ILLUSTRATED BY

Candace Maté

PHOTOGRAPHED BY THE AUTHOR.

Volume I Interior

137   illustrations
62   photographs

DISTRIBUTED IN THE U.S. BY W.W. NORTON
500 FIFTH AVENUE, NEW YORK

To Susan and Eric Hiscock,
for their inspiration

Philosophically

There is little joy in creating junk. Boats live a long time and so do people, and so does the spark of pride in a lovingly crafted piece of wood or canvas. Have patience, enjoy every step. You may never get the chance to do it again.

Specifically

Start big. Begin with the project that requires the largest piece of material and you'll definitely be safe, for then if you miscut or misdrill or misthink, you can always pretend that you were actually working on the next size down object in the first place, and you wanted a smaller piece of whatever anyway, and you're not *really* as big-a-stupid as the puzzled onlookers think you are.

Of course, there are limits. If you began with a piece for the boom gallows, and ended up with eight pounds of teak toothpicks, stop and reflect, then yank out a chunk of old line, and just tie the bloody boom to the backstay. . . . Stupid.

Generally

I'm not familiar with every skylight, dinghy chock or awning in the whole wide world. As a matter of fact, I have an acquaintance with only a few of each, so by no means does this book contain *the ultimates*. But all things in it have been tested, or built, or at least dreamt about thoroughly, and within those limits they all worked. . . . More or less.

Thankfully

Our thanks to the many kind people, from Antigua to Hawaii, whose yachts we invaded with cameras and notebooks and tape measures.

Our gratitude to Jean Koefed of Charles Scribner's Sons and Eric Swenson of W.W. Norton, and the gracious people at Princeton Tools, Detco Marine, Garrett Wade Company, Leichtung Tools, The Adjustable Clamp Company, Faire Harbour Ltd. and Spyglass Catalogue for their help and photographs.

TABLE OF CONTENTS

SECTION I: GALLEY

SECTION II: HEAD

SECTION III: CHART TABLE AND NAVIGATION

SECTION IV: SALON

SECTION V: LAMPS AND STOVES

SECTION VI: ENGINE ROOM

SECTION VII: STOWAGE

SECTION VIII: BIBELOTS

galley

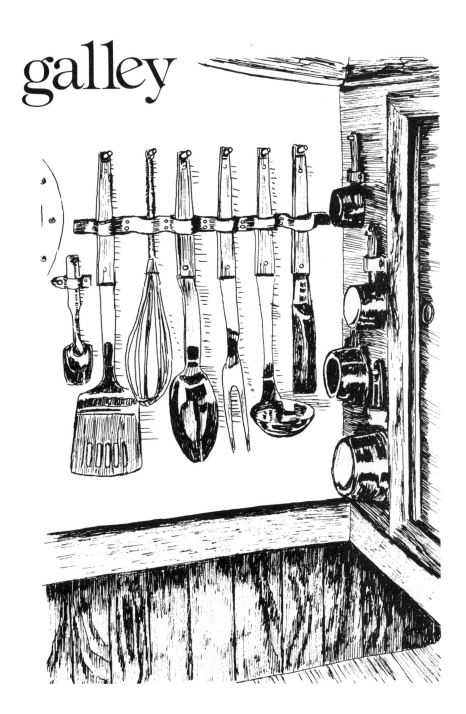

SINK BOARD WITH DRAIN TRAY

Since chopping boards are rather a pain to stow aboard a yacht at the best of times, perhaps the best solution is to have one fitted over the sink where it: a) will provide extra counter space, and b) can be stowed when the sink is not in use. For chopping board construction, see section under that name. One special caution should be taken, however; only long strips of wood should be used for this operation, since the board will be supported only at its edges, unlike a standard board which is evenly supported on a counter top.

So make your chopping board as you wish, leaving a 1″ overhang all around the sink. Next, you'll have to devise a way to keep it from sliding about. Two methods can be used: a) for 1″ or thinner boards, run an open corner frame of cleat stock around the bottom of the board, so it will fit reasonably tightly into the sink. I mentioned open corners, for most sinks have theirs generously radiused, and the effort spent trying to get your cleat stock modified to accommodate that radius would be totally wasted, and b) for 1½″ or thicker boards, a more difficult, but aesthetically pleasing, job can be done by rabbeting (with two cuts of the table saw) a 3/4″ × 1″ rabbet into the lower edges, so part of the board will slip into the sink and act as its own restrainer. Once the cutting has been done, you will have to rasp away the corners to suit the radius of the sink, but this should pose no more than ten minute's work. It may behoove you to rasp a dimple into the leftover lower edge on all four sides, so a finger can slip under the board for lifting. Of course, if you don't mind stripping your fingernails from your fingertips, don't bother with this detail.

The acutely aware will recognize the need to relocate the board when the sink is to be used. The best place, of course, is right next to the sink, upside down, where it can be used as a drainboard for dishes. To make this drainboard leak-proof in the simplest way possible, trot down to your corner supermarket or hardware store and purchase a little plastic container (the largest that will slip into the sink upside down), then trot home and attach it with epoxy or plastic container attacher to the bottom of your chopping board.

Voilà. A perfect little drain tray and an impeccable bath tub for midgets.

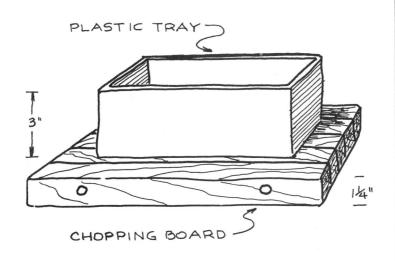

PLASTIC TRAY

3"

1¼"

CHOPPING BOARD

SINK BOARD WITH DRAIN TRAY

COOKWARE STOWAGE

I think it of vital importance that the ship's cook be kept as happy and complacent as possible, for few things are less appetizing than a bitchy cook stirring sock-stew in his cauldron. To this end, all cooking gear should be exposed and readily accessible, but *noise free*. An attempt should be made to purchase a set of cookware with similar size holes in the handles to eliminate the need for reaming and other such nonsensical modifications. When all possible gear has been gathered (including the fine little measuring pots), determine the amount of space you will need for the whole show, and mark in the locations for the 1/4″ dowels to be used as hooks. These will be inserted as in the "Pot Rack." One difference here is that no more than 3/4″ of dowel can be allowed to protrude, for any more length will not allow the utensils (limited in movement by the fixed leather strapping) to slip over the long pegs and into place.

Be sure to take the same precautions as mentioned in the "Pot Rack" section regarding thin bulkheads and cabinsides. If the cabinside is the only resort, and it is made of unreinforced ultra-thin fiberglass, cut a length of 1″ × 3/8″ by whatever length stock, insert and glue the dowels into it, and then epoxy that to the cabinside.

Next, cut a length of 1″ wide leather strapping, about one and a half times the length of the row of utensils. A nice old leather belt will do just fine here. Tack one end down past the first utensil, loop it somewhat loosely over it, then tack down, and so on. If you have a thin cabinside, cut another piece of stock, same width and length you need to mount the pegs, epoxy it to the cabinside, and drive your tacks into this. Be sure you place your strapping no lower than 4″ from the top of the handle, or you will require entirely too much unobstructed space below your tools for maneuvering.

If all this gleaming hardware doesn't make cooky happy, throw the bugger overboard.

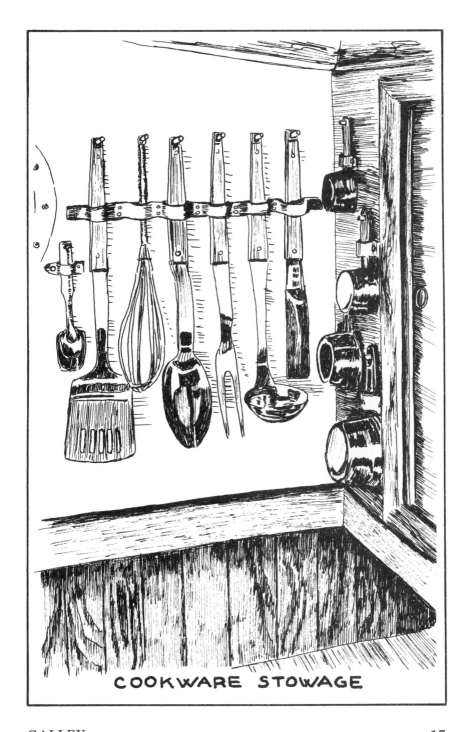

COOKWARE STOWAGE

CUTLERY RACK

No proper yacht would have loose cutlery beating itself to death in a drawer. Drawer space is a precious commodity in any galley and should be saved to store ugly things like spatulas and rubber bands. Tasteful eating tools should have a rack of their own where they will be: a) removable with one hand, and b) tight and quiet. This rack should be of modest size. Contemplating something like grandma's silver set case with each fork in its own velvet nook is an absurdity. Cutlery for six need not have a case larger than $7'' \times 7'' \times 3\frac{1}{2}''$ if the cutlery is sensibly selected, that is, one with modest curvature. One-quarter-inch solid stock should be used for all sides and interior baffles, while a single piece of $1\frac{1}{2}''$ stock $1/2''$ narrower than the exterior width of the rack will do for knife stowage.

The inside compartmentalization should involve four spaces plus the knife block: $1\frac{1}{2}''$ for six spoons, $1\frac{1}{4}''$ for six teaspoons, $1\frac{1}{4}''$ for salad forks, and $1\frac{1}{2}''$ for dinner forks. The remaining width will be consumed by the baffles and the two sides. The $1\frac{1}{2}''$ stock for the knives should have slits cut on $3/4''$ centres. Mark slits wide enough to house the knife blades and part of the handles as well. In a $7''$ high rack, you should have no difficulty immersing at least $3/4$ of the average knife.

Since delicate $1/4''$ stock is being used, it would be prudent to let in and glue all the pieces instead of using brass tacks or screws and plugs. Again, as in all box construction, the face should completely cover the edges of the sides. You will find it advantageous to designate the two central compartments for the short tools (salad forks and teaspoons), and then cut a semi-circular piece out of the face to allow finger access to these mostly submersed pieces. The bottom piece must have at least one drain hole per compartment to facilitate cleaning.

Mount it in any available area in the galley, making sure adequate space exists above for smooth removal, especially of the long knives. We made the mistake of mounting ours too close to our brass chronometer and have suffered numerous hairline scratches on the brass ring as a consequence.

If mounting screws can be inserted from behind, by all means attempt it, for it will save marring the teak face with plugs.

KNIFE
SLOTS

1/4"
DRAIN
HOLES
FOR
CLEANING

1/4"
BAFFLES,
SIDES
AND FRONT

PLAN VIEW

CUTLERY RACK

SPICE RACK

Any vessel used even only a few weeks a year, should have its own spices and its own spice rack. Hauling spices back and forth from house to boat and back again is usually self-defeating, for not only will you forget the spice you need the most, but the odd shapes and sizes of the containers will create a noisy and unsightly mess in galley lockers.

Once the number of spices required has been decided upon, a set of containers must be found. Tin cans are out of the question: they rust within weeks. Honed out wood containers are nice, but few woods are transparent and great amounts of time will be spent label reading — hardly a pleasant occupation in a seaway. That leaves glass spice jars. They can be obtained of heavy glass, with fine plastic lined stoppers, at the reasonable cost of fifty cents each, unfortunately full only of air. Full of spices of various colors and texture, they are extremely appetizing. The jars are usually 1½" in diameter and 4" in height, including the stopper. A marvelously simple and appealing rack can be constructed out of four pieces of wood and a piece of heavy fishing line.

Determine the length of the rack by the number of jars you will need, and rip a piece of 13/16" stock to that length by a 2½" width. Rip another piece to the same length, but a 3½" width. This piece will be the back of the rack and will allow 1/2" of the jars stoppers to protrude for easy handling. Cut the end pieces to a 2½" width by a 4¼" height, cutting off the top corners, or radiusing them, to reduce visual severity and awkwardness. Glue and screw the back piece onto the shelf. With an extremely fine drill bit, drill a hole in one end piece about 1/4" in from the face and 2½" from the bottom. Countersink this very slightly on the outside with a slightly larger drill bit. For the other end piece, secure a tuning peg from a ukulele and drill a hole in the end piece the size of its shank. Fix the end piece in place with glue and screws. Next, fetch a length of heavy gauge fishing line and tie a tidy knot in one end, then thread it through the small hole of one end piece and out the shank hole (via a perpendicularly drilled hole) of the other end piece. Wrap a few turns of line onto the tuning peg, make fast, and cut off the rest. Insert the peg in the hole and twist to a tune of G Major. Secure the rack to a bulkhead or cabinet with three staggered screws. Pop the little jars in place. Lovely.

THE FINELY FITTED YACHT

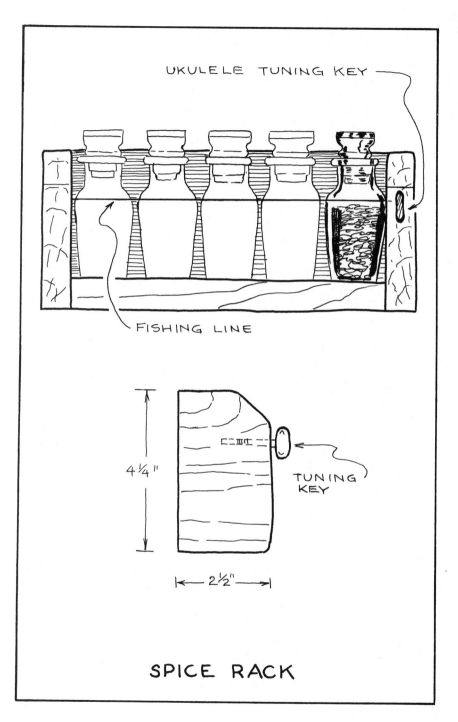

UKULELE TUNING KEY

FISHING LINE

4 ¼ "

2 ½ "

TUNING KEY

SPICE RACK

PAPER TOWEL RACK

Possibly no other expendable item is expended in as great a quantity as paper towels. Now, it is quite probable that I'm measurably neurotic who's constantly cleaning, wiping, dusting and mopping, but even if one was only half as neurotic as I, using merely half the amount of towels, the quantity would still be quite astounding. For this reason, I feel paper towels require a well thought out, well located holder of their own. The holders fall into two general varieties: exposed and discreet.

Exposed

These are close kin to the store-bought plastic ones, but infinitely more decorative. Cut 3/4″ stock to a roughly 4″ × 4″ piece, drastically radiusing the front corners. Bullnose all but the back edges. Cut a piece of 1/2″ dowel to a length of 13″ (most paper towels come in 11″ rolls). In the centre of the radiused front, drill a 5/8″ hole to a depth of 3/8″. On the inside of the other piece rout a 1/2″ wide and 3/8″ deep reverse "J". See diagram. This will enable you to have the two end pieces fixed, and have fresh rolls easily dropped in from the top with the dowel the only moving part. Attaching the towel rack can be performed at this stage, if the bulkhead, cabinet, or whatever has access from the rear. You can drill pilot holes from the front, positioning your two end pieces in place, and drill and screw from the back. If no rear access exists, a back will have to be made of 1/4″ solid wood onto which the ends can be mounted, then this, in turn, can be screwed to bulkhead, etc. It seems the three major towel consuming centres are the galley, the engine room, and the cockpit, therefore, location near the companionway would be desirable.

Discreet

For those who do not find a roll of paper particularly decorative, a simple dispenser type system exists. This involves cutting a 1/4″ × 12″ slit in the face of any cabinet or bulkhead, behind which an accessible 6″ × 6″ × 12″ space exists. (Paper towel rolls are usually of 5″ diameter.) Simply dropping the roll in place and feeding it through the slot will not be sufficient. You will have to have a dowel axle system. A hole in the bottom of the cupboard will seat the dowel while a deeper hole in the top will let you slip it up and then down into place. If the space is not of appropriate size, a store-bought plastic holder will do nicely here.

PAPER TOWEL RACK

THE PROPER PUMP

Well now. Let's roll up the shirt sleeves, clench the fists and start swinging, for I'm sure little will be accomplished by reasoning about pumps, for all of you have your favourite one that you cuddle and cherish. But when it snorts and burps and sputters and comes apart in your loving hands, you'll be happy you have read the following.

Very few of the mobile home conversion pumps, which many small boat manufacturers insist upon, have any long-lasting value. My niece's doll house has better built equipment. First of all, these pumps had a poor upbringing: they spit. The water from them does not flow, it comes in restless little ejaculations and even that, only after one nervously whips the delicate little handle back and forth a few dozen times. But heaven forbid thirst at sea, for the delicate little handle was designed to be used with perfect muscle and weight control, so the slightest lurch or shifting that places more than 18 ounces of pressure on the little jewel will result in its becoming a chromed pretzel.

Electrical pumps are cute and funny. You haven't really laughed until you've seen the owner of a $100,000 floating palace lying on his belly sucking water out of his tanks after the cute electric motor has given up the ghost.

Foot pumps are great as long as they're out of the way, like in a drawer or in the basement.

Now for the real pumps. Nothing in the world can replace the old-fashioned draw pump. Various designs have been used for hundreds of years, drawing jillions of gallons of water in their lifetimes. The Romans used it, the Arabs used it, the Italians still use it, so who are you to snub it? Most are built like cannons, heavy brass that's hard to bend and harder to break, and also hard to pump, but then two pumpings will fill the largest tea mug. The handles swivel 180° to accommodate right or left handers; they come beautifully chromed or irresistably polished with large solid knobs that fit snugly in your palms, and the insides are all brass, and they never need priming, and they never bend, never stick and never break, and ours have worked flawlessly for three years, one in the head and one in the galley and one in a little lighted niche for daily adoration.

THE PROPER PUMP

HINGED COUNTER

A very simple and fine solution for adding working surface to a galley without cutting permanently into any walking areas, is the addition of a small fold-down table to the end of a counter. Granted, it will not have the strength and usability of a fixed cabinet, but it will be a great help during food preparation when a place is needed to put a pot while a stove is lit or icebox lid opened.

The hinged counter in its simplest form can be a piece of 1/2″ plywood, painted, oiled or varnished, and trimmed with 1/2″ teak or mahogany. If the counter is to open into a fore-and-aft passageway, one would be wise to reach a compromise in design to allow a person to at least squeak by the open counter, if absolutely necessary. A counter I've seen that, in use, completely blocked a passageway was eventually ripped out by the owner because he got sick and tired of crawling under it. For support, the store-bought collapsible metal arms will do nicely (brass would look the best) unless one wants to save money and fabricate a hinged plywood knee (see seat for "Forepeak Desk Conversion"). In either case, the trim must be run about one inch past the bottom edge of the plywood to create a space for stowing the hinged support. I can see no need for fiddles on the counter top, for I very much doubt that anyone would undertake a meal at sea elaborate enough to require the additional counter space. The trim should be cut on 45° corners, glued, and screwed to the plywood with #8 P.H.S.M. screws and plugged. If desired, brass tacks can be substituted to save time. Round the corners of the trim generously. Affix a barrel bolt to the cabinet face, and drill a corresponding hole in the edge of the hinged counter to keep it from swinging when folded down. If nothing else, it will make a perfect little shelf for a vase.

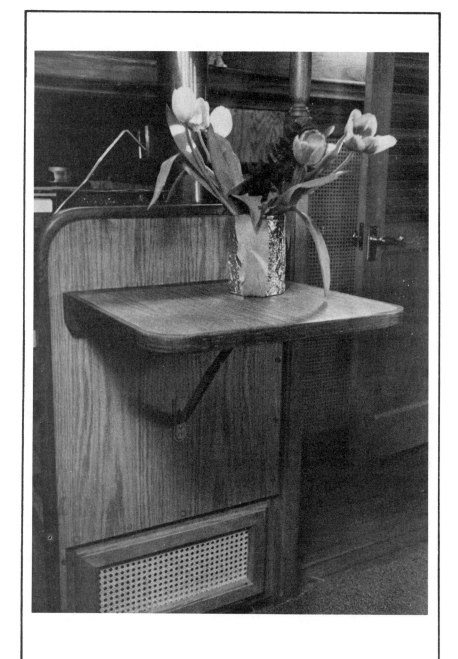

HINGED COUNTER

POT HOLES

Why would anyone in his right mind want pot holes in his boat, you ask. The answer is simple: to keep pots in, of course. The source of this most ingenious idea is again Susan and Eric Hiscock, who have, aboard *Wanderer IV*, more pot holes than all of Tijuana's roads combined. They are very close to being the perfect solution to pot stowage — enabling removal of any single pot without disturbing others, eliminating the possibility of any rattling and clanging at sea, and being extremely simple to construct and adapt to any vessel's cabinetry. Beyond all that, they have one great advantage over any other pot stowage method I can think of, in that the lid to each pot can be stowed *in* the pot, again eliminating endless digging and searching through some bottomless pit. When at sea, the lids can be stowed upside down in the pots to lower their center of gravity and make less likely their escape.

Into most above-counter cabinets, at least two shelves of holes can be installed. The pots having the largest surfaces should be on the top shelf where the curvature of the hull usually allows more room.

Rough cut 1/2" sheets of plywood to fit, then lay out all your pots and pans and arrange them in the most economical order. Don't forget to leave space for the handles in such a fashion that they will be readily accessible. Draw in the shape of each pot and cut out the hole with a jigsaw very accurately, remembering that any overcutting will result in irritating rattles under way. Very shallow pots, like frying pans, whose handles prevent them from slipping into a hole to sufficient depth will require the fabrication of chocks, the height of which will be determined by the lip. Three short ones will do. Install these to make a very snug fit. Round the edges of the holes with sandpaper to prevent splintering. Next, lay out the position of the shelves inside the cabinet and install either 3/4" cleat stock or quarter-round as shelf supports. Glue and screw them into place. Sand all edges of the shelves, then screw the shelves onto the cleats. Do not use glue here, for you may one day get sick of your current pots or you may one day lose some of them overboard and logic tells me that it would be infinitely easier to make new holes for the new pots, than to hammer a pot to fit properly into the old holes.

POT HOLES

POT HOLDERS

Pots and pans in cupboards take up vast amounts of valuable space and make much noise. Every effort should be made to relocate them onto a bulkhead, where they can hang out of the way with the counterspace below them still fruitfully utilized. Of course, if your pots are ugly, forget this suggestion and store the damned things in the bilge.

Decorative copper-bottomed pots are not all that costly, and with a bit of regular polishing they look splendid on any yacht.

If your pots have no metal loops at the ends of the handles, you will have to drill an eighth-inch hole and fabricate a leather loop yourself.

Arrange your pots in order of size, and mark the end of the loop of each on the bulkhead. In aligning them, it is best to use a centreline through the middle of the pots. Lining up tops or bottoms tends to look less balanced.

At each mark on the bulkhead, drill a 1/4" hole downward at 45°. Drill about 3/4" deep, bulkhead permitting. Next, cut 1/4" dowel stock into 1¾" lengths. Round the fresh edges with sandpaper, then glue them into the holes. Try to have even lengths protruding.

From soft leather, cut one 1¼" × 5½" strip per pot. Trim the corners to a radius — it looks more civilized. Have a canvas shop insert grommets (or do it yourself if you have a grommet press) for twist-locks at one end of the strap. Install the straps on the bulkhead at the base of the handle with a single screw. Be sure to use a finish washer. It looks better, and it will keep the leather from ripping out. Attach the twist end of the twist-lock to the bulkhead in a position where firm tension will be placed on the straps. Your pots will remain silent in even the roughest seas.

Just keep those bottoms gleaming.

THE FINELY FITTED YACHT

POT HOLDERS

KNIFE BLOCK

Those most circumspect will realize that I call this a knife *block*, and not a "rack". A knife rack, which somehow grips the handles and allows the sadistic little blades to whirl about at sea, has no place on a boat. The blades should be fully sheathed and securely pinched so they remain benign carving tools.

The simplest method of construction involves one piece of 2″ X 6″ or 2″ X 4″ (depending on how many knives you want to stow). The length of wood required is twice the length of the longest blade, plus an inch.

Thus, step one is to buy the knives. No way on earth can you hope to make a perfectly fitting block for an imaginary set. Blade length and thickness will determine all measurements.

Try to buy a set that will: a) last, and b) be easily replaceable in case a member of the first set decides to dive into the sea. Nothing is more difficult to remodel than a knife block. Except maybe a needle.

Without cutting the piece of board into two halves, secure the thinnest table saw blade possible, and cut the slits for each knife with the saw blade set at *half* the depth of the widest part of the specific knife blade. Be sure to cut the groove to the exact depth, otherwise the blades will wander about in a rolling or pitching boat and irritatingly dull themselves.

Once grooved, cut the board into two equal pieces and mate them, like closing a book. Your grooves will be perfectly aligned. Now, drill four holes between the grooves (from the back so that the holes won't show), and glue and screw the halves together. Bullnose the edges of the front and top. Next, drill two mounting screw holes from the front, and countersink them judiciously. If you're setting the block on a countertop, place a bead of silicone around the perimeter of the bottom to prevent a stagnant pool of water from forming beneath.

The location is obvious. Leave enough room above to allow removal of the longest knife. A narrow part of the counter that's unusable as a working surface would be an ideal spot. The block is more suited to sit on something anyway, so its bulk will be reduced visually.

Try to mount it athwartships. If mounted fore and aft, the rolling of the boat may cause the heavy handles to pendulum with the blades hacking the block on every roll. Galley knives are not for wood chopping.

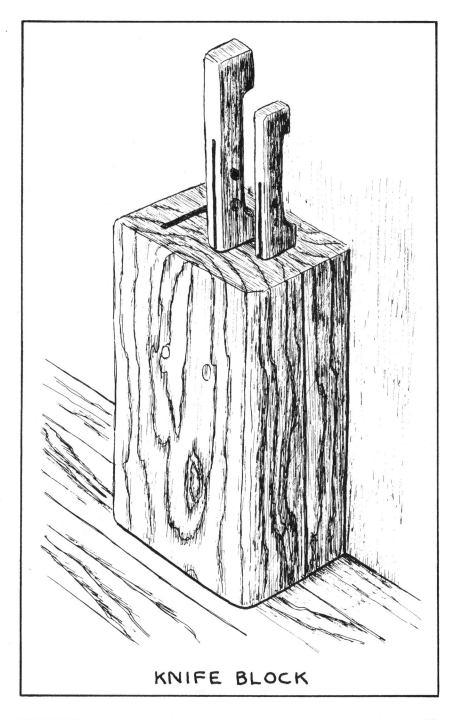

KNIFE BLOCK

TOASTER

Having gone through a number of store-bought, stove top toasters made of landlubber tin that rusts at the first whiff of salt air, and little stainless steel ones that toast one pathetic side of two flimsy pieces of bread at one time, I've been forced to design one of my own.

This one can be made of either stainless or brass sheeting of a fairly light gauge, and brass or copper wire of about 8 or 10 gauge.

It will very nicely toast one side of five pieces of bread at one time to a fine, even hue.

First, cut the sheeting to the shape shown, making the width of the base roughly the same as the diameter of your burner. Then draw concentric circles, spaced about 3/4″ apart, onto each half of the base plate. *But* stagger the radiuses from one plate to another, i.e. if the largest radius on your bottom plate is say 2 5/8″, then make the largest radius of your top plate 2¼″ (a reduction of one-half of the 3/4″ spacing). This is done to get the heat to circulate a bit between the two plates so that it will be fairly even by the time it reaches the toast. Now drill 1/16″ holes every half inch along each circle. Stagger these as well from bottom plate to top plate. Drill your screw holes as well for assembling the base, then bend the plates along the dotted line to 90°, but leave closing the jaws (bringing the two plates together) until later when you've bent the support wires into place. Actually, you should do that right now. Bend four pieces of the wire to the dimensions in the diagram, then slip them into the drilled holes and bend the last 3/4″ under sharply, as shown. Now pull them all together tightly, and join them in the upper corners with short bits of wire.

Lastly, pull the jaws together and secure them with #8 P.H.S.M. screws through the six screw holes indicated.

Not only will this unit toast your bread very efficiently, but after a few hours of heat, the metal will turn all sorts of beautiful colours.

Oh yes, the fifth piece of toast is laid over the tops of the four standing ones like a house of cards.

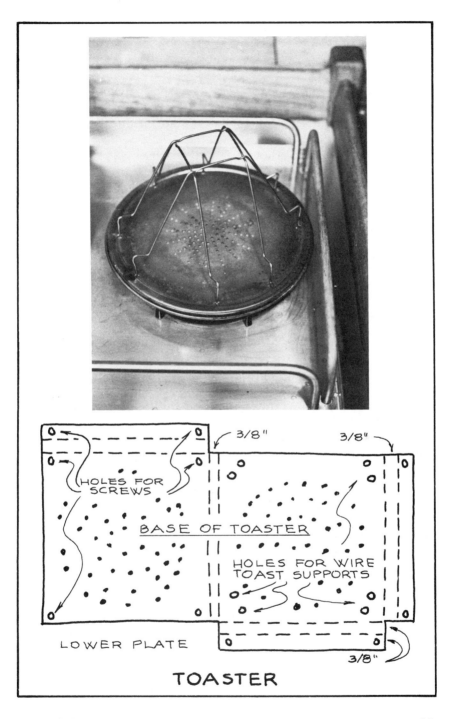

3/8"   3/8"

HOLES FOR
SCREWS

BASE OF TOASTER

HOLES FOR WIRE
TOAST SUPPORTS

LOWER PLATE

3/8"

TOASTER

SINGLE BURNER PRIMUS

In cooler northern climates, most yachts are equipped with a diesel cooking stove that also doubles as the ship's furnace. These units produce enough heat to keep the yacht cozy on the coldest of days, but their heat is too general and excessive for making a quick dinner or boiling water for tea on a warm summer day without overheating the entire cabin.

A good solution, although it may seem somewhat redundant financially and spacially, is to install a single burner, double-gimballed, kerosene stove (see illustration). The most reliable one is an all brass one made by Optimus which uses the same heavy duty burners that fire the best large kerosene stoves. The stove itself is mounted in the classic heavy cast aluminum bracket which mounts with four screws onto any bulkhead. The most beautiful aspect of the whole unit is that a single set-screw near the bracket's base quickly releases the entire apparatus, so if its mounting can be accomplished only in a somewhat inconvenient area, it can be kept stowed on most occasions and pulled out and inserted in place on very short notice. While storing, care must be taken not to turn the control knob to "ON", or the stove will leak kerosene everywhere. It should be stored in the most vertical position possible. The major drawback of the kerosene system is that the burner must be preheated with either alcohol or other priming fuels. This results in spillage on some occasions, so effort should be made to mount the stove over as resilient a surface as possible. The galley sink is best, your favourite bunk is worst.

The entire unit sells for under a hundred dollars, and judging by the testimony of yachtsmen who have suffered through summers with the heat-blasting diesel stove, the investment pays wonderful dividends.

A word of caution that's worth repeating everytime one discusses kerosene burners — the tiny hole, where the vaporized kerosene is released to the burner, is closed off and cleaned with a very delicate built-in needle. If the control knob is turned too violently to the "CLEAN" position, the fragile needle is liable to break off and render the burner useless. Because replacement parts are so difficult to find, you'll probably have to replace the entire burner at the rather formidable price of $30. So use tact. This is a fine mechanism, not a wrist exerciser.

SINGLE BURNER PRIMUS

STOVE UNDER CHOPPING BOARD

On all small cruising vessels galley space is extremely precious. With the inclusion of the bare necessities such as a sink and stove, extremely little free counter surface remains for food preparation. A most useful area above the burners of cooking stoves that can, on almost any vessel, yield a 24″ × 16″ chopping board *cum* work surface, remains to be exploited. I found the most thoughtful of these retractable boards on the Dutch ketch "*Areité*."

The board consisted of two long pieces hinged in the middle, that, in turn, hinge up together, out of the way, behind the stove (see diagram). The stock used should be 13/16″, preferably two solid pieces whose combined widths equal the depth of the stove. If you already have a chopping board and need only counterspace, the solid wood will still be less expensive in the long run than plywood with formica over, because of the vulnerability of formica to heat which may cause it to bubble. The ideal wood for a chopping board is maple, but any other, like oak, would suffice. Avoid teak, for it tends to flavour foods.

Cut your stock to fit over the stove allowing 1/4″ clearance at each end between board and cabinetry. Next, cut two lengths of cleat stock to run along the cabinets and act as supports for the board. Bullnose the free edge for a nice effect, then glue, screw, and plug. Round the edges of the boards slightly with sandpaper.

Acquire some very thin copper or stainless steel sheeting (so thin you can bend it with finger tip effort) in a quantity sufficient to cover one side and all edges of each board. I think this is mandatory for even though the board will be held away from the stove with barrel bolts when flames are present, the possibility of a "slip" still exists which would let the boards fall over the exposed flames. The sheet metal will give considerable protection in such an event. So, cut the metal, lay the board over it, then cut in at the corners and fold the metal onto the edges and tack every three inches with small brass tacks. Now, using four 2″ hinges join the boards together on the undersides and, in turn, join the board to the cabinetry behind the stove so the boards will fold up and stow in this vertical position (see diagram). Affix a single barrel bolt to the top inboard corner of the inboard board and drill two holes in the adjoining counter to hold the boards in either their open or closed position. Oil lightly with mineral oil.

THE FINELY FITTED YACHT

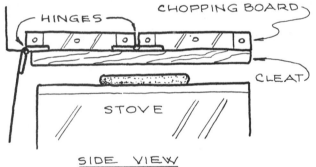

HINGES — CHOPPING BOARD

CLEAT

STOVE

SIDE VIEW

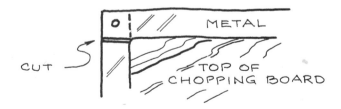

METAL

CUT

TOP OF CHOPPING BOARD

CHOPPING BOARD OVER STOVE

STOVE GUARDRAIL

If your galley is U-shaped with your stove aligned fore and aft (I defy you to gimball a stove mounted athwartships), a stove guardrail must be installed. Contrary to its name, the rail guards not the stove but the cook, from a flaming belly flop. As well as being a fence, which prevents inadvertent twisting of knobs by careless hips and derrières resulting in overruns of kerosene or alcohol, it is also a terrific place to hang dish towels. In short: build it!

Purchase two sets of stainless steel or brass dinghy gudgeons and pintles, and install the gudgeons on the cabinet sides so the rail when installed in the pintles will line up with the counter searails. Be certain to allow sufficient space between rail and stove so that the latter can swing freely. This setup will let you remove the rail at will without causing any damage.

A single piece of 13/16″ teak about 3″ wide will be all the wood needed. This should be cut to a length that will fit snugly into the pintles while in the gudgeons. Radius the corners, bullnose all around, and bolt on the pintles.

To keep the cook from falling *away* from the stove, a padeye should be installed at each end of the rail. These must be through-bolted. If masterfully planned or craftily re-bent, the holes in the padeyes and the pintles will be aligned allowing the use of a single bolt. Use cap nuts. No chef likes to get his wrists scratched before having them slapped.

A length of seat belt (measurement depending on the obesity of the most frequent cook) should have a snap shackle sewn onto either end. It can be clipped quickly into place in heavy seas. Do not make the belt too tight — give the cook room to turn and twist. Just provide a secure brace so his hands will remain free to stir the browning sugar for the Crème Caramel.

GUDGEON
AND
PINTLE

STOVE GUARDRAIL

THE GALLEY SEAT

We hunted down this beautifully crafted piece on *Scorpion*, a sleek 46' Argentinian ketch, cruising in Antiguan waters during Antigua's Sailing Week, which is an absolute must see for anyone who likes pageantry, gallant yachts, and wonderful people from as far away as Norway and New Zealand. Where was I? If you don't have a U-shaped galley, accept my profound sorrow, and begin building your galley seat.

Brass or stainless tubing of 1½" or 2" diameter makes an ideal main support. You need about a 5' length. If you have access to a plumbing or machine shop that can put a 90° bend into the pipe, have it bent making the vertical leg 26" and the horizontal piece as short as possible. As obvious from the illustration, this sort of an arrangement is not the easiest to anchor, so the shorter you can make the horizontal lever arm, the fewer problems you'll have with heavy leaning bodies. Under no circumstances should you have the two pieces cut at 45° angles and then welded. The vicious point you'd be creating would be massacring thighs daily. Have a 4" diameter base plate welded to each end with two triangulated supports to reinforce the welds. While at the welders, have him attach a small plate where you will be putting the wooden seat pad.

Drill 1/4" holes in your base plates and, using a single backup plate instead of large washers, bolt the base plates to the cabinet and cabin sole. Now, fabricate a seat from 1¾" × 4" × 6" teak. Anything larger would be a waste. This is not a throne. It's a place for the cook to rest momentarily before he returns to the bubbling cauldron. Whatever shape your seat, round the corners and bullnose the edges. Attach it to the bracket with #10 sheet metal screws. Now, invite down your *mom-in-lawus gargantuanus* to test it.

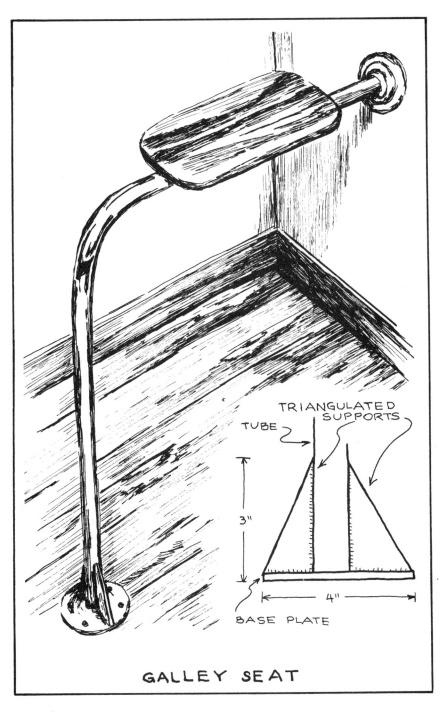

TUBE

TRIANGULATED SUPPORTS

3"

4"

BASE PLATE

GALLEY SEAT

CHOPPING BOARD

Construction of a comely chopping board can be a rewarding investment of one's time. There are no real finicky touches, no delicate measurements, and the results are, in most cases, delightful.

The hardwoods best suited are the non-oily ones like maple or oak, although people have mixed many woods with different tones and grains for effect. The only types to be avoided are woods like teak which have so much oil that they tend to transfer some of it along with a definite unpleasant flavour to foods left on them for any length of time.

Longevity can best be guaranteed by using end grain for the chopping surface. If the grain of the wood is laid along the surface, grooving and slivering will quickly occur and total board death will not be far behind.

The board should not be extravagantly large. Hardwoods are very heavy and no sea cook need be burdened with the task of controlling a behemoth at sea. If such a thing as general size can be given, then the figure of 100 square inches is probably a good one. Thickness should be 1½". The board will be of a manageable weight and size and can double as a cheese and bread board, obviating the use of a number of plates.

The actual measurements should be guided by possible stowage locations. Since it is a weighty object, it can gain momentum at sea unless carefully corralled. We have an 11" counter space in a corner of our galley framed athwartships by cabinet face and the searail, thus, measurements of our board became 11" X 9". Stowed here when not in use, it has become an ideal base for hot pots and pans which would otherwise damage the varnished countertops.

Ideally, wide boards should be acquired to minimize the work involved; since you only need about one lineal foot of a 2" X 8" board, acquisition should be no problem. Any woodworking shop would be happy to sell you an end piece that size if you can't find it in a lumber yard. Be certain that the board is not warped or your task will be impossible. Sand and fair both sides of the board, then cut it into 1½" strips and glue and bar clamp. Use waterproof plastic resin or resorcinol glue only. Remember to assemble end grain up. Try to have the surface of each strip flush with the others for end grain is very difficult to plane and almost as difficult to sand. Allow it to set overnight, then remove the clamps and detail. Oil with a couple of coats of flavourless mineral oil.

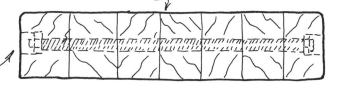

ENDGRAIN ON TOP

1/4" ALL-THREAD TO KEEP BOARD FROM DELAMINATING UNDER CONSTANT EXPANSION/CONTRACTION OF BEING SOAKED, THEN DRYING OUT.

CHOPPING BOARD

THE DISH RACK

If you think, for a moment, that the teak dish rack in the illustration is a complicated thing to fabricate, then you're absolutely right. But so what, a good mind thrives on challenge.

The very first step is to determine location. The rack drawn is in *Warm Rain*, directly over the ice box, which is built athwartships between the galley and the salon. With its very open design, the rack allows a flow of air and light and conversation through the ship, yet it does serve as a bit of a visual divider, making the salon a secluded area. As a further division, Candace usually slings a net of fresh fruit below the rack from one end to the other. The openness of the rack has another most practical aspect in that the dishes can be reached from the salon without one's having to actually leave the table.

The entire rack can be made to hang from the overhead without the benefit of support from the inboard pole you see in the illustration, however, a little reinforcement can go a long way, especially when it can double as a handhold as well.

The construction of the dish rack is similar to a drawer with partitions. Its bottom is of 1/2" plywood, the rest is 13/16" teak.

The size of the rack should be dictated by two factors: 1) the amount of space available, and 2) the amount and size of dishes you regard as indispensable to preserve the style to which you are accustomed. This latter point is no laughing matter. To function perfectly and look its possible best, the dish rack will have to be designed for a certain set of dishes, so choose most thoughtfully and thoroughly.

And here a few words on dishes may be meritorious. Yacht dishes are like no others in the functions they are called upon to perform in the most absurd of conditions. Peas and soups are required to stay inside them on the most absurd angles, gravy is not to be spilled from them even if they're going back and forth like a teeter-totter, and they're morally bound to keep various foods warm while the crew saunters off for a sail change or a look-see. Thus, four points can be deemed to be of top priority when the selection is being made: depth, stability, height of rim, and insulative ability.

Depth

This is most important in mugs and soup bowls. A deep dish, half filled, will have a much lesser chance of spilling when tilted than a necessarily fuller shallow one. This is vital when food is being carried, or being eaten from the lap.

THE FINELY FITTED YACHT

DISH RACK

Stability

This is of utmost consideration. Most plates or bowls with sloping sides and wide rims need only to be tapped anywhere along the perimeter and they'll willingly spill half their contents before they stabilize themselves again. A totally flat-bottomed dish, on the other hand, would take a fat lady from the circus standing on its rim before it would behave in an unhousebroken manner (see diagram).

Height of Rim

A landlubber rimless plate has no place on a yacht. Even an experienced tightrope walker would have difficulty keeping his food corralled, and I speak not only of stormy sea conditions, but of any time a runabout passes by or someone steps off the side deck. Plates with vertical lips of as little as 1/2″ will very nicely hold gravy, salad dressing, rolling peas, toast and even sliding ice cream, safely in place.

Insulative Ability

A heavy ceramic plate or mug, if preheated, will keep food and drinks warm for a long time. Light ceramic or plastic dinnerware has the insulative characteristics of a Kleenex.

With these four factors in mind, we searched store after store for the proper dinnerware and after much frustration, ended up having a dear friend make us a heavy earthenware set to our own specifications. The bottoms of all dishes are completely flat, as Plate B in the diagram. The plates have lips, the soup bowls are deep, and the mugs are large and heavy enough to be used as weapons. With the weight, their one disadvantage is that if dropped they leave dents in the woodwork, but we've been taking anti-oaf lessons and getting much better.

So pick your dishes, then decide the approximate surface area for each shelf and lay it out on a piece of paper. Your mugs should be no problem, just arrange a shelf wide enough to house them. The handles can hang out of slots as shown. Take your plates and bowls and arrange and rearrange them until a balanced and accessible pattern has been found, containing as little wasted space as possible. Don't forget to allow 13/16″ between the dishes for the divider baffles.

Next, establish how the outboard end of the rack is to be secured. We worked ours into the grab/drip rail of the edge of the underdeck. If you own no such rail, just run about 3″ of the shelf under the side decks and fasten it to same with glue/mishmash and screws. The inboard end, as mentioned, is best supported by a pole,

a. REGULAR PLATE

PRESSURE ON
POINTS INDICATED
BY ARROWS
WOULD FLIP "a"
BUT NOT "b"

b. FLAT-BOTTOMED PLATE

DIAGRAM A   -   DISH STABILITY

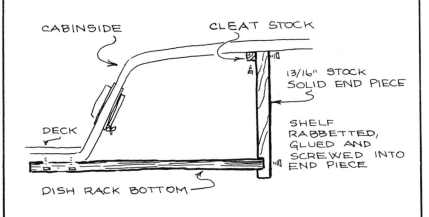

CABINSIDE

CLEAT STOCK

13/16" STOCK
SOLID END PIECE

DECK

SHELF
RABBETTED,
GLUED AND
SCREWED INTO
END PIECE

DISH RACK BOTTOM

DIAGRAM B - RACK SUPPORTS

DISH RACK

but if that's not possible, a solid end piece can be attached to the shelf and secured to the overhead with cleat stock (see diagram). To assist somewhat, the sides of the rack will be rabbetted to let in the shelf then, with the means of cleat stock, secured to the cabin side.

If you are going to use a post, then, from 1½" stock, cut a square post and bullnose all edges with 3/8" bullnose. Now, cut away half of the post stock on its first 6" to make room for the ice box, or whatever the lower end is to be fastened to. Next, from the point where the bottom of the low side of the rack is to intercept the post, dado the post as in Diagram C. You'll have to clean out the last couple of inches with a chisel.

For the sides of the rack, try to determine a good average height, one that will safely keep your plates, but not one that looks absurdly weighty. Remember, it's aesthetically much more pleasant if all the sides and baffles are of the same height, instead of jutting up here and poking out there like some sort of unsolved Chinese puzzle. Mark the centre of each compartment onto the low side pieces.

You will be butting up all baffles to sides, so just cut them to length and assemble them dry and keep checking the fit from time to time with the dishes. When everything is cut and fitted, pencil in all your baffles onto the shelf and drill pilot holes every six or so inches, brush a bit of glue onto each baffle, put them back into place one by one and, using the pilot holes as guides, countersink from the *bottom* of the plywood shelf, and fasten the baffles to the shelf with #10 P.H.S.M.'s. Where you have access, put a screw through the side of one baffle into the endgrain of another. At other places, just brush glue onto the endgrain and stick in place, and let the bottom screws do the work.

The small dead spaces can be left open for storage of odds and ends, or if they are too narrow to be of any use, just fashion a small lid out of 1/4" teak and glue it over the crevasse, otherwise, it'll just become a filthy, fallow hole.

Round all edges smartly and oil.

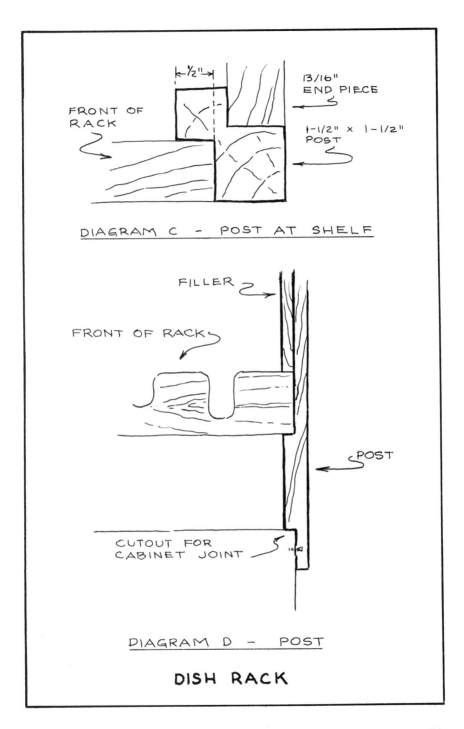

½"

13/16"
END PIECE

FRONT OF
RACK

1-1/2" x 1-1/2"
POST

DIAGRAM C - POST AT SHELF

FILLER

FRONT OF RACK

POST

CUTOUT FOR
CABINET JOINT

DIAGRAM D - POST

DISH RACK

THROUGH-BULKHEAD ACCESS

Now we're getting down to the bizarre details that make a yacht such a place of wonder. In numerous instances, small access holes through bulkheads would be most advantageous to flip a switch, or turn a valve, or just to have a quick glance into the engine room to verify that all is as should be. This quick removal hatch can obviate the need for unhinging steps and doors and drops.

I shall concentrate on the engine room bulkhead for: a) that is the one most frequently needing this little critter, and b) the critter for this bulkhead is the most complex to make because it is usually sound insulated.

Since we are normally concerned with a finished bulkhead of either oiled or painted wood, the utmost care must be taken when work is being done so as not to damage any surfaces. First, ascertain the location of your access hatch, remembering that wrists and fingers bend but forearms don't. Next, with a 1/4" drill bit, drill a hole through the center of the assigned area. A 4" hole saw will be needed for the hatch itself. (Four inches seems to be large enough for the mightiest fist.) With the bit set long to act as a guide, carefully cut the hole. Hold the drill motor steady or you'll make a hell of a mess of the bulkhead. Once cut, remove the piece from your hole saw and, for heaven's sake, don't throw it away, for this will comprise the hatch itself. Sand the edges of the hole and hatch to avoid chipping, and plug the 1/4" hole with a wood plug. Chisel off and finish. Attach a small brass padeye to the center of the hatch for a handle. Cut a thick strip of leather, and stretch, glue, and tack it around the circumference of the hatch. This will act to hold the hatch snug when in place, and seal off any engine noise. The hatch is now ready to use, working much like a cork in a bottle. Attempting to hinge it would prove unsuccessful, both functionally and aesthetically for: a) a snug fit would not be possible and through the crack would come engine noise and engine smell, and b) a hinge, no matter how small, would look sort of silly, and would most likely necessitate the use of a latch as well.

BULKHEAD PIECE WITH LEATHER
WRAPPING FOR TIGHT FIT

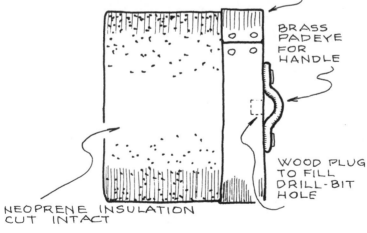

BRASS
PADEYE
FOR
HANDLE

WOOD PLUG
TO FILL
DRILL-BIT
HOLE

NEOPRENE INSULATION
CUT INTACT

BULKHEAD CUTOUT DOOR

THROUGH-BULKHEAD ACCESS

LA BOÎTE DE GARBAGE

Everything has been tried: plastic bags, paper bags, buckets, and old boots, yet none has proved to be an ideal garbage container for a yacht. Unsupported plastic bags collapse, paper bags leak, buckets roll about, and boots smell. A container, firmly affixed, easily accessible, and quickly removable, must be fabricated. Two major varieties exist: the slip-in top-loading, removable top type, as found on Bristol Channel Cutters and CT 38's, or the fixed-onto-hinged-door types, as found on Ontario 32's. These are both extremely functional, the former, because it can be located on top of a galley counter and things can be swept rapidly into it, the latter, because it can be fabricated with much ease.

Top-Loading

The basic structure of the top-loader is a box built of 3/8" plywood and thoroughly painted. If you can find a top-loading galley locker that is not now used to its fullest advantage (ho-ho-ho), then you are halfway there. Line the rim of the opening with milled or laminated seating cleats. Since drilling and screwing will be well nigh impossible from within, unless you are a retired India rubber man, just glue and clamp the cleats in place.

Fabricate your plywood box to slip past the cleats, and line its top with a holding cleat of 3/8" plywood, protruding 1/4" all the way around. This should be glued and screwed in place, or, if preferred for added strength, a 5/8" cleat stock can be run around the inside perimeter; the holding cleat may then be secured to this. The latter is a more positive configuration, providing a little hand hold, as well, for removal. Paint the inside of the box thoroughly with a couple of coats of good gloss paint, and line it with throwaway plastic bags.

Hinged-Door Type

Find a front loading locker whose inboard end is scarcely used, and find a plastic waste paper pail that will fit nicely onto it, and screw it to the door. And you had to buy a book to find this out. Oh well!

LA BOÎTE

DROP DOOR GARBAGE STOWAGE

A drop door equipped with a small plywood bin seems to be a perfectly ideal garbage container. The box should be formed as shown and, if made as large as possible, it will more or less accommodate the plastic garbage bags that usually measure 20″ X 20″.

On one side of the box, a shallow sleeve will hold the spare plastic bags, while an even smaller sleeve will be made to accommodate the wire or plastic twisties that seal the bags.

The depth of the box need be no more than 6″ at the bottom, flaring to about 12″ at the top. The angle of the top of the box is critical; it should slope away from the door in such a fashion that measurement X on the diagram will be about 1/2″ less than the height of the door opening.

To construct, cut 3/8″ plywood to form the bottom and three sides, assemble using cleat stock, glue, and screw. Cut a small slit about 1″ deep and 1/8″ wide into the tops of the sides of the bin where it meets the door. This is to accommodate the edge of the plastic bag which can be slipped down into the slit to keep the bag from collapsing. The sleeve for spare bags and twisties can be made from a single piece of 1/8″ plywood, set on a frame of 3/4″ cleat stock. The size of the sleeves should total about 7″ X 7″, with the twistie taking up about 1″ of one side. Paint the interior of the bin generously to seal off any cracks; you do not want leaky garbage leaking all over your lockers.

To minimize the odours drifting out and about the yacht, cut a simple lid from 3/8″ plywood and hinge it from the door. Line the edges of the lid with weatherstripping (self-adhesive foam strips are available in rolls at hardware stores) for a perfect seal. If you're fussy, install a hook and eye to keep the lid closed securely. Paint or varnish the lid to keep it from warping or staining.

Lastly, attach a length of brass chain a few inches from the bin, both to the door and the cabinet, to keep the door from flying wide open and dumping the garbage on the cabin sole. Make the end of the door a permanent attachment, but make the cabinet end detachable (just slip the last link of the chain over a cup hook), so the door can be lowered into a fully open position, should access to the locker's bowels be required.

DROP DOOR GARBAGE STOWAGE

GALLEY   57

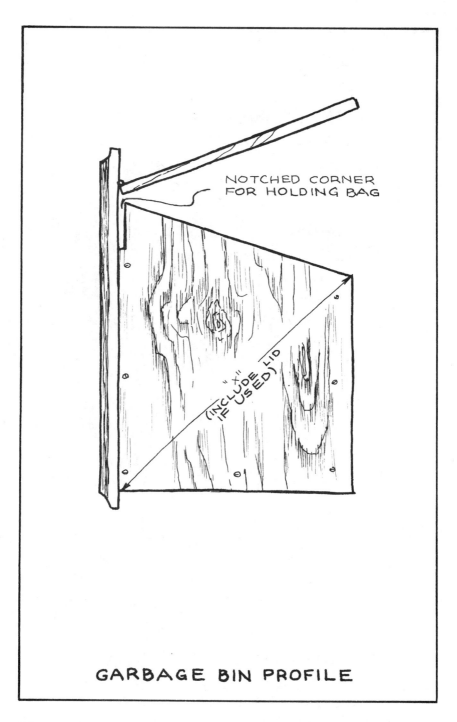

NOTCHED CORNER
FOR HOLDING BAG

"X"
(INCLUDE LID
IF USED)

GARBAGE BIN PROFILE

SOAP DISPENSER

More often than not I'm against anything that's unnecessarily mechanized, believing strongly in simple things that have no breakable parts like a plastic bottle of liquid soap. Yet now, there exists such a beautifully designed and carefully crafted dispenser that I must mention and even recommend it for all galleys, and perhaps heads.

As shown in the photo, the visible chrome part is only 2½″ tall, and the entire thing requires less than 2″ of horizontal space on a counter, spout included. It is visually appealing and quite nicely eliminates the unsightly Joy bottle which, after a few days, collects dirty fingerprints, and with its label half soaked and smeared, creates a disgusting sight even among dirty dishes, and that's bad.

The dispenser requires one hole in the counter top for installation. Choose your location well, keeping in mind that the spout should overhang the sink, but that sufficient space must be left beneath to unscrew the refillable bottle, which itself is 7″ × 2″. As mentioned, it could be put to good use in the head as well, if you don't mind smelling a little like a department store washroom. One of the more splendid locations for one of these critters would be, I feel, in a cutout near the cockpit where fish cleaning and clothes washing as well as hand and dishwashing often occur. It can be totally out of the way in a niche and refilled simply from below; and best of all, no one need ever worry about slipping on a bar of soap.

head

TEAK FOLDING SINK

Back when fine work was a point of pride with most craftsmen, beautiful things, such as this sink, were a common sight. It consists of solid teak or mahogany, and some profound stainless steel work. If you are satisfied with a 10″ diameter sink, the entire cabinet need be no more than 24″ × 18″ × 4″.

Begin by building the frame of the cabinet (the part to be fastened to bulkhead). Rip 13/16″ stock to 3¼″ width, and butt them and screw them, or dovetail them, with a jig (see "Tools"), and glue them to make up the 18″ × 24″ frame. Next, cut the fixed face piece to a 6″ width and screw it temporarily to the lower part of the frame. Drill a 1″ diameter hole in the centre of the bottom of your frame for a drainpipe. Now, from a 5′ piece of 6″ wide board of 13/16″, teak, cut the trapezoid shaped pieces for your sink base as shown in Diagram A. Join them together as in the illustration with the help of a doweling jig (see "Tools"). Next, mill from similar stock 1½″ pieces to make up an on-edge frame of 16″ × 18″ o.d.

When the glue has dried on your assembled trapezoids, draw a 10″ diameter circle in their centre and cut it out with a jigsaw to make room for the sink. Now, screw and glue the 16″ × 18″ frame to the trapezoids leaving a 1″ perimeter around the sides and top, which will force a 2″ part of the frame past the bottom of the trapezoids. This will make up the drain lip once the stainless steel is in place. Since the whole cabinet is to be lined with stainless, you will have to allow a little room for it when the drip lip becomes vertical. This can be accomplished by rabbetting the overhanging two inches of the frame by running it through the table saw for two cuts. See Diagram B. Now, take all the pieces and the illustrations down to your favourite sheet metal man and watch him die of laughter. When he resurrects, discuss what you need, explaining carefully that the lower portion of the cabinet, behind the temporarily attached 6″ piece, is to be a watertight well into which water will pour when the sink is tipped. With that in mind have him: a) weld a 3/4″ drain pipe to its bottom, b) hammer a lip around the edge of the frame to keep stray water in, and c) leave a 1/2″ wide lip bent to a 45° angle hanging *past* the 2″ drip lip frame. Now, tell him you don't want any rude talk, you just want your sink hammered out and adjoining parts made and installed a.s.a.p., and walk out. When you've restocked your savings account, leave on a hunt for a beautiful brass pump that mounts on the bulkhead, and fits snugly into a 10″ diameter sink.

Bon voyage.

FOLDED UP

TEAK FOLDING SINK

MEDICINE CABINET

Although I don't care a great deal for this idea, I do think that since you have to have a mirror in the head anyway, you may as well put a box behind it. It should *not*, of course, be used to contain the equipment of the first-aid kid. That should be put in a transportable container, like a good fishing tackle box, so the whole thing can be taken quickly to the injury, instead of dragging the injury down below and getting yuk all over the cushions.

Now, design the size of your cabinet to fit unobtrusively into the head, being certain that the mirror won't shatter against the bronze portlight on first opening of the cabinet door. General size need be no more than 12″ × 15″, but most importantly, it should be no deeper overall (door included) than 3½″. This leaves a useable shelf depth of 2¼″, which will accommodate most things yet will prevent the stacking of things behind each other.

Rip the four sides from 13/16″ stock to 2¾″ width. Rip your 1/4″ thick shelves to the same width, less 1/8″ to allow for the plywood back. Allow enough length so that 1/4″ of the shelf can be let into the sides. Leave a space of about 6″ between two shelves, and 4″ between the others. Next, set your table saw at 1/8″ height and, leaving 1/8″ between the blade and the guard rail, run each shelf and the two vertical sides through once. This slight groove will accommodate searails of 1/8″ plexiglass which: a) takes up little space, and b) allow you to see what's behind them. Next, rabbet the back of the sides to 1/8″ depth to let in the plywood back. Glue everything well, and tack and glue the back onto the shelves as well as the frames. Measure for the door. Cut your frame pieces from 13/16″ stock. Put a double rabbet into each frame to accommodate a 1/8″ thick mirror backed by 1/8″ plywood. See diagram. Lap joint your frame, glue and clamp, and allow it to set overnight. Drop in the mirror and the plywood and hold it in place with tacks running parallel to the plywood.

Next, cut 1½″ strips from 1/8″ plexiglass, remembering to add the 1/4″ in length to allow for the grooves in the cabinet sides. Sand the edges, and pop each strip into place by bending it gently, then slipping it right down into the groove of the shelves.

Four sheet metal pan heads (with large washers beneath them) through the cabinet back should be sufficient mounting *if* you've glued and tacked the back on well. If not, good luck.

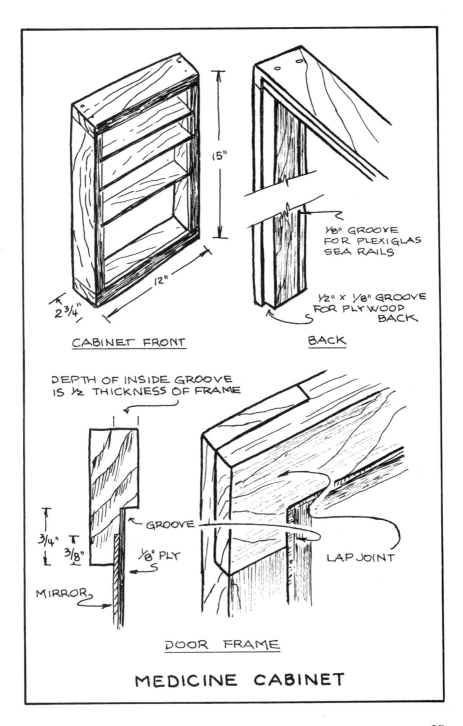

15"

12"

2 3/4"

CABINET FRONT

1/8" GROOVE FOR PLEXIGLAS SEA RAILS

1/2" x 1/8" GROOVE FOR PLYWOOD BACK

BACK

DEPTH OF INSIDE GROOVE IS 1/2 THICKNESS OF FRAME

GROOVE

3/4"

3/8"

1/8" PLY

MIRROR

LAP JOINT

DOOR FRAME

MEDICINE CABINET

HEAD

TOOTHBRUSH AND CUP HOLDER

As shown in the photos, beautiful ready-made ware is available in brass and porcelain, neither inexpensive, and both very functional. The porcelain is Italian, and it's in *Warm Rain* mostly because we thought it would be easier to keep clean than brass.

Fabrication of toothbrush and soap dishes out of wood is promoted by many, but to me seems to be the height of folly, for both soap and toothpaste have a habit of soaking deep into teak and leaving unsightly stains. If home fabrication is to be attempted, the only logical material seems to be plexiglass.

For the toothbrush and cup holder, cut on a band saw from 1/2" plexiglass stock, a 3½" square piece, radiusing all corners, and lightly sanding all edges with 100 grit to make them less sharp. Cover the surfaces of the plexiglass with masking tape during all fabrication, to avoid scratches. Insert the piece face-up in a vise, using wooden padding to keep the plexiglass from getting marked, locate the centre point, and very carefully drill a 1/8" pilot hole. Measure the diameter of the cup you will be using, at a point two-thirds up from the bottom. Remember not to use a perfectly cylindrical glass, for obvious reasons. Next, get a hole saw of that size, and drill through as vertically as possible. Now, in the four corners where the most available space exists, scratch in with a nail the shape of the stems of your favourite tooth brushes, then find a drill bit whose diameter is equal to the narrowest part of your pattern, and drill it through the centre. You will now have to gently play the drill bit back and forth until the entire area inside your nail line has been removed. Have only half the length of your drill bit in the hole, and try to avoid excessive up and down movements, lest you go down too far and the chuck of the drill gouges the plexiglass.

Now, sand all edges, then, from 1/4" plexiglass stock, cut a piece 1½" × 2", radius the corners, and drill four 1/8" holes in its corners, 3/8" in from the sides. Using a square and an awl, lightly scratch a line parallel to the long sides, 1/2" from the bottom. Using this line as a guide, cement the plate to the back of the holder with methylene chloride solvent, aligning the line with the bottom of the holder. Mount with round heads through the 1/8" holes, and brush away.

TOOTHBRUSH HOLDER

HIDE-A-SINK

In any small head where the head itself faces athwartships a sliding hideaway sink can be installed to save space. To use, the sink slides out over the head and to stow, it slides outboard to the hull just below the side decks. The backrest attached to the inboard edge of the sink serves to hide the hole in the fore-and-aft bulkhead, which is necessary to allow the sink and related plumbing to slide "through."

The choice of sink will be determined by the amount of space available behind the head. When choosing, do not forget to allow for some sort of pump or faucet. Because this is a sliding platform, one would be unwise to equip it with a behemoth hand pump that might put unnecessary strain on the supports.

Cut the platform to fit from 3/4″ plywood, allowing space for 13/16″ trim on each end, plus 1/8″ for clearance. Thus the platform length = space - 1 7/8″

From 13/16″ stock, cut two 1½″ high rails to act as slides below the platform. Install them on the two athwartship bulkheads. Cover your platform with formica, etc., then cut it, and install the sink and pump. Now trim out the platform with similar pieces fore and aft and inboard, and a 4″ wide piece outboard. Arrange it so that half of this piece will stick up above the platform and half below. The "above" part will hide hoses and other apparatus while the "below" part will act as a stop to keep the platform from sliding out of its track. With this in mind, notch the ends of the stop to make space for the rails.

Next, attach the drain and intake hoses to the sink for a dry run just to determine how much of the fore-and-aft bulkhead will have to be cut away. Cut it and trim it out. With the trimmed out platform in "stow" position, lay the two top rails (to hold the platform down) into place, leaving 1/8″ clearance between it and the platform, and mark the back-stop for notching. Cut notches, then slide the platform back into place, install the top rails permanently and hook up the plumbing.

To fabricate the backrest, use 1/2″ plywood attached to the platform with two or three sturdy pieces of angle iron or "L's". Make the backrest overhang the rim of the hole by 1″ on all three sides so the rim can take up the sitter's weight. Upholster to taste.

The sink platform in the photo has been constructed with permanent searails to keep splashed water from running over all four sides. If you're a sloppy face washer, by all means emulate.

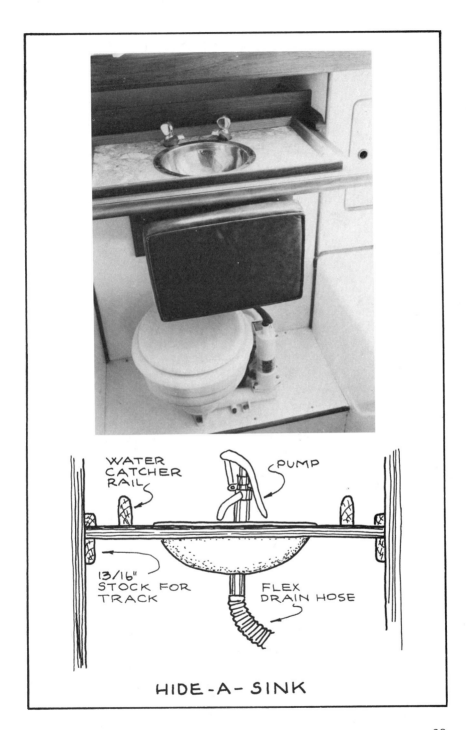

WATER
CATCHER
RAIL

PUMP

13/16"
STOCK FOR
TRACK

FLEX
DRAIN HOSE

HIDE-A-SINK

TOILET PAPER HOLDER

It's always sad to see a beautiful new yacht, spiffy and polished, well-outfitted in every detail, with a totally inappropriate chromed toilet paper holder streaking rust down a lovely white bulkhead.

Few fittings below are as vulnerable to salt as those in the head, since it seems to be common practice to leave the head portlight open for ventilation while the yacht is underway.

Consequently, toilet paper holders should be made of only brass, wood, or plastics. They should be small, so they're out of the way as much as possible; strong, so they can take the weight of misdirected bodies; and extremely easy to disassemble for roll change. If you're inclined to build Chinese wood puzzles, just take a deep breath, forget about it, and let the chrome monster run its streaks.

The following holder may be made of either wood or plastic. From 13/16″ stock, cut two identical 3½″ square pieces for the sides. Radius the outside corners well, or cut and curlicue to your heart's content. Three-fourths-inch in from the radiused front, centre and drill a 1/2″ hole right through one piece, and half way through the other. Sand the edges so they don't splinter or chip. Cut two 6″ long pieces of 1/4″ × 3/4″ stock, and let these into the backs of the sides 1/2″ from top and bottom. Glue and screw with #6″ flatheads. These bars will be used to mount the rack on a bulkhead.

From 1/2″ dowel stock, cut a piece 5-5/8″ in length, slip it through the through-hole, and into the half depth hole to fit. If it's too long, adjust now, for it must fit flush. Cut out a tear-shaped piece of brass, or thin rigid plastic, with the bulbous end 3/4″. Drill a fine hole through the elongated part, just large enough to fit a small brass tack. Nail the tack to the side of the rack so the bulbous shape fits over the hole and keeps the dowel from slipping out. Paper roll change can be effected by slipping the dowel completely out of the hole, inserting the new roll, slipping the rod back into place, then sliding the flap shut to hold it there. Mount with four flat heads through the mounting bars, in a low spot, out of the way of hips and knees.

If a nearby locker has unused interior space, a very nice concealed mounting can be used. See "Concealed Paper Towel Holder" for details.

HEAD

TOWEL RACKS

The major concern with towel racks is the material to be used. One should immediately eliminate the chromed atrocities from bathroom shops, for the chrome plating can be of an extremely poor quality that will chip and flake in a salt air environment. Solid brass racks can be found in shops that specialize in marine antiques, and we luckily found one from the *Queen Mary*. Brass racks from bathroom shops may be just plated, so beware.

Very fine racks can be fabricated once the material has been chosen. As lovely as teak is, it is a poor choice, for wet towels can cause it to mildew. Varnishing will, of course, help prevent this, so if you don't mind the upkeep, proceed. Cedar can be used to a most pleasing effect. For some reason, it seems to be more impervious to mildew than teak. The most ideally suited material, though, is clear plexiglass. It's easily workable, it looks very nice, and the cost of the material is most reasonable. A 1/2" plexiglass rod can easily span 18" without danger of breaking. The end blocks can be made of 3/4" stock, while the back can be 1/4" or less, or eliminated altogether.

Cut the two end pieces to 2½" X 1½", radius the front corners to eliminate nasty points, and, 1/4" back from the front face, drill a 1/2" hole about half way into the 3/4" plexiglass. Cut your rod to length, and glue it into place with plexiglass solvent. This last bit must be performed on a very flat, very even surface with the end blocks sitting squarely on their to-be-mounted sides, to insure that they will remain parallel for mounting.

At this point, a choice is to be made. If the back of the bulkhead or cabinet face, on which the rack is to be mounted, is accessible, then set the rack in place, mark the perimeters of the end blocks, and drill four pilot holes (two each) from the head side. Now, go to the other side of the bulkhead, and while someone holds the rack in place over the pilot holes, drill with a tapered bit into the rack, using the pilot holes as guides. Countersink the bulkhead, screw, and plug. If rear access is not available, a mounting plate of thin plexiglass will have to be used. Cut this to fit flush all around the end blocks, glue it onto them with solvent, and mount with four screws.

A note on placement. Do not put towel racks in a spot where sitters may be tempted to use them as hand rails, or if you must, install an unmistakable teak grabrail nearby.

TOWEL RACKS

FOLDING WASH BASIN

This is a pretty little Simpson Lawrence unit which comes totally assembled, ready to install. It's a perfect solution in small heads and even better on small boats where only a toilet exists. On large vessels, it provides tasteful and unobtrusive washing units in cabins. The basin is of high density plastic. Overall dimensions are a conservative 16″ high, 13½″ wide and when folded, only 6¼″ deep. The sink itself extends sufficiently when open that side access to it can be gained, so mounting can be done at 90° to the user if limited space so demands. Dumping the water is achieved by lifting the sink into its "folded" position. A tap (tap-shaped plunger pump) is available with the unit for about $20, but if you have a preferred unit, by all means use it. A simple soap holder is built in.

You will of course have to plumb it in yourself, providing a fresh or salt water intake and a waste outlet. Since additional seacocks are to be avoided at all costs, improvisation is in order. If the marine toilet is anywhere nearby, the task should be simple.

Waste

Since the outlet is for a 3/4″ hose, which usually is a manageable and discretely installable bit of tubing, the simplest thing would be to run the hose in a tasteful and tidy fashion between the hinged part of the seat and the bowl, terminating it just as it enters the bowl. A hoseclamp on the tubing as near the bowl as possible and screwed to a bulkhead or partition will do nicely to keep it in place. Admittedly you'll have to pump out the bowl every time you use the sink, but that seems a small price to pay for a "no-hole" in the hull. Besides, every toilet could use a nice soapy flush now and then.

Intake

A regular "T" takeoff from any part of the freshwater supply will do fine. If you're a freshwater-saver contemplating a salt water pump, the ideal thing to use would be a "T" takeoff from the toilet intake, *if* and only if the intake is *well forward* and *well above* the head outlet. Pumped effluent spreads over a great area; if you don't believe me, just look over the side next time you pump. If you're in doubt about the sufficiency of the locations of your intake and outlet, forget the whole thing and just tap into your freshwater system. Better to die a thousand times of thirst than to brush your teeth once with shee-shee.

FOLDING WASH BASIN

chart table/
navigation

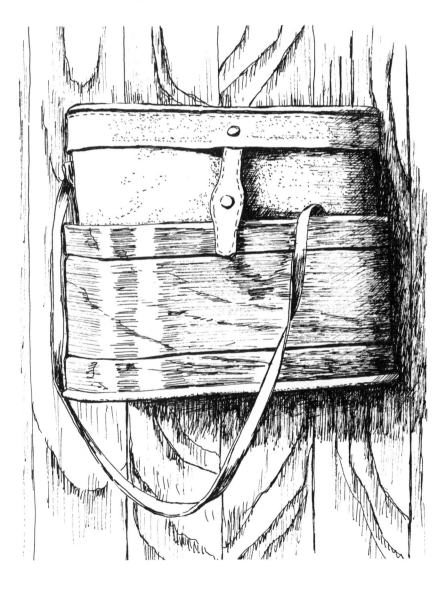

ENDLESS NOTE PAPER

This is a must. It is the handiest thing since the invention of toilet paper rolls. Using a roll of adding machine tape, and fabricating a holder for it inside a cabinet (see "Concealed Paper Towel Rack"), will give one an almost limitless supply of note paper.

The best location for it is in a high cabinet, near the chart table or galley. Here, notes can be left for oncoming crew, check lists can be written, and on lonely nights, yards of paper can be used up playing solitary tick-tack-toe.

Adding machine tape varies in width, so get the widest possible and cut a slit in the cabinet to suit, then, if you can't get the exact width in a Madagascari fishing village, to replace the roll, you can always get narrower stuff and make do.

Cut the slit with drill and jigsaw, then work the edges round and smooth by running folded sandpaper through. Next, fetch a piece of thin copper or brass sheeting and cut it to 6" length. This will be your writing surface; without it the wood cabinet would be grooved with pen and pencil lines in no time. Make the width 1" wider than the slit. One way to keep the paper flat against the writing surface is to cut two cross pieces from the brass stock and bend the edges under to allow space for the paper to slip through. Fit these to the upper and lower ends of the brass pad. Brass tacks through the ends of the cross pieces will be the only things needed to attach the whole rig to the cabinet. The lower cross piece can double as a tearing edge.

Mount the pad at least 1" under the slit. If you mount it higher, you'll have a hell of a time feeding the new rolls through the brass guide.

If the pad is located away from the chart table, where writing utensils are always accessible, an elegant touch would be a single holed pencil holder fitted directly next to the pad. See "Pencil Rack."

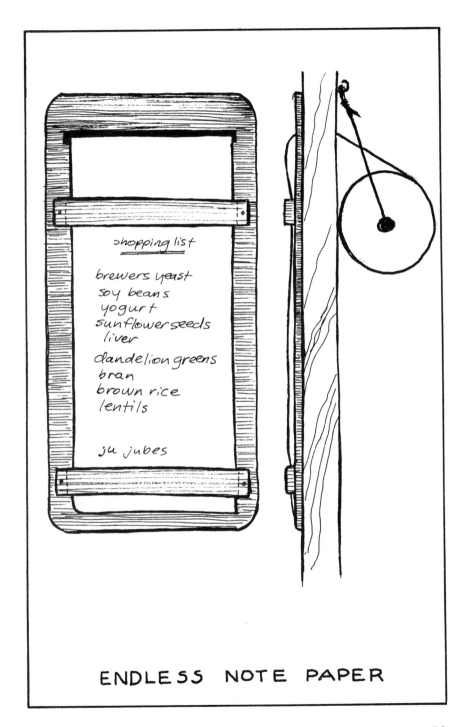

ENDLESS NOTE PAPER

HAND-HELD COMPASS STOWAGE

One of the most vital tools for coastal navigation, one which can get a fix on a vessel's position within one minute, is in many cases subjected to unnecessary abuse. This condition seems all the more preposterous when coupled with the reverence given to the fixed ship's compass. I'm not for a moment advocating that the main compass be mis-managed to create a more egalitarian state of affairs, I merely suggest that this delicate and costly instrument be given better treatment than being stuck in a feeble little metal bracket provided by the manufacturer. The bracket will, of course, provide sufficient bondage, but it still leaves the compass exposed to physical violence of all kinds. In short: box it.

The more pricey compasses do come with an optional box for about 40 modest dollars — usury at half the price. Construction of a tiny box takes no genius. If you are reluctant to get involved with a dovetailing jig, simply construct a butt-sided box from 1/4" stock. A 5" wide by 10" high by 4½" deep box will do for most compasses. To be totally accurate, make the interior of your box 1/2" wider than the widest part of your compass, the height 1" more including the prism, and the depth 1/4" greater. Thin plywood stock will do nicely for the back. Glue and brass tack the whole thing together.

Next, you'll have to fabricate blocks to hold the compass immobile in the box. Set the compass inside the box as perfectly aligned as possible to both axes. Measure for small blocks of 1/2" stock to hold the shoulders of the face *down*, and fit for a U-shape block of 3/4" stock to firmly accommodate the base of the handle. Don't be pompous, scrap bits of soft woods will do nicely here. Line all wood surfaces that will be making contact with the compass with thin self-adhesive weatherstripping, or felt. Once the compass is snugly in its home, find a point (somewhere at the joint of the handle and the base would be most ideal) where a 3/8" dowel can be slipped from side to side for support. Drill through one side from the outside, and continue with the drill bit half way through the next side. Cut a dowel to length to fit flush when inserted. From light gauge brass, cut a tear-shaped piece about 1½" X 1", pin it with a brass tack through the narrow part to enable the flap to pivot and alternately cover or expose the end of the dowel. Varnish the box inside and out. Mount the box with the open side facing aft to enable the compass to act as a course verifier down below. Now that loops shippy.

THE FINELY FITTED YACHT

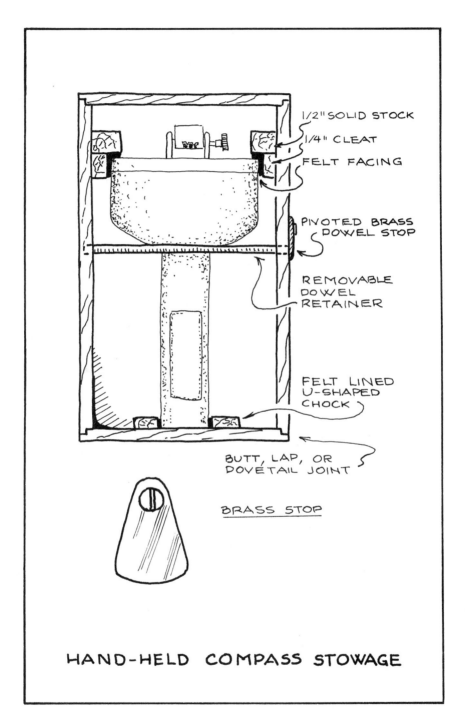

1/2" SOLID STOCK

1/4" CLEAT

FELT FACING

PIVOTED BRASS DOWEL STOP

REMOVABLE DOWEL RETAINER

FELT LINED U-SHAPED CHOCK

BUTT, LAP, OR DOVETAIL JOINT

BRASS STOP

HAND-HELD COMPASS STOWAGE

THE FLIP-UP CHART TABLE EXTENSION

A most commendable improvement in many recently designed yachts has been the inclusion of a chart table. By necessity, these have been allotted relatively small areas and more often than not, are of the sit down variety, frequently employing the foreward end of a quarter berth for the seat. This makes for a handy place to sit and work out navigation details and future trips, or fill in the log, but the small surface area of the table itself is the most inappropriate for actual chart work involving navigation tools and large charts. With the addition of a hinged extension, these severe limitations can be easily overcome.

If the chart table has its own independent seat, the solution is simplest, for then the back of the seat can support the hinged piece. This can be made of 1/2" teak or mahogany plywood with the appropriate trim on all sides. The trim must be flush top and bottom to avoid complications in either the stowed or engaged position. The prudent will affix the extension with a piano hinge, since occasional heavy pressure in the form of leaning bodies will be unavoidable. Securing the extension to the deck itself will not be such an enviably simple matter. Barrel bolts inboard and out do not provide sufficient support, and even if they did, their positioning would not be very hygienic. Knees hinging out from the aft face of the desk have been used with moderate success, their largest drawback being that they're rather unattractive when not in use. Possibly the most clever arrangement I've ever seen involves two sliding rods which stow fore and aft inside the desk. When required, they slip out through holes in the desk face (they themselves plug holes when not in use) and fit snugly into two corresponding holes in the back of the seat. This seems the least complicated of any system, requiring only two 1" dowels or similar sized stock, and a 1" hole cutter or a chisel.

If the desk is of the quarter berth add-on variety, the problems begin. The extension must be hinged from the hull itself. A 2" wide piece of 3/4" plywood, bonded to glass hulls or epoxied to wood ones, should be used as a base for the hinge. *Do not* screw anything into the hull. A tidy 3/4" × 3/4" cleat can be added to the aft face of the table to support the forward edge of the extension. The aft part can be supported by a hinged leg added on to the extension which can rest in an indentation on the inboard edge of the quarter berth.

With either extension, you'll be able to tackle any size chart without having to fold it to the size of a Sunday hankie.

THE FINELY FITTED YACHT

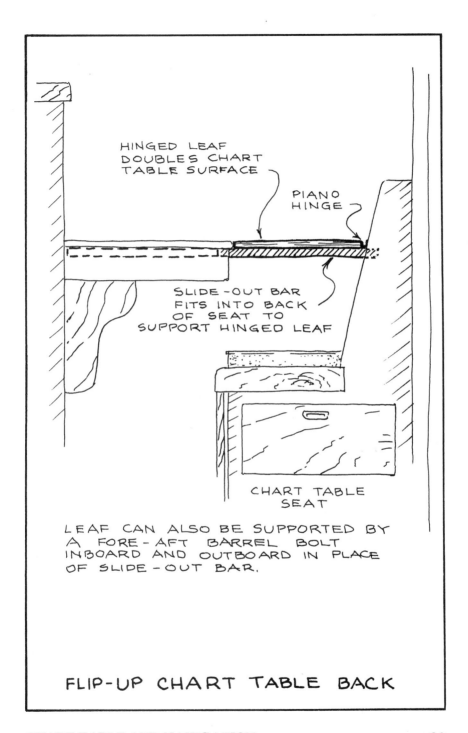

HINGED LEAF
DOUBLES CHART
TABLE SURFACE

PIANO
HINGE

SLIDE-OUT BAR
FITS INTO BACK
OF SEAT TO
SUPPORT HINGED LEAF

CHART TABLE
SEAT

LEAF CAN ALSO BE SUPPORTED BY
A FORE-AFT BARREL BOLT
INBOARD AND OUTBOARD IN PLACE
OF SLIDE-OUT BAR.

FLIP-UP CHART TABLE BACK

CHART TABLE AND NAVIGATION   83

STOP WATCH HOLDER

An hour's work can produce a tasteful stop watch case from either plexiglass or wood, or a combination. Scrap pieces will do nicely since the case is small, exceeding the watch's diameter only by 1/2″ on three sides, and not at all at the top.

The case will be made of three layers. The thickness of the front and back can be 1/4″, while the centre piece need be just under the full thickness of the watch.

Cut the back to final size. Be sure the top is low enough to allow manipulation of the reset and "stop" and "start" buttons without the need of removal from the case. Cut the middle and front pieces to similar shape, then set them one at a time into a vise, and drill the following holes with hole saws. The hole in the thick middle piece should match the diameter of the watch, while the hole in the thin front piece should have the diameter of just the watch's crystal. This will make for a secure fit, yet allow total visibility of the face. It would be a mistake to leave the front piece solid plexiglass for then the face of the watch would rub constantly against it, scratching both surfaces to opaqueness. Now cut out the pieces above the holes to form a "U". Round off the edges of the holes in the front piece with sandpaper, then glue and clamp the three pieces together. When dry, finish off the edges with a file or sandpaper, depending how closely matched your pieces are. Mount with a single screw just behind the watch. Line it with felt.

If properly placed, high up within reach of the companionway, the navigator taking celestial shots will be able to use it safely, instead of having it dangle precariously from a lanyard around his neck. Using a sextant from the security of the companionway is in itself heartwarming, then simply one-fingering a firmly affixed stop watch, would make the process a dream. Since most navigation areas directly adjoin companionways, the watch can then be left untouched until the time is entered in the tables.

Besides, it looks professional.

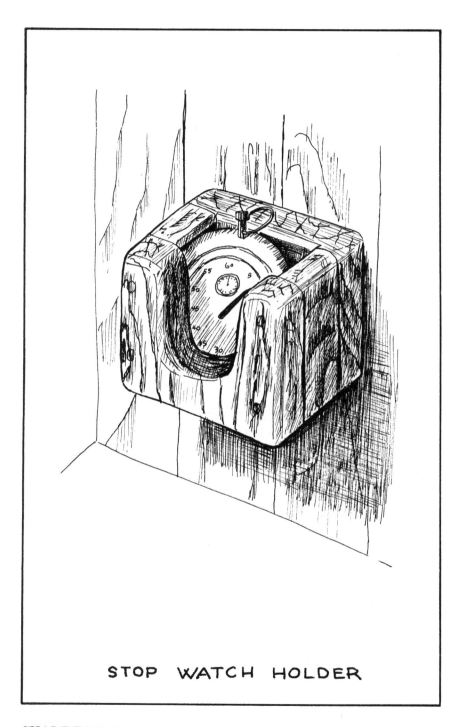

STOP WATCH HOLDER

RADIO RACK

One of the most precious pieces of equipment aboard any yacht is the radio receiver. Since most of the best ones, like the Zenith Trans-Oceanic, are of a design that somewhat resembles a portable transistor radio, the temptation to treat it as such is fairly hard to resist. As a consequence, the radio will be found lying all over cockpits, and foredecks and lockers, or wherever the whim of the music lover carries it. A great mistake. The radio should have a permanent and very secure place below decks from which it should not be moved, unless it's being used as a direction finder, or if reception in that particular position is insufficient and a new locale must be tried.

One basic rack design will function very well for most situations (see diagram). The only adjustment necessary depends on the amount of space available above the unit. If the rack will be simply attached to a bulkhead, then it can be made to be top loading, i.e. the rack will need to have no moving parts. If, however, the radio will be located directly below a shelf or the deck, then front loading will become necessary, entailing one hinged side and a removable frontal retaining bar.

Top Loading

Three pieces of 13/16" teak or mahogany should be cut: the bottom just 1/4" longer than the radio itself and about 2" wider. The two sides will be identical in width to the bottom and should have a height closely equal to that of the radio. If a side control exists as it does for band selection on the Zenith, a cutout somewhat larger than the control itself will provide access. The frontal support bar should be cut of the same stock to a width of no more than 1¼" or it will impede working of the front controls. Position the bar, quite high up, interfering with as few vital knobs as possible. Although end-screwing the bar through the sides would probably be adequate, a small routed or chiselled recess in the sides would give more security. The bar should be no more than 1/2" away from the face of the radio.

Assemble the parts as shown, using #10 1" S.S. P.H.S.M. screws. Countersink, glue and plug. To affix the rack to the bulkhead, hold the rack in place, draw a light pencil line around its bottom and sides, then remove rack, and drill pilot holes through the outlines. Three per side and three on the bottom should suffice. Have a friend hold the rack back over the outline and drill and screw from the

ROUT HALF THICKNESS FOR BAR

BARREL BOLT

HINGED TO RELEASE BAR

RADIO RACK

CHART TABLE AND NAVIGATION

other side of the bulkhead through the pilot holes. Use plastic resin glue and 1½″ #10 P.H.'s.

For the front loading unit, mill the identical parts (bypassing the bottom, if the radio is to sit on a shelf or a counter) making sure you rout 3/8″ deep recesses for the bar this time. Install one side permanently, but fit the other side with two small hinges on its bottom (outside), and a barrel bolt at the top to hold it in its vertical position. This side can then hinge down so the bar can slip out and the radio be removed.

Happy listening.

OVERHEAD COMPASS

A must for single handers, and a nice bit of luxury for others on passages of any length, is an overhead compass. Catalogues recommend "fixing above the owner's bunk to observe how the yacht is heading," in other words, to make sure the helmsman hasn't skipped off to the rum locker.

Whatever the excuse required, it would be pleasant to be able to glance up in a half-sleep and, without actually disturbing one's dreams, verify the ship's heading, then quickly return to matters of greater import. The sensible size of this bit of decadence should be, of course, *small*. The most commonly used ones seem to be rather bulky — 4½″ high and over 8″ in overall diameter — which I fear would be more of a skull-cracker than a mind-settler. But if you have height over your bunk and money in your pocket, by all means indulge. What the hell, you only live once.

OVERHEAD COMPASS

NAVIGATION TOOL BOX

This is another item most requisite on small yachts where a regular chart table with its wanted drawers is spacially uneconomical, but it's a beautiful thing on any yacht. It is essentially a 14″ × 3″ × 3″ box with a hinged drop front (much like the overhead chart cabinet but on a smaller scale) constructed to accommodate pencil lead, parallel rules, pencil sharpener, erasers, and for those unwilling to construct a proper stop watch case, a stop watch.

Three-sixteenth inch stock is needed to house the screws and the hinge, but a thin 1/4″ piece will nicely suffice for the back. The top, bottom, and sides should be butted and screwed, or dovetailed and glued, while the back can be brass tacked and glued, since it will not be visible anyway. The solid drop door should be bullnosed. Note that the piece for the front covers all end grain of top, sides, and bottom. A 7/8″ or 1″ finger hole should be drilled and bullnosed. Small butt hinges should be let into both drop door and bottom edge with a very small 3/8″ chisel for a perfect fit. Because of the lack of weight in this door, even the hated bayonet snap-lock should be sufficient to keep it tightly closed in most conditions. To attempt installation of the more positive locking, finger-tripped elbow catches in such a tight space would prove to be a challenge, even to those well-versed in building brigantines in bottles.

A searail 1/2″ high would be a nice touch just inside the door to a) keep things from falling out when the door is open, and b) prevent things from rolling between the hinges when the door is being closed. The latter could easily rip out the small hinge screws.

One small note. You'll realize I mention storage for pencil leads. We have constantly found the reloadable draftsman's pencil superior to ordinary ones. First, if the lead snaps, a flick of the finger will bring on a new tip without the lengthy interruption of pencil sharpening. Second, avoided are the horribly stubby creatures one inevitably ends up with, that are too short to sharpen, too short to store, and too short to find. A pair of draftsmen's pencils are a solid investment, especially if neatly stored in a pencil rack. Oh yes. For the less ambitious who store their stop watches here or other sublet areas; sew the poor thing a little pouch out of scrap leather. The crystal will remain legible much longer.

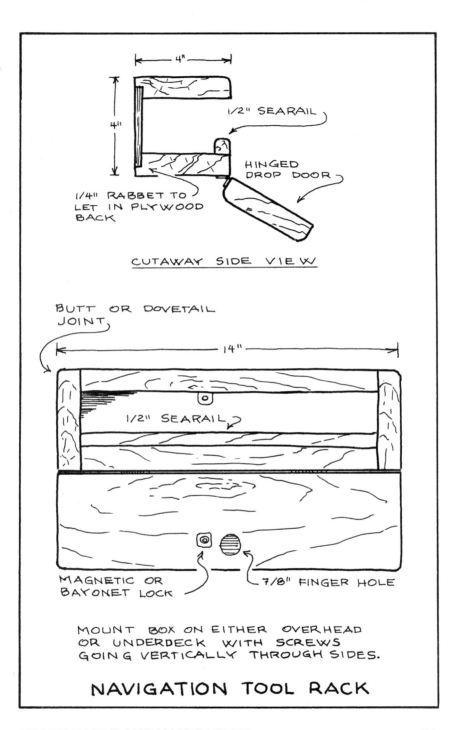

1/2" SEARAIL

HINGED
DROP DOOR

1/4" RABBET TO
LET IN PLYWOOD
BACK

CUTAWAY SIDE VIEW

BUTT OR DOVETAIL
JOINT

14"

1/2" SEARAIL

MAGNETIC OR
BAYONET LOCK

7/8" FINGER HOLE

MOUNT BOX ON EITHER OVERHEAD
OR UNDERDECK WITH SCREWS
GOING VERTICALLY THROUGH SIDES.

NAVIGATION TOOL RACK

DEPTH SOUNDER BRACKET

Great controversy boils over the ideal location of depth sounders. The new digital types with succinct bright numbers can be placed in the cockpit, totally ideal indeed for the helmsman steering in a fog by the fathom lines, or doing tight navigation in foreign ports, but this leaves a void down below for the navigator who has to work at night.

A good compromise with any sounder (especially with the traditional ones which must be kept out of the weather) is the hinged mount. This can be focused in or out, serving double duty.

A block of 13/16" teak is ideal, cut and decorated to match the boat's personality, and hinged on a sturdy brass or stainless piano hinge. Mount the sounder on this block, and attach a smaller block to the cabin side, and affix the hinge between them. Make sure your mounting block has enough room beside the sounder to clear the trim around the companionway. Since a lot of play will be required in the wires, the best solution is to use a piece of coil cable, such as found on telephone receivers. Two sets of hooks and eyes are needed. One at the unhinged end with the eye in the pad and the hook in the cabin side to fix the bracket for use down below; the other at the hinged end with the eye (the smaller obstruction) in the companionway trim and the hook on the hinged pad to hold it in the open position for cockpit use.

Companionway positioning is admittedly awkward, endangering life and instrument, so a preferred alternate would be to install a small portlight in the aft face of the cabin and hinge the sounder in front of it for cockpit use. Whatever the location, make certain that the read out face is always shielded from the sun, for (especially on the traditional spin types) the soundings are virtually impossible to read in direct bright light.

THE FINELY FITTED YACHT

DEPTH SOUNDER BRACKET

OVERHEAD CHART RACKS

In many small yachts where no space is available for large chart drawers, the traditional leaning has been toward stuffing charts under bunk cushions; a totally needless venture into decadence. Ample unused space is available overhead, and two very simple stowage bins can be constructed, one for "folders" and one for "rollers". Both schools have reasons for their madness.

For Rollers

This is actually a magnified pencil rack. Three-quarter-inch stock can be used, ripped to 4″ widths, with 3″ diameter holes cut with a hole saw on the centrelines. The length of the rack and the number of holes depend on the amount of space available. Do not attempt to drill smaller holes. Rolling a chart tighter than 3″ will lead only to prolonged wrestling matches. One advantage of this rack is the potential for exterior markings at the bottom of each chart hole. If you're using the same ten charts year after year, you could get really fancy and have tiny brass plates made up with the name of each chart engraved. Now that's decadence!

Mount the racks about 20″ apart in a place where you can easily reach the outboard piece of the rack. You'll need to, to thread some rambunctious charts that have a tendency to unfurl.

For Folders

A very tidy, flat, suspended chart box can be made out of a piece of 3/8″ plywood slightly larger than a twice folded chart, and 3″ wide solid 13/16″ stock. If you want it to look beautiful, fit the back of the box flush against the curve of the cabin sides. Cut the plywood to width and rough cut to maximum needed depth, i.e. be sure to have the short side cut at least as long as the longest folded chart. Add to this the difference of cabin curvature over the width of the box to arrive at the rough length of the long side. Fit as close as possible with the inboard end running parallel to the keel. Scribe it with a compass from end to end with the pencilless tip on a constant line of the cabin side (on a constant vertical plane). You've got your curve. Cut with a jigsaw on a slight bevel to match the slope of the sides. Use the same angle to cut your 3″ wide frame ends. Fit the sides on and glue and screw into the plywood at 12″ centres. Mount on overhead with glue and screws. Don't drill or screw right through the cabin top. If you can mount it against a deck beam, so much the better. Use two simple butt hinges on a piece of solid stock cut to 3″ width to make up a drop door. Secure the door with a barrel bolt.

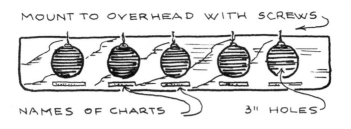

MOUNT TO OVERHEAD WITH SCREWS

NAMES OF CHARTS   3" HOLES

DIAGRAM A
CHART RACK FOR "ROLLERS"

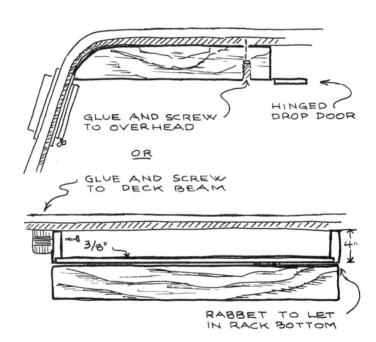

GLUE AND SCREW
TO OVERHEAD

HINGED
DROP DOOR

OR

GLUE AND SCREW
TO DECK BEAM

3/8"

4"

RABBET TO LET
IN RACK BOTTOM

DIAGRAM B
CHART RACK FOR "FOLDERS"

OVERHEAD CHART RACKS

SIGNAL FLAG RACKS

Signal flags are cute. They can be run up to celebrate arrival and departure of friends, as well as send messages in inconvenient moments, like the sinking of your ship. These little flags will prove totally useless if randomly stuffed and jammed into a sack or a drawer. Ready access to all flags is essential, and ready access to each specific flag at a specific time, without rummaging and searching and cursing, is mandatory.

Since each flag is clearly stamped with the letter or number it represents, stowage will have to be arranged so each of these stamps is clearly visible. A set usually contains 40 flags: 26 for letters, 10 for the numbers, three repeats, and one for "code". When individually rolled with the stamps showing, each flag occupies a minimum space of $2\frac{1}{2}'' \times 2\frac{1}{2}'' \times 3''$ for depth. The total area needed for proper stowage need be no more than about $14'' \times 22''$, or any combination yielding 308 square inches.

The material should be solid, stock cut to $1/4''$ thickness and $3''$ width. Cut it to whatever length you've decided on. If unavoidable, $1/4''$ plywood can be substituted. At $2\frac{1}{2}''$ intervals, a $1/4''$ wide let in should be cut to one-half the depth, in this case $1\frac{1}{2}''$. Slide the pieces into each other until a honeycomb has been assembled. A touch of glue on each joint might be used for added security. Frame the whole thing in $1/4''$ stock. Butt the joints and glue and nail with brass tacks. Two small brass "L's" on top and bottom (inside the pigeon holes so they don't show) should be used to mount on bulkhead or whatever.

No door or outer covering is compulsory, especially if the rack is mounted athwartships. Neatly folded, the flags look very shippy and colorful nestled in their little homes.

SIGNAL FLAG RACKS

MAGNIFYING GLASS HOLDER

You may frown upon esoteric yacht gear such as a custom fitted magnifying glass holder, but it's these fine details that ultimately distinguish a yacht from a pick-up camper or a wheelbarrow. The specific one in the photo adorns a bulkhead next to the chart table of *Wanderer IV,* and is used very frequently to discern chart details in unfavourable lighting.

One must begin by searching through antique shops to find a beautiful specimen of a classic magnifying glass. Next, cut a piece of solid stock down to the same thickness as the thickness of the handle, and width and length to border the handle by at least 1″ at any point. Lay the handle upon the wood, draw its outline, then cut it out with a jigsaw. Lightly bullnose all edges and sand.

Next, from half-inch stock, cut a small piece (3/4″ X 2½″) with the grain running along the length, then drill a hole through its center so that a #10 flat head brass screw will turn in it, somewhat stiffly. Then, drill into the holder itself as shown, insert the screw, and tighten only to the point where the "lock" will still turn but not fall into a vertical position on its own. Now, slip in your magnifying lens and enjoy. If that's not shippy, I don't know what is.

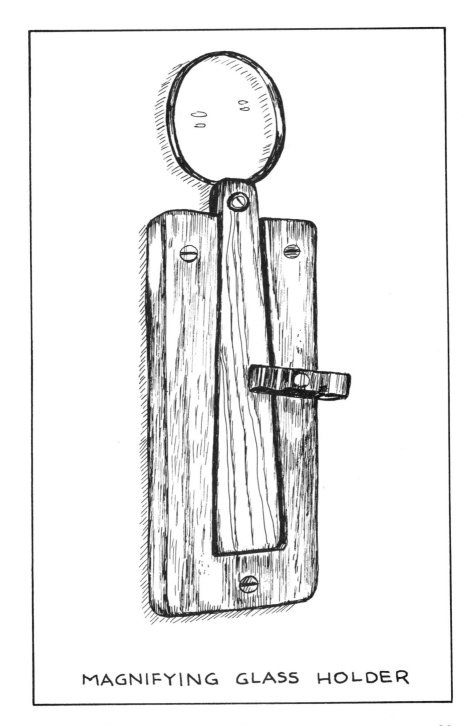

MAGNIFYING GLASS HOLDER

FLASHLIGHT AND FLARE RACKS

I feel that the presence of a flashlight very close to the companionway is mandatory, whether a yacht is to spend the night at sea or at anchor. Any emergency situation contains more than enough surprises without one's having to resort to little games like "flashlight flashlight, where is the flashlight?"

The bracket illustrated will not only guarantee protection and ready access to the flashlight, but it will also free some valuable shelf or drawer space. It requires a vertical space somewhat less than one and one-half times the light's length and only very slightly more than its width.

You'll require two square pieces of wood cut from 1/2″ solid stock. Let the size be 1″ greater than the diameter of the flashlight's handle to give you a 1/2″ shoulder all around. Cut the mounting plates from similar stock to an identical width and 1½″ height. Next, insert each bracket piece in a vise, mark the centrelines, and with a hole saw whose diameter is equal to that of the flashlight, cut completely through one piece and about two-thirds of the way through the other (to be the bottom piece). Now, butt one piece to each mounting plate and glue and screw with #8 P.H.S.M.S. Allow them to dry overnight. Install the brackets in such a way as to make sure the flashlight switch will not cause the flashlight to hang up on the upper bracket. Now that you have the bracket, make sure you use it.

The bracket for the flare is done in a similar fashion for a similar purpose. If a tapered hand flare is to be used, the best and simplest thing is the U-shaped bracket (see photo) that consists of two sides and a back. This has the advantage of taking a flare straight in, unlike the flashlight holder which requires much space above to allow the flashlight to be dropped in. If a flare gun is to be used, the bracket will, of course, be rather complex and designed to fit the individual gun, but, in either case, the location for the bracket is vital, for the flares should be kept safely out of both weather and traffic. The Hiscock's flare (see diagram) is stored both high and well back beneath the bridge deck, where it's accessible, but safe.

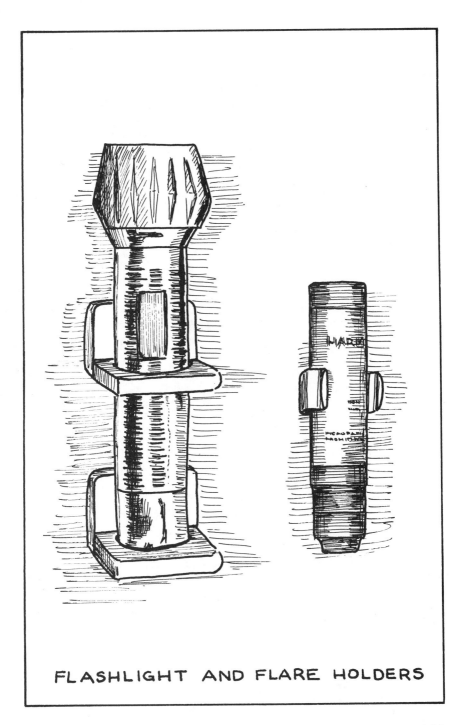

FLASHLIGHT AND FLARE HOLDERS

PENCIL HOLDER

This little critter is so painfully simple, I'm almost embarrassed to write about it; but here goes.

Rip a piece of 2″ by about 8″ long strip from 13/16″ stock of whichever wood you prefer. Remember *rip* means with the grain. Round the ends and edges with a file and sandpaper. If you want the rack to look more graceful, bevel the ends with a jig or bandsaw. Now, place the piece of wood with a 13/16″ × 8″ side up into a vise using flat scrap pieces of wood to absorb the toothmarks. Scribe a light centreline down the length of the long side and mark points on 3/4″ centres along it. At the 1/3 and 2/3 points, leave gaps for mounting screws. Leave the last 2½″ space for one-handed dividers. These have about 2″ diameter hinged necks. Mark for a hole 1¼″ from the end for the dividers. Drill all holes with a 3/8″ bit, but first read on.

Be certain to wrap a piece of masking tape around the drill bit 1¾″ from the tip, and *do not* press into the wood beyond that point. Few things look less sophisticated than a person of average intelligence placing a pencil in the top of a rack, only to have it slip immediately out the bottom.

Since your piece of wood is quite thin, be sure to sight straight down the top of your drill, and drill as vertically as possible. If you have access to a drill press, the above need for caution will be obviated.

With your holes drilled, turn the wood wide-face up in the vise, and draw a centreline along the length of it. Where you skipped spaces, mark and drill two holes in the centre of each half. Drill with a tight, tapered bit and counter-sink. These are for housing mounting screws. Now, take the thing out of the vise and rip it lengthwise into two 1″ wide pieces. Voilà. All your holes will line up.

Sand and detail completely before installing. Some people like to make a single piece rack about 3″ deep. This is not advisable. Frustration can reach its apex when one spends endless hours fishing broken pencils, or junior's hard-packed gob-balls, out of 3″ deep pencil holes.

Mount 2″ apart with a dab of glue behind each. If you mount them further apart, your pens with pocket pins will dangle feebly from the top bar.

PENCIL HOLDER

CHART TABLE LIGHT

There seems little doubt that the flexible gooseneck lamp, if well situated, is the most ideal chart table light. If mounted on the underdecks over the chart table, the neck will sweep over a 12" arc and throw enough light to cover an 18" square area very well at any given time. Its solid black hood keeps the light out of the rest of the cabin so as not to disturb the sleeping crew. Even more important is that most lights come with a slip-on red plastic sheath, that can be put quickly over the light bulb to protect the navigator's night vision.

The better goosenecks have an arrangement whereby the shade or cowl is retractable if a more general lighting is required. The mounting base usually contains the on-off switch. Mounting can be accomplished with two screws. If mounted under the side or aft decks, the neck of the lamp can be bent up out of the way to give free access to areas behind it. Most units are available for 12 or 24 volt systems.

If you feel these lights render insufficient light for things when you would like the whole chart table floodlit, then the *Solite* fluorescent lights might be a good idea. They are quite compact (13½" X 2" X 1¾" deep), have very low current consumption, and what's extremely important, they have a circuitry that's protected to reduce radio interference. Available from Thomas Foulkes for about $15.00.

CHART TABLE LIGHT

BINOCULAR HOLDER

This is not merely a decorative item. It's a must. To spend a small fortune on good binoculars only to have them shuffled from shelf to drawers is madness. They will scratch and become unusable in little time. Keeping them safely stowed in their original cases which, in turn, will be hidden in some dingy hole shows similar mental instability, for need of binoculars is usually immediate and the elusive buoy with the vital number on it in a viciously shoal harbour will have been long swallowed by fog by the time you unearth and unpack your precious toy.

Since little direct force will ever be placed on the box (hopefully), 1/2" thick teak should suffice. Twenty inches of an 8" wide board will be plenty if cautiously cut, and eight #8 panhead sheet metal screws will be enough for fasteners.

Cut the wood to dimensions shown, remembering that this case is made for binoculars with 2" diameter lenses and a fully-open width of 6". If yours differ, adjust accordingly. Take care that you align the grain of the front piece with the grain of the bulkhead, or ceiling, or whatever you intend to mount it on. Nothing looks less thorough than criss-crossing grains. Butt, glue and screw all pieces, *after* the bullnosing has been completed with a router. Do not forget to rout a good 3/4" diameter hole in the bottom piece to allow for cleaning. Don't make the hole any larger than that, or the small lens covers shall incessantly fall through and roll astray.

Space permitting, the best place for a binocular case is just inside the companionway, within easy reach of the helmsman. Mounting in the cockpit should be avoided under any circumstances, for lenses cake and smear in salt air (not to mention the metal parts corroding), and when the poor sailor on watch most dearly needs them, he will see nothing in the distance but streaky fog and fingerprints.

Interior placement should be on the aft ceiling (cabinside) and as high up (to keep dry) as possible, but not so high that you can't yank the thing out of the case without crushing most of your fingers against a deckbeam.

One last note. A binocular case should never be used as a handy storage bin for keys, or screws or bottle openers. Deep scratches in expensive lenses have caused more deaths to scratchors than all other binocular deaths combined.

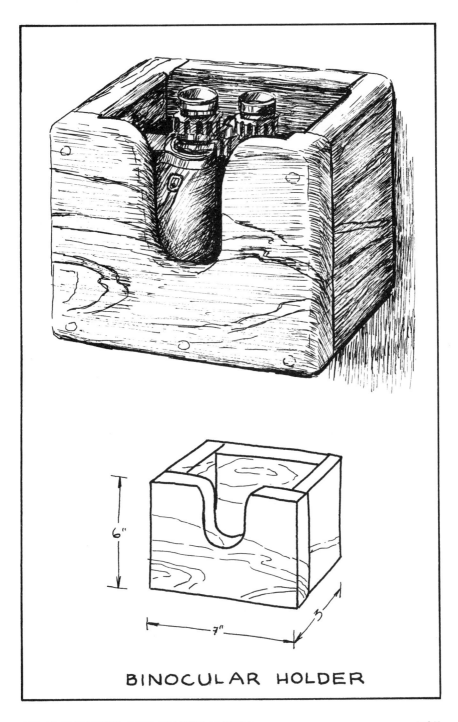

BINOCULAR HOLDER

SEXTANT/HAND HELD COMPASS MOUNTS

I was rather surprised once to see an expensive sextant aboard a yacht being stowed in a feeble tin bracket, exposed to dust and steam, on the excuse that the owner demanded quick access. Folly. The most secure place for a sextant is in the box designed specifically for it, and the most secure place for the box is on some nice protected shelf to which it can be securely screwed.

Susan Hiscock explained to me the additional importance of being able to work through the entire box-opening-sextant-removal operation with one hand when seas are rough and the yacht skittish. On these occasions, one hand will be required for survival.

To enable one to do this, a way will have to be found to hold the lid securely open so it will not come crashing down on the delicate mirrors and adjustment screws as the sextant is being removed. The sextant box will have to be located so that the open lid will be close to the hull on a bulkhead. Cut a 2" long block to the thickness of your lid and fasten it to the bulkhead directly above the opened lid. Then with a single screw, loosely attach a small wood swivel (1/2" thickness is plenty) to the block, and have this act as a lock to hold the lid open. The box latch can then be tripped with one hand, lid opened, swivel lock turned, and when the lid is secured, the sextant removed.

Hand Held Compass

A second compass aboard a yacht is most advisable. To risk the safety of crew and vessel on a single compass would be thoughtless. Many yachtsmen prefer a fixed back-up unit below decks so the yacht's course can be checked without venturing topsides. This seems a redundant expense. The better hand held compasses come in a very presentable wooden box complete with a little window and an external switch which, when flipped, places pressure on the finger trigger in the compass, illuminating it for night use. The box need only be screwed to a bulkhead or shelf (mounted fore and aft will save adding or subtracting 90°) and a perfectly functional fixed compass is now in operation. Care must be taken that no metal be located near the compass, or it will be helplessly thrown out of kilter.

THE FINELY FITTED YACHT

Sextant box screwed to locker top for one-handed operation.

CHART TABLE AND NAVIGATION

LEAD AND LINE

Depth finders are lovely little instruments that spin and flash or just coolly blink exact little electric numbers at you. I'm first to admit that they are an absolute joy to use and play with, but one should prepare for their unscheduled demise and not be in a helpless state of tears when it comes. Having a proper lead and line aboard can enable a crew to proceed just as safely, if not quite as conveniently. They worked wonderfully well for centuries so they should more than suffice in a modern emergency. Since chandleries that carry a lead-line are few and far between, one should undertake making his own.

First, either buy six pounds of scrap lead, or take the old dusty car battery from the corner of your garage and go at it with an ax (after having dumped out the very last drop of battery acid of course). Now get out an old pot you've always hated (actually a tin can will do just as well), put it over a hot flame, and throw in your lead, little by little. While it is melting, take two tomato paste tins (about 2″ diameter) and cut out the bottom of one and tape it with heavy duct tape to the open top of the other to form about an 8″ tube. Have nearby a galvanized eyebolt with a good 3″ stem and 1″ eye and you're ready for the fun. Set the tin tube up vertically using some rocks or bricks around it to make sure it won't tip and spill the spoils, then cautiously pour the molten lead into it. Fill it no higher than 1/2″ from the top, then quickly get hold of your eyebolt with a pair of plyers, and holding it by the eye, stick it into the molten lead until only the eye shows. Hold it there until the lead sets. When it's set, hammer off the tin can tube and voilà, you've got yourself one hell of a billy club.

Now fetch a 10 to 20 fathom line of about 1/2″ diameter (anything less will cut uncomfortably into hands) and splice one end of it to the eye, then, with careful measurements, mark in the fathoms according to the standard method which allows identification in the dark by feeling with hands or lips. These can be tucked into three-strand line or sewn onto a braid. Mark the first 10 to 20 feet with a simple marking for shoal water cruising.

The best method of stowing is to smartly coil the line and hang it in the rope locker on a piece of leather stripping (see "Rope Locker").

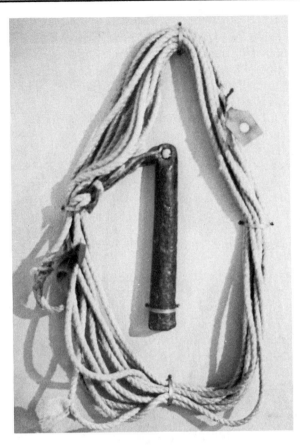

```
 2  FATHOMS - LEATHER WITH TWO ENDS
                   (MARK TWAIN)
 3      "      - LEATHER WITH THREE ENDS
 5      "      - WHITE CALICO
 7      "      - COARSE RED FABRIC
10      "      - FLAT LEATHER WITH HOLE
13      "      - THICK BLUE SERGE
15      "      - WHITE CALICO
17      "      - COARSE RED FABRIC
20      "      - CORD WITH TWO KNOTS
```

FATHOM MARKS

LEAD AND LINE

CHART SURFACE FOR CHART TABLE

This is such a clever idea that I'm surprised I didn't think of it myself. I found it on Ginny and Peter Marshall's beautiful Spencer. They are planning to cruise the Pacific Northwest for the next few years, so they laminated their most general chart of that area onto the surface of their chart table.

This should be done on most vessels, for not only does it look more attractive than vast expanses of formica or veneer, but it also provides wonderfully quick reference without searching through chart drawers and unfolding charts.

To laminate the chart, sand the existing surface lightly with 100 grit sandpaper, then take a *new* unfolded chart (anything with creases will be very difficult to laminate properly), and crop out the section you are most likely to use. Crop it so it fills the entire chart table surface from fiddle to fiddle. Do a dry run to make sure it's a perfect fit. Next, tape off around the area where the chart is to be laid, because you'll be using a spray adhesive and taping sure beats scraping. Now, take a can of said adhesive (available at most art and stationery stores), and spray the chart table surface judiciously, but evenly. With the help of a friend, hold the chart over the table and begin to lay it in place starting with one corner. Lay down only a 6" square area at first, then press thoroughly to work out all air bubbles. From here on, lay the chart in inch by inch pressing firmly and thoroughly as you go.

When you're done, wipe the chart well and, without removing the surrounding masking tape, lay on two or three coats of satin finish varnish (the high gloss would throw too many reflections and would be more slippery), allowing sufficient time to dry between coats. A light sanding with 400 grit between coats would yield the best results.

When you decide to do extended cruising in a new region and feel that a new general chart would be of more use, you can easily replace the existing one by either peeling it away or better still, just leaving it and laying the new one over it in a similar fashion. It will be sometime before your accumulation of charts reaches the tops of the fiddles.

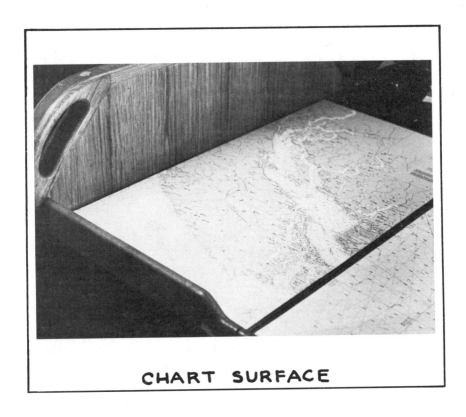

CHART SURFACE

salon

THE FINELY FITTED WET LOCKER

It strikes me as somewhat droll that most designers create a vertical space of about 48″, slap a door on it, and call it a wet locker. And indeed these places live up to their name, for whatever you put in them will stay forever soggy and dank. Well, maybe not forever, just until they mildew. Apart from the physical space required to hang one's foul weather gear and stow one's boots and harnesses, three vital points must be considered and wet lockers modified accordingly. These are drainage, ventilation and proper stowage.

Drainage

Gear will have difficulty drying if it must forever dangle in its own drippings. In a fiberglass boat with a built-in liner, a small plastic through-hull should be fitted into the low spot of the locker and a hose led back into the bilge. As a further precaution, a grate can be installed in the locker to encourage passage of water away from the gear.

Ventilation

Surprising as it may seem, neither a small finger hole nor even a cut out in the shape of a tiny anchor in the door of a wet locker, will provide sufficient air circulation to dry clothes quickly. The most sensible solution is to replace the door provided with one having a cane insert. An alternate step and one perhaps more easily effected, would be to cut a very nice hole out of any part of the bulkhead that makes up the locker. This must be cut with great care and the edges thoroughly bullnosed. The corners can be radiused for a nice finished effect. The same caning can now be installed from the inside of the locker, using 1/4″ stock for securing and trimming. Some people advocate drilling holes in a pattern. Unfortunately these do not provide sufficient air circulation and seldom look any better than what they are: a bunch of holes.

Proper Stowage

Plastic hangers should be used for all clothes. Rust stains on foul weather gear look very unsightly. Shallow shelves of netting should be installed so boots and gloves and hats don't sit in a hopeless soggy heap on the bottom of the locker. Wooden pegs (dowels) about 1¼″ long can be used on 45° angles to provide space for safety harnesses. Use no cup hooks or metal fasteners in a wet locker. Expensive foul weather gear can be needlessly torn by such an oversight.

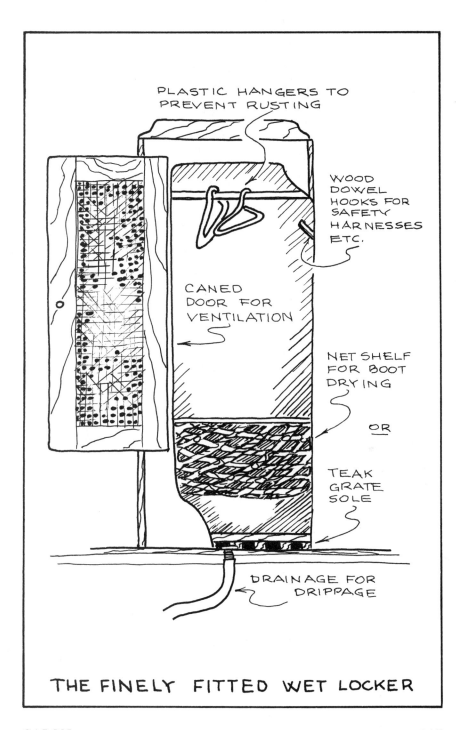

PLASTIC HANGERS TO PREVENT RUSTING

WOOD DOWEL HOOKS FOR SAFETY HARNESSES ETC.

CANED DOOR FOR VENTILATION

NET SHELF FOR BOOT DRYING

OR

TEAK GRATE SOLE

DRAINAGE FOR DRIPPAGE

THE FINELY FITTED WET LOCKER

GIMBALLED FLOWER POT HOLDER

All people who live aboard and most people who spend a lot of time on their boats like to have at least one live plant, but are usually deterred by the constant dirt sweeping and replanting which follows most sailing trips, unless they take place in an aquarium. A rather sophisticated looking, but basically simple-minded device, can be fabricated to keep the plant swinging, but in place. Granted, the pot will have to be small, about 4″ in diameter, basically eliminating your average palms and redwoods, but nicely accommodating bonsais or herbs. You'll have to go first to your local plumber and with a straight face, ask for a 3/4″ *length* of 4″ copper pipe and two 3/4″ lengths of 4½″ pipe. He'll mutter and curse, but he'll cut them for a nominal cutting charge on his magical pipe cutter.

Take home your treasures and drill two holes on opposite sides of the smaller ring and four holes on opposite sides of the larger ring. Cut a slit in the second large ring, and bend it into a "U", with a 5″ diameter mouth. Drill a hole in each end and one in the centre. Assemble the three rings with small flat head bolts and shallow nuts as shown in diagram. Use nuts as spacers. You will now have a double gimballed pot holder that will spill nothing and hit nothing. To attach, bolt through the centre of the "U" and back it up with a nice sized plate or washer. If through-bolting isn't possible, flatten the belly of the "U" and drill three holes in the pattern of a triangle, and attach with sheet metal screws.

Happy gardening.

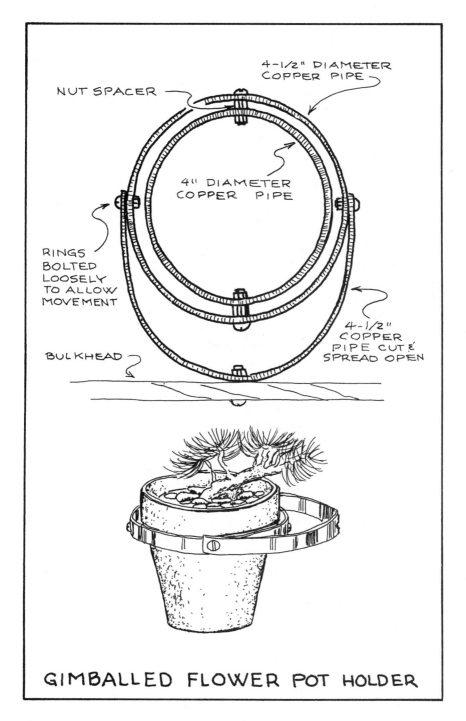

NUT SPACER

4-1/2" DIAMETER COPPER PIPE

4" DIAMETER COPPER PIPE

RINGS BOLTED LOOSELY TO ALLOW MOVEMENT

4-1/2" COPPER PIPE CUT & SPREAD OPEN

BULKHEAD

GIMBALLED FLOWER POT HOLDER

MAGAZINE RACK

They're everywhere. *New Yorkers* and *Elles* and magazines about sailboats and magazines about sailplanes clutter *Warm Rain* as if she were a used book shop. I throw out piles daily, but the publishers keep printing and Candace just keeps bringing. What can I do? All I can do is built racks to contain the beasts.

Fortunately, this is a fairly minor project, but one that will reap reward year after year, rag after rag.

The first thing to do is to find a nice flat vertical surface about 10″ × 12″ upon which the rack can be installed. Next, track down a 10″ × 9″ × 1/2″ piece of teak, or whatever you wish to use, and get two matching pieces for the sides about 3½″ × 9″. Be sure all your grain runs vertically. A piece of 1/2″ plywood will do for the bottom, unless your rack will be located up high so the bottom will show, in which case you'll need another 3″ × 10″ piece of stock. Cut the sides and the face with 45° angles where they are to meet. One-half-inch from the bottom, rabbet both sides and the face to let in the bottom piece. Assemble everything dry and measure the exact interior distance between the sides, then cut a dummy piece from scrap to fit. Now, glue all joints and assemble, slipping the dummy in at the unsupported top of the rack. Clamp with a short bar clamp to hold the sides and two C clamps to hold the face to the bottom piece and also to the dummy piece. Let set overnight.

In the morning, bullnose all edges and sand and oil or varnish. If you have done a good job, the rack will seem to have been hewn from a solid block of wood. If possible, mount on bulkhead or cabinet face by drilling and screwing into the sides from behind so the face of the rack can remain unmarred. Oops, almost forgot: drill a good 3/4″ hole in the bottom for cleaning.

Upon installation, you'll realize two things. One, the titles of most magazines will be visible over the rack; two, the rack holds only about ten magazines. If more than that find their way aboard, just store them carefully behind the companionway in a little container marked "garbage."

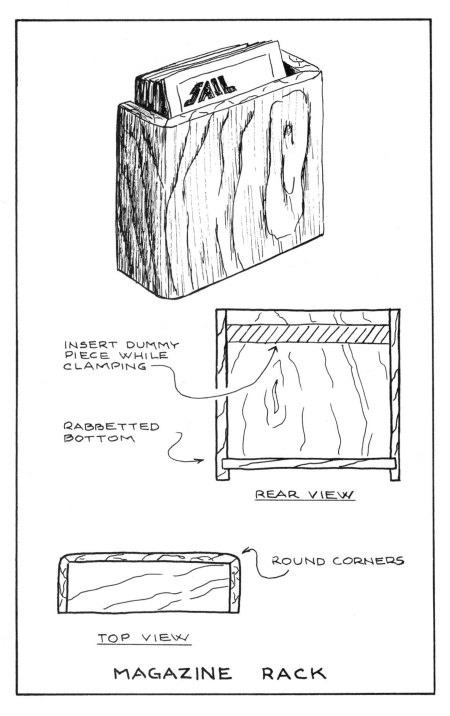

INSERT DUMMY PIECE WHILE CLAMPING

RABBETTED BOTTOM

REAR VIEW

ROUND CORNERS

TOP VIEW

MAGAZINE RACK

OVER BUNK FOOT LOCKER

When you're a crew on someone else's yacht, it's difficult to feel totally at home unless you receive your own cabin, an event which occurs seldom to never. The next best thing is your own bunk. It can feel so much more personal if it has above the foot a nice little locker where a few of your more precious things can be kept. The locker need not be enormous, indeed it is limited in height by the proximity of the deck, since, in most cases, we are speaking of quarter berths and pilot berths and bunks in the forepeak and aft cabins.

Their use should not be limited to visiting crew. Since each member of the family usually frequents the same bunk, a very private locker would seem a most useful idea.

Even over the narrowest bunk of 20", having a clear vertical space of only 24", a very neat little locker of 10" in height, 20" in width, and 16" in depth can be built. The opening should be fore and aft to keep things from slipping out.

The first 5" against the hull must of course be dedicated to books. Without books, there can be no civilization. This space should be no more than 6" deep, which of course means that there will be a bizarre area behind it, but that can be accessible with a little arm bending. This should be fitted with a half height baffle, and it will then hold a miraculous number of socks and underwear. Granted the sweaters in the adjoining area would have to be removed, but then, that's life. If you want lots of open space, move to the moon. The central area should be free for things like the aforementioned sweaters, but the last 5" should be saved for two 4" X 4" X 16" deep drawers, one above the other. Nothing holds tiny knickknacks from watches to razors to strange metal things you find on the beach and have to keep, better than a drawer, especially if it's divided into fore and aft sections.

The top and bottom and outboard side of the locker can be of 1/2" plywood, the inboard side of teak or mahogany. The locker will be too large to survive on butted joints alone, so cleat stock must be used where any large pieces meet others. Cleat stock will be needed along the underdecks to suspend the sides and partitions of the locker. The drop door should be of teak, equipped with a bayonet catch and a brass chain stopper. Doors and drawers should have 1" finger holes as handles. Sand and bullnose everything. Do a nice job. This little item will bring ooh's and ah's from even the coldest hearted visitors.

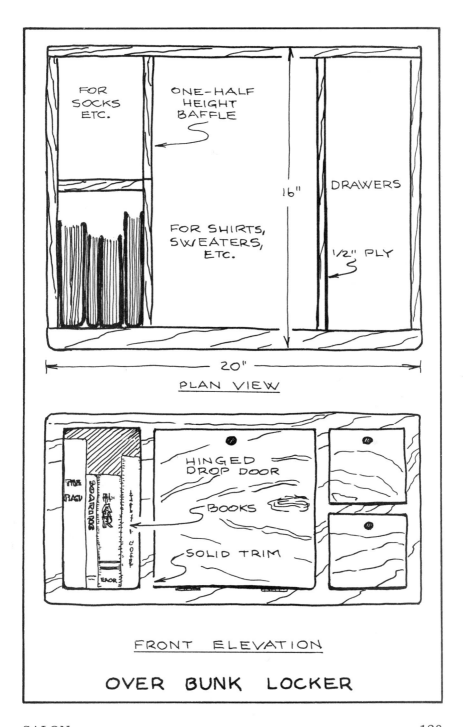

PLAN VIEW

FRONT ELEVATION

OVER BUNK LOCKER

BOOK SHELVES

A yacht without books is a sad place indeed. Apart from the basic almanacs, pilots and scattered reference books, a goodly library is needed.

Size

Since most books today are leaning toward a standard 6″ × 9″ measurement, one major set of shelves can be based on these dimensions, adding an inch vertically to allow one book to be lifted over the searail without disturbing the others. The minimum depth should exceed 6″ by about 1/2″ and no more. The tighter the book fits behind the rail, the better.

A second shelf should be designed for paperbacks. These are totally standardized in the publishing industry to 7 1/8″ × 4¼″. Again, allow a spare 1″ vertical space and 1/2″ horizontal space. A large area should be left open for the above mentioned almanacs, sight reduction tables and loose-leaf binders. Most of these measure 10″ × 12″.

Quantity

Any available space should be made into book shelves. If they go unused, other items can be kept on them, such as recording barometers, transoceanic receivers, VHF radios, etc.

Location and Construction

Ideally, book shelves should be built athwartships, for then the need to hold them in place with lines, chains, or bars will be eliminated. The appearance of most bulkheads will be enhanced by orderly book shelves. See photo.

The most aesthetically pleasant shelves are those let either partially or totally into the bulkhead. These have the basic advantage of not depriving the main salon of space, and, in addition, most of the construction can be of inexpensive 1/2″ plywood since the bulk of it will be located in the head or forepeak or whatever it adjoins.

Determine your goal and make the bulkhead cutout. Construct a plywood box with a matching sized opening and let in 1/2″ plywood shelves. Assemble with 3/4″ radiused cleat stock on the *outsides*. This will hide the cleat from the main salon as well as make the box look less boxish from the other side. Trim the opening with "L" trim of teak or mahogany, or, if the bulkhead is painted, simply bullnose the edge of the opening and paint it without trim. An accent will be provided by the searails.

One important point: when milling your searails for shelves, be sure to make the rabbet at least 1/4″ higher than the shelf itself. See diagram. This way the searail can overhang the shelf, and when screws are inserted, it will not split as it would almost surely do without the extra 1/4″.

If delicate "L" trim is to be installed, finishing tacks should be used instead of screws. These will have to be drilled for as well, but you will not run as great a risk of splitting the wood as you would with even the smallest screw.

Fore and aft bookshelves are, of course, more simple to construct since the space is usually already defined by the hull and bulkhead, and cabinets, requiring only installation of a shelf, a searail, and some magical means of keeping the books in place.

Scribe and fit the shelf and install. Do not use cleat stock. That entails extra work and it looks messy. Attach the shelf by screwing through cabinet and bulkhead into the shelf ends. The same can be done with the searail, eliminating plugging. Glue everything well; you'll need the strength. If your shelf exceeds 20″ in length you'll need a knee beneath it for additional support. This will have to be of solid wood. Scribing and fitting of the knee should be done before installation of searail.

For the fore and aft shelves, some method of keeping the books in place must be arranged. Some people suggest shock cords, but I find the idea quite impractical for unless the cord is absurdly taut, it will stretch and the books will dive effortlessly over it onto the cabin floor. The following three solutions seem to be reasonable in function and amount of work involved.

Brass Chain

Attached to padeyes on either end, brass chain works very nicely. The two end links will have to be bent so the chain will be taut yet removable without broken fingernails.

Wood Rods

A simple 3/4″ dowel rod or 3/4″ teak bar slipped into U-shaped wood chocks will do nicely and can be stored behind the searail when in port.

Hinged Searail

This is the most complex of the three, requiring a 4″ high bottom hinged drop board. With a barrel bolt at either end, it provides very nice support, but it seems to be a bit too much work for what it accomplishes.

THE FINELY FITTED YACHT

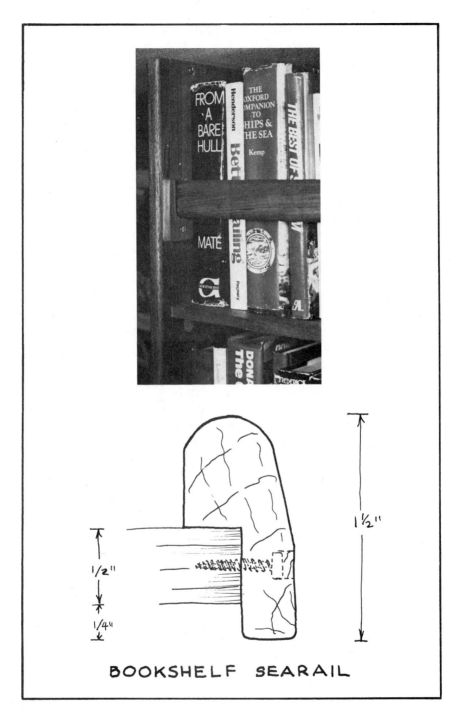

BOOKSHELF SEARAIL

1 ½"

½"

¼"

TABLE TOP STOWAGE

Whether your salon table is of the dinette or dropleaf variety, valuable storage space is probably being lost just below its surface. Most dinettes are wide enough to have a shallow 7″ wide box run down their spine and almost all dropleafs can facilitate the same.

This size stowage would do nicely for placemats, cutlery, serviettes, salt and pepper, etc., enabling attainment without leaving the table.

The first step is to decide the size of the box. Take into consideration under-table hardware and, more importantly, knee space. No one can have a pleasant dinner leaning over the table from a distance like a crane, so if your table is too narrow for both the box and knees, let the knees reign. Boxes can live elsewhere, but knees can only thrive on legs.

Once you've decided on the size, build the box of 1/2″ plywood with internal cleat stock. At this point, assemble only the four sides. In the bottom piece, drill a 1/2″ hole (to serve as a cleaning outlet) for each compartment that you plan. Affix the bottomless box in place to the underside of the table with cleat stock.

Measure in and outline the size of the lid you'll be cutting out of your table top, being sure you leave 1/2″ all around the inside perimeter to which you'll be attaching seating cleats that, in turn, will support the lid. See illustration. From below, drill four 1/8″ pilot holes in the corner of your drawn outline to establish the corners on the top where you will be doing your cutting. Cut out the lid most precisely with a hack saw blade and a jigsaw. Round all fresh edges with a very fine file and sandpaper.

The best, as usual, is left for last. Select a beautiful piece of solid 3/4″ wood for your lid. If your table top is dark, pick something light like ash or oak or maple; if it's light, use teak. Place the piece over the hole and, from below, scribe in the shape, then cut it. Cut your seating cleats to 1″ widths from 3/8″ plywood. Screw and glue them around the perimeter from below. If your table top is less than 3/4″ thick you'll have to rabbet your edges of the lid to fit. Mark the amount to be removed from underneath by running a pencil along the seating cleat. *Now* you can install the bottom of the box. Drill a 1″ diameter finger hole in the lid for a handle and enjoy.

THE FINELY FITTED YACHT

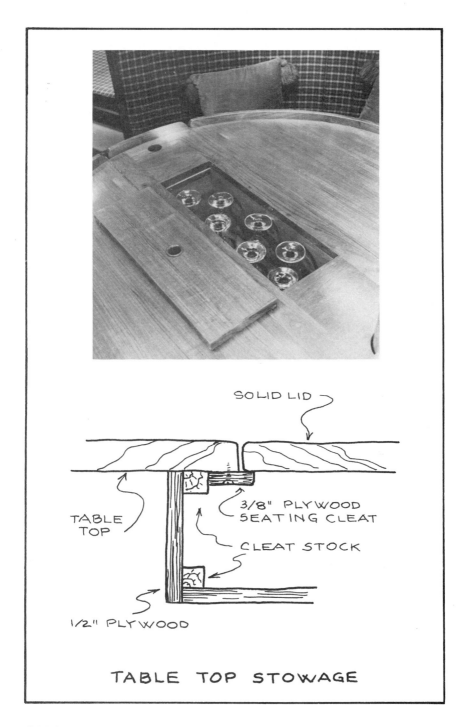

SOLID LID

TABLE
TOP

3/8" PLYWOOD
SEATING CLEAT

CLEAT STOCK

1/2" PLYWOOD

TABLE TOP STOWAGE

OPEN FOOT LOCKER

Most salons with a centre table arrangement tend to have full length berths running fore and aft. Many of these are never fully utilized as seats, for seldom are there six to eight people in a salon perched along them; thus, a great amount of valuable storage space is lost.

A very simple conversion can be made, requiring only three pieces of plywood, some cleat stock, and a bit of searail. This structure will provide an open locker for pillow and bedding, and a fine flat surface for mounting anything from a small stove to a moose head.

The dimension of the structure will depend on the layout of your boat and what sort of additional space you require. On *Warm Rain*, the main bulkhead extends clear to the mast support post, so we decided to run our foot stowage about 14″ past the face of the berth, and create a top loading locker for wood and coal.

The top of the locker should be cut to about a 12″ width, and whatever length you desire. The foot hole portion will need to be 13″ high for large feet, plus 1½″ to accommodate cleat stock and searails.

To join the two vertical plywood pieces together, mill a teak corner post (see "Desk" for details). Cut and fasten needed lengths of cleat stock onto the settee back and bulkhead, to form supports for the face and the top. Cut and attach cleat stock to the top edge of the face to form the last piece of foundation for the top. Glue and screw the face to the settee back, then glue and screw the top onto the fixed cleat stock. In both cases, try to do all the drilling and screwing from the inside, that is, from the cleat stock into the plywood, to avoid as much plugging as possible. If you are building a front loading cabinet, install all shelves *now* before you install the fore and aft cabinet face, then cut the face to fit, furnish with the cleat stock and fix into place. For door construction, see "Cane Doors." It's time to install the searails. If you wish to use traditional corner pieces, see "Searails Corners"; if not, read on. Get a piece of stock searail, slip it over the top of your new locker, mark for length, and cut on a 45° angle. Now, install this piece permanently in place. Take a rough-cut short piece of searail and mark on its face the distance between the bulkhead and the tip of your freshly cut 45° piece. Mark, cut, and install. Trim the foot hole with "L" trim. Paint or oil.

OPEN FOOT LOCKER

NON-SLIPPERY COMPANIONWAY RUNGS

Some companionways, be they ladders or removable steps, seem to come perfectly varnished and perfectly slick; ideal for slipped disks. Four very simple antidotes to ladder diving exist:

Macrame Pads

This is probably the most charming of the available ideas, doubling as a dirt catcher as well. Two fine examples made of hemp or old dacron, are the Flemish coil mat and the ultimate Ladder Step Mat. Their construction is wonderfully described in Harvey Garrett Smith's "The Arts of the Sailor," a fine book on rope work written 25 years ago that no mariner should be without.

Permanent attachment of any mat would be a mistake. Small bits of Velcro should be sewn beneath the mat and glued onto the step as well. These will trammel the mat very effectively, yet enable removal for cleaning beneath or washing.

Cast Brass Pads

These were in profuse supply some decades ago, but now seem to be impossible to find. They completely protect the step, and with their heavily textured surface, the stepper as well. Where they are now, nobody knows.

Silicone Non-skid

The fine grained silicone used in conjunction with paint for deck non-skids, can also be used in varnish with fine success. Simply tape off the area to be varnished or, if you're creative, make a stencil out of cardboard, cutting out either the boat's name or something useful, like "No Smoking." Lay in a coat of varnish, then sprinkle thoroughly and evenly with the silicone particles. When the varnish has set, vacuum or brush off the un-adhered surplus, and add another coat of varnish.

Meat Mallet Special

The owner of the vessel that had some of these pads in service wished to remain anonymous. Read on and you'll know why. Cut light gauge brass or copper sheeting the size you need, then place it on a medium dense towel over a piece of plywood or cement. Take a good metal-studded meat mallet and place it over the sheet metal, studs down, then whack it with a hammer. This will create neat little protrusions that will act as ideal non-skid. Move the mallet to the next area and whack again.

Well. Any grown man who'd do this would skip naked down Fifth Avenue at midday, singing fullthroatedly "Daisy, Daisy give me your answer true."

NON-SKID RUNGS

WINE CABINET

A finely fitted yacht must have a few bottles of white Burgundy aboard to wash down the poached salmon and moules marinière. Even though I had considered myself well versed in the ways of the world, it was pointed out to me by a dear friend that stowing wine aboard wrapped in sweater sleeves and sweatsocks did not really constitute the ultimate in elegance. Since then, we have installed a sort of a piece of plywood with holes in it into one of our lockers, but it comes nowhere close to the first class wine cabinet built into Grand Banks motor yachts (see illustration).

The entire unit is mobile, being equipped with four casters, so maximum access is gained to even the deepest part of the rack with minimum effort. The most limiting factor is, of course, size, for not only does the unit occupy 18″ of athwartships space in its "out" position, but it demands a similar run of flat cabin-sole inside the cabinet as well. The dimensions can be reduced, however, to about one-quarter the volume by removing the upper level and halving the depth of the rack. With a little shrewd spacing of the holes, one could still end up stowing six wine bottles in comfort.

So, first determine the absolute amount of space you can afford, then cut the hole in the cabinet face with a jigsaw. Next, cut the outboard piece (back) from a piece of 1/2″ plywood, and make up the front piece to the same dimensions out of four 3½″ wide pieces of 13/16″ stock patterned into a frame. Use either lap joints or dowels to secure the corners (see "Tool" section for doweling). Fill the area between the frames with teak plywood, cane, or louvers. Next, measure the absolute depth of the cabinet, including the front and back pieces. You will need to know this to make the fit as tight as possible so all play and movement can be avoided. Cut two shelves from 1/2″ ply to the depth of your space, minus 1 5/16″, and a width that's 1/2″ less than the width of your front piece. You'll need that 1/2″ space to trim each side of the plywood shelves with 1/4″ teak strips. Next, get your most favourite bottles of wine and liqueurs and lay them out over your shelves in the most economical way possible. A 3/4″ space between bottles is quite sufficient. Cut out the holes with the appropriate hole saws, or, if those are unavailable, use a jigsaw. To expedite matters, clamp the two shelves together and cut at once. Lightly sand all the holes to remove splinters. From 1/4″ plywood, cut a piece identical to the shelves, and glue it and clamp it to the bottom of the lower shelf. This is to keep the bottles from falling through and dragging on the cabin sole.

WINE CABINET

You will now have to purchase a set of four casters. To do without them and just use wood slides would result in too much friction with such a substantial weight as six bottles. Once you've bought your casters, you will be able to determine how high you can install your lower shelf. Leave at least 1/4″ clearance between the face of the cabinet and the cabin sole. A 4″ space between the upper and lower shelves will be enough. Use cleat stock per diagram and #10 P.H.S.M. screws. Do not drill or screw through the face of the front piece. Now, decide how far you want the cabinet to roll out, and run a piece of cleat stock across its path to act as a stop against the back wheels. Lift the rear wheels over the stop and slide the cabinet into place.

With such weight and mobility, a very positive lock system should be devised to keep the cabinet in check. The use of three, high quality, barrel bolts would be advisable, one on top and one in each side. The top one is, of course, the safety that will naturally "fall" in any vibration and keep the cabinet closed.

If, at some point, you develop a taste for a new wine whose bottle fits too loosely into the shelf holes; don't panic; just slip it in a sweat sock and put it back in place; which puts us aesthetically back to where we were before we started building this edifice to bloodshot eyes.

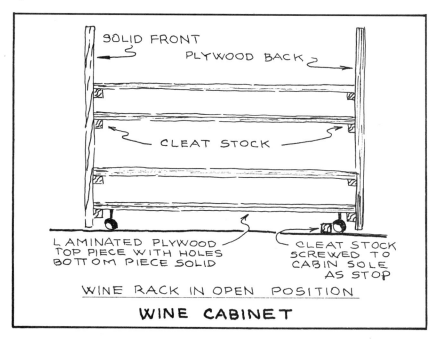

WINE CABINET

PIPE BERTHS

Once upon a time, before the major goal of yacht designers was to try to fit 67 berths into a 30' boat, extremely pleasant wooden yachts were built with two comfortable settee berths in the salon and sail storage in the forepeak. This was a very sensible and suitable arrangement for couples but left a lack on those occasions when guests were to spend the night aboard.

Pipe berths became popular at that time, and some beautifully made ones, like those found on the graceful cutter "Nan of Clynder" from Greenock, Scotland, should deserve consideration on any modern yacht. Instead of having the salon inundated with bunks until it looks like a boy scout hut, pipe berths can be fitted over each settee to serve as cleverly disguised settee backs during the day, and when hinged up, comfortable quarterberths by night.

Although various combinations of materials can be used, ranging from wooden boxes with bedspring bottoms to handsome bent aluminum tubing with slip-on covers, the most serviceable ones, from the standpoint of both construction and appearance, seem to be the galvanized pipe berths with a stretched and laced dacron base and an upholstered, slip-on foam mattress.

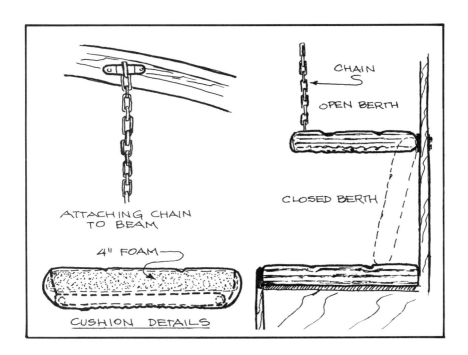

ATTACHING CHAIN TO BEAM

4" FOAM

CUSHION DETAILS

CHAIN

OPEN BERTH

CLOSED BERTH

Standard 3/4″ galvanized pipe is very inexpensive and if the berth measurements are accurately taken, any plumbing shop will cut the pipe to the required lengths and treat them appropriately. Be sure to tell them that the pipes will be assembled into a closed rectangle so they can cut you an elbow with reverse thread to enable you to assemble the last piece suitably. When measuring for the pipe berth, leave a 1/2″ space between the ends of the berth and the bulkheads for ease of maneuvering. The gap can be largely covered up when fabricating the upholstery. The width of the berth will be determined by the current height of the settee's back, but a good guideline would be 20″ for cold climates and 24″ for hot ones.

Assemble three sets of brackets as shown and bolt them onto the back of the settee. To keep the pipe berth from sliding fore or aft, drill two 1/8″ holes in the pipe directly fore and aft of the bracket at the foot of the berth, tap the holes, and screw a 1/8″ machine bolt into each. The heads of the bolts will act as stoppers.

Next, use a piece of discarded sailcloth to form the bottom of the berth. Good dacron will stretch and sag much less than canvas or any other material. Allow for fold-under flaps of at least 4″. For extra strength where the grommets are to be installed, run a piece of heavy dacron tape and triple fold the hem. The lacing should be set up as shown. A 3″ or 4″ thick foam cushion should be cut to the exact length and width of the berth and upholstered as described in the "Cushions" section with one exception. Run the fabric an extra four inches to form a flap under the berth, sew a tubing into it, and fit it with a draw cord. This will enable you to readily remove the cushion for cleaning etc. You will of course have to leave cutouts for the hinges in much the same way as you did for the dacron base. Leave gaps on the inboard edge for two chain supports as well, but make the cushion full in the corners. To support the berth in "back-rest" position, screw a block on each bulkhead to hold the berth in the angle desired. A 15° slope is quite comfortable.

To support the inboard edges of the pipe berth in the "up" position, bolt two padeyes through two deck beams about 18″ from the foot and the head of the berth, then secure a length of 3/16″ chain to the head and foot of the berth respectively, then hook the ends into the padeyes. You may find it advantageous to leave a bit of extra chain so slight adjustments can be made to the plane of the berth on prolonged and excessive heels.

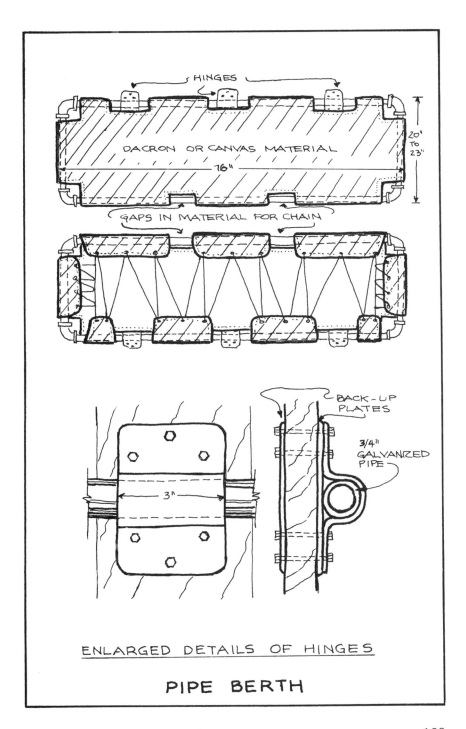

HINGES

DACRON OR CANVAS MATERIAL

76"

20" TO 23"

GAPS IN MATERIAL FOR CHAIN

BACK-UP PLATES

3/4" GALVANIZED PIPE

3"

ENLARGED DETAILS OF HINGES

PIPE BERTH

CUT FLOWERS ABOARD

Few things add as much simple beauty to a well-equipped cruising yacht than some freshly picked flowers collected on the most recent jaunt ashore. If kept aboard, they will bring back fine memories for some days after the port has long been left behind. The problem, of course, is where do you find a vase that won't tip over during the first heel. The answer has been discovered by Susan Hiscock who found a beautiful little half-vase during their cruise in the Greek Islands. A half-vase is a creature that has been cut in half lengthwise and thus, has a flat back, usually fitted with a hole through which it can be secured to a bulkhead. Because it is so high, with a bulbous lower half, almost no water will spill, if one cleverly fills the bulbous part only half full. This principle will only work if the vase is mounted on an athwartships bulkhead, otherwise, spillage will quickly occur along the flat side.

The second alternative is to have a long container held in a gimballed bracket similar to ones that hold kerosene bulkhead lamps (see "Gimballed Plant Holder"). Any ceramic container that fits in the bracket should suffice, although special attention should be given to having the vase's bottom weighed down (a few large pebbles should do) to encourage gimballing. The vase should not be filled higher than the bracket.

The third and most permanent way to display your favourite flowers would be to press them (in a book), dry them, and mount them under glass in small picture frames. These will enhance almost any bulkhead.

The processes of preservation are many. Some people advocate spraying the flowers very lightly with varnish, while others simply mount them on paper and frame them. Whichever way you select, they will rekindle beautiful memories for a long time.

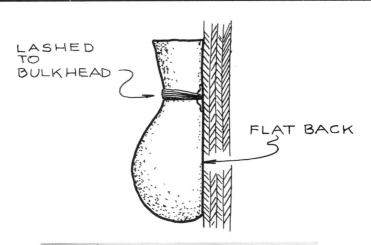

LASHED
TO
BULKHEAD

FLAT BACK

CUT FLOWERS ABOARD

FOLD-UP TABLE/MAGAZINE RACK

Most multi-functional inventions frighten me. As a matter of fact, I have developed such an aversion to them that I now refuse to wear a reversible jacket; but this combination flip-up table and magazine rack I find captivating. It would serve very well in narrow walkways plus have the advantage over a regular flip-up table in that it functions as a magazine holder in its "down" position. A removable crossbar holds the magazines in place. A hinged butterfly support holds the table in the "up" position.

II. & L. Marine sells a very handsome ready-made version, but if you want to build your own, here's how.

From 13/16″ teak or mahogany stock, cut one 2½″ × 16″ piece, and two 3½″ × 13″ pieces. Shape one side of the two short pieces as in the diagram, leaving a 1/2″ high by 4″ long bulge in its center. Route a 1/2″ × 1½″ hole about 1/2″ back from the edge. These holes will house the crossbar for the magazines. Bullnose all long edges of these two pieces. Next, 5/8″ in from the edge of all three pieces, dado a 3/8″ × 3/8″ groove running the full length of the 16″ piece and terminating within 3/8″ of one end of the two 13″ pieces. If you forget to terminate there, you'll have two bizarre little holes showing in your table front. Now square out the end of these grooves with a 3/8″ chisel and cut a piece of 3/8″ mahogany plywood to a 12½″ × 16¾″ shape, glue mercilessly, and slip it into your grooves. Reinforce the whole thing by side screwing (countersunk of course) the two sides of the table to the front piece, and by running a couple of screws (#8 by 3/4″ is plenty) through the sides directly into the plywood. Plug and trim.

The last remaining step is the butterfly support. The butterfly is much to be preferred in these situations because it allows the horizontal piano hinge to run almost equal amounts on both sides of the support. To achieve an ideal fit, both the fixed and the mobile parts should be cut from a single paddle-shaped piece of 1/2″ plywood whose overall height can be 10″ and width 14″. Cut the paddle into two pieces per the diagram and after cutting piano hinges to length with a hacksaw, install them before securing the fixed piece to the bulkhead with five or six 1″ P.H.S.M. screws.

FOLD-UP TABLE/MAGAZINE RACK

STEREOS AND SPEAKERS

There is something inexplicably emotional about being on a vessel that's moved only by the wind, but what's unavoidably tear evoking is having Bruch's *Scottish Fantasy* or Beethoven's *Pastorale* rising joyfully from belowdecks. Show me a man aboard with dry eyes and I'll show you a man with a dead hearing aid.

But beautiful music requires at least adequate equipment, otherwise you can bypass the whole thing and just hum old tunes. The most ideal system appears to be a stereo cassette. The quality exceeds that of eight-track, the machine itself is noticeably smaller, and the cassettes themselves have a more civilized appearance than the oaf sized eight-track tapes.

If undertaking lengthy cruises upon which new friends from different areas will be met, a cassette with recording abilities should be considered. It is truly a great joy to listen to forgotten voices. Another fine advantage of such a system is its ability to record from the AM and FM radio which usually accompanies it. Something like a Sanyo FP33M AM-FM cassette recorder, which retails at about $150, seems ideal. The speakers purchased should be the best car speakers available. Jensen's 9″ ovals (about $60 a pair) with built-in tweeters have less distortion than most and put out a generally fine quality sound.

The awful plastic facing must be removed and tasteful speaker boxes should be built of teak and fabric. The Jensen speakers can be nicely accommodated in a space 12″ wide, 7″ high, and 6″ deep. Try to pick shallow, hard to use corners in bookshelves, etc.

The sides (an existing bulkhead can make up one side) should be fitted to the curvature of the hull and underdeck from 3/4″ teak, mahogany, etc. Cleat stock it in place. Place the vertical cleat stock 1″ back from the front edge. This will serve as a mounting base for the face. Bring the wires through into the box with a good 15″ to spare.

From 1/2″ plywood, fabricate a face to fit snugly between the sides against the cleat stocks. Cut a hole sufficient for the speaker and mount same in the face. Cover the entire face with fabric that's left over from your cushions (not naugahyde), wrapping it clear around the back and affixing it there with brass or monel staples. Hook up your wires and slip the face in place. Attach it there with two brass round head screws. Use no glue. You never know when you need to get in there. Now slip in *Pastorale* and get out the hankies.

THE FINELY FITTED YACHT

STEREOS AND SPEAKERS

SLIDING DOUBLE BERTH

Most boat owners, myself included, demand a comfortable double berth on board. On large vessels, this need creates no problem to designer or builder, but on a vessel of 30 feet or less, the only solutions seem to be a forepeak with a V-filler or a converted dinette. Both have severe limitations. The former usually results in very cramped quarters caused by the low foredeck, and also gives birth to a cumbersome filler-cushion for which space must be found when not in use.

The latter is a major problem because its prerequisite is the existence of a dinette that, in most small boats, means extremely uncomfortable seats (the outboard edges of most dinettes are wedged beneath the side-decks which causes one's head to bend so far forward as to make any movement of the jaw impossible), as well as the destruction of an extremely valuable seaberth.

With this in mind, I propose that the illustrated sliding berth found on CT 37's is the work of a genius. It can convert a single berth in the main salon into an ample, airy double, while preserving the integrity of the single seaberth.

Most salon berths can be remodelled at a very moderate expense. The top of the existing berth can be left (if solid, i.e. non-sliding) and the new slats can be installed directly on it. If the current berth is sliding (i.e. a narrow settee converting into an acceptable single), just remove the original slides and, using the existing fore and aft foundation, install the new slides.

The slides will be fabricated from 1″ stock ripped to 4″ widths. To figure out the number of lineal feet you'll need, measure the width of the bulk (berth face to hull) at its middle to get the average width, then divide the bunk length by four and multiply the result by the average width, i.e. L/4 × average width.

Dado both sides of each piece removing one-half the thickness *plus* 1/16″ to a width of 3/8″. The extra space (1/8″ total) will allow for swelling. Lay the first board next to a bulkhead with dado down, tongue up. Allow this, as well as all other pieces, to overhang the berth face by at least 3″. Glue and screw inboard and out. Beside this, slip in the next piece with tongue down. Using a 1/16″ spacer on either side, put down the third piece (tongue down), and glue and screw it into place. Remember to use spacers on both sides of the loose piece *and* on both its inboard and outboard ends to keep everything parallel and avoid jamming. Repeat this procedure until you run out of bunk. At the end, your last piece will have to be

THE FINELY FITTED YACHT

SLIDING DOUBLE BERTH

tongue up and screwed down firmly. If your order doesn't come out that way, throw out the last *loose* piece and make your *fixed* piece as wide as need be.

Next. Cut a piece of 2″ × 3″ to match the length of the berth, slip it wide-face up below the 3″ overhang of the slides, and screw and glue it to every *loose* piece with two countersunk 1½″ #10 P.H.S.M.S. per slide. Remember your spacers again, this time on the inboard end only. Now, trim off all ends flush to the inboard edge of the 2″ × 3″, and trim out with a piece of teak or mahogany as shown. Allow trim to form a searail 1½″ to 2″ above the slides to hold the cushions in place.

To support the berth when it's pulled out, you'll need two legs about 18″ from either end. These can be of either wood or metal. If you choose wood, make it 3″ wide with a 3″ wide hinge on its top so it can swing up and out of the way. Hold it up with a small barrel bolt.

If you choose metal, you'll have to find two receptacles per leg which will stabilize the leg as well as keep the cabin sole and berth from being worn through. In either case, a stop will be needed on the lower face of the slides, at least 4″ from their outboard ends. One length of 3/4″ cleat stock screwed from below with a single screw to each slide will do nicely. It will also help to rigidify the whole structure.

Your cushions will have to be the same thickness as the seat and of such a width that the seat plus the back will fill in the extended bunk.

Now cuddle up.

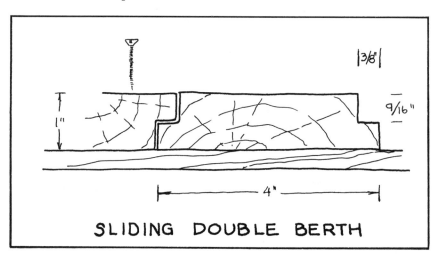

SLIDING DOUBLE BERTH

lamps/
stoves

WOOD AND COAL BIN

Any well-fitted yacht north and south of the 30th latitudes will probably have a little solid fuel heater, for those nasty winter nights when nothing can replace the comfort of flickering flames. Such a solacing companion as a wood burning stove deserves a special place for storing its food.

Even though these marvels barely nibble at the fuel compared to the amount of heat they produce, a two-cubic-foot storage space allotment would be a consummate notion. Unused vertical space is most ideal, like that next to the foot of a settee berth, or at the end of a fore and aft salon table. Of course, proximity to the stove is most desirable. Since possibilities for shapes and sizes are unlimited, I will humbly describe the one in *Warm Rain* as an example. We designated space for our bin at the junction of our centre table and the berth foot locker top. The space remaining allowed us to construct a bin $12'' \times 9'' \times 30''$ deep, yielding a volume of 1.8 cubic feet. We had a stainless steel, open-topped box welded to fit the space, and installed it with screws around the rim. The rim was caulked to keep dust from disappearing in the space between steel and plywood.

We had been told by many that a simple painted box would suffice, but we felt that a steel box would be the easiest thing to keep clean, and, in case of fire which could well occur in a place where bits of dry wood and paper are stored, control and containment could more easily be provided by steel. Of course, light gauge copper or brass sheeting would have been equally desirable, and as I recall, stainless was used either because of availability, or price, or a combination. For fuel, we frequent beaches for driftwood, or hardwood shops and boatyards for leftover scraps of oak and ash and maple. Hardwoods ignite less easily than softwoods, but burn longer. Of course, we have alder tidbits for the sweet smell of their smoke. In case of an emergency, machine pressed logs, chopped to thin slices, work very nicely; not too romantic, but quite warm.

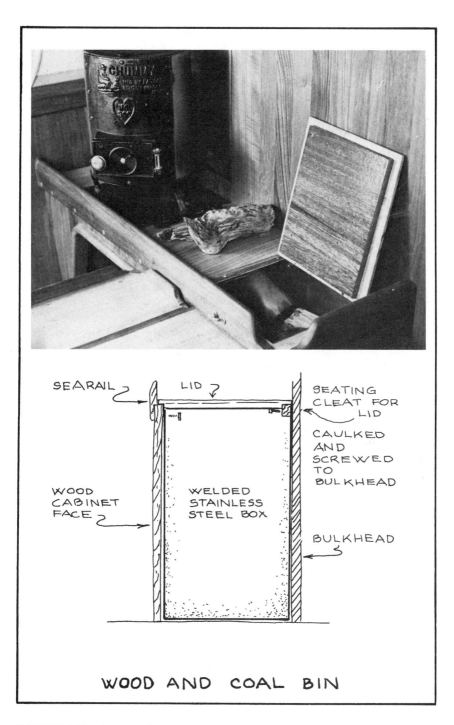

SEARAIL

LID

SEATING CLEAT FOR LID

CAULKED AND SCREWED TO BULKHEAD

WOOD CABINET FACE

WELDED STAINLESS STEEL BOX

BULKHEAD

WOOD AND COAL BIN

TRAWLER LAMP

One of the most beautiful and functional items that no yacht should be without is the Trawler Lamp. This is an all-brass, hanging, kerosene lamp with a white enamelled reflector hood and a circular wick whose circumference is over three inches. It is this combination of wick and reflector that creates a light strong enough to read by, yet one not nearly as cold and impersonal as the pressurized or mantel type lanterns.

Because of its large wick, the lamp throws enough heat to take the chill off most spring and autumn evenings; but because of this heat, caution must be taken when finding the lamp a permanent living space. If the cap of the lamp is closer than 8″ to the overhead, a brass reflector plate will be required, otherwise the heat emanating in copious quantities all around the cap can scorch the wood. The diameter of this plate need be no more than 8″; shallow spacers (1/8″) will be enough to create a dead airspace between it and the overhead.

Another small project required will be to tether the lamp when the vessel is underway since it tends to pendulate rather furiously. "S" linked brass chain is the most ideal material. Open the last links on each, then close them (with pliers) over the cap-supporting brass pillars. Next, install two small brass padeyes on bulkheads, salon table etc. so the chains will form a 35-45° angle. Now pull the chains tight and separate at the last usable link to the padeyes. Leave these last links partially open to facilitate removal when in port, for the chains tend to be bothersome during cross conversations.

Cleaning the glass chimney is vital at least once a week during constant nightly usage. Cleaning the white reflector should be effected periodically. The wick trimming is only an occasional task but it must be seen to. After many hours, the wick will lose its perfect horizontality, and small "high spots" will develop. These tend to burn with much greater intensity than the rest of the wick, and consequently, will be the first bits to smoke when the wick is turned too high (smoking should always be avoided to prevent flying, oily soot). To trim the wick, simply remove the globe, set the wick to the lowest setting where a bit still shows all around, then take a razor blade (tape over one edge so you don't amputate any fingers) and run it clear around, using the brass edge as a guide. Now light it up and let it roar.

TRAWLER LAMP

MICA DOORS FOR WOOD-BURNING STOVES

All solid fuel burning stoves can become much more exciting if their flames can be seen from the cabin. Just opening the door is no real answer, for smoke and sparks can soon escape; but replacing a solid door, with one having a mica centre or a screen, would do the job safely and handsomely.

Since most stove doors are of the simplest type, with a gudgeon and pintle hinge arrangement, and have even simpler locking mechanisms, like a gravity-held tongue, replacing them with a mica door or screen is quite a pleasant and undemanding project.

Of the two, I would strongly recommend the mica door, since most tiny stoves are rather harshly affected by even the slightest change in their intake of air, to the point of turning into blast furnaces if uncontrolled quantities of oxygen are introduced.

The cast iron doors on most stoves are virtually impossible to modify, hence, a new door must be fabricated of brass. The simplest method involves cutting two sheets of medium gauge brass sheeting to the size of the door, leaving on a tongue as an integral part of one side, and two small leaves of sufficient length, to be slightly bent to act as parts of the new hinge. If the gauge of the metal is heavy enough, only the outside sheet needs to have this arrangement of appendages.

Cut out the central area of both sheets, leaving at least 3/4" of metal all around. To accomplish this, drill a hole with a 1/2" drill bit somewhere within the area to be removed, and inserting a jigsaw blade (hacksaw teeth) through it, proceed slowly to cut out the four corners. File all edges and corners as round and harmless as possible. Have a shop weld pieces of rod to complete your hinges, but be sure to have your whole door along as a pattern, so no mistakes in placement are made.

Gather seven of the tiniest machine bolts you can find, and drill holes (per diagram) to fit their shanks. Be sure your holes are drilled far enough in from the edge to allow for the nuts to fit on the inside, and not obstruct the shutting of the door. Cut your sheet of mica (sometimes it can be rescued from old irons) to fit well within the holes. Now you see why the 3/4" minimum perimeter was necessary. Slip the mica between the sheets of brass, insert the nuts and bolts, tighten, and fit the door into place. Now, just sit back and watch the beautiful firelight flicker on the bulkheads. My, oh my.

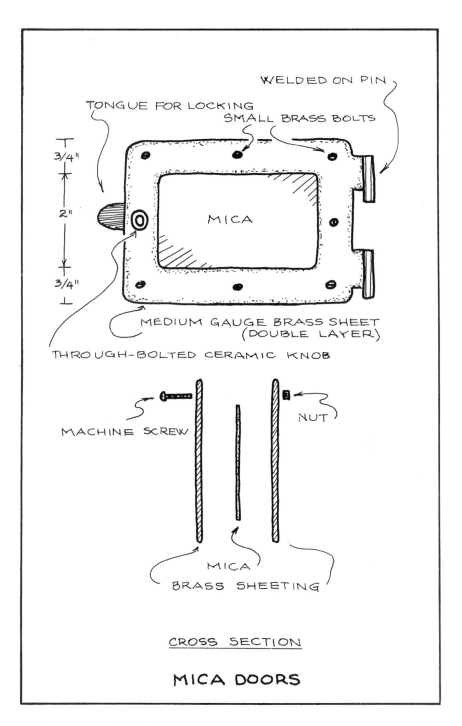

WELDED ON PIN

TONGUE FOR LOCKING

SMALL BRASS BOLTS

3/4"

2"

3/4"

MICA

MEDIUM GAUGE BRASS SHEET
(DOUBLE LAYER)

THROUGH-BOLTED CERAMIC KNOB

MACHINE SCREW

NUT

MICA

BRASS SHEETING

CROSS SECTION

MICA DOORS

LANTERN REFLECTORS

A reflector not only decorates and moonlights as a sometimes mirror, but it also makes a tremendous contribution toward keeping oil from sizzling, paint from bubbling and varnish from blistering on a precious bulkhead. It's one of those-to-be-cherished rare projects that one can actually finish in less than an hour, with most of one's self-esteem and hair untorn.

Very light gauge brass is an excellent and inexpensive material to use here, and although it doesn't have the reflective qualities of mirrored glass, it does look more shippy. For the average gimballed lamp, cut a 5″ × 8″ sheet with a pair of tin snips. Round all corners. Drill, or stamp with a sturdy nail, a hole in each corner and ·one in the middle of each side. Mount with brass tacks. For unlined glass sides, skip the holes, and after totally cleaning the fiberglass with acetone, epoxy the plate in place. There is no need to use the customary spacers between the plate and bulkhead. As long as the brass is well-polished and the lamp is the common non-pressurized variety, the added insulation gained from the spacers will not be required. Even if you are possessed enough to crank the lamp up to ridiculous luminosity, you need not worry about disfiguring your bulkhead; your coach roof will be ashes by then. Which brings us to the next point.

All kerosene lanterns should have either factory-made caps, or reflector plates above them. In the case of bulkhead lanterns, the factory-made mushroom caps will function infinitely better than cabin roof mounted plates. Because a gimballed lamp can, on a heel, actually lean as much as 45°, an average lamp with an average chimney of 5″ height, installed 12″ from the ceiling, will require a ceiling mounted plate of nearly 20″ diameter if it is to function adequately in such drastic situations.

At the same time, a 5″ diameter mushroom cap extending out from the bulkhead on an arm, will cover the steepest heels, if placed no more than 2″ or 3″ above the glass chimney top. If you insist on using a home-made plate, calculate your range of deflections, and size your sheet of brass accordingly. This will, however, require spacers, for the heat from the wick will be coming directly at the ceiling, and it can be quite intense. The simplest spacers are those cut from 1/4″ copper tubing to the desired length. Finishing washers can also be used. An 1/8″ space between ceiling and plate should not be considered pathologically overcautious.

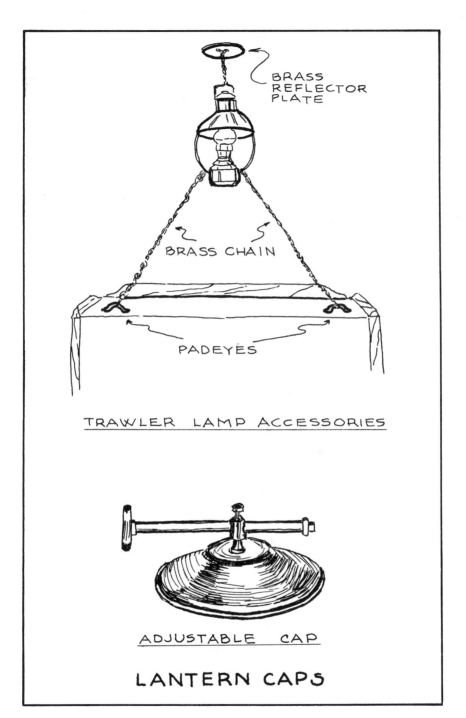

BRASS
REFLECTOR
PLATE

BRASS CHAIN

PADEYES

TRAWLER LAMP ACCESSORIES

ADJUSTABLE CAP

LANTERN CAPS

SMALL KEROSENE LANTERNS

Gimballed Lamps

For small areas, like the galley, chart table and forepeak where no room exists for the rather space consuming trawler lamp, the small and elegant two-way gimballed lamp can be used. The good ones have circular wicks and throw adequate light for most operations, excluding, of course, lengthy writing and reading. They hold about one-half pint of fuel, which even at full luminosity will last five long evenings. Installation of their caps and reflectors are mentioned elsewhere.

Anchor Lights

A well fitted yacht will most certainly carry a kerosene anchor light, if for no other reason than as a backup to the masthead or stern light. It can also act as a spare interior light or an efficient hand lantern for nightly deck inspection. I have often taken great joy in wandering on deck on a starry night, unhooking the glowing lantern from the gallows and taking a turn checking anchor line, halyards, or just ambling about searching for an excuse to linger and have the dark breeze ripple on my skin.

If gallows are unavailable, a brass ring lashed to the backstay will make a nice hanging place. Take care not to leave the main boom directly under the lantern for it may drip and damage sail covers and sails. The only special attention the lantern requires is during daytime storage. It should have a hanging place belowdecks with a short chain attached to its base to keep it from swinging wildly about. If placed on a shelf or the like, it may leak on a drastic keel. The simplest solution is to stick it in the oven of the gimballed galley stove. Just remember it's there. No one likes overcooked anchor lights.

KEROSENE FILLER RIG

On most yachts, refilling kerosene lamps and the small pressure tank for the kerosene stove is a major operation at best, a kerosene bath at worst. The kerosene, usually stored in a five-gallon jug, is impossible to handle with any delicateness (of which great amounts are required) when filling a half-pint lantern.

A sensible storage system and a simple apparatus for redistribution must be fabricated. A small stainless tank of say five to ten gallons can be custom made for about $60. It should be designed to fit some otherwise unused space, preferably directly under the deck, so a deck fill can be installed for major fill-ups. Try to locate the fill directly above the tank intake hole so an ordinary graduated dip stick can be used to check the fuel level; otherwise, it's virtually impossible to keep track of fuel used when an assorted number of lamps and a stove are involved. If possible, the tank should be mounted high to facilitate gravity feeding, and its outlet should be fitted with a 90° petcock. A copper tube should be run into the galley area and terminated in an accessible space (ours is below the galley sink). Affix an aviation grade flexible fuel line to the galley end of the tubing and affix another petcock on the end of this with a hose clamp. The length of the flex hose should be dictated by two factors: a) it must reach the stove's pressure tank, and b) it must reach the galley sink where the filling of kerosene lamps should take place. A word of caution here. When refilling lamps, spillage will often occur. The spilled kerosene must not be allowed to float on top of the water next to rubber or neoprene drainhose walls. Always have a bottle of liquid detergent handy, and when the first spill comes, squirt in copious quantities to neutralize the kerosene.

Back to the filler hose. The petcock on the filler hose must be safely stowed or it will open and spill the goods. We have managed ours without incident for three years by coiling our flex hose into a tidy loop and hanging it up high — in the narrow space between the sink and the cabinet wall — by means of a leather loop and cup hook. See "Rope Locker" for detail. We have also taken the added precaution of having the petcock on the tank itself accessible directly from the galley, by means of a hole-door (see "Through Bulkhead Access"), so we can be double sure of preventing a major kerosene catastrophe.

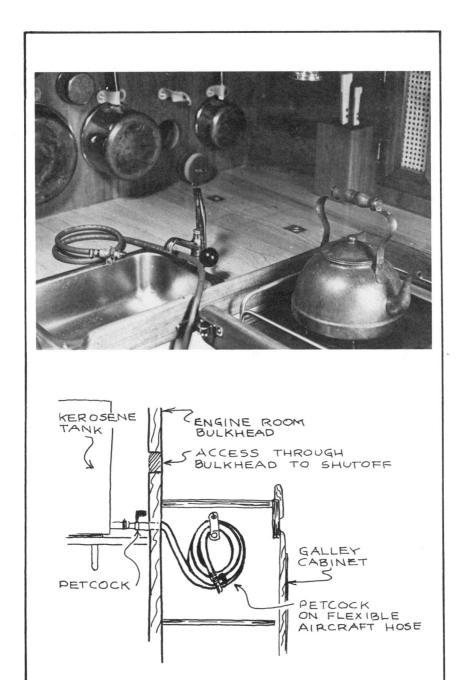

KEROSENE
TANK

ENGINE ROOM
BULKHEAD

ACCESS THROUGH
BULKHEAD TO SHUTOFF

GALLEY
CABINET

PETCOCK

PETCOCK
ON FLEXIBLE
AIRCRAFT HOSE

KEROSENE FILLER RIG

KEROSENE TANK PRESSURIZING RIG

If one's personal repertoire lacks having experienced total frustration, the immediate remedy is to attempt pressurizing the tank of a kerosene stove with that little insult of a pump that most manufacturers provide; somewhat akin to building the pyramid of Cheops out of ice cubes in July.

Step one to a better life is to heave the thing overboard. I normally abhor all pollution, but no one should be deprived of the inimitable pleasure brought about by the splash of this venomous little bastard. Do not throw away the threaded fitting that held the original pump in place. Keep the rubber gasket too. Next, purchase a small, good quality, bicycle pump, and buy a couple of spare rubber things that fit on the end. Now, scrounge up an old bicycle tube and remove the nipple intact, or better still, live it up and get two. Solder each of the nipples into a circular piece of tin, the diameter of which is determined by the opening of your tank. Reassemble the unit with the rubber gasket between the tank and the tin disk. The only task you'll have is screwing the bicycle pump fitting onto the tank each time and pumping a few strokes. Do remove the pump after using the stove and release the pressure. Not only will this prevent leaks caused by someone accidentally turning on the control knobs, but it will also help to keep fuel from building up in the manifold which will cause poorly combusting burners, smoke and big naughty flames.

THE FINELY FITTED YACHT

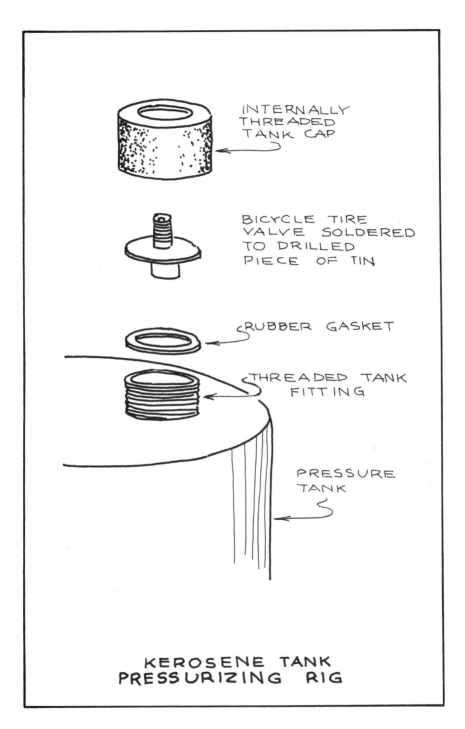

INTERNALLY
THREADED
TANK CAP

BICYCLE TIRE
VALVE SOLDERED
TO DRILLED
PIECE OF TIN

RUBBER GASKET

THREADED TANK
FITTING

PRESSURE
TANK

KEROSENE TANK
PRESSURIZING RIG

SOLID FUEL STOVES

Every cruising yacht should have a small salon stove of the wood burning variety to keep the cabin free of dampness, quickly dry wet foul weather gear, and, most importantly, to add an undeniably romantic aura belowdecks. Few things are as lovely on a cool night as listening to the rain patter on the decks,and watching the flames of a little wood fire.

Scraps of driftwood can be found almost anywhere and,with the aid of a sharp hatchet,they can be trimmed down to size with little effort. Most of the small wood burners are of a very old design, having comforted fishermen and tugboaters for decades, so their engineering has reached a very high efficiency, to the point where two handfuls (not armfuls) of almost any wood will keep a small yacht warm through all but the coolest of evenings.

The two basic kinds of wood-burning stoves are the bulkhead mounted, and the sole, or flat-surface mounted ones. Most of the modern ones, made of medium gauge tin or stainless steel, are of the bulkhead mount type. The more traditional ones, usually of cast iron, are generally sole mounted. *Warm Rain's* stove, aptly named "Chummy", is of the latter variety, and is affixed to a shelf with a bolt through each of its legs.

The stoves of either kind seldom take up more space than 16″ × 10″ × 10″, so lack of room is no excuse for their exclusion. The one important factor when selecting a stove,is the size of its top area. I feel that all stoves should be able to heat up a pot of tea or warm a dinner if the need arises. The traditional place for stoves is in the salon adjoining the main bulkhead. They should be located at least 18″ off the centreline to avoid smoking the sails, sail covers and halyards. "Chummy" is rather far outboard, so its stack comes through too close to the coachroof's edge, and has, on occasion, snared a staysail sheet or two. Halfway between the mast and coachroof edge seems an ideal compromise.

No major alteration should be needed for the installation of a stove. It can be installed as close as two inches from a bulkhead,so long as a sufficiently vented reflector plate is mounted for protection. Similar caution should be exercised wherever the stove pipe passes near any wood surface. A metal plate below the stove will not only afford safety,but facilitate cleaning up the occasional spilled ash as well.

Definite and strict procedure must be followed, however, when the smokestack is being fitted through the coachroof. The keystone

SOLID FUEL STOVES

of this entire operation is the double-walled, air-cooled, through-deck fitting, a proven one of which must be purchased and installed. A complete representation of the necessary parts is given in the illustration. One should not rear in horror upon first glance, for everything shown is a very standard, and not prohibitively expensive, manufactured item made especially for marine use, hence, of all stainless steel or a corrosion resistant alloy. The most common size of stock and fittings is 3″ diameter, and that's fine, because most marine stove fabricators know this, but if you purchase a stove with an unusual smoke outlet diameter, be prepared to have some time-consuming custom work done. If the above does occur, try to have an adapter piece made to fit directly onto the stove so that, after that single custom piece, you can return to buying standard parts.

The Charley Noble (chimney cap) is always a point of discussion and derision among yachtsmen, but general consensus has it that the round, flat cap gives very few problems in any wind, and on almost any point of sail. When things become rather extreme, one would be showing poor judgment by keeping the fire going and risking spillage of hot coals. We have used the flat cap on *Warm Rain* for the past three years and have received flawless service, even during a 40 knot gale.

The two key factors in having a properly functioning draft are to have as long a run on the smoke pipe as possible, with as few drastic turns as possible. The former can be attained by mounting the stove as low as practicable; directly on the sole is not a bad idea, except that potentially useful space above it must then be sacrificed. I have been aboard many yachts, ours included, where stoves have functioned perfectly with a straight stand of pipe of no more than 30″ between stove top and coachroof. As for the turns, one should completely avoid all 90° ones, and substitute 45° ones in their place. This can be accomplished by resetting any of the store-bought 90° elbows. Just get one and start twisting, and you'll see what I mean.

Specific Installations

The heat reflector panels behind the stoves should be of 20-24 gauge brass or stainless. The shinier the plate, the more effective it will be. It should be large enough to overhang the stove by 2″-3″ all around. If you dislike the idea of having asbestos and asbestos dust around as much as I do, then simply set the plate about 1/4″ away from the bulkhead by means of spacers. The air circulating behind the plate provides a very reasonable alternative to the asbestos. A

THE FINELY FITTED YACHT

CHARLEY NOBLE

 DECK FITTING

DECK

 NUT SPACERS

 FLANGE

 BUSHING

 DAMPER

STOVEPIPE

 ELBOW PIPES

FITTINGS FOR STOVE

second very attractive but more patience consuming alternative is the use of ceramic tiles all around the stove. Describe the use to your tile store and ask for a demonstration on tile cutting; it will save you a whole pile of tiles. Lighter gauge brass sheeting can be used in areas where bending or forming will be required.

To install the through-deck fitting, assemble the stove, complete with as many pieces of the stack as the coachroof will allow, set the smoke pipes in their final position, and scribe a light pencil line on the coachroof around the pipe. Now remove the pipe, find the centre of the circle, drill a pilot hole right through, then follow with a hole saw. Cut only halfway from the inside, then cut the other half from the outside to avoid chipping the gelcoat or splintering the wood. Clean all dust out of the area, wipe with a damp cloth, then caulk generously with polysulfide, and install the through-deck fitting.

If you're planning to be in a warm climate where use of the stove would be infrequent, it may behoove you to invest in a threaded bronze deck fitting into which a flat plug, or the Charley Noble, can be screwed.

Now stoke up the fire and bring on the hot toddy and a good book.

STOVE ALCOHOL STOWAGE

It seems that the tiniest of inventions on a yacht often bring the greatest pleasure, and it is definitely so in the case of the alcohol stowage mount.

Like most kerosene cooking stoves, ours came with a little plastic bottle that holds the alcohol used in pre-heating the primus burners. The nasty little critter, of course, had no sealable top, and no matter where we stood it and wedged it, it got free, threw itself about, and spilled its precious contents, until all our food and clothing smelled like an old stairwell on Skid Row.

When Candace had enough of this, she took a piece of copper plumber's tape (a perforated copper strapping 3/4″ wide used to hold plumbing pipes in place), attached its ends to the side of a cabinet just behind the stove, about 2″ up from the shelf where the little bottle sits, and it now lives continually upright unspilling and very accessible.

Yet a better container exists than the plastic thing. It's a beautiful brass oiling can, which holds three times the volume and four times the glamour. Its flexible nozzle allows you to pump evenly, without the unavoidable spills so common with the plastic jug; spills that turn the stove top into a pyre.

Our gallon container of alcohol is kept in the lazerette, well away from anything flaming or even warm, and we keep a one pint container of it in the same cabinet as the pre-heating bottle, similarly kept captive by a length of plumber's tape.

All this mess can, of course, be avoided by the installation of a propane stove, but then a propane stove might just send you on an unscheduled sightseeing flight over the islands, *sans* airplane.

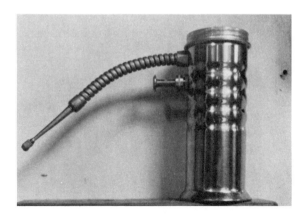

DIESEL STOVES

North of Norfolk or San Francisco, any live aboard yacht, or one used frequently in the winter months, should be equipped with a diesel heating *cum* cooking stove, or a diesel heater. Diesel stoves have been used by the fishermen of both coasts for over three decades, and are now engineered so that they will operate with a minimal output of soot. Indeed, if installation and maintenance instructions are carefully adhered to, the units will operate soot and trouble free, and what's most important, they'll do so at a heel of up to 40° on either tack.

Most of the galley stoves are not much bigger than an average kerosene or gas cooker, measuring around 24" in width, 17" in depth and 20" in height.

Not only will they keep the cabin cozy day and night, and supply the yacht with wonderful quantities of hot water (through internal coils), but they will also cook and bake magical dinners.

In the summer, when the heat (emitted somewhat generally by the stove) would make belowdecks uncomfortable, a single burner Primus could be substituted, while the flat smooth stove surface is used as counter space.

The foremost manufacturer of diesel stoves is Dickinson Marine of Vancouver and Seattle. They furnished me with the following installation procedures and general comments, many of them applicable to most diesel heaters and ranges.

General Description

Operation consists of fuel oil being metered through a metering safety control valve to a combustion chamber of stainless steel.

The burner is welded to a rigid crisscross framework of stainless steel, which in turn is surrounded by fire brick, an inner connected mesh of stainless, and grouted with furnace cement. The walls in most models are layered stainless with insulation sandwiched between.

Being directly heated by the burner, the aluminium alloy top is fast to warm and quick to cool. The oven damper provides for continuous circulation of heat within the range. Through its use and that of the metering valve, regulation of the desired oven temperature and cabin temperature is easily achieved.

The products of combustion along with the accumulated moisture are expelled to the outside atmosphere through the flue pipe and do not enter the vessels circulation system.

One of the best-drawing Charley Nobles.

Diesel galley stove with very intelligently designed guardrails. The small gimballed Primus stove beside the diesel is for summer use.

With proper installation, the heat created by the unit (allowing for heat loss up the flue pipe), is absorbed through radiation into the boat from the top, the oven or the inboard flue pipe.

In addition to the production of warm dry air, the range or heater is capable of supplying hot water through installation of stainless steel coils seated in the fire box.

The factory has made the coils "field installable" for the ranges. However, the ranges are limited to a maximum of two turns of coil due to space.

The heater operates in the same basic manner as the galley range.

Installation Instructions

1. *Locating Your Stove*

Special considerations for a power boat are not required because the heel and pitch associated with this type of vessel is not normally of a long enough duration to effect the flow of oil from the control valve to the burner.

Because sail boats inherently are on either a port or a starboard heel while underway, special care must be taken in locating your stove to insure continuous operation. Most models are designed to be located athwartships on sail boats. In this position fuel will continue to flow from the control valve to the burner at angles up to 40° (either port or starboard).

If the standard model is mounted in line with the keel, it will operate on one angle of heel but only up to 10° on the other; i.e., if mounted on the port side it would operate on a port heel but go out on a starboard heel after 10°.

To remedy the situation described, the standard model can be altered to operate "in line or parallel" to the keel. This is accomplished through the use of a kit which is designed to secure the metering valve at the proper height, parallel and perpendicular axes, on the left hand side of the range. This will extend approximately three to four inches. If space is a problem, the valve could protrude through the adjoining bulkhead into a locker or compartment. If the control valve is to be located in any other location, extreme care must be given to keep the float level (line on the side of the valve) 7/16″ higher than the bottom of the burner and all axes relative to the line of the burner must be in alignment.

With the above modification complete, the range will operate on angles of heel up to 40° on either port or starboard tack.

For sail boat operation on a gravity feed system, consideration must be given to the location of the tank and the outlets. The fuel

Stainless steel, diesel cabin heater with a large enough top surface for a single pot. Note fiddles around same. The nicely designed nook is finished off with stainless sheeting and ceramic tiles.

level at varying degrees of heel must not drop below the feed level of the metering valve, otherwise the supply will be cut off from the burner.

No unit should be installed where there is danger from combustion vapor, i.e. gasoline motors, propane equipment, etc., as such vapors can reach the flame in the fire box and cause an explosion.

Where necessary, combustion air can be ducted from the outside to the burner area.

2. *Preparation of Location Area*

To ensure a seamanlike installation, all combustable surfaces adjacent to the range should be covered with 1/8"-3/16" asbestos board and light gauge metal — stainless steel or brass gives the most pleasing effect. The height of the covering should extend slightly above the stove's top. Temperatures radiating from the stove would not likely ignite these surfaces but could char them.

A metal pan should be placed under the valve. In the unlikely event of any oil overflow the drops will be caught in the pan.

3. *Fuel Supply*

A 5- to 15-gallon tank would be ample for most day and weekend sailors. For most vessels, consumption is from one to three gallons in a 24 hour period.

The preferred method of supplying fuel is from a tank located higher than the level of the valve.

If gravity tank is your choice, it should be positioned so that the bottom is at least 12" higher then the control valve. It must be vented and a 3/8" copper fuel line brought to the stove for connection to the control valve. A good quality fuel filter complete with a positive shut off valve should be fitted into the feed line adjacent to the unit.

If the vessel is "diesel" powered, a small 3 to 5-gallon day tank can be located as suggested above, and a supply line run from it to the main fuel tank. A small hand pump can be placed in the supply line to replenish fuel in the day tank. If possible a day tank should have a site glass to eliminate the operator from overfilling.

A third method is possible for diesel powered vessels, namely the use of a small electric pulse pump to supply fuel directly from the main tank to the control valve.

We have reservation about the last method for the following reasons:

1. A fuel pump is one more mechanical device which can break down.

2. If the pulse generated by the pump exceeds 4 PSI, there is a danger of overflowing the valve and the burner, although there are low pressure regulators available to limit this problem.

3. Pulse pumps operated from a battery source and are subject to the charge available.

4. Should the fuel supply line prove defective, i.e. a puncture, fuel will flow unchecked.

4. *Securing The Stove*

The stove should be set as level as practical and fastened to the floor of the recess with bolts.

5. *Connecting The Oil Line*

With the stove securely in place, the oil supply line can be run in and connected to the control valve. The air must be bled from the system at all joining fittings along the supply line enroute to the control valve.

Flare fittings do not require any further sealant if the line has been properly prepared.

Do not over-tighten fittings but do tighten snugly.

In no circumstances should the overflow be plugged. Under some operating conditions a few drops of oil may drop from the overflow outlet, i.e. in rough weather. Therefore, a small metal container should be placed under the hole to catch spills, or a line can be run into the bilge and a container placed there.

Do not run a return line from the overflow to an engine tank because under certain conditions the oil may surge back up the line and overflow the valve.

engine room

ENGINE ROOM INSULATION

Engines are beautiful to look at, but never to listen to A deafening beast can be made into a purring pussycat with a few hours of effort and a pocketful of money. The two most effective insulators are sheet-lead and sandwiched neoprene, both very costly. I have seen boats use pressed paper tiles of the variety used in recreation rooms, but these are extremely fragile and frighteningly flammable. They can be sprayed with a fire-proofing compound, but then, the expense mounts to where it almost equals that of lead or neoprene.

For the ease of handling the variety of surfaces it can be applied to, and mostly for its lightness, I have always been a fan of neoprene. The stuff used for sound insulation has a layer of fibrous compound sandwiched between the layers of neoprene. Cutting can be accomplished with razor-knives or handsaws, and adhesion can be achieved with the aid of either screws, or a variety of glues and tile adhesives.

If screws are to be used, they must be accompanied by the largest possible washers to prevent ripping through, especially in areas where the insulation will be "hanging," e.g., the undersides of decks and cockpits.

Insulation should not be limited to partitions only. Any surface in the engine room that can act as a sound reflector should be covered to make it into a sound absorber. If only partial insulation is contemplated, then at least the following surfaces should be dealt with: bulkheads, doors, ceilings (underdecks or cockpit soles) and the exposed hull.

The next, single, most effective area to be dealt with is the engine pan. This is usually either of fiberglass or of stainless sheet metal, but whichever it is, it acts as a perfect drum, multiplying every engine vibration and transmitting it to the hull and to the ears. A simple way to dampen this effect is to build a plywood filler under the low end of the pan, then pour in tested quantities of two part liquid urethane foam. I mention *tested* because the stuff expands with an unimaginable force that could potentially deform or break away your pan. So experiment with it in a can or box until you get the knack, then pour in sufficient amounts that, on expansion, completely fill the space between the pan and the hull. If the space below the pan was used to allow seepage to pass from the stuffing box to the bilge, simply cut a piece of 2" PVC pipe in half lengthwise, and lay it, like a tunnel, under the pan *before* you begin pouring foam.

ENGINE ROOM INSULATION

ENGINE ROOM SEAT

I have always found fumbling about an engine room quite enjoyable, made painful only by the absence of a decent place to sit. Since *Warm Rain* is a double ender, and her engine room is well aft in her pinched stern, bracing oneself on the sloping hull is somewhat akin to pressing with your knees on the walls of a crevasse, hoping like hell you won't slip to the bottom. All this is complicated by the presence of the shaft and stuffing box, neither of which I want to test with my weight, so the only solution was to build a seat above them.

I cut a piece of 1/2″ plywood to fit a certain point on both sides of the hull. A width of 12″ was deemed quite enough. Next, with a bevel square, I determined the slope of the hull at the points where the plywood rested, set a table saw at that angle, and ripped two lengths of 2″ × 2″ fir, equal in length to the length of the angled sides of the seat. Both of these needed minor adjustments, which I performed by means of a table sander and eventually a file. I then marked the hull around each end of the seat, removed the paint from the fiberglass with paint remover, then rinsed the hull with acetone. The seat was then put back into place and its bottom edges were scribed onto the hull. The angled fir pieces were then placed just below these marks and bonded to the hull with single layers of mat and cloth. When the resin went off, the cleat stock was painted, the seat put in place, and the four centres for mounting holes, marked. The seat was removed and the holes drilled in it, then it was placed over the cleat stock again and a pencil was used to mark the holes onto the top of the cleats. Once again the seat came off, and the drill was furnished with a wrapping of masking tape 3/8″ from its tip to be sure I would not drill too deep and end up with the ocean pouring through the hole. The 3/8″ holes were drilled and the seat was attached to the cleats with the four 1″ panhead screws. These were not countersunk or plugged, so the seat can be quickly pulled if the shaft or stuffing box has to be removed.

Some people suggest simply bonding the seat to the hull without use of the cleats. This, of course, would be totally inappropriate, for major demolition would then be required to perform even simplest replacement of the packing gland.

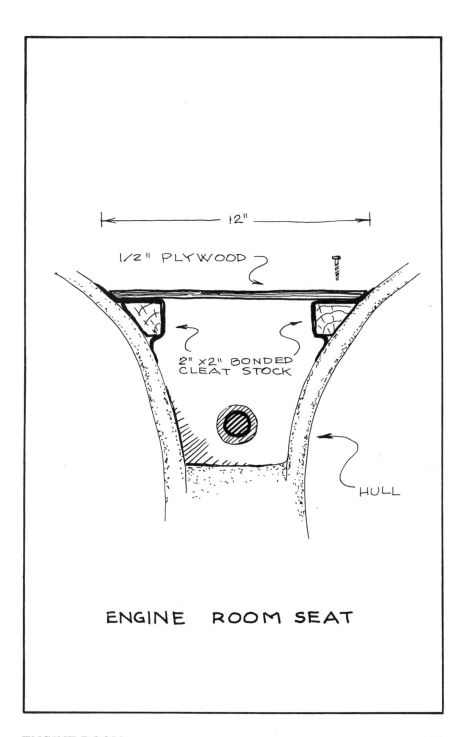

ENGINE ROOM SEAT

ENGINE ROOM TOOL RACK

Perhaps some deem this a bit luxurious, but it's common knowledge that most engine rooms are extremely cramped, and once one is comfortably positioned, he will not want to leave to fetch a forgotten screwdriver. All engine rooms should have their own tools (this is the place most tools are used with greatest frequency anyway), and they should all be neatly and accessibly stowed in their own rack. Hours of searching and frustration will be saved in the long run.

I'm not advocating fabrication of shelves to accommodate a 150 piece Craftsman set. A careful study should be made of the most common tools needed and a rack constructed accordingly. As a general guide, I feel the following to be minimal: combination screwdriver, adjustable pliers, crescent wrench, magnet with flexible shaft, flashlight. Thought should be given to the tool kit most engine manufacturers include with their engine. They know which size wrenches, etc. are most frequently needed. If you have space, include them all. The minimal items above should fit handily onto a 5″ high by 7″ wide by 3½″ rack, if arranged as shown in illustration. Since this rack will be going into the engine room, virtually any leftover 3/4″ stock can be used. Cut out the 7″ X 3½″ piece first with radiused corners, then lay the pieces over each other in a vise so you can drill both sets of holes at once. I feel that the double rail system is necessary to avoid noise from rattling. If you're adamantly set against it, just do a single. I don't really mind.

Using your tools as templates, draw your cutouts and drill them. Attach the rails to a backing board of leftover stock. Glue and screw from behind. Now attach the whole thing to a convenient bulkhead, and just watch your next outing to the engine room become a pleasure.

ENGINE ROOM TOOL RACK

ENGINE OIL DAM

On some production fiberglass boats, I have been surprised to find no engine pan below the engine. In practice, that means that all fuel and oil drippings are free to proceed into the bilge to stink up the whole boat and mix with bilge water creating an awful mess. Belated installation of an engine pan is a mammoth task, but a considerably less demanding alternative exists. The bilge area directly foreward and aft of the engine can be dammed off so the oil will at least be confined.

There is no need to build monstrous edifices here, for the average small diesel seldom holds more than five quarts of oil, and in the event that all of that is somehow lost, your smallest worry will be cleaning up. So, fabricate two small dams or bulkheads from 1/2″ plywood and fit them into place. Next, take a 2″ diameter PVC tube and cut it in half lengthwise, sand the edges smooth, and set it below the engine so it just protrudes past each of your new bulkheads. Mark the bulkheads for the holes to let the tube penetrate, and cut to suit. The tube will become a sealed off tunnel, allowing seeping water from stuffing box, etc., to flow unimpeded to the bilge where it can be pumped out. Next, sand the convex side of the tube with as coarse a paper as you can find (a file would be better) to roughen up the surface, then clean off all the paint and dirt from the hull, and set the three pieces back in place. Using 6″ fiberglass tape cut in half lengthwise to make it more manageable, bond the bulkheads and the tube to the hull and each other, making sure you seal off every little crack to keep the oil in. Bond the bulkheads only on the sides that face the engine; remember, this is just a container, not a structural reinforcement. Be certain you smooth down all loose fibres while the resin is still wet, otherwise, they'll become savage little pins when hardened that will forever tear your skin when you're working below the engine. Finally, grab a little container of not too expensive enamel paint and slosh it generously over your new bulkheads to protect them from water.

Every few months, just dab up the oil drippings with a paper towel. It'll sure beat scouring out the whole bilge.

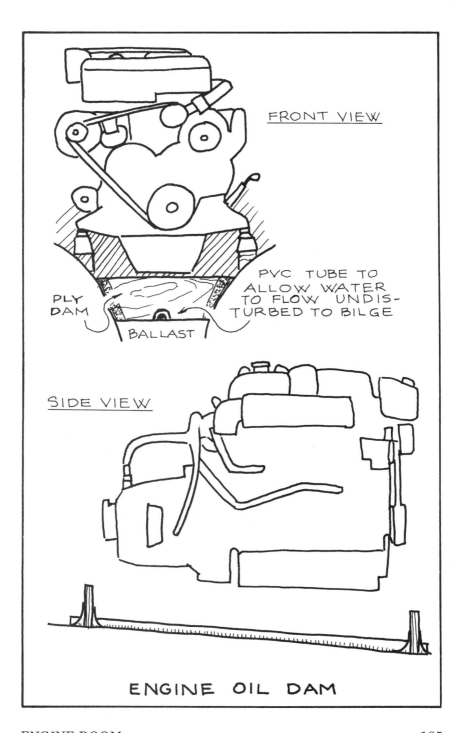

FRONT VIEW

PVC TUBE TO ALLOW WATER TO FLOW UNDISTURBED TO BILGE

PLY DAM

BALLAST

SIDE VIEW

ENGINE OIL DAM

SEA WATER FILTER

I think most people will agree that some sort of screen or filter system should be installed on all engine intakes to prevent the possibility of something big and ugly being sucked into the engine, causing blockage of cooling water and eventual overheating and seizing of water pump or main bearings. Admittedly, an on-hull-screen can be blocked by a plastic bag or other non-destructable matter thrown overboard by some mentally disorganized, but at least, one will have a single problem spot to investigate instead of having to tear down the engine bolt by nut. Some through-hull fittings have a screen cast into them as an integral part, obviating the need to insert extra screws in the hull. A regular bi-weekly check overboard just to make sure nothing has wedged in the screen would be a commendable idea.

A more costly and complex system, but one that allows instant inspection and cleaning from the engine room, involves the purchase of a salt water filter (see photo). This unit has four major advantages. One: it contains a cylindrical screen with a few hundred perforations through which the water is filtered after it circulates at a rapid speed around the cylinder. During this circulation, whatever has managed to find its way in through the seacock is violently rasped against the screen until it is eroded to "digestible" chunks, i.e. chunks that will fit through the screen and pass harmlessly through the water pump, et al. Two: the salt water filter is made up of a tempered glass cylinder so you will be able to tell at a glance if something is caught in it. Three: the large brass wing nut on top opens the entire top, making removal of blocked material very rapid. Before you loosen the wing nut, make sure your intake seacock is shut off so you won't flood the boat. Four: on boring afternoons in the doldrums, you can sit and watch seaweed and seaspiders and little fish swim around in the glass bowl.

Admittedly the system has another drawback besides cost in that it requires additional fittings in a water system, and of course fittings are usually the first to develop leaks. The potential danger of this can be minimized if thought is given to the location of the filter (just inside the engine room door would be ideal) so that inspection and adjustment can be done quickly and effortlessly. The wing nut, like most other brass fittings exposed to salt air or water, should be cleaned and oiled at least once a year. But don't forget to shut off the seacock first.

THE ENGINE ROOM FIRE EXTINGUISHER

This fast to fabricate item could save many serious burns and many serious yachts. Fire extinguishers are, of course, mandatory in engine rooms and they serve very well as long as the fire is small, or discovered quickly, or both. If the fire has spread to any degree, access to the engine room may be impossible, and even if not, the opening of an engine room door may be all that's needed to turn the fire into a blaze by providing a fresh supply of oxygen. To cover the above possibilities, a fire extinguisher should be installed *just outside* the engine room bulkhead. Access to this extinguisher must be unimpeded. The installation involves no new equipment, except for a piece of copper pipe. Affix the extinguisher bracket to the bulkhead so that the nozzle points straight at the bulkhead into the engine room. Pay special care to have the trigger accessible without removing the extinguisher from the bracket.

Next, fit a piece of copper pipe over the nozzle and feed it into the engine room through a hole in the bulkhead. Have the pipe fit as tightly as possible. If you have to force the pipe through the hole with a mallet, so much the better. Have the pipe terminate just inside the bulkhead so the chemicals won't spray right over a part of the engine room. To seal the pipe-to-nozzle joint, slip the nozzle into the pipe as deep as it will go, then lay a bead of polysulfide along the seam.

Some yachtsmen have substituted rubber or plastic hoses for the copper. This is a grave mistake. In case of fire, the engine room end of the hose can melt, sealing perfectly the entire apparatus and rendering it totally useless.

A side note. If you feel the fire to be large enough to warrant use of this extinguisher, do not "crack open" the door just to check. Very bad facial burns have been suffered like that. First, pull the trigger and empty the extinguisher, *then* investigate.

An afterthought. It would show good seamanship to investigate different access apertures to engine room fires, e.g., vents, lazarettes, etc. just as a drill, so less time will be required during the fire for contemplation and discovery.

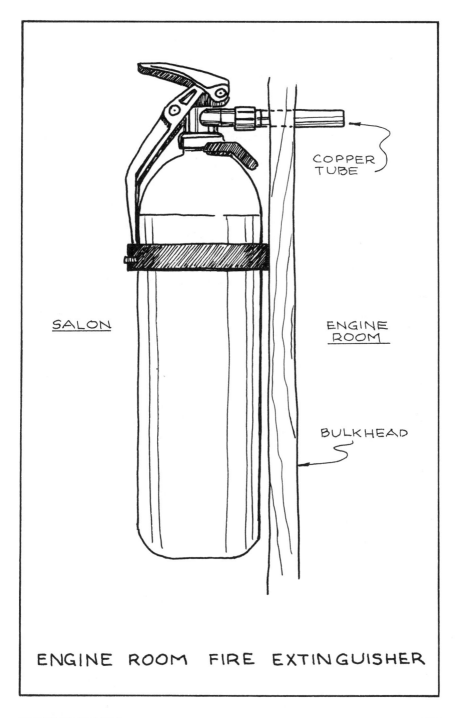

COPPER
TUBE

SALON

ENGINE
ROOM

BULKHEAD

ENGINE ROOM FIRE EXTINGUISHER

ANTISIPHON SYSTEM

In all vessels where the engine is located below the waterline, an antisiphon valve must be fitted into the cooling water circuit line to prevent the engine from flooding. The valve is, of course, located above the waterline, and all it actually does, is break the flow of water by allowing air to get into the system; this causes the water in both hoses (up-to and down-from the valve) to drain off.

Even though most store-bought valves do work very well (especially the U-shaped bronze ones with float balls), I hesitate to use them in the engine room because even the best serviced and maintained valves seem to seep occasionally. This of course causes no problem in an area like the head, but in the engine room where vulnerable wiring and machinery is exposed, any amount of corrosive salt water should be considered a threat. The valve we installed with our Volvo diesel didn't actually seep, it actually sprayed, so after consultation with the naval architect and some engineers, a most satisfactory, foolproof system was arrived at that's one-tenth as expensive as the original and twice as useful. The conversion required no new hose, for fortunately, the old lengths worked well, so the only purchase made was a 1/2″ bronze through-hull vent (see diagram).

We discarded the antisiphon valve and mounted a vent in the cockpit directly above a drain. This position got the valve high enough to have it act effectively as a siphon breaker and its exposed location enabled the helmsman to glance at the valve occasionally to insure that cooling water was getting to the engine. On a normal yacht, that can only be determined by hanging over the side and looking for water coming through the exhaust, consequently, it's quite possible to run the engine dry for some time, unless, of course, someone keeps an eye on the temperature gauge which few people ever do. With the vent in the cockpit, a very steady trickle is emitted when the engine is running, a small enough quantity that it causes no deprivation to the engine, but large enough to be easily visible.

Some friends mounted the vent overboard. This has two disadvantages: a) it is not easily seen from the cockpit, and b) since it has to be mounted very high to be effective, usually near the sheer, the trickle of water it emits will stain the hull considerably. This stain, of course, occurs in the cockpit as well, but here it is shorter, less noticeable, and easier to clean.

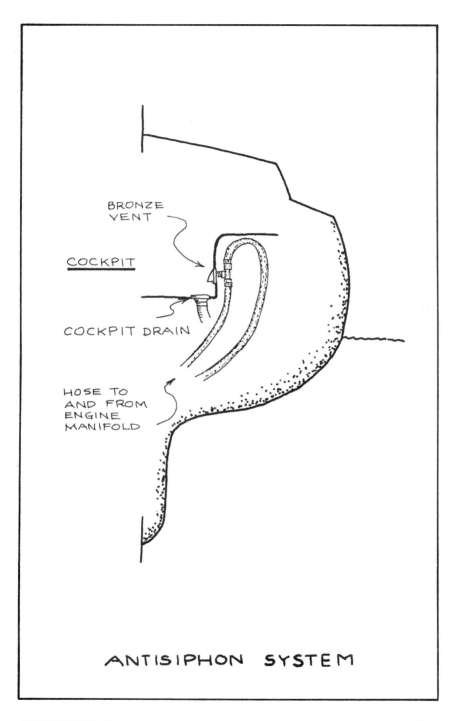

BRONZE
VENT

COCKPIT

COCKPIT DRAIN

HOSE TO
AND FROM
ENGINE
MANIFOLD

ANTISIPHON SYSTEM

EXHAUST SIPHON PREVENTER

Many yachts have suffered engine failure and significant engine damage after following seas, entering through the engine exhaust through-hull, have set up a siphoning action that consequently flooded and seized up the engine.

I've been told that attempted looping of the exhaust hose and even installation of an antisiphon valve have proved futile, the former because the vessel's deck limits available height, and the latter because the corrosive fumes of the exhaust quickly rendered the valve immobile, thus inactive.

A recent idea incorporates the function of the highly looped hose and adds to it a safety precaution in the form of a hefty gate valve (see diagram). It is of course mandatory that the gate valve be readily accessible and it is most preferable that this access be gained from the cockpit where the helmsman on watch can shut it off as soon as he notes that sea conditions so warrant. On *Warm Rain*, the gate valve is mounted inside the lazarette at the very top of the lazarette bulkhead. Mounting is effected by two very large, all stainless hose clamps, which have first been completely opened, then drilled through the centre and screwed to the bulkhead. Before drilling and screwing you should do a dry run to determine at exactly what point the clamp must be drilled to have the clamp screw end up facing upward. If this bit of forward planning is done, both installation and later servicing will be made very much easier.

Care must be taken to run the hose well up out of harm's way, for I know of few other places inhabited by as dangerous a group of loose, nasty junk as a lazarette.

It would probably reflect excellent seamanship to have the valve closed at even the slightest danger of flooding. I'm told by the experts that one need not worry about forgetting to open it back up because the engine will simply not start if the exhaust is blocked. Be that as it may, we take the extra precaution of removing the key from the ignition everytime we close the valve, and slipping it into a little container inside the lazarette. This way we can never forget to open the valve when we reach for the key.

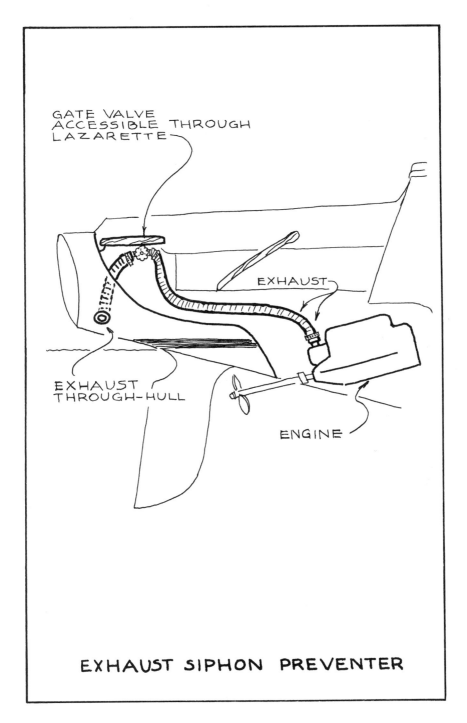

GATE VALVE
ACCESSIBLE THROUGH
LAZARETTE

EXHAUST

EXHAUST
THROUGH-HULL

ENGINE

EXHAUST SIPHON PREVENTER

ENGINE ROOM LIGHTING

I have always been shocked by people who regard their engine rooms as horrible black holes. We have managed aboard *Warm Rain* to bring in sufficient light, both natural and artificial, to make the engine room into a most pleasant place to work, or even just to sit around and lovingly fiddle with the old green diesel.

If the engine is located beneath the cockpit, the most practical and multifunctional source of light would be the installation of an opening portlight in the cockpit side that could house the ignition and other switches. (See "Portlight for Ignition.") If this is, for some reason, undesirable, then the most inexpensive method would be cutting a rectangular hole in the cockpit side and bolting a piece of 1/4″ plexiglass over it. If the cockpit side is of unreinforced fiberglass, i.e. no balsa or plywood core, one should consider putting the plexiglass on the inside to prevent any potential knee scrapings. The bottom of the hole should be cut on a bevel to facilitate water drainage. All sides of the hole should be sanded round and re-gelcoated. The plexiglass should be cut large enough to overlap the hole by 1/2″ all around. Bed it in silicone and secure it with round-headed bolts (head out) every three inches.

In wood, or wood-cored cockpits, the plexiglass should be placed on the outside to protect the end grain exposed by the cut. In this event, the outside edge of the plexiglass should be generously bullnosed.

The ultimate solution is of course to make the entire cockpit sole out of 3/4″ plexiglass. This thickness is not sufficient to bear the load alone required of a cockpit, so strongbacks should be installed on the sole's underside (see diagram). To prevent the engine room from becoming a greenhouse, both sides of the plexiglass should be sanded with 100 grit paper to make it opaque. Because it will be sanded anyway, the plexiglass you purchase could be a salvaged or scratched piece. To make the surface non-slippery, 1/4″ × 2″ teak slats will have to be glued and screwed to it.

By far the most sensible electric light for engine room use is the fluorescent wand. This is a small plastic tube (unbreakable) with a handle and a spring coiled cord and it works on 12 or 24 volts. It throws generous quantities of light exactly where you want it, and if needed as a general source, it can be slipped onto a bracket mounted on a bulkhead.

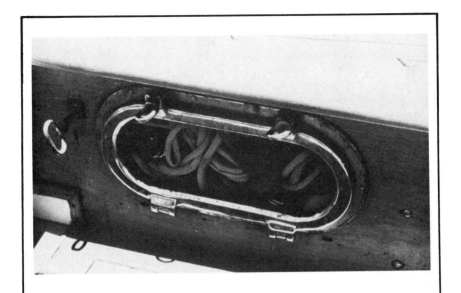

PORTLIGHT WITH PLEXIGLASS BOX
OVER ENGINE ROOM PROVIDES
LIGHT AND STOWAGE.

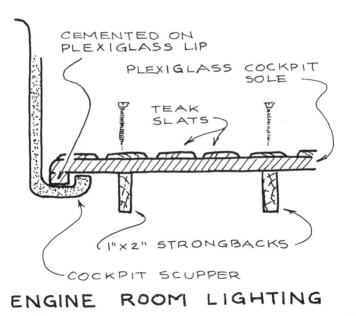

CEMENTED ON
PLEXIGLASS LIP

PLEXIGLASS COCKPIT
SOLE

TEAK
SLATS

1" X 2" STRONGBACKS

COCKPIT SCUPPER

ENGINE ROOM LIGHTING

ENGINE ROOM STOWAGE

Possibly nowhere in a vessel will one find as great a need for stowing obnoxiously-shaped objects as in the engine compartment. For the many odd pieces like spare alternator belts, oil sump pumps, and spare injectors, one will require nooks and crannies that are both secure and readily accessible. Both points are vital; first, because weighty flying objects can do horrendous damage to themselves and to delicate things like petcocks and glass filter settling bowls, the second, because lack of accessibility in choppy seas can lead to quick frustration and seasickness.

Tools should have their own special place, as should space demanding things like cans of spare oil, therefore, more will be said about them in following sections. For general stowage, the slat faced bins seem to be most practical. Through the slats, adequate vision can be gained of the bin's content and because of the slats, construction can be rapid. The bins should be narrow, about 8″, and moderately deep, about 12″, to allow most things to be wedged into place to prevent unscheduled flights. To help this wedging effect, the sides of the bin should be angled about negative 15°. If one end of the bin is a bulkhead, simply affix cleat stock at the mentioned 15° and make up the other end of a partial bulkhead of about 8″ average width, reaching from the lowest accessible point on the hull right to the underdecks. Fasten this new bulkhead to the underdeck with cleat stock and bond to the hull with fiberglass tape of mat and cloth. Bond on either side. On wood hulls you can screw, or clamp and glue, directly to a rib. This newly created vertical space can now be converted into bins with their plywood bottoms cleat stocked to each bulkhead and enclosed with 1/4″ solid stock slats cut to 1½″ width. All slats should be screwed to cleat stock or bulkhead, while the topmost slat should have a butt hinge at one end and a small barrel bolt at the other to affect a gate. The bins are now ready to house anything compatible.

One small point: spare engine parts are best left and stowed in their cardboard boxes. Not only will the boxes afford vital protection to delicate things like gaskets, but they'll provide a quick record of part names and numbers for the reordering and restocking which should be done as soon as possible after the part is used.

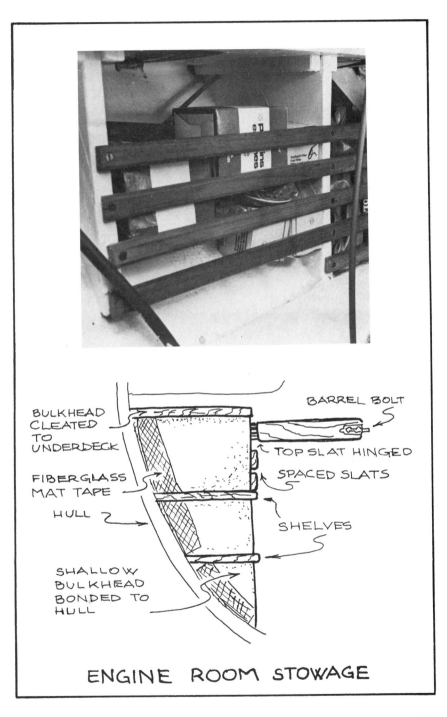

BULKHEAD
CLEATED
TO
UNDERDECK

BARREL BOLT

TOP SLAT HINGED

FIBERGLASS
MAT TAPE

SPACED SLATS

HULL

SHELVES

SHALLOW
BULKHEAD
BONDED TO
HULL

ENGINE ROOM STOWAGE

ENGINE ROOM   197

BILGE PUMPS BELOWDECKS

Without going into the history of lovely old pumps, let us acknowledge that in a well fitted yacht, a substantial manual bilge pump system is mandatory. An electric bilge pump is a nice convenience, although it tends to lull the crew into complacency regarding the surveillance of bilge levels which can often lead to discovery and repair of a leak. On the other hand, the electric pump is a useful warning system when the vessel is left unattended, alerting nearby yachtsmen with its constant buzzing if a major leak is present. Until the battery dies.

The ideal cockpit bilge pump is described in the following section. For belowdecks, a larger diaphragm pump like a Henderson or a Whale 25 would be ideal. The latter can move 25 gallons per minute quite successfully if thought has been given to its installation. Functioning in an emergency usually imposes great strain on a crew; so someone performing the doubly strenuous duty of working the pumps should be assisted by at least having: a) a comfortable place to brace himself, and b) copious quantities of fresh air to avoid seasickness. With this in mind, a location very near the companion-way would be the most favourable, having the added advantage of quick communication with the cockpit. On *Warm Rain*, we installed a Whale 25 directly over the bilge, just under the bridge deck, at the entrance to the engine room. Being directly over the bilge eliminates the need for curves which increase friction and, consequently, the amount of effort required to move the water overboard. Being so close to the bilge also gives very rapid access to the strum boxes (strainers, see drawing) in case they plug up and require cleaning. Being at the entrance to the engine room, the pump man can act quickly when it's time for drastic measures like closing the engine intake seacock, cutting the hose just above it and sticking it into a strum box and into the bilge to gain the assistance of the engine salt water pump in saving the vessel. An average engine pump will discharge about 20 g.p.m. at 2000 engine rpm.

The pump should be mounted at a height where the least strain will be required in its operation. If the pump man is to be standing, the pump should be chest height. Clear access should be provided so that the pump man can pull the handle toward himself, then push it away on the return stroke, like rowing. In both cases, body weight can be applied instead of relying on sheer muscle power, which indeed would be the sad case, if the pump handle had to be worked by moving it from one side of the body to the other.

Care must be taken at installation to leave sufficient space around the pump so it can be quickly torn down and cleaned should the need arise. To prepare for this eventuality, one would be well advised to tear the pump apart while lazing on deck on a sunny day with tools and manufacturer's diagrams handy. The pump should be torn down and cleaned and the bolts greased annually as standard maintenance.

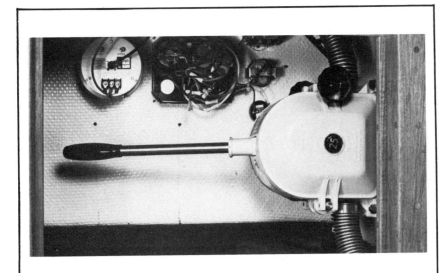

BILGE PUMP

stowage

STOWAGE GRATES

Almost any yacht will require a half dozen grates for sundry uses. Most of these will be rather small, necessitating only light construction and will be, therefore, relatively easy to make. Unlike larger grates in the cockpit or shower, which are called upon to support large weights, the stowage grates need only have one set of dadoed cross pieces. The uses for these grates will be many.

Ice Box

Since most good ice boxes are top loading, vast vertical space is normally wasted because no one likes to unpack the whole ice box to get at one little thing on the bottom. If the ice box liner doesn't have molded ridges to support shelves, seating cleats will have to be installed. Cleats 3/8″ × 3/4″ should be used on edge. All wood inside an ice box must be varnished or it will mildew. If room exists for a number of shelves, the upper shelves should be narrowest, with lower ones getting increasingly wider. At no time should any shelf take up more than two-thirds of the surface area, for access beneath it will be impossible, necessitating total unloading — which is what it's trying to prevent in the first place.

Against-Hull Stowage

No food or clothing should be placed directly against any uninsulated hull, or mildew will instantly attack it. This is true for fiberglass, aluminum, steel, and ferro cement because of condensation, and of wood because of seepage. The simplest way to keep air circulating beneath stowed items is to place light grates against the hull. These, too, must be completely spray varnished or painted to be mildewproof.

Construction

These light grates require 3/4″ stock as wide as possible to minimize work. Out of a 36″ × 6″ board, enough grate stock can be cut to make a 36″ × 12″ grate, since one-half of all grates is air. Set a table saw with 3/4″ dado blades at 3/8″ depth, and run the board through widthwise, allowing 3/4″ space between the dadoings. When a whole board has been dadoed, rip it into 3/4″ strips. Next rip 3/4″ stock to 3/8″ thickness. Cut both the dadoed and 3/8″ slats to required length and assemble using a 3/4″ spacer between the dadoed stock. Glue with resorcinol and weight down. The sides can be trimmed with 1/2″ trim, and attached with resorcinol glue and #6 screws. For ice box shelves, a searail of 2″ height should be utilized to prevent playing the food version of Fifty-Two Pick-Up.

THE FINELY FITTED YACHT

STOWAGE GRATES

THE DOLLAR FORTY-NINE ROPE LOCKER

There are few sadder sights than a dacron snake-pit. Anyone who stores hundreds of dollars worth of lines as if he'll never use them again, should be hung by them all at the same time. On the other hand, great pleasure can be derived from lifting the lid of your counter, reaching confidently into an accustomed spot, unhooking a leather strap, and coming out with the exact piece of line you were after. Now that's living. Some may argue.

Almost any spare lines (sheets, halyards, etc.) can be whipped into a modest coil and hung into a space no wider than 6". Thus, a narrow locker 24" X 8" can house as many as eight staggered coils on its walls, and still have two hooks left over, one for the sail repair kit bag and the other for a small canvas bag housing odd lines. This little bag you will find your best friend, yielding long-forgotten treasures at the most dire moments, like when your belt buckle breaks.

The fastenings required are laughably simple, an even greater reason for installing them immediately. Leather straps 10" X 1" will be needed with an awl hole at either end to act as loops for the coils. These will be hooked to brass cup hooks. Only one end of the strap will be mobile when releasing or fastening the lines, the other can hang permanently on the hook.

If this isn't function in its simplest form, may Frank Lloyd Wright spit on my grave.

ROPE LOCKER

BAFFLES FOR DRAWERS AND LOCKERS

Most yacht lockers are rubbish heaps, those of our friends and acquaintances not included, of course. Due to their huge single spaces, they become bottomless pits for everything from shoes to onions, which then proceed to out-rot and out-smell each other for untold months, until a flood or a fire cleans them out.

Drawers

Any large flat drawer can easily be divided off into small civilized areas by using either 1/8" wide plywood baffles or ready-made plastic trays. The latter have many advantages over the plywood and should be used in places where things may be spilled or leaked, like in the head and galley. Cleanup can then be effected by removing and rinsing one tray only, without the need to unpack the entire drawer. The plastic trays couple nicely together with molded grooves and tongues so they will not shift and slide about.

If you use plywood baffles, cut them 1/2" lower than the sides of the drawer. Each piece should be let in half its height where it intersects with another piece. In plywood of 1/8" thickness, any radial arm or table saw blade will be enough to cut the let in. Assemble without any glue or permanent cleats. If well measured and cut, the baffles will have enough tension to hold themselves in place and still be easily dismantled and removed for cleaning or modification.

Lockers

All lockers, whether top or front loading, that are used to stow drygoods, equipment, cans or vegetables, etc., should have a baffle every 12" or 18". These should, for the sake of flexibility, be readily removable. If little weight is involved, and ventilation is of prime concern (as it is with food such as dried fruits and vegetables), then baffles made of netting should be used. They can be attached by means of brass hooks that are screwed into the cabinetry, *not into* the hull. If the bottom of the netting needs to be secured, wedge and glue a piece of scrap fir or mahogany 2" × 2" along the bottom of the netting, attaching ends to cabinetry, and screwing the brass hooks into it.

If ventilation is of no major concern, as with canned goods, a 1/8" plywood baffle, carefully cut to fit the hull curvature and cabinetry, will do nicely. There is no need to affix these to anything, for the force of the cans will be enough to keep them in place.

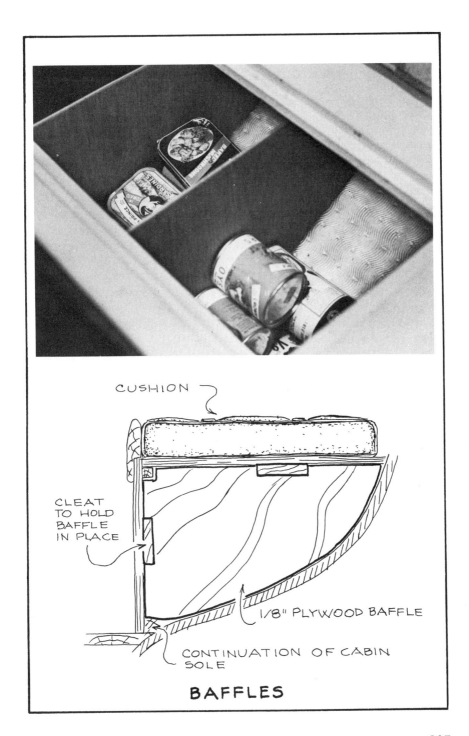

CUSHION

CLEAT
TO HOLD
BAFFLE
IN PLACE

1/8" PLYWOOD BAFFLE

CONTINUATION OF CABIN
SOLE

BAFFLES

STOWAGE

NETS

Nets are great: you can fish with them, slick your hair down with them, and catch butterflies with them. They are also one of the most important materials one can use for stowage, both exposed and concealed.

Exposed

We have found many uses for exposed netting on *Warm Rain*. These are the self-contained nets with hemmed edges and loops in the ends, for either hanging or carrying. We have one dangling from the dishrack, just above the icebox, for fruit. The fruit lasts much longer when not sitting against an unbreathing surface, the net doubles as a shopping bag, instead of the silly paper bags that rip, and it utilizes space that otherwise would be quite vacant.

In the forepeak, two larger ones are used — one, just below the foredeck where we stow our bedding during the day; the other, a smaller one similarly installed over the outboard uppermost part of the double bunk where it serves as a *necessaire* for late night goodies like books, flashlights, and teddy bears.

Finished nets are useful everywhere for endless knickknacks and most useful up high near the companionway for sailing gloves, strobe lights, suntan lotion, sunglasses, etc. On nice days, the net can be unhooked, taken out (contents and all), and hung conveniently from the gallows or lifelines, near the cockpit.

Concealed

In lockers, nets are a marvel. Finished nets can be filled with different fruits and vegetables and hung inside lockers, ventilating and out of the way. They are perfect for storing paper products, like napkins and paper towels, which usually take up great space and often become wet in locker bottoms.

Unfinished nets in lockers are also of great value and I saw a marvelous boat in Camden, Maine, whose name I cannot recall, using it most cleverly in all closed lockers, instead of solid plywood shelves. They greatly aid in venting, keeping clothes, towels, and shoes fresh.

The best netting to use is un-dyed cotton, for it's easily washable and it will not stain clothes. It can be purchased in bulk and cut to the required size; the loose strands can then be tied to a 1/4″ hemming line running clear around the net, with a loop at either end for handles. It can also be hemmed by sewing a ribbon of cotton around the perimeter, with an occasional 3/16″ grommet to be used for suspending.

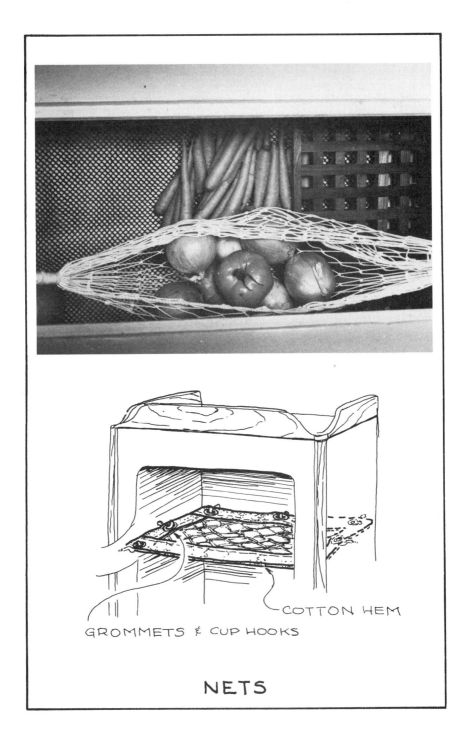

GROMMETS & CUP HOOKS

COTTON HEM

NETS

STOWAGE IN COMPANIONWAY LADDER

Small compartments in accessible areas are at an absolute premium in most yachts and few better places meet both requirements as well as companionway ladders, into which small lockers can be built to house everything from flashlights and bilge pump handles to suntan lotion and sandwiches. Since most ladders hinge up to give access to spaces beyond, the overall weight has to be considered as well as the allowance of sufficient foot space for normal travel.

Willi de Roos' *Williwaw*, the first sailboat to sail through the ice of the Northwest Passage, has a ladder constructed somewhat pyramidically so the depth of the compartment increases toward the base. Between each rung is a hinged or sliding door, giving access to the compartments.

Since ladders vary in slope and depth, I shall describe here only the very simple adaption that could be applicable to most.

The one thing that cannot be tempered with on a ladder is the surface of the rungs. They need to be at least 5" deep for good footing, hence, the storage to be added must be in the form of an upside down pyramid, with maximum stowage space gained just beneath each tread.

Step One involves sealing off the rear of the ladder. This can be accomplished by a single piece of 1/8" plywood that is set into rabbets in the back of the ladder and glued and tacked onto the rungs and the sides. Next, install cleat stock angled from the back of the top of each rung to within an inch of the front of the bottom of the rung above. The face of the storage space can be of 1/4" plywood split horizontally in a ratio of about two to three. To explain. The lower 8" of a given face of 12" will be fixed permanently to the cleat stock while the remaining 4" will hinge *down* from two small butt hinges adjoining the two facial pieces. If you erroneously hinge the whole face, good luck. Every time you open it you'll be playing Fifty-Two Pick Up. Since most things stored here will be light, a single barrel bolt to one side will be sufficient. Space permitting, this would be an ideal location for a concealed paper towel rack (see Paper Towel Rack).

A word of logic, place the heaviest objects near the top rung and the lightest near the bottom rung. The ladder will be much easier to lift. Remember the wheel barrow.

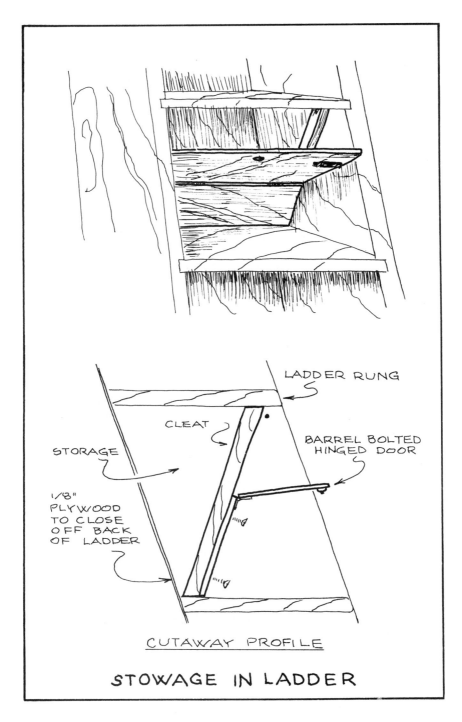

LADDER RUNG

CLEAT

STORAGE

BARREL BOLTED
HINGED DOOR

1/8"
PLYWOOD
TO CLOSE
OFF BACK
OF LADDER

CUTAWAY PROFILE

STOWAGE IN LADDER

LOCKER VENTING

Keeping all areas of a vessel well vented is mandatory, regardless of the material used for hull construction. In wooden hulls, dry rot starts beautifully in lockers and bilges where rain water has ventured; in metal hulls, the danger of rust is ever present; and, of course, rot can start in fiberglass yachts, whose plywood bulkheads are very vital, but very vulnerable, structural parts. Actually, the danger is considerably greater with fiberglass, since condensation is such a major problem, and if you think this is being nit-picky, just run your hand along the inside of your hull on a cold night after you've finished cooking a steamy dinner.

The first step in fending off dry rot, etc., is to provide each locker with a drain hole in its lowest part; this way, any stray water will drain off into the bilge before it has an opportunity to soak into any surrounding wood. The drain hole need be no more than $3/8''$. Periodic cleaning will be required to ensure flow. Sufficient ventilation can be provided to most lockers by substituting solid doors with louvered ones, or ones with cane inserts, or at least jigsawing out ventilating holes in a large attractive pattern, say in the shape of Dolly Parton's left boobie. For top loading lockers, whose lids are usually covered by cushions, holes can be cut in the locker faces, which can then, in turn, be filled with louvers, grates, or cane.

To facilitate inter-locker ventilation, drill three or so $1''$ diameter holes in the non-structural bulkheads between them. Drill these as high up as possible to be sure they won't get covered over by clothes or other objects. With all lockers thus interconnected, a further step can be taken to increase air flow. Lead a pipe from a dorade vent well forward into a locker in the bow, creating a sort of forced system which can flow through the locker and out through an aft vent. If the engine is aft, with its own vent, the lockers could be allowed to simply feed into the engine room and be extracted from there.

Use as many grates and vents as possible inside lockers, to facilitate air passage close to locker surfaces. If your anchor chain is fed below, through a piping system, into a locker which vents into the bilge, use of a dorade-shaped deck pipe, instead of the top closing flat kind, would be most prudent, for then at anchor, or on good days, the flap gate could be left open, creating a perfect air feed down through the bilges.

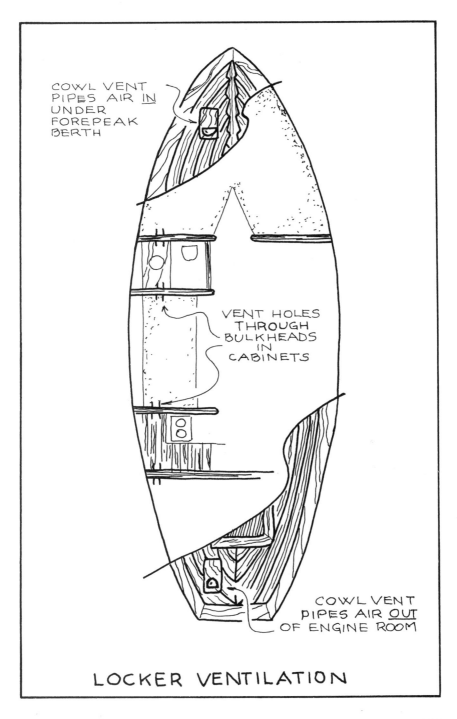

COWL VENT PIPES AIR <u>IN</u> UNDER FOREPEAK BERTH

VENT HOLES THROUGH BULKHEADS IN CABINETS

COWL VENT PIPES AIR <u>OUT</u> OF ENGINE ROOM

LOCKER VENTILATION

FISH ROD RACKS

I don't like fishing. I don't mind dangling bits of nylon and chrome over the side, and I don't even mind paying for more chrome and nylon after some stupid fish makes off with the first set, but what I don't like is unhooking the slithering beast, bludgeoning it with my only hammer, carving flimsy bits of meat from its carcass, and ending up with two bits to eat and a cockpit full of guts to clean up. But those two bits are so good that I've buckled under and now regularly dangle, bludgeon, etc.

Of course, now there's a new problem: the stowage of fishing gear. Nothing is less entertaining than a hook in the seat of one's pants or other private places, so a most secure rack must be fabricated and used religiously.

Solid 3/4" stock will be required in two 3" × 12" pieces for two rods. Add about 6" more for each additional rod. The rack is made for collapsible rods, so for each rod, a large hole will be required for the handle, a small hole for the base of the tip and two small "J" ends. A 1½" hole should suffice for the rod base, and about 3/4" for the base of the extension. The "J"s should be routed to about a 3/8" width. To save space, the second set of rods should be reversed, that is, the holes switched places with the "J"s. The ends of the "J"s should be equipped with locking tabs made of brass plate or hard plastic, secured loosely by a single screw or brass tack.

The mounting board of 1½" width should be screwed and glued onto the edge of each rack. Mounting can be effected on either the overhead or bulkheads.

If you're to engage in activities such as cleaning and bludgeoning, you will require an official fish board. For the sake of stowage, this should be thin (1/2" plywood is just fine), and about 18" × 8". All your cleaning and filleting can be done on this board. Drill a hole half way through in one end to accommodate a mounting spike, which you'll have to drive through the end of the skin when separating the fillet from same. A real hole at the other end with a lanyard through it would be a great idea to enable you to dangle the board over the side for a good salt water rinse. A scrub brush should be used to clean the board thoroughly after each use.

Botulism is no fun.

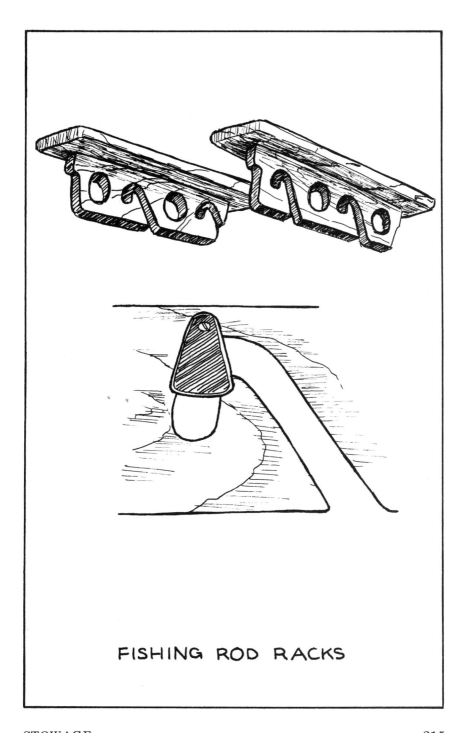

FISHING ROD RACKS

FOUL WEATHER GEAR DRYER

It's all ugly. Being wet and cold and having fingers like pale prunes, and lips like grape-sicles, and teeth that chatter nerve-wrackingly is all ugly, but it's even uglier when you have to sit in a cabin after all that with ugly dripping clothes dangling all over the place.

The best solution for both you and your soaked gear is to start a good roaring fire and hang the clothes in a well-ventilated place to dry, but preferably out of sight so they won't be constant reminders of your prunishness.

A major factor here is location of your heating stove. It's nice to have it on the bulkhead adjoining the head. Any further discussion will be based on the assumption that this is possible. Directly behind the stove, cut a hole about the size you had your reflector plate. On the head side of the bulkhead, cover the hole with fine brass meshing and staple it to the bulkhead with monel or brass staples. Trim the hole with "L" trim on the salon side and with a rabbeted frame on the head side.

The rabbeted frame should be constructed as follows: from 3/4″ stock, rip two 1½″ wide strips with lengths of twice the height of your hole. Also rip two smaller pieces whose length equals the width of the hole. Next, groove the centre of all pieces with a 1/2″ deep groove the width of your saw blade. Affix the two sides and the bottom onto the bulkhead like an open frame. Acquire a moderately gauged piece of copper or brass or stainless sheeting to fit the frame and cover the hole, and overhang it (downward) by 2½″. Attach a small porcelain handle to the bottom of the plate. Across the top of the hole, fit a 2″ strip of 1/4″ plywood, then affix it so that the plate will cover the entire piece when in a down position. Slip the plate in place and install the grooved top of the frame. Gravity will keep the plate in a closed position. To keep the plate in an open position, slide the plate up and drill a 3/8″ hole in its lower two inches, continuing the drilling through the 1/4″ plywood sealer. Use a 3/8″ dowel as a keeper. To facilitate circulation, a hole of about 4″ × 8″ should be cut in a wall of the head very close to the cabin sole and fitted with a grate. Good circulation will now be insured with the plate open, and then retention of the heat for the salon can be achieved when the plate is closed. The head can be strung with wet gear out of sight and out of mind.

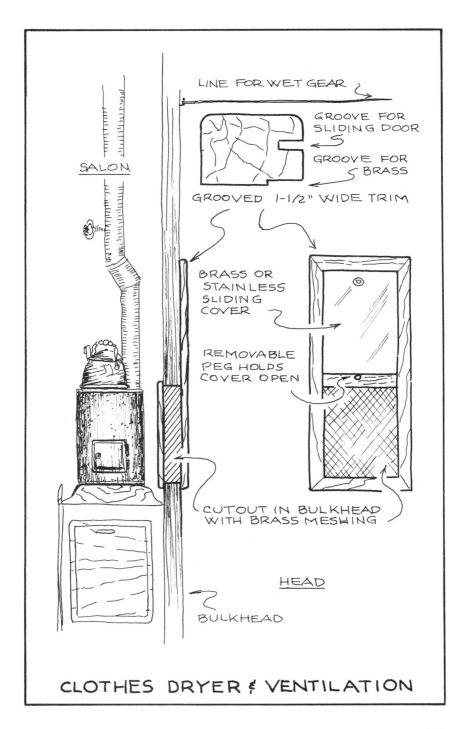

LINE FOR WET GEAR

GROOVE FOR SLIDING DOOR

GROOVE FOR BRASS

GROOVED 1-1/2" WIDE TRIM

SALON

BRASS OR STAINLESS SLIDING COVER

REMOVABLE PEG HOLDS COVER OPEN

CUTOUT IN BULKHEAD WITH BRASS MESHING

HEAD

BULKHEAD

CLOTHES DRYER & VENTILATION

CANE DOORS

Ventilation of lockers is always of primary concern, especially in steel, fiberglass, and ferro cement hulls, where much condensation forms. Solid doors, in spite of the finger holes and cutey sweety anchors routed in them, provide only pathetic little puffs of air. Something much more drastic is required. On *Warm Rain*, all the doors have inserts of woven cane, so we're able to keep all lockers mildew and condensation free. Fabricating doors is no small task, so be prepared to spend time — about an hour and a half per door.

Cut the door frames to about a 2½″ width, from 13/16″ stock, and assemble with single dowels in each corner using a mitre jig. Glue with resorcinol, and clamp. Wipe off all excess glue immediately or it will seep deep into the grain and cause permanent stains, removable only with an ax. Let it set overnight.

Rout a 3/16″ groove 1/2″ in from the frame's edge. This will accommodate 1/8″ caning beads, which you can buy by the roll from furniture finishers. Rough cut a piece of cane, with at least a 3/4″ overhang past the groove all the way around, and soak in warm water. Whatever you do, *do not* skip this step. The cane must soak thoroughly, and this can take up to half an hour. An eastern boat manufacturer saw the cane doors in *From A Bare Hull* and decided to put them on all his boats, but he somehow managed to miss the paragraph on soaking, and ended up with limper, saggier looking things than the mammaries of a 90-year-old African grandmother.

Lay a bead of glue clear around the groove (Elmer's glue will do), towel the cane dry, and lay it in place, making sure the pattern runs parallel to the frame. Lay in the caning bead and hammer it into place with a mallet. Next, lay in the opposite caning bead and, while stretching the cane to the utmost, hammer it into place. Do likewise with the remaining two sides, keeping as much tension on the cane as possible. Wipe off all excess glue with a damp cloth and, while the cane is still wet, trim the protruding ends with a razor knife. You can belt sand off what little stubble remains, when it's dry and stiff. When dry, spray both inside and out with non-gloss shellac to prevent moisture re-entering the cane, causing the aforementioned sag. For single doors, drill 7/8″ finger holes, and bullnose. For double doors, simply attach a double-hinged cabin hook and eye. Finger holes here will be redundant, for the brass fittings are sufficient handles. Install the doors with brass hinges and watch your guests turn green with envy.

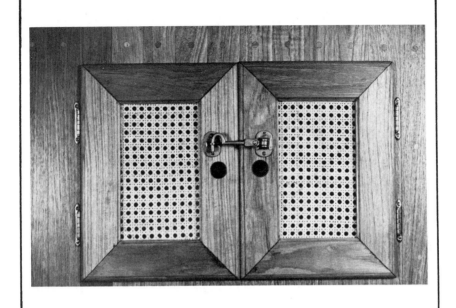

3/16" CANING GROOVE

CROSS SECTION OF FRAME

CANE DOORS

LOCK STOWAGE

Nothing has caused man more worry and agony than a boat's padlock at rest. When needed, it is never to be found. When not wanted, it's everywhere: on big toes, in wine glasses, in the garbage, or right between the cream cheese and capers in the lox and bagels.

It has caused marital flare-ups and breakdowns, and, indeed, the second-most frequent question Candace asks me after, "What on earth are you talking about now?" is "Where is the lock?!" The lock is where it wants to be. Nowhere special, but always in the place where discovery consumes at least 23 minutes.

But salvation is here. I found a simple solution to this complex dilemma aboard the ketch *Glaucus*, the only other boat at a quiet anchorage called Sturt Bay. Here is how it's done.

On a 1½″ thick piece of teak, about 3″ × 3″, trace the shape of your lock. The body only. The tongue should always stick out to indicate whereabouts. Rout the pattern deep enough to house the body flush. Bullnose the edges of the face on the two sides and the bottom. Slightly sand the top edge. From 1/4″ teak stock, cut a piece to fit the back, creating an enclosed pocket. Mounting a backless holder, that is, using a bulkhead or cabin sides as a back is a mistake. The constant in and out moving of lock will scratch the area directly above resulting in endless maintenance.

Mount with one screw on either side and plug. Locate it right next to the main hatch and use it.

A timely note on locks. The combination variety is awfully handy obviating the use of keys, which disappear at least as frequently as the locks themselves. The only drawback with this is that night time operation is difficult unless you're a bat or an owl, so placing of a flashlight in an unlocked and handy area is essential. Also, be certain that the tongue is casehardened. We had the misfortune of neglecting this small point, and were relieved of a tidy heap of equipment when someone neatly cut our pretty, but putty, padlock clear off.

3"

SPACE
ROUTED OUT
FOR LOCK

1/2"

1/4" PLYWOOD BACK

LOCK STOWAGE

SLIDING DOORS

Cabinet Doors

If you desire to close off an area for storage, whether in the engine room, galley, or around the chart table, the least time consuming and least expensive method would be to fabricate a partial bulkhead and equip it with sliding doors. The doors can be of either 1/8″ plexiglass or 1/8″ veneer depending on how ugly a thing you're trying to hide.

First you will need to fit the new 1/2″ plywood bulkhead into place and secure it there using cleat stock, glue and screws. Next, mill the track for your sliding doors as shown in the illustration. Mill enough to cover the entire perimeter of your bulkhead opening, using the 1/4″ deep slotted pieces (see dotted line) for the bottom and sides, and the 1/2″ deep slotted pieces for the top. This way, you can put the sliding door in place by pushing it up into the 1/2″ slot, then dropping it down into the 1/4″ slot and still have 1/4″ of track lip on top to hold it in. So, mill the pieces and glue and screw them into place drilling from the front through the 1/2″ wide "L," then countersinking and plugging. Next, cut your sliding doors from veneer or plexiglass, making the height the size of the opening (with rails in) plus 1/2″, and the length, one-half the opening plus 1″ to allow for a slight overlap. Sand all edges lightly to avoid splintering. The simplest handle for the doors is of course the finger hole, providing it's at least 7/8″ in diameter. Anything less will result in stuck fingers and a lot of cursing.

Cabin Doors

Since few small boats have enough space for hinged doors to provide privacy, the alternative can be sliding doors. These can only be used if a clear surface exists on the bulkhead adjoining the passage to be closed off. The one disadvantage you will suffer with this system is that you'll have to put in a permanent low bulkhead (4″ will probably suffice) across the opening for your lower slide to be mounted on.

Cut your door from a piece of 1/4″ plywood and frame it with 13/16″ stock cut to 3″ width and grooved as shown. Lightly bullnose all edges, cut the corners to 45°, glue all grooves, then assemble along with plywood filler and screw diagonally across the corner joints. An occasional screw through the frame and plywood, about every 18″ or so, would be good insurance.

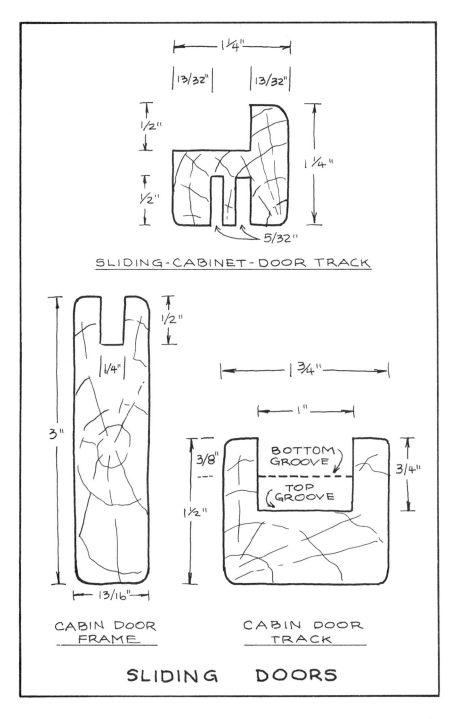

SLIDING-CABINET-DOOR TRACK

CABIN DOOR
FRAME

CABIN DOOR
TRACK

SLIDING DOORS

The track, as shown, can be milled from solid 1¾" stock or built up of three individual layers. The groove of the upper track will be twice as deep (3/4") as the lower track (3/8") (see above). Cut your track to such a length as to allow 2" overhangs past the door in both open and closed position. Glue and screw both tracks onto the bulkhead using the measurement of the finished door to determine spacing. Be certain the tracks are perfectly parallel. For stoppers, glue filler pieces into both ends of each track. Wax the tracks with good heavy wax. A candle will do.

To keep the door from sliding inadvertently, drill a 1/8" hole through the track and door, in both closed and open positions, and insert a small removable eyebolt to hold it wherever you like.

SLIDING DOORS

LOCKER PADDING

Although I do sometimes get carried away with gadgets and tinkering, I think that locker padding is a must in most yachts. First, it should be used to save the hull. Heavy tumbling objects, like cans, chains, wrenches, and winch handles, can gouge wood, chip paint, cause rust on steel, and crack the gelcoat on fiberglass liners. Secondly, the stowed goods should be protected. Tiny leaks will quickly cause rust, spoiling the last can of rum cake that you were just dying to bite into.

Most padding can be readily and cheaply bought, the most common type being solid heavy gauge plastic. Although the varieties and sources are limitless, we chose the rug-saver for our lockers. Often used in semi-finished buildings, where the carpets are being protected from wear, this usually comes in a 24″ width on a virtually endless roll. It's a very heavy, yet flexible, plastic sheet with nobbies on one side, and a smooth surface on the other. The nobbies are perfect for allowing air to circulate beneath the plastic, and the smooth side is easily kept clean. It is thick and rigid enough that it will remain in place even against the steepest of hulls, so no adhesion is necessary. We use it in our lockers under cans and heavy tools, and in our chain lockers, under the anchor chain. Maybe I'm over-reacting, but at 69¢ a running foot, who can afford to wait and see.

Another ideal material we've found, through a friend who works for the airlines, is an open webbing made of flexible plastic. The walls of the webs are about 1/8″ high and the diamond-shaped cells take up one-half square inch each. It makes very good padding, as well as great non-skid under plates, etc., but seems much more difficult to clean if something mucky and gooey is spilled into the tight little cells.

bibelots

INTERIOR GRABRAILS

Virtually all production boats, as well as many time-tested yachts, suffer from a lack of interior grabrails. These are an absolute must if the crew is to operate safely in a seaway.

Grabrails fall into two general categories: the traditional looped type, and the underdeck-supported solid-trough type. Both are extremely functional, and have a place belowdecks in different locations.

Trough Rails

If at all possible, most vessels should be fitted with cabin-length trough rails running along where the cabinsides join the underdecks. These rails have three major functions: a) they serve as an uninterrupted grabrail that can be clutched at any spot, b) they act as a trough for water coming in through forgotten portlights, and c) they serve as a marvelous little shelf to stuff all sorts of knickknacks into, from keys to small change.

Construction is quite basic, consisting really of an "L" of hardwood. The horizontal piece should be of 3/4" stock and have an average width of 5". Since most cabins taper toward the bow, it will be necessary to cut some of these from stock as wide as 8" or 10", depending, of course, on how drastic the curve is. I advise using templates of 1/8" plywood to eliminate experimentation with expensive hardwoods. Of the 5" width, 3" should be used to fit against the underdeck, the other two will form the bottom of the trough. The inboard edge of the support should be cut on a bevel that matches the cabin sides. In wood boats, fastening will be child's play, since you'll just be screwing into hefty hanging knees. On most fiberglass boats, underdecks have a plywood core and occasionally a secondary plywood lining. The combination of the two make for an excellent base. One must first establish the thickness of each of these (especially if only a plywood core is present) with information from the manufacturer before any drilling is begun, or one may find sunlight pouring in through the little drilled holes. With wood on wood, use glue; with wood on fiberglass, use mish-mash.

The rail itself should be ripped from 3/4" stock to a width of 2½". Bullnose all edges, and with the bottom of the rail overhanging the support by 1/2", glue and fasten with 1¼" #10 F.H.S.M. screws on 6" centres. You will probably need someone to hold the rail in place while you drill and screw, especially if the sheer of your vessel is drastic. Run a tiny bead of silicone sealer between the support and the cabin side to make the trough watertight.

THE FINELY FITTED YACHT

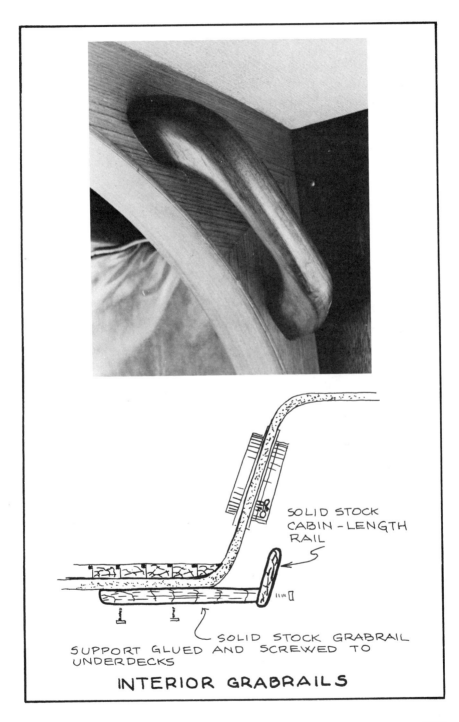

SOLID STOCK
CABIN - LENGTH
RAIL

SOLID STOCK GRABRAIL

SUPPORT GLUED AND SCREWED TO
UNDERDECKS

INTERIOR GRABRAILS

Loop Rails

Some people advocate the use of these directly overhead or about 1½' off the keel line. I feel that, in most yachts, the trough rail would be of much greater value, unless you're an ardent commuter of trains or buses who automatically reaches up for support when the going is lurchy. If so, read the section on exterior grabrails for information.

I do feel, however, that the looped rail has great value in its single loop format, around places like the sides of companionways; above difficult to get in and out of berths; in the head; and in nearly any other place in the yacht where support is needed. For up and out support, you'll just have to think hard and pretend you're in a blow; but for general location, a simple experiment involves sectioning off the cabin sole into one foot square areas, then standing in each of these, and literally throwing yourself into all imaginable directions. If it hurts, that's the place you need a single loop of grabrail.

The size of single loops should generally be determined by the space available, with the maximum loop hole of 8" length supported by 3" flat ends, tapered as in illustration. Fabrication is described under "Exterior Grabrails."

Installation should be by means of 1/4" S.S.R.H. machine screws (bolts), with flat washers and nuts for support. If this is not feasible (as in some companionways), #12 sheet metal screws can be used with generous portions of resorcinol glue. Whichever you use, be sure you don't over-tighten; few things split as easily as these damned grabrails.

GRABRAILS

BERTH CURTAINS AND PORTLIGHT CURTAINS

Perhaps I'm over the hill and consequently approaching the age where people whisper the adjective "stodgy" behind my person, but I love few things more after having a fine lunch of cheeses, smoked salmon, and a glass of wine in the solitude of a northern anchorage, than crawling into the pilot berth and catching 40 winks. It's a special little thing that divides the day into manageable halves, but it's a thing that could not be done without a well-curtained berth. Like many people, I cannot sleep with the sun blazing through my eyelids.

Since the upper part of the foot of the berth is open onto the chart table, one wing was installed as an "L". Since a 6'5" curtain rod would have looked completely terrible, we used single strand stainless wire, stretched very tightly between two padeyes, with a brass U-nail in the centre. All this is nicely hidden by the 1/2" overhang of the solid grab rail that runs the length of the cabin. One must not use multi-strand wire for curtain suspension because it can fray and cause absolute havoc with both curtain and fingers. When open, the curtains are held at either end by a sash whose two ends have been fitted with small pieces of Velcro. One end is tacked to the bulkhead. You have to try it. You haven't slept so well since you were in the cradle.

Portlight Curtains

I have never had an affinity for traditional curtains on portlights. They flip-flop nauseatingly at sea, they don't lie quite closed enough for privacy, and they seem to destroy the preciousness of beautiful bronze portlights with their bulky housiness. Of course, for non-opening large windows, they are the only solution. For others, a simple device exists that dispenses with the rods and curtain ties and can be best described as a portlight cap.

Use material that matches your cushion covers, and cut out a circular piece 1" greater in diameter than the widest dimension of your portlight. Do not neglect to include the dogs and hinges. Now cut a strip of cloth 1" longer than the circumference of the portlight (including dogs and hinges) and 1½" wider than the portlight's depth. This will be the side. Sew the side onto the circle using a 1/2" seam allowance, and hem it, leaving a space for elastic. Insert the elastic with a safety pin, and what have you got? A flat-topped shower cap. It can be quickly put on and more quickly stowed neatly inside another cap, leaving the beauty of the portlight undisturbed during the day.

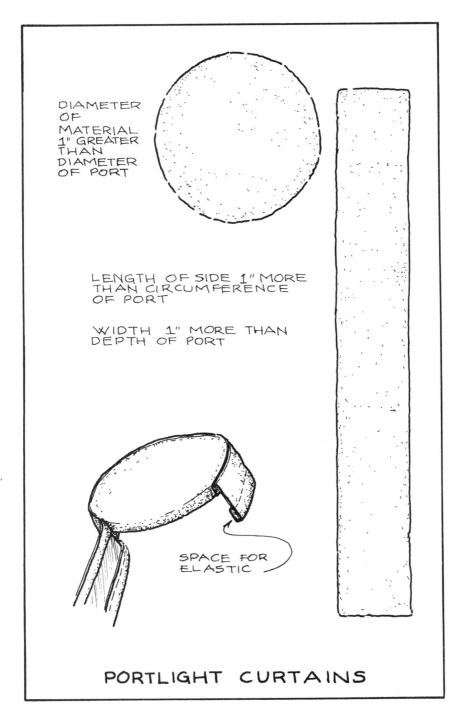

DIAMETER
OF
MATERIAL
1" GREATER
THAN
DIAMETER
OF PORT

LENGTH OF SIDE 1" MORE
THAN CIRCUMFERENCE
OF PORT

WIDTH 1" MORE THAN
DEPTH OF PORT

SPACE FOR
ELASTIC

PORTLIGHT CURTAINS

BULKHEAD HAND GRAB

If your cutaway-bulkheads are not equipped with posts, that's too bad. Although this oversight can provide a boat with unbroken visual volume, you should add a bit of security to un-grabable and un-hugable space by fabricating and installing the illustrated hand grab.

For strength, a triple laminate has to be constructed. The rough size will be about 3″ × 8″. The middle piece should be the thickness of the bulkhead, and the two outside pieces, the size of the overhang of the existing trim around the bulkhead. The central piece should be end grain (in the completed hand grab), while the outside pieces should have the grain perpendicular to the central piece. Glue with resorcinol and clamp.

Cut the bulkhead trim 90°, then cut the bulkhead corner itself to a 45° angle with as clean a cut as possible, remembering that the existing trim is to remain intact (hopefully) for all but the very corner. Measure from the inside corners of the leftover trim pieces, determine the bottom length of the hand grab, then mark from these points, flaring out, following the angle of the cut trim. You will now have to rout or dado out the bottom of the piece to bulk and thickness. Dado to a depth so that the grab's base edge will meet the inside tips of the existing trim pieces.

If you have, by some saintworthy miracle, managed to follow the instructions thus far with your chunk of wood and sanity intact, take a deep breath, for you're over the hump.

Now, you'll want the hand hole itself about 4″ long and 1¼″ wide. That should accommodate even the sausagiest of fingers. The ends of the hole can taper, so on 3″ centres, cut two 1″ holes with a hole saw (leaving 1/2″ of wood on the bottom of the grab), then finish cutting out the rest of the grip with a jigsaw. To establish the cutting lines, make your lower cut parallel to the bottom of the grab; make your upper cut by scribing an arc joining the tops of the holes. Make a centre space 1¼″ wide. To get the outside radius of the hand grab, re-fit the piece, and scribe a line from the top of each old trim, following the upper curve of the fresh-cut hand hole. Cut with a jigsaw, and round all edges to match the existing trim. Glue and screw vertically into the bulkhead about an inch from the ends, and plug. Nifty, isn't it?

SEARAILS

Strangely enough, even in this day and age, when you'd think everyone would have gotten the word, many boats still arrive from the manufacturers without searails. How they expect things to remain on counters and tables in any seaway, heaven only knows.

What is probably worse than no searail at all, are the silly things made of little spindles with a toothpick of a rail along their tops. These frivolities will last through exactly the first five minutes of a good wind, until someone grabs them or leans against them, whereupon they turn instantly into kindling.

Searails should be of solid stock 13/16" or better, 2" high (clear), rabbetted, and screwed, and glued firmly to the countertops. If you are contemplating future alterations to your vessel, you will be well advised to mill a backlog of searails all at one time, for then you will be sure they match perfectly, since you will be performing all the milling with the same machine settings.

A much improved version of the old solid searail has been born. I first saw it on a Fast Passage 39 from Philbrook Shipyards in Sidney, B.C. They very thoughtfully incorporated grab loops into the searails, providing excellent security. These I would think to be indispensible around chart tables, galleys, heads, and engine rooms; anywhere hands may be in need of a quickly available support.

The overall height of these rails must be at least 2¾", since the height of the hand hold should be 1 1/8", the handle itself 3/4", and the bottom rabbet 7/8". Beveling the top should be bypassed in favour of the extra strength. The length of each loop hole is optional, ranging from a minimum of 5" to accommodate most hands, to a maximum of 8" to provide minimum strength. The solid parts between the loops can range anywhere from 2" up. The rails should be thoroughly bullnosed with a 3/8" bit, along the top and bottom, as well as inside the loops.

They can be installed either as in the photo, or the illustration, with open or closed corners. The closed corner has the obvious advantage of strength, but has the disadvantages of: a) restricting sweeping of counter tops, b) having nasty things lodge in the inside of the sharp corners, and c) being a pointed weapon against hips and pelvises. If properly rabbeted, glued, and screwed, the open corners can provide quite sufficient strength.

SEARAILS

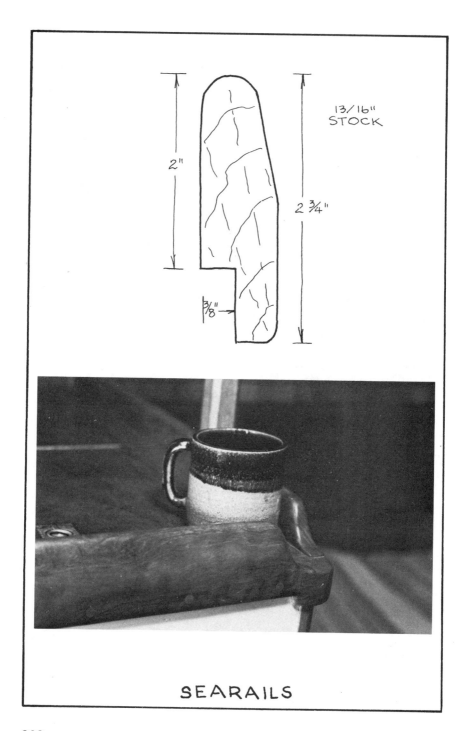

13/16"
STOCK

2"

2 ¾"

⅜"

SEARAILS

THE FINELY FITTED YACHT

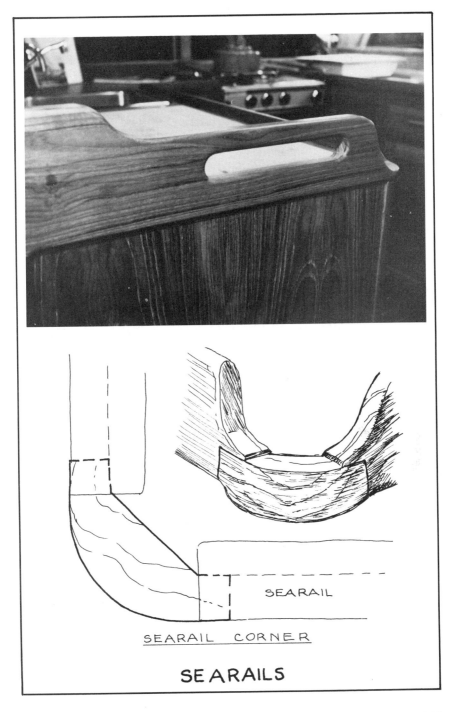

SEARAIL

SEARAIL CORNER

SEARAILS

DESK

Desks are magical places aboard a yacht. You can just sneak behind one, spread out papers and pens and, after sitting there an hour staring vacuously into space, you can come out and feel like you've actually done something. A number of people who have read *From A Bare Hull* have written asking for details about our desk (I euphemize it as my "study"), so here they are. The elevation and layout are shown in the illustrations.

To achieve comfortable foot space, a 6″ riser was built to provide a 20″ wide flat surface instead of a 14″ one. A small drop-hatch provides access to the space beneath it. The area of the desk was by the location of the bulkheads made rather claustrophobic, so we cut away the inboard upper third of the main bulkhead (the desk faces aft) opening up a very wide vista into the salon. An opening portlight in the cabinside directly over the desk, and what additional light we've gained by allowing light from the skylight to come through the cutout in the bulkhead, have turned this into a very pleasant work space. The weakening of the bulkhead through the removal of a portion of it was compensated for by the addition of a 2″ × 2″ post on the bulkheads inboard edge. Not only is this of a structural benefit, but it's also a perfect thing to grab in overreactive seas. The lower portion of the post was dadoed to allow insertion of the bulkhead into it. They were glued and screwed together. The upper end of the post was fitted under the deckbeams and secured there by means of a routed pad into which it snuggly fit. The pad was in turn glued and screwed to the deckbeams.

So now we were back where we had been before we started butchering the bulkhead, except that we had a nice flat floor. The choice to have the desk facing aft was fairly obvious for: a) the hull was turning in rather abruptly so about 25° more floor width could be gained for feet, and b) the salon was a brighter area to steal light from than the forepeak.

Next, we installed a short fore and aft 1/2″ ply bulkhead at the outboard end of the designed 28″ seat. This was secured to the main and forward bulkheads with the aid of cleat stocks and bonded (on its outboard face) to the hull. Over this bulkhead came another major structural piece in the form of a 1/2″ plywood "L" which was to become the horizontal (fixed) bottom of the desk, the armrest, and the bottom of both the bookshelf and the shallow cabinet beside it. This was tied into all three bulkheads by means of 3/4″ cleat stock, and it was supported on the inboard end with a solid teak knee cut from 2″ stock.

THE FINELY FITTED YACHT

The seat was fabricated from three pieces of 1/2" plywood (top, aft side, inboard side) with a drop hatch to give access to its rather spacious interior. Plywood seating cleats, 1/2" × 1½", screwed to the underside of the top kept the lid from falling through.

The rough work for the bookshelf and adjoining cabinet were next. The cabinet needed only an inboard face and an aft side, but the problematic part was to join the two pieces at 90° and end up with a presentable job. Plywood endgrain is not too shippy, and I don't really fancy "L" trim, so we decided to mill a corner piece from solid teak that would serve as a structural support for the sides and finish off the endgrain at the same time. The corner post shown was used to finish off the 3/8" plywood ends; it can be milled simply on a table saw by following the shown measurements. The short bookshelf was fitted in place and to avoid unsightly cleat stock supports, we just made sure it was a tight fit, glued the ends, then screwed into them from the other side of the bulkheads that the shelf adjoined. When screwing into the edge of plywood in this fashion, care must be taken with the amount of force used, for it's extremely easy to become over-zealous and rip out the delicate threads you've just cut.

Then the teak work on the desk was begun. The free standing corner of the desk was cut on an angle to reduce the likelihood of injury. The two sides and the front were cut from 13/16" stock, and were attached to the desk bottom with the aid of cleat stock. The narrow fixed piece of the top (from which the lid is hinged) was put in in a similar fashion.

The frame for the lid was made up of five 3" wide pieces, using lapped joints. A groove was routed in the bottom of the frames so a 3/8" plywood could be let in and glued in place. Another piece of 3/8" was used to fill in the space to within 1/16" of the tops of the frames. The last 1/16" was filled with leather to form a very excellent writing surface. The leather was laid in with contact cement (starting in one corner to eliminate wrinkles) and pressed firmly down with a cotton-gloved hand to avoid staining. Round hinges were recessed into the lid and the fixed piece of the top. A small cabin hook was affixed to the outboard edge of the lid to keep it hooked to the underdeck if extensive, two-handed rummaging is required inside the desk. A brass lamp provides good reading light.

It's such a cozy nook I almost never leave it.

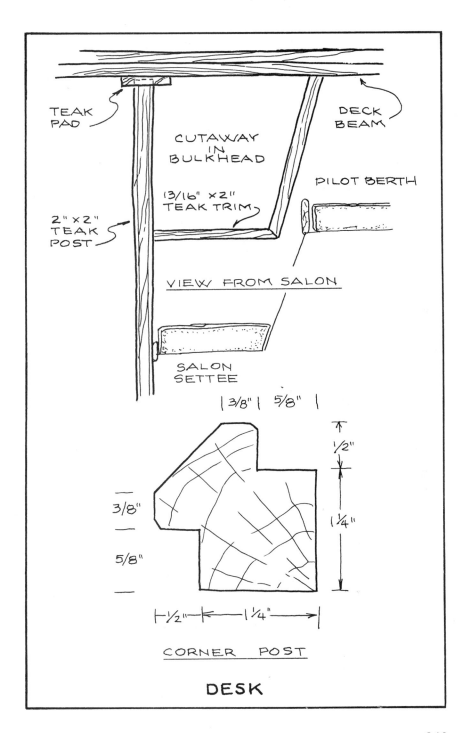

TEAK PAD

DECK BEAM

CUTAWAY IN BULKHEAD

PILOT BERTH

13/16" X2" TEAK TRIM

2" X2" TEAK POST

VIEW FROM SALON

SALON SETTEE

| 3/8" | 5/8" |

1/2"

3/8"

1¼"

5/8"

|—½"—|←—1¼"—→|

CORNER POST

DESK

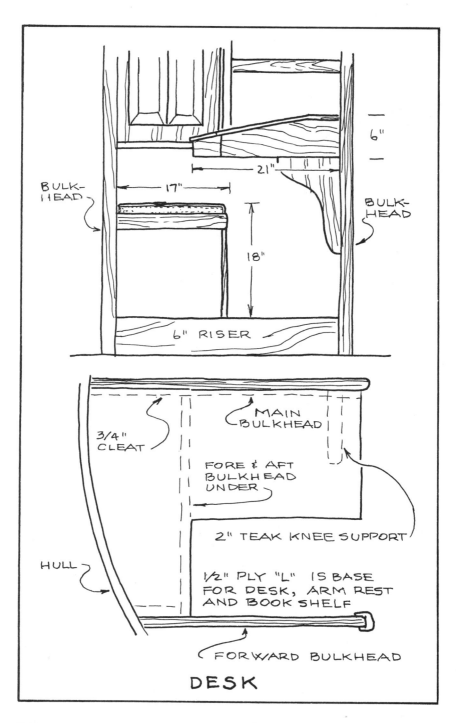

6"

BULK-
HEAD

17"

21"

18"

BULK-
HEAD

6" RISER

MAIN
BULKHEAD

3/4"
CLEAT

FORE & AFT
BULKHEAD
UNDER

2" TEAK KNEE SUPPORT

HULL

½" PLY "L" IS BASE
FOR DESK, ARM REST
AND BOOK SHELF

FORWARD BULKHEAD

DESK

THE FINELY FITTED YACHT

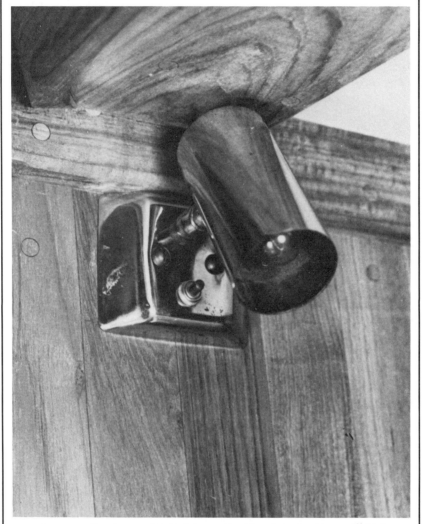

Brass reading lamp with high intensity 12 volt bulb. About 4″ high.

THROUGH-HULL PLUGS

All cruising and racing boats should have plugs aboard, for neither is immune to failed seacocks. Indeed, many offshore racers are required to carry them as standard safety equipment. It would not seem overcautious to have at least two plugs for each size of seacock just in case trouble really does come in threes.

Only softwood should be used for plugs. I have heard the tragic tale of a hard-as-steel oak plug which, when driven into the seacock by an overanxious crew, split the housing like a blooming rose; so use softwood (cedar is perfect), and use your head. If you have no access to a lathe, fret not, an hour's whittling will supply you with 50 years worth of plugs. For the large ones, cut 5″ long plugs from 1½″ stock, tapering them from 1½″ to 3/4″. After your first two cuts, it would be nice to place the plug into a vise (fat end only) so that two more tapering cuts can be made with a jigsaw. Next, get out the shoe rasp and rasp away. If your wood is well chosen, rounding the plug with a rasp should not be too demanding. Round the ends to avoid splintering. Drill a 1/4″ hole through the fat end and run a generous lanyard through it. With this the plug can be tied to the seacock it is to serve, for both storage and as a safety line to hold it in place if the need ever arises. When needed (heaven forbid), just tap the plug into place and wrap the lanyard around the base of the seacock (or the greasing plug and seacock handle) to keep the water motion from spitting the plug back out.

For smaller seacocks (3/4″), cut your plug from 1″ cedar (the 1″ is minimum), make it 4″ long, and taper it to 3/8″. Inspect plugs each year for checking or cracking. A little oil now and then wouldn't hurt.

THE FINELY FITTED YACHT

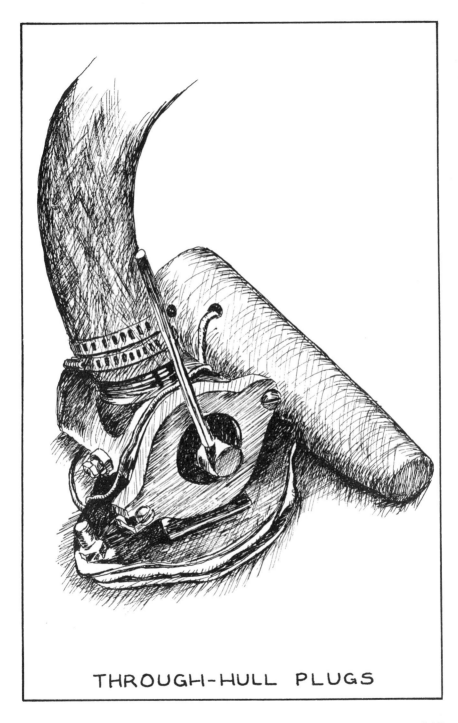

THROUGH-HULL PLUGS

COMPANIONWAY LADDER

Warm Rain's original design called for a companionway equipped with a number of slide out, lift up, yank away steps, all of which, when removed to make way to the engine room, made into a pile of rubble over which one constantly tripped. In other words, it didn't work worth a damn.

Every effort should be made on a yacht to abandon all overcomplicated hybrids, and the companionway is a good place to start. The traditional ladder is the ultimate solution. Its lovely rigid sides can house any number of hand holes, and with the help of some fine hinges at the top and a snap shackle on a short lanyard below the bottom rung, it can be swiftly lifted up out of the way and made fast to a padeye on a deck beam.

The sides of the ladder should be cut from 13/16″ stock, to a width of no more than 6″. If the ladder is sloped even just a little, very comfortable 7″ wide rungs can be fitted to the 6″ sides. If space demands, 4″ wide sides are tolerable. Radius the tops of the sides pleasantly, as shown. Draw in your treads allowing for 13/16″ stock. They should be spaced as far apart as you can conveniently make them (13″ is not excessive), remembering that the farther your rungs are spread, the easier it will be to come down the ladder facing forward. The tread length (ladder's interior width) need not be more than 12″. Dado in the space for your rungs on each side (not forgetting to mark the inside surfaces of the sides first) with your dado blades set at 3/8″. Check your setting on a piece of scrap wood before you cut the ladder.

Now, with your table saw blade set on the same angle as your ladder slope, trim the forward and aft edges of your rungs to match. Now, set your router at a depth of 7/8″ and rout a 1½″ × 4½″ hand hole near the top of each side. (A drill and jigsaw can be substituted for the router. See "Boarding Ladder".) For young sailors, a second set of hand holes can be cut between the second and third rungs. Bullnose the hand holes and edges of the ladder sides except: within 1/2″ of the rung slots, the footings, and the area where the hinges are to fit. Assemble the ladder with plastic resin glue and two or three 1″ #10 P.H.S.M. screws per rung end. When the glue has set, attach the hinges to the ladder, install the snap shackle and padeye, and lock the bottom of the ladder up to the deck beam, and have a friend hold the top of the ladder in position while you screw the hinges to the aft face of the cabin.

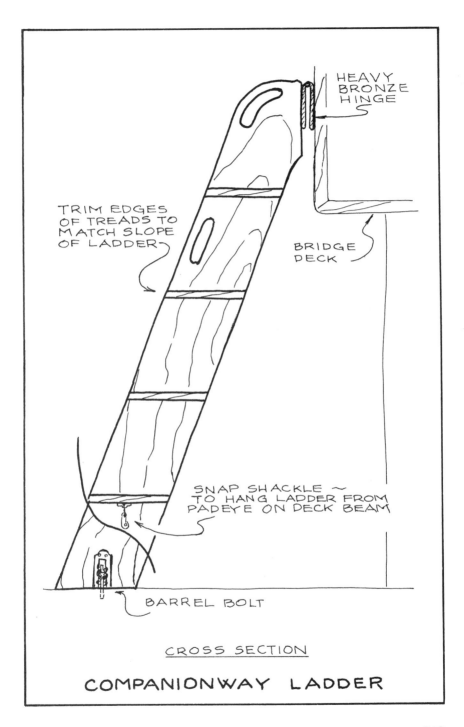

HEAVY BRONZE HINGE

TRIM EDGES OF TREADS TO MATCH SLOPE OF LADDER

BRIDGE DECK

SNAP SHACKLE ~ TO HANG LADDER FROM PADEYE ON DECK BEAM

BARREL BOLT

<u>CROSS SECTION</u>

COMPANIONWAY LADDER

FOREPEAK DESK CONVERSION

Many vessels have spacious forepeaks which, with a small crew, are mostly unused or worse, become a junk mine for rummage sale organizers. One of the better ways of eliminating this waste is to eliminate one berth, and install in its place, a desk-cum-storage area.

First, determine how wide you'll want your desk top — 20" seems minimal, over 36" on anything smaller than the Queen Mary seems obscene. At the determined point, cut out your berth face and top with a jig saw. Remove all old cleat stock that supported the pieces you've just cut out by digging out the plugs, unscrewing the screws, then *gently* prying the cleats away with a chisel. Gently. This is a minor remodeling job, *not* a housewrecking.

If there is bonding to be cut, remove the blade from your hacksaw, wrap one end with tape so the teeth won't gnaw away your milk-toast palm, then, after cutting a starting hole with an *old* chisel, proceed to cut along the bond as close to the hull as possible. To insure that the hull will remain unmarred, wrap a piece of tape around the last two inches of the tip of the blade as well.

To close off what's left of the berth, install a full-height 1/2" thick bulkhead (see Chapter 14 of *Bare Hull*) establishing the inboard edge 1" inboard of the berth face. To trim, rip a 1½" piece of teak or mahogany to a 1½" width. Dado a 1/2" wide by 3/4" deep dado into it. Bullnose all four edges with a 3/8" bullnose bit.

Put glue into the dado, then slip the trim onto the bulkhead and screw to the bulkhead edge. One screw every 18" is plenty. Countersink and plug.

Next, from 3/4" plywood, cut and fit a desk top using the same scribing and cutting procedure as you did for the bulkhead. To speed things along with the fitting, it may be prudent to install the cleats on which the top is finally to rest, at this time. Three-quarter-inch cleat stock glued and screwed to each bulkhead will be fine. If your desk top is no wider than 30", you will not need to support it on the hull; cleats on the bulkheads alone will suffice. When installing the cleats, remember the cabin sole-to-desk distance must be at least 26". When measuring this height, do so halfway between the outboard and inboard edges of the top so that the curvature of the hull will be taken into consideration. If you don't, you may end up writing in a dead-man's float position.

Glue and screw the cleats onto the bulkheads. Fit the desk top into place but *do not* install it. Remove it to a nice open working space and cover it with whatever surfacing material you like: wood,

FOREPEAK DESK CONVERSION

formica, leather, etc. (see Chapter 18 of *Bare Hull*). Do all the edge finishing, then lay glue over your cleats and drop the top into place. Drill and screw from below, taking care to mark the drill bit with a piece of tape so that you won't drill too far and come through the top. Next, trim out the inboard edge. If you've fabricated the corner as shown in the illustration, i.e. well rounded, it will be most economical to use three separate pieces of 13/16" or 1½" teak milled to a 2" wide "L", with a 3/8" × 3/4" (or 3/4" × 3/4") cut out. Putting searails on a desk is the height of folly, for it will create an unbearable writing surface unless you have well notched lower arms.

The corner piece will take a lot of hand fitting but it will look beautiful. Install it unfinished, that is, not trimmed down to final thickness. You can file and sand it once it's glued into place. Holding the thing while the glue sets is no small feat. You'll have to screw a small cleat temporarily to the bottom of the desk against which a C clamp can bite. You may of course invest in an esoteric little tool (see photo) called an edging clamp, which will be valuable if you're doing other moulding trim on tables or bulkhead edges, but it does cost over six dollars, so if it's for a one-time use, use a temporary cleat with a C clamp and to hell with professionalism.

To augment the desk, cabinets or bookshelves can be installed above it, with a directional reading light (not the dome light that Candace is trying to mislead you with in her illustration). If the forward hatch is solid, one should contemplate installing a deadlight in it for more natural light.

The space forward of the new bulkhead can nicely incorporate a net-shelf to house bedding, sails, etc.

Now, a minor detail. Since neither reading nor writing has made any great inroads as a stand-up sport, effort should be made to fabricate a modest, yet comfortable, seat. The most functional would seem to be one that hinges up from the face of the remaining berth. It can be about 16"-18" wide and 13" deep at its shallowest point; it can be cut from 3/4" plywood and upholstered with sturdy fabric. To support the seat in its horizontal position, two hinged knees should be fitted below it. These hinge "under" when needed as supports and hinge "out" of the way against the seat bottom when not. To make space for them when the seat is folded down, cut a hole in the face of the berth. The hole width must equal the distance between the pins of the hinges at the two knees, and no more. The very edges of the hole will be supporting the knees when the seat is opened up. To make sure all these hinged beasts are kept from flapping madly about at sea, install a tiny barrel bolt on the berth

THE FINELY FITTED YACHT

face and have its shaft slip into a hole drilled into the seat. (Elbow catches or bayonets will do almost as well.) To be sure all will remain intact, use only piano hinges, and to stop the knees from "slipping" out from below the seat, let two 3/8″ dowels into the end of each knee allowing them to protrude about 3/8″. Round their tips. Drill corresponding holes into the berth face into which the dowels can slip.

There. Now, sit down and write your dearest a letter. Momma will love ya for it.

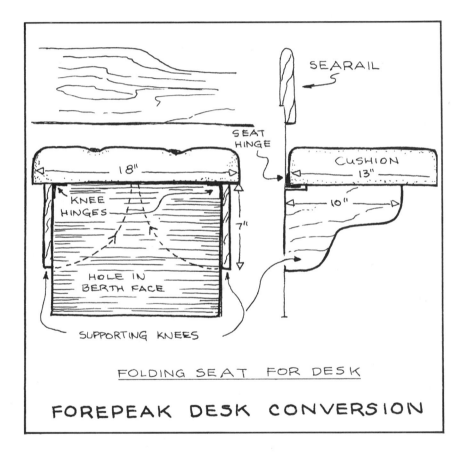

FOLDING SEAT FOR DESK

FOREPEAK DESK CONVERSION

DEADLIGHTS AND PRISMS

It seems that no one in the history of sail has ever had enough natural light in his vessel. This is especially true of ocean cruising and racing boats whose vulnerable glass surfaces have to be kept to a minimum, resulting in black holes of Calcutta below decks. Fortunately, designers have lately been rediscovering deadlights as practical alternatives.

Deadlights in decks, cabin tops, hatches,or drop-boards transmit wonderful quantities of light through relatively small areas. They fall under three general types: traditional deadlights, prisms, and fiberglass light spots.

Traditional Deadlights

Here, I speak of the bronze-rimmed, heavy-glassed, non-opening ports, which can be purchased at better marine stores. Ranging in size from 3″ to 8″ in glass diameter, they are easy to install in cabin tops, hatches and dropboards. Their major flaw for decks and cabin tops is that the thick brass rims remain forever toe stubbers and sole scrapers. In wood decks and hatches, the problem is not totally unsolvable,for the rim can be let in flush by routing the wood surface and bedding the port in polysulphide. If this method is chosen, a 3/16″ square channel should be routed all around the rim to provide space for a decent bead of caulking. In fiberglass decks and cabin tops, you'll have no choice but to mount the port on top of the fiberglass. Since most cabin tops and decks are plywood core reinforced, and since most deadlights come without interior finishing rings, the simplest method of providing an acceptable finish would be to bullnose the cut plywood edge and hope for the best.

Two areas where the use of deadlights should be avoided are the hull and often-walked surfaces. Deadlights in the hull will tend to condense horribly in cold waters where they're constantly buffetted by cold spray. If placed in often-walked surfaces, they become dangerously loose footings when wet.

Prism Deck Lights

When copious quantities of light are required in a specific area a prism-type deadlight can be used. These come in two basic shapes: rectangular, with a lens that looks like a wedge, and round, in which case the lens looks something like an orange squeezer. They both come with brass outer frames, and both transmit and distribute light

DECK PRISMS

fabulously. The prisms are infinitely more resistant to breaking than the straight glass types and of course infinitely more expensive.

Fiberglass Light Spots

One of the cleverest methods of transmitting light below decks in a fiberglass boat is to leave off the gelcoat from an area of fiberglass and leave out the reinforcing plywood or foam core below. This method has the great advantage of not disturbing the boat's outer surfaces, thereby eliminating potential leaks and foot damage. Belated conversion is not difficult but it does take forethought.

Having ascertained that both the inside and outside of the future light spot are free from fittings, wires, etc., tape off the area topsides and sand off the coloured gelcoat. Clean with acetone and re-gelcoat with clear gel.

In the interior, carefully measure the location using beams, mast supports, etc. for verification, and draw in the area of interior liner to be removed. Remember that a very small area, say 4″ diameter, will seem down below as if a spotlight has been turned on, so there is no need in removing acres of plywood, thereby jeopardizing the structural integrity of the deck.

Next. If you can't find out from the manufacturer the thickness of the deck core, you'll have to explore. Take a 1/8″ drill bit and with your drill motor on low speed, begin drilling. (The more prudent might use a hand drill for this occasion.) Most cores (plywood, balsa, foam) are much softer than the fiberglass, so with a little attentiveness, you will be able to tell when you've passed through them. But do be careful and pay attention. If you're a klutz, drill in 1/32″ at a time, then pull out the bit and see if you have brown sawdust or white fiberglass. Drill until you hit the glass, then stop. Having thus fathomed the depth, set your router with a straight bit at that depth, and clean out the whole area. A thorough man would now replace the removed core with a layer of fiberglass mat and cloth.

If considerable condensation is encountered, a thin piece of plexiglass can be cut to shape, and installed with a strip of weather proofing foam around the inner surface of its perimeter. This will create a handsome air pocket and eliminate condensation.

Whichever of the three methods you use, the results will be remarkable; you'll be forever reaching for your sunglasses.

An 8″ diameter area where gelcoat has been removed lights up the belowdecks like a spotlight.

DRIP CATCHER

I have yet to see an opening portlight on a yacht that does not somehow manage to collect just enough water to viciously soak your favourite pillow upon opening. *Warm Rain's* portlights, I think, hold the unchallenged world record in this department. During a common drizzle lasting no more than a half hour, they are able to collect enough water to drown your average family of four *plus* the dog. They were helped to attain such heights by their idiotic owner who insisted to the church bell foundry that they make his portlight sleeves extra deep to keep out the blazing tropical sun. I have since spent many hours trying to figure out a way to hack off the bloody sleeves without having to tear out the whole portlight.

Where was I? Right. I found a very pleasant solution to the drip problem on a rather famous vessel, the St. Roche, a gaff schooner of 320 tons, built in 1928 especially for Arctic service. She was the first ship to navigate the Northwest Passage, a feat accomplished under the command of H.A. Larsen of the R.C.M.P. in 1940-42, a feat mostly designed to establish Canadian supremacy over the Arctic Ocean.

Take a piece of 1½″ stock cut to a width of 2″ and length of about 4″, and hollow out a part of it with a fair whittling knife, as if you were building the port half of a dugout canoe. Bullnose the outside edges with a 3/8″ bullnose and attach just under the portlights (see diagram) using a bead of silicone sealer to make it water tight, and a couple of countersunk #8 screws to hold it in place. Alternately, you can substitute plastic resin glue for the silicone, and, by opening the portlight, you can make room for a C clamp to hold the trough in place until the glue sets. Be sure to wipe off any dribbles with a damp cloth.

Not only will these little troughs make excellent water catchers, but they're also perfect little storage places for sextant box keys, ignition keys, rings, nuts and bolts and little stuff you find in your pants pocket just when you have to heave them into the laundry. Just think, a veritable tiny treasure chest under each portlight.

THE FINELY FITTED YACHT

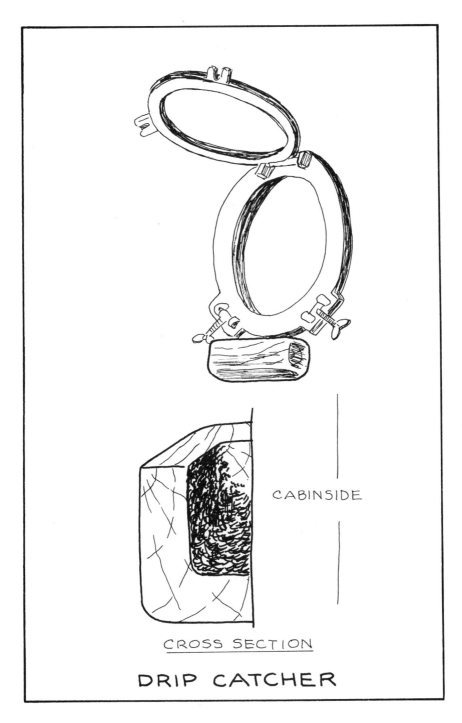

CABINSIDE

CROSS SECTION

DRIP CATCHER

INSTRUMENT COVER BOXES

All cabin face-mounted instruments, whose backs protrude into the cabin, should have boxes built to protect them and keep them out of sight. The best solution is a hinged box, giving ready access for repair and cleaning. If the whole box is hinged, the need for painstaking door fabrication is eliminated. It should be built as shallow as possible to take up as little cabin volume as necessary, and the hinges should be placed on the bottom so it hinges down and rests with its open side up. This way tools, parts, etc. can be laid into a safe and accessible place while work on the instrument is underway.

Since very little strain will ever be placed on such a box, a light construction of 1/2″ teak or mahogany stock will be quite sufficient. If at all possible, a single box should be made to cover all instruments. This task will of course be made easier if forethought was given to placement of the instruments.

If the instruments are up high, that is, close to the overhead, construction of a three-sided, bottomless box should be contemplated, for then it can be closed tight against the overhead. Of course you will have to side-hinge such a box, but then that's a small price to pay for purity of design.

For the sake of simplicity, construct the box with all parallel sides, then hold it in place, scribe in the angle of the cabin top, then just run it through a band saw and cut the whole thing at once, taking care not to run through any screws.

The assembly of the box can be done with resorcinol glue and #8 or #6 F.H. screws. Butt ending will of course be satisfactory, unless you wish to use your dove-tailing jig and do a masterful job.

To secure the box in the closed position, a barrel bolt can be attached to the cabin side and a corresponding hole can be drilled in the box, eliminating the need for the brass end fitting. Of course if you prefer, there's always the ol' hook and eye.

One word of caution — these little boxes are irresistible hiding places for junior's secret little toys like old keys and magnets, both of them very dangerous when stuck only a few inches from a compass. Just remember the old adage: "Spare the rod, and you'll run aground."

INSTRUMENT COVER BOXES

THERMOS MOUNT

I customarily react quite adversely to gadgets, but this one, seemingly very sensible, forces me to recall all those lovely cups of tea and hot chocolate that I've missed on cool night watches simply because I couldn't face the prospect of going below and digging out the thermos from its hiding place where it had been wedged so it wouldn't roll about, then hanging on with my feet while I unscrewed the thermos lid, held the cup, spilled the stuff, rescrewed the lid, etc.

This little invention allows one to perform the whole operation with one hand. It consists of a stainless steel bracket very much like the one that holds fire extinguishers to bulkheads, a bulkhead mounted holder for mugs or cups, and a threaded plastic spigot which fits most vacuum bottles with #4 stoppers. The removal of the thermos itself can also be done with one hand, so the only tricky activity remaining would be the initial pouring of the hot fluids into the bottle.

The whole thing seems to be such a good idea that thought should be given to having two sets of mounting brackets and cup supports aboard, one located somewhere in the galley, companionway area, the other placed brilliantly in a locker accessible from the cockpit, or if such a beast doesn't exist, then in the cockpit itself. But since both brackets are rather on the frail side, i.e. not expressly designed to be stepped on, or kicked, or bashed with winch handles, thought should be given to perhaps building a little niche in the cockpit wall. As previously mentioned, much unused space usually exists around a cockpit, so why not utilize it shrewdly. For construction, see "Winch Handle Holders."

I could think of few things nicer on a cold starry night than just reaching out, flipping the little spout, and coming back with a steaming cup of something, all without having released the tiller for an instant. Besides, the niche could be a nice place to keep things like beer cans and juice glasses in the daytime. Salut.

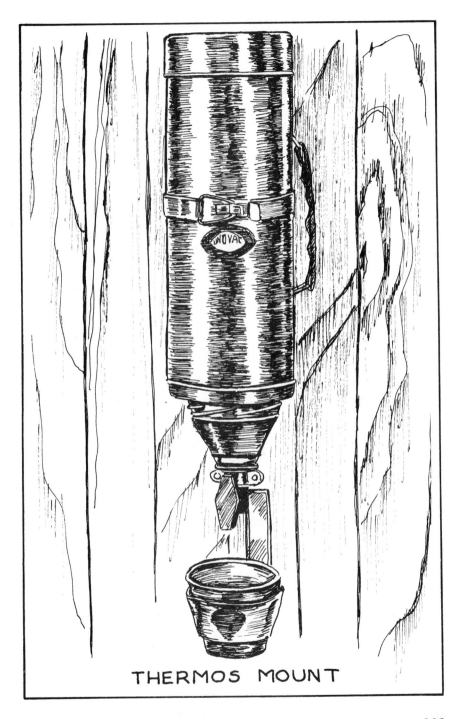

THERMOS MOUNT

THE METAMORPHOSING DOOR

It must be true that there's no better teacher than experience, for it cannot be coincidence that *Wanderer IV* has so many novel, but totally practical, ideas. One of the best the Hiscocks have devised is their cabin door for all seasons. Since their centre cockpit is rather deep, entrance to the main cabin is gained through a door that's over two feet high. An opening of such a size is a tremendous potential source of both light and air, but then, it must also be protected effectively in violent weather.

Their solution was to have the door built up from a sturdy frame, using 1″ solid stock cut to 2 3/8″ widths. The corners were overlapped. A 1/2″ wide by 1/4″ deep groove was let into the inner edge of the frame. Into this groove can be laid either a piece of plexiglass or a sheet of mosquito netting, either of which can be held in place by strips of teak molding held on by woodscrews (see diagram). So this way, in a warm buggy climate, the mosquito screen can be unrolled and, in cold cloudy climates, the plexiglass can be slipped into place.

At sea, both such delicate conveniences can be stowed (the plexiglass would love to live in an old pillowcase where it can't be scratched), and a single piece of 1/2″ thick plywood (varnished of course) could be slipped into the frame over some not too sticky bedding compound like dolfinite, then screwed down directly to the frame by-passing the moulding all together.

As an extra precaution whose necessity is brought about by the largeness of the door, *Wanderer IV* is equipped with simple, but sturdy, gallows just inside the door into which a solid wood bar can be slipped to reinforce the door, should the yacht be overtaken by heavy seas.

In all, this is a most practical idea for cruisers who spend extended periods in greatly varying climates.

MOULDING ONLY SCREWED,
NOT GLUED, TO DOOR FRAME

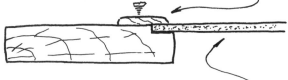

PLEXIGLASS OR
MOSQUITO SCREEN

THE METAMORPHOSING DOOR

INSECT SCREENS

In the dead silence of the night when you slip away to slumber, they come humming and buzzing around your eyes and around your ears, and you slap and swat and swear and scream. Such a waste of good dreams.

Every yacht in any latitude must have insect screens. I have come to this conclusion after battling sandflies in Costa Rica, man-eating mosquitoes off the B.C. coast, and goat flies, the kind that lay eggs in the corners of your eyes, in Hawaii.

Companionway

Whether drop boards or doors are used, the method is the same. From 1/4″ solid teak, rip two 2″ wide pieces. The length should be equal to the height of the outboard sides of your drop boards or doors. Now, also from 1/4″ stock, rip two 1″ wide pieces equal in length to the lower and upper width of the opening of the companionway. With four 1/4″ wing nuts and bolts, assemble the frame, making sure the holes in the vertical pieces are centred near the inboard edges. An aggregate of two 1/4″ boards plus a wing nut will not fit into the slot made for the drop boards. I have been told that strips of Velcro will do nicely in place of wing nuts, since the frame is of such light construction. Next, stretch plastic mosquito netting over the frame, allowing it to hang 1″ past the *backs* of the sides, cut the corners away as shown in drawing and sew open-ended tunnels on all four sides, into which the wooden frame can slip piece by piece. This will enable you to disassemble, roll up the screen and stow in a very small place.

Hatches

As simple as wetting the bed, my dear grandfather used to say. Cut a piece of plastic screening to overhang your hatch openings by 3″, hem 1″ each side, sew the corners, and slip in a piece of elastic. When needed, just slip it over the hatch opening just like a shower cap. To stow, wrinkle it up like a dirty sock and throw it in some corner. Now why didn't you think of that?

Portlights

Bend ten gauge or heavier solid copper wire to snugly fit into the ports. Overlap the ends 1/2″, hammer flat, and solder. Fold brass screening over the ring, allowing it to overlap in the back by 1/2″,

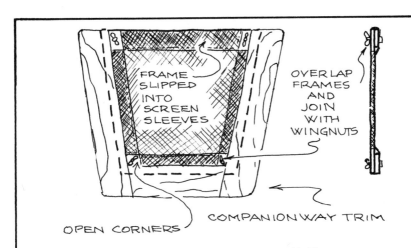

FRAME SLIPPED INTO SCREEN SLEEVES

OVERLAP FRAMES AND JOIN WITH WINGNUTS

OPEN CORNERS

COMPANIONWAY TRIM

FOR COMPANIONWAYS

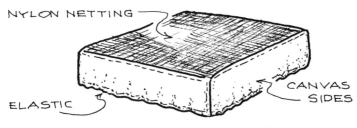

NYLON NETTING

CANVAS SIDES

ELASTIC

FOR SKYLIGHTS AND OPENING HATCHES

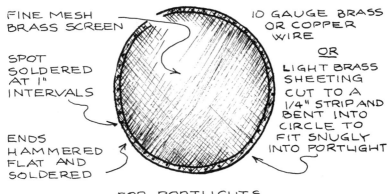

FINE MESH BRASS SCREEN

10 GAUGE BRASS OR COPPER WIRE

OR

SPOT SOLDERED AT 1" INTERVALS

LIGHT BRASS SHEETING CUT TO A 1/4" STRIP AND BENT INTO CIRCLE TO FIT SNUGLY INTO PORTLIGHT

ENDS HAMMERED FLAT AND SOLDERED

FOR PORTLIGHTS

INSECT SCREENS

and solder it every 1″ with a small spot to the ring. Slip it into the portlight sleeve,and leave it there until it rots.

Note: nylon netting does break down after prolonged exposure to the sun. Since it is so inexpensive, one would do well to carry a small roll of it on long voyages. If nothing else, you can trade it in Bora Bora with some poor bug-chewed fool, who is desperately trying to make screens out of his wife's pantyhose and some old ladles. Don't be greedy. Her gold earrings and diamond ring should do.

THE FINELY FITTED FAN

A yacht is a wonderful place when sea and land breezes eddy in the cabin, but when the winds die and the sun beats down, things can become depressingly hot. I was aboard a yacht once in Puerto Vallarta when the wind died and the air just hung there as if it were nailed to the bulkheads, and the entire belowdecks turned quickly into a steam bath. Because of the modest interior volume of most yachts, overcoming this uncomfortable condition can be done with the help of a low drain, no noise, 12V electric fan.

Ready-made models are available from most automotive supply stores, but their great drawback is that they were designed for non-marine use, hence, their delicate metal parts can corrode rapidly to the point where the little motor will seize up. Aside from that, the little critters are, as a rule, quite unattractive.

A small shippy model can be fabricated for just a few dollars using a small electric train motor, available from most hobby shops, or from junior's model train set. If he complains that his little engine doesn't run anymore, tell him to get a rubber band. When selecting the motor, look for a plastic or aluminum housing, and ask for the quietest one they have. Tell them what you'll be using it for, so they can then give you the one that's best sealed.

The blades for the fan can be made from either thin brass sheeting or teak stock milled down to 1/8″ thickness. In both cases, the central mount would be brass.

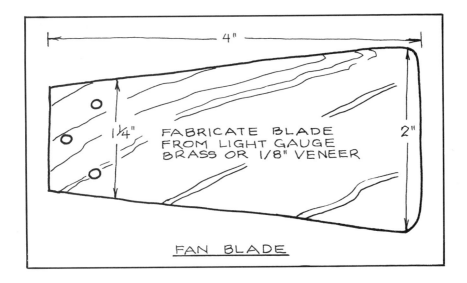

FAN BLADE

To fabricate the central mount, cut a piece of brass into the shape in Diagram A. Cut a pattern first from paper. Scribe in the 1″ diameter circle, then draw in the arms as shown. Drill 7/8″ diameter holes in each arm for mounting the blades, plus a hole in the centre of the mount for the motor shaft. Next, insert one blade at a time into a vise, bringing the dotted line even with the tops of the jaws, then hold the central part of the mount, just along the edge of the circle, with a pair of pliers (see diagram) and twist without changing the plane of the pliers, very gently and evenly until the small triangle between the vise jaws and the plier jaws is in a nearly horizontal position. This will give the arm about a 25° pitch which is quite ideal for moving air. Continue to twist each arm in the same way, making small adjustments as you go to give each arm an identical pitch. Next, cut your blades from either brass or teak to the shape in the diagram. The dimensions will give you an overall fan diameter of 9″. If this is impractically large for your boat, by all means shorten each blade an inch. You will still have ample air movement for now your engine rpm's will increase.

The most ideal place to mount the fan would be directly in front of an open portlight. To accomplish this, fabricate a hinged mount (see "Hinged Fathometer Mount" for details). The best portlight would be one on the aft cabin face to set up a good wind tunnel in the cabin. From this location, you can run the wires nicely concealed beneath the bridge deck to the breaker panel. Use a combination breaker on-off switch or a simple toggle switch. If a solar-charger panel is installed aboard, the fan can be hooked directly into it.

Bring on the mint juleps.

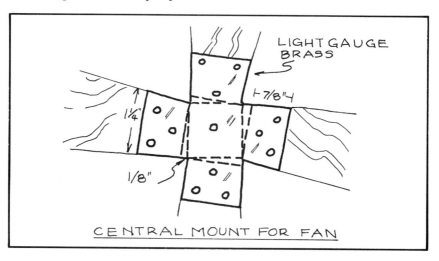

LIGHT GAUGE BRASS

CENTRAL MOUNT FOR FAN

THE FINELY FITTED YACHT

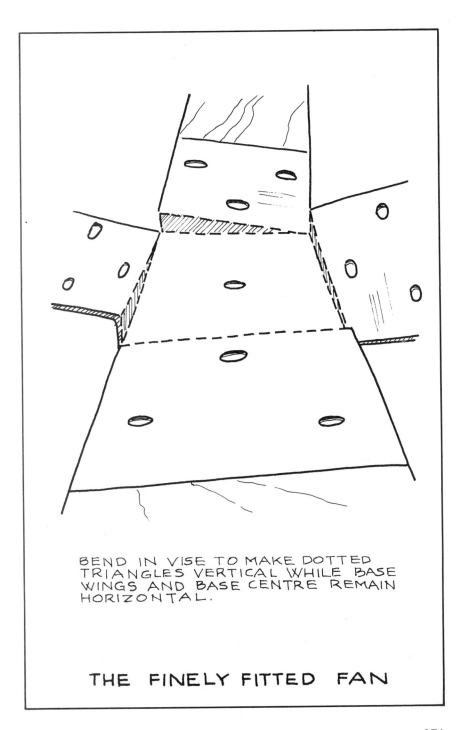

BEND IN VISE TO MAKE DOTTED
TRIANGLES VERTICAL WHILE BASE
WINGS AND BASE CENTRE REMAIN
HORIZONTAL.

THE FINELY FITTED FAN

INSULATION

One common complaint of all fiberglass boat owners is that their hulls "sweat". This condition is more aggravated in colder climates where condensation is more frequent, due to the great temperature difference between the heated interior and the very cold exterior.

Many excellent thermal insulators are available to boat builders and each has its own very valuable place.

Styrene

This material is a very good insulator. A half-inch of styrene has the "K Factor" (insulative quality) of two inches of common house insulating glass wool. It is easy to cut with a sharp "exacto" knife and a metal straight edge. It's very light, quite inexpensive (about 20¢ a square foot), and very uncomplicated to attach. Any common tile cement applied to a few critical spots will hold it in place until a hard covering of wood liner is laid over. It is perfect to lay onto a hull, cabin side, or cabin top where tongue-and-groove or plywood can be used to cover and protect it. It is most impracticable inside cabinets or in a place where no protection over it is planned, because even a paternal tap with a can of anchovies will cause a rivulet of cascading foam chips. Such an accident is messy and affects the life span of the foam quite adversely.

To cover over styrene with either plywood or solid wood strips requires some ribbing to which one can fasten the covering wood. Two methods can be used for ribbing, one a little more expensive, the other quite dumb because it consumes a tremendous number of hours.

The Dumb Way

— rip 3/4" plywood into 1½" wide strips
— cut to 24" lengths
— run it through a table saw with the blade set so high that it will cut all but the last two layers of veneer
— slit in this fashion at 1" intervals
— mix a batch of mish-mash and using a putty knife squeeze it into the cracks. Leave a judicious layer over the rest of it.
— acetone hull where rib is to fit, then fit it into place. It should bend easily. Now the only problem is holding it there. Brace it, however, with whatever you can until the mish-mash goes off.

When using mish-mash the catalyst must be stirred into the resin first, then the asbestos or whatever, added. It is advisable to practice on a small quantity until you ascertain the amounts of catalyst you require.

Once the mish-mash has gone off, bond at least one layer of mat type over the rib just to be sure. You can nail or screw into the ribs as well as slip 1/2″ sheets of styrene in between them. The centres need not be more than 18″ if you are using 3/8″ plywood or tongue-and-groove. If you are butting slats without any tongue-and-groove or other overlap, use 12″ centres.

Decks and cabin tops usually have a plywood core for stiffness; thus the ribs can be fastened with screws while the mish-mash is going off so that awkward bracing won't be required.

The More Expensive Way

In the same fashion that you scribe plywood to fit the hull, scribe ribs out of 1¾″ stock of fir, mahogany, or other easily workable wood. Ribs may have to be cut from as wide as 6″ stock if the hull's curvature is drastic. Because once cut out these ribs have no tension forcing them straight, mish-mashing and bracing can be bypassed. A single layer of mat will bond them to the hull quite securely. You can fabricate your ribs to the thickness of styrene you wish to use.

Needless to say, I did our ceiling the dumb way. That's why I know it so well.

Rigid Urethane Foam

To insulate the rest of the hull, inside the cabinets, etc. is a grueling two-day job, but it may save mildewed clothes and soaked underwear. I at first thought it a simple matter, believing it feasible, economical, and rapid, to simply spray with urethane foam and then glass over it. You can rent a sprayer and the bonding should be no big thing.

This method has one giant failing: it's impossible to spray on a smooth even coat of urethane, even for the most experienced craftsman. The result, at best, would be wartish to the extent where a solid week is required to bring the surface to a condition smooth enough for bonding over. The week would be spent at planing, curving, and grinding the foam, a dusty, itchy, miserably unrewarding task. Avoid it.

The remaining alternative is fitting and installing solid urethane foam sheets into cabinets. This procedure is no dream job either since you'll have to crawl into spaces you've previously considered too small for a dog and work often in very dim light with very little air. The foam can be cut with a knife. If the surface is large and curved, the foam should be sliced to allow small straight pieces to form the required arch. A few spots of tile cement will suffice to hold the pieces in place until bonding.

Since bonding over the foam is necessary to protect it, one must use urethane. Like styrene, urethane comes in sheets of varying thickness and, although it is more expensive than styrene, it has two advantages. First, it is a 30 percent better insulator. Second, it will not melt when used in conjunction with polyester resin. It is usually green or tan in color, is very brittle, and is much itchier than styrene but you have to use it.

Because it is almost impossible to measure and cut large accurate pieces of mat to fit over the odd curves and angles of a cabinet's belly, I used 6″ mat tape (the same that I used for bonding plywood to hull). A single layer of ounce and a half mat (with edges overlapped an inch) proved sufficient after numerous stress tests. The tests were quite basic, involving little more than dropping a quite ordinary hammer from assorted heights. If you can devise more profound testing, proceed.

One noteworthy point. When you are putting in the foam, leave a 2″ gap between its upper edge and whatever plywood surface you have above it. When you bond over the foam, finish off the bond only onto the hull and not onto the plywood. We had made the mistake of doing the opposite. When water found its way onto the horizontal plywood surface, it ran behind the bond and into the sealed pocket formed by the lower bond. We didn't discover this mistake until installing a transducer. I was drilling from outside the hull, waiting to see light, only to be showered by brown stale water. We ended up tearing part of the insulation out and rebonding the whole cabinet. So beware.

Perhaps a few inconspicuous drain holes through the bottom of the bond would not be overcautious, but try to be sure that you don't drill through your hull. In bonding, do as clean a job as possible, leaving no hard strands or upturned ends.

Once bonded, paint over all surfaces, first with a coat of undercoat (Z-Spar 105 or equivalent) then with one or two coats of easy-to-clean gloss or semigloss enamel. It's best to get mildew-proof paint. Although manufacturers' of marine paints insist that their product exceeds all others in quality and wonderfulness, I have been reassured by those who know that paint is paint is paint. So use almost any exterior mildew-proof oil base. The cheaper the better.

THE FINELY FITTED YACHT

Soft Urethane Foam

Some people advocate the use of soft urethane foam (like cushion) with a vinyl cover, contact-cemented to the hull. I think that it is quite satisfactory under a wood cover, but I cannot see how a clean tidy fit can be achieved inside cabinets, for the shapes created by compound curves are almost unimaginable. Apart from aesthetics, if heavy objects such as cans and tools are to be stored, the soft foam will collapse to such an insignificant thickness that its insulative qualities will be decimated.

I do, however, believe that neoprene foam (preferably the non-flammable type) is ideal for soundproofing the engine room. This material represents an expensive venture, but diesels are annoyingly noisy; therefore it may be worthwhile. Thickness of up to 1½″ may be required to be effective (see "Engine Room Insulation").

BOAT CUSHIONS

Before we delve deeply into the construction aspects of boat cushions, let us get a few things into perspective.

As far as I can make out, most of us spend hundreds of dollars on various upholstery materials to cover up our foam mattresses because we consider them: a) unpleasant to sit on, and b) ugly. Now the point that needs clarification is why so many people choose materials that possess the above two qualities to an even greater extent than the thing which they're trying to cover up.

The smooth vinyl upholstery is admittedly very easy to keep clean and will resist most spilled things, but it also repels most humans. It has a general tactility that rivals the skin of a just-dead toad; in cold weather, it's at least 50° colder than the surrounding air; and in hot weather, it will quickly generate such quantities of moisture in one's lower garments that it will make the wettest diaper of one's memories seem like a patch of the Sahara desert.

Then, of course, we have the woven polyesters, which usually do their utmost to imitate old Irish weaving, but are betrayed by their crisp, shiny fibres which have the texture delicacy of an average Brillo pad.

Long forgotten by most, but still clinging tenaciously to last century's furniture, and just begging you to come close and touch and stroke and cuddle, is beautiful, delicate, as soft and soothing as a mother's breast; cotton.

It comes in the world's most beautiful natural colours, and it looks fresh and new year after year, and I was told by the proprietor of the finest furniture store in Newport that it will outlast, and outwear, any Shinyester or Jerkulon material, and that's a lot to say because cotton cushions are forever sat on, fondled, and used.

We've had raw cotton cushions on *Warm Rain* for over three years. She was our full-time home for at least half of that time, and all our cushions still look brand new even after washings, even after cups of spilled tea and a whole bowl of fish soup.

The choice in good upholstery cotton, with rubber backing that keeps it from sliding and stretching, is limitless. It ranges from corduroys and gabardine to the most elegant velvets and brocades. They are, of course, fairly pricey, but so is a Mercedes Benz. You get what you pay for.

Foam

Good quality polyurethane foam seems to be the best choice for cushions of a yacht. Foam rubber breaks down in the heat, absorbs

THE FINELY FITTED YACHT

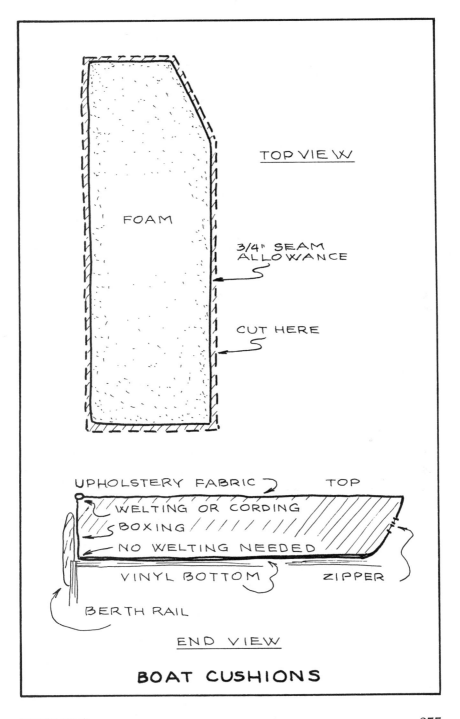

TOP VIEW

FOAM

3/4" SEAM ALLOWANCE

CUT HERE

UPHOLSTERY FABRIC TOP

WELTING OR CORDING

BOXING

NO WELTING NEEDED

VINYL BOTTOM ZIPPER

BERTH RAIL

END VIEW

BOAT CUSHIONS

water insatiably, and develops a rather strange odour in time. But it does retain its firmness better than the poly.

A good foam person will describe to you the best type (in terms of firmness) to get, depending on your personal tastes. Do beware when you are choosing. I once made the mistake of purchasing a 4″ foam mattress that was actually harder than the plywood berth it was on. A good solution if you want a firm mattress, but no bruises in the morning, may be to select, for a 4″ overall thickness, 3″ of very firm foam, and have the foam person glue on top of it 1″ of medium firm foam. You will then have the initial welcoming softness without the "bottoming out" that's such a frequent occurrence on the less firm foams.

Liners

Since, because of their limiting shapes, very few yacht cushions can be turned bottom up and used, the undersides of cushions should be made of vinyl. Mildew and stains are easy to remove from it and, of course, it will cost considerably less than the velvet or the corduroy.

Threads, Zippers, and Welting

The best all round thread is polyester, mostly because it will not be weakened by mildew as a cotton thread may. Zippers are costly critters, especially if you buy them made to length. Delrin (plastic) zippers are available on rolls by the yard, and if you have a whole boat of cushions to do, you may as well buy them as such, cut them to length, and slip the sides on yourself. This way if you make a mistake on your cushion, you will not have to fix and patch; you can simply make your zipper shorter or longer than planned. The plastic zipper doesn't bind as easily as its metal counterpart and, of course, it won't rust.

To calculate the length of the zipper per cushion, measure the back of each cushion and subtract between two and five inches, but no more. If the zipper is too short, getting the foam back into that envelope will be like wrestling with an alligator.

The welting is the thin sausage that circumvents the upper joints (side to top) of cushion covers. It helps to hide stitch irregularities and adds firmness to seams as well. It is actually made up of a cord or a nylon worm sewn into a tube of the upholstery material which is then, in turn, sewn to each of the pieces it borders. The material for welts should be cut on a bias (45° to the weave) if the material lacks rubberized backing. This is to avoid fraying. On material with a

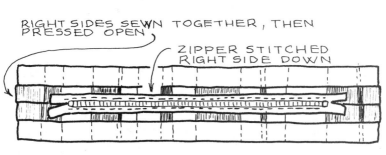

RIGHT SIDES SEWN TOGETHER, THEN PRESSED OPEN

ZIPPER STITCHED RIGHT SIDE DOWN

ZIPPER INSTALLATION

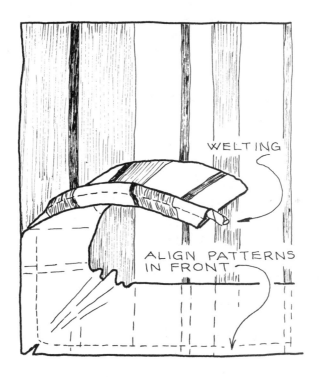

WELTING

ALIGN PATTERNS IN FRONT

STITCHING SIDES TO TOP

BOAT CUSHIONS

backing, this precaution can be bypassed and the welting can be cut to a width of 1″-1½″ (with the usual 1/8″ diameter nylon worm) from a single strip of fabric.

Construction

Patterning

For anything but a completely regular cushion,you should make a pattern out of brown paper. If you're simply recovering an existing cushion, just use the foam as your pattern piece.

Next, lay the fabric "wrong" side up (that's a sewing term for the side you don't want to see) and lay your foam or paper pattern over it,and outline the shape with tailor's chalk. If you use a felt pen or a ballpoint, the ink will bleed through the first time the cushion gets wet. Outside the line you've just drawn, draw another one from 3/4″ to 1″ away. This will be for what is known in sewing as *seam allowance*. The generous width will absorb any cutting mistakes.

Cut along the seam allowance, and label the pieces with tailor's chalk. Mark all your pieces as you lay them out, not only with their name, but also with specific references, like "forward edge," "top edge," etc. Now, cut the long and short side pieces (known as *boxing*). It's always advisable to use the factory-finished edges, for then you'll have at least one true edge per piece. Don't forget the 3/4″ seam allowance on *each* side (all four) of every piece (see diagram).

When laying out the sides, it's advantageous to cut the entire run (all the way around), except for the zippered end, as a single piece. This will save you two extra seams. One word of caution. When pinning the sides to the top, be sure you align the pattern at the front (visible) side of the cushion; the hidden sides be damned. The zippered side will be the same width as the other sides plus one inch, cut horizontally in half. The "right" sides of this zippered end are then sewn together, allowing for a 1/2″ seam, at the ends where the zipper will terminate. Open up the material, iron the seams flat, and lay the zipper, right side down, in the centre of the seams. Baste it in place, then stitch it. You'll be going through three layers, so don't rush the machine.

Next, lay out the bottom of the cushion on coated vinyl and mark and cut as you did the top.

Finally, in the cutting department, cut sufficient lengths of welting material (the house for the worm) to a width of 2″, as you will need to run all around the seams where the top joins the sides.

Since the lower edges of most cushions are hidden by searails, this welting hocus-pocus can be bypassed there.

Sewing

The sewing should be done in the following order: (a) cord to welting, (b) welting to side, (c) zipper into side, (d) side to top, (e) side to bottom. Some sewing books advocate the melting of (a) and (b) together to eliminate one step. Whichever way you choose, lay the cord into the centre of the welt strip and fold the strip so the two edges match. With the zipper or cord foot on your machine, sew along the welting strip as close to the cord as possible. Leave the last 2″ unfinished so the ends of the welts can be mated.

To attach the sides (boxing) to the top, pin the boxing to the *centre* of the top cover front edge, then proceed with the pinning away from the centre and around the corners. If you find that your zipper will be a touch off centre in the back, don't worry about it, worse things have happened. Take care to put equal tension on the top and the boxing, and smooth both equally, or you will end up sewing in permanent wrinkles. To make the cover a nice tight fit, cheat on your pinning and reduce the top piece by 1/4″ all around.

Now, turn the pieces inside out and sew them together, running the needle as close to the cord as possible. Sew in the bottom in similar fashion.

Turn the covers right side out, and take your foam and stuff it.

DETAILING

At the joyous moment when the completion of your project flutters just above your fingertips, you will be faced with the grandpop of all icebergs. Somehow, somewhere, someone christened this horribly fidgety, monstrously time-consuming, and penuriously rewarding task, "detailing." This cultured term refers to resanding, repainting, regelcoating, recleaning, and generally rebuilding the entire thing you've just built.

At any rate, there are a few short cuts and precautions which can be pursued to achieve a completely satisfactory job in minimum time. The greatest time saver, of course, is sufficient preparation and careful rough assembly. If you did the job well, the task now facing you will be minimal.

Painting

It seems, through practice, that short grain woods, like mahogany, make for a better surface than wider grained ones like fir. Though you may be considering covering plywood cabinetry with paint, it may well be worth the extra two dollars per 4 X 8 foot sheet to use mahogany plywood instead of fir. You may argue that with dedicated sanding the fir can be brought to just as fine a finish. Quite the contrary. The more you sand, the deeper will be the softer grains and the more highlighted the more pitchy, harder ones.

One solution that does improve fir is painting the wood while still unsanded with a coat of undercoat, then sanding, then painting, then sanding, etc. By this process, the softer grained areas will be protected by semi-hard covering. I had to use this method on one piece of fir plywood that I recklessly substituted for mahogany. Not only did sanding take an unimaginably long time, but it possessed the added featurette of covering the minutest surface with a thorough coating of white dust that lifted and thickened the air every time I blinked. So try to use mahogany; if you can't, suffer.

Your painting chores will be much easier if you mask unpainted adjoining areas with tape. This practice is admittedly time-devouring, but not nearly as bad as scraping blobs of paint from wood. Since the paint will penetrate into most woods (the drier the deeper) overslop could lead to major problems. To get out all the unwanted paint, you will need to carve irreparable gulleys with sandpaper. In solid wood, such repairs are less noticeable than on plywood. On plywood, very slight over-zealousness can result in your penetrating the thin (with teak plywood only one mil thick) top layer of veneer. I have not yet heard of a satisfactory method of veneer repair.

So tape off the perimeter of your areas and you will save hours of frustration. To help even further, seal off the area adjacent to the masking tape with a clear wood sealer and acid brush. This procedure should prevent any paint from seeping under the tape. If it does not, at least the paint will not penetrate the sealed wood and it will be easy to remove.

On the painted surface, use a quick drying undercoat. Z-Spar 105 is very satisfactory, although I'm not convinced that other oil-based undercoats perform any less commendably. Even if you use mahogany ply, it is a good idea to sand well between coats. The first undercoat will be almost completely removed if you want a good job. Brush strokes are left by the finest brushes; if left unsanded, they will become more accentuated with each following coat. I'm not advocating a formica-like finish, but a soft smooth finish will bring hours of pleasure in silent dawning light.

Although Z-Spar 105 is a wonderful undercoat, I cannot recommend Z-Spar products for subsequent layers. Their finishing paint is very thick (I'm told that a good finish paint should be no thicker than fresh milk) resulting in a multitude of runs and brush marks. Apart from this problem, it has the irritating habit of never drying, thus clogging up a four-cent quarter-piece of sandpaper on the first stroke.

Interlux makes excellent finishing paints in many beautiful quick-drying shades. It also is difficult to sand, not because it fills the sandpaper, but for quite the opposite reason. It has a very hard protective finish.

A good rule is to use two undercoats (as mentioned) and two finishing coats. Some people advocate four or five finishing coats, but then some people mow their front lawn five times a week. After the last coat of paint has dried, don't leap to tear off the masking tape. If you do, you'll tear half the paint with it. Some paint will have overflown on to the tape and you will find a tendency for this overflow to pull the other paint with it instead of breaking conscientiously where the tape ends. To avoid pulling off paint take a sharp knife and literally cut the paint around the tape's edge. You can then pull the tape off cleanly and admire your masterpiece.

Masking tape will come in handy during procedures other than painting. If you are sanding a surface which is at right angles to another, you will be endlessly either hand sanding grooves into the other surface, or gouging it repeatedly while you use a vibrator or belt sander. To avoid the unnecessary repairs that will have to follow, tape the edge of the surface you won't be sanding, the wider the tape the better. WARNING — As exceptionally beneficial as masking tape is, it does have one villainous quality. If left on over a long period in a place where direct sunlight hits it, the glue will penetrate the surface it's on and cling tenaciously while the paper backing will crumble in your hands. We once left a strip of tape all around the fiberglass bulwarks when we caulked our teak decks. Absurd as it may seem, Candace and I spent 18 tearful hours scraping off 64 feet of one-inch wide tape. It was about as much fun as practice bleeding.

Sanding

If you are sanding wood, no matter how solid and thick it is, use sandpaper of no rougher grit than 60. You can still shape wood rapidly with 60 grit, if necessary. Any rougher grit will leave deep gouges (especially if you are going cross-grain) which will be very difficult to remove. Cross-grain sanding should be avoided if at all possible. On exterior surfaces, I can see no need to go finer than 150 at the most. If you are oiling exterior teak, to go finer than that is a waste, because the grain of the wood will rise drastically within two or three days no matter whom you know. If you are varnishing, you may consider going to 220 on your last run on the wood, but then varnish immediately because the grain will rise as soon as the dew falls. Two hundred twenty is acceptable to use between coats, although some say to use 400 before your last coat.

If you can afford to (and you almost can't afford not to), buy sandpaper by the sleeve. A sleeve usually contains 50 or 100 sheets. It is cheaper and you will end up using it all, especially common grits like 80, 100, and 150.

On interiors, you may consider using 220 on all your woods. If you are varnishing, you will need to; and if you are oiling, you may as well for then you can oil the wood and immediately run over it with 600 grit to achieve a nearly hand-rubbed finish.

Oiling

The only important point here is to wipe down the wood with an acetone dampened cloth before oiling. Keep turning the cloth to get all of the sawdust out of the grain. If you don't, it will have a tendency to darken once the oil is applied, rendering the wood lifeless and dark.

The first coat of oil you apply should be of a resin type, like Watco Interior Danish teak oil. It does have a pungent odour, but it seals and protects wood better than wood sealers. Later coats can be of resinless variety, like lemon oil.

Be sure to wipe all excess oil (that which has not absorbed) no more than 20 minutes after application. If you don't, it will become tacky and attract every speck of dust and fluff as well as make the surface unsightly with patches of unequal sheen.

For the exterior, use oil recommended for that purpose only. Watco makes one that has a tendency to turn grey and unappealingly black within a very few weeks. Others, like Tip-Top Teak Oil, blacken to a lesser extent. Light sanding is highly recommended before a new coat of exterior oil is applied. A very fine product called "Te-Ka" cleans the wood better than sandpaper because it penetrates deeper. A very good idea after sanding a coat of varnish or a coat of oil, instead of using acetone which may be spilled and cause patches, would be to use a product by the name of "Tac-Cloth." It is a messy, toadish feeling cloth that is treated with a substance which absorbs fantastic quantities of dust from even the graniest woods.

Varnishing

As mentioned, you may want to prepare the surface with 220 grit sandpaper. Then, a thinned-down sealing layer (about 20-25% paint thinner) should be applied followed by light sanding, then a full strength varnish coat. It is a fallacy that each coat has to be sanded to the point where no hairline is left untouched. Unless you want a glasslike finish, light sanding will do nicely. Apply the varnish in thin coats. Five thin coats are better than three thick ones which may run and curdle when touched, even days after application. After sanding, wipe with a Tac-Cloth or similar product.

Be sure your varnish is applied at least three hours before the dew falls, if you are doing exterior wood. In climates where the day may have been cooler than 60 degrees, try to have your varnishing finished by mid-morning or the dew will ruin your precious work. For the eccentrics it might be a great matter of pride to use refrigerated varnish. Varnish, thus cooled, will have a tendency to dry "from the inside out" and consequently have a better hold. I was told this by an eccentric and I never did quite figure out what he meant, but it might be worth a try.

Do not be frugal. Buy a good quality brush and clean it meticulously after using. There's nothing worse than picking molting hairs or kernels of hardened varnish from your otherwise perfect surface.

Filling

Small marks which are deep or irreparable can be drilled and plugged. A teak or mahogany plug out of place does not look as bad as a worm hole or a blob of white paint or a deep gouge. If the spot is large, patching could be considered. Patching is nothing more than the old art of inlaying wood. If you have a bad area, chisel it out very carefully and fill it with a piece of wood. If the grains match perfectly, that's wonderful. If they don't match at all, it looks good, and if you use entirely different kinds of wood, it looks even more intentional. Whichever you use, cut your filler piece to size first, then use it as a pattern on the damaged wood to scribe in the perimeter, then chisel out the damaged piece. Use a very sharp cutting tool or you will cause more damage through chipping than what you set out to repair to begin with. Keep a wetting stone handy.

If you suffer long splits in wood like we did with our hatches, the repair is simple. Many people use just glue or glue mixed with sawdust. I find either solution most unsatisfactory. You will end up with very dark coloured seams or cracks which probably look worse than the crack itself. The best way to fill cracks in wood is to use wood. Cut long wedges, cover the sides with glue and drive them into the cracks with a mallet. Then chisel and sand off the remaining bulk.

If you pick your wood colour to match, the inserted wedges will be unnoticeable.

Gelcoat Touch-Up

If chips in the gelcoat occur, follow this procedure:
— Clean the area with acetone.
— Fill the crack with body putty.
— Sand with 400 grit sandpaper.
— Spray on gelcoat.
— Spray on sealer.
— Peel off the tape before the gelcoat hardens.
— Wash off sealer with water.
— After it has gone off, sand the whole area with 600 grit. If you don't do your final sanding immediately following the catalyzation of the gelcoat, you may run into another problem, especially if you had taped off the area round which you sprayed. Very likely you will have a sharp edge of fresh gelcoat protruding which, if not feathered in immediately, may result in chipping. So sand with 600 grit and feather in.

Other Problems

If you do have stubborn problems with over-cooked masking tape or polyethylene which the sun baked onto your mast, deck, or caprail, only one economical remedy seems possible. People have attempted to use acetone, thinners, heat guns, and fingernails to no avail. The only thing that seems to work is steam cleaning. You can rent portable units or find companies which will come out to your aid. If your mistake is portable (like a boom), take it to the nearest do-it-yourself car wash and do-it-yourself.

THE
FINELY FITTED YACHT

Ferenc Maté

ILLUSTRATED BY

Candace Maté

ALBATROSS PUBLISHING HOUSE

vancouver bc canada

Other Books
By

Ferenc Maté

"FROM A BARE HULL"
An Encyclopedia of Boatbuilding

"WATERHOUSES"
Houseboats and Floating Homes

THE
FINELY FITTED YACHT

BY

Ferenc Maté

ILLUSTRATED BY

Candace Maté

PHOTOGRAPHED BY THE AUTHOR.

Volume II Exterior

169 illustrations
58 photographs

DISTRIBUTED IN THE U.S. BY W.W. NORTON
500 FIFTH AVENUE, NEW YORK

Édesapámnak

Philosophically

There is little joy in creating junk. Boats live a long time and so do people, and so does the spark of pride in a lovingly crafted piece of wood or canvas. Have patience, enjoy every step. You may never get the chance to do it again.

Specifically

Start big. Begin with the project that requires the largest piece of material and you'll definitely be safe, for then if you miscut or misdrill or misthink, you can always pretend that you were actually working on the next size down object in the first place, and you wanted a smaller piece of whatever anyway, and you're not *really* as big-a-stupid as the puzzled onlookers think you are.

Of course, there are limits. If you began with a piece for the boom gallows, and ended up with eight pounds of teak toothpicks, stop and reflect, then yank out a chunk of old line, and just tie the bloody boom to the backstay. . . . Stupid.

Generally

I'm not familiar with every skylight, dinghy chock or awning in the whole wide world. As a matter of fact, I have an acquaintance with only a few of each, so by no means does this book contain *the ultimates*. But all things in it have been tested, or built, or at least dreamt about thoroughly, and within those limits they all worked. . . . More or less.

Thankfully

Our thanks to the many kind people, from Antigua to Hawaii, whose yachts we invaded with cameras and notebooks and tape measures.

Our gratitude to Jean Koefed of Charles Scribner's Sons and Eric Swenson of W.W. Norton, and the gracious people at Princeton Tools, Detco Marine, Garrett Wade Company, Leichtung Tools, The Adjustable Clamp Company, Faire Harbour Ltd. and Spyglass Catalogue for their help and photographs.

Our very special thanks to Gerri Gilbertson for her essay "Sewing Canvas," and her many long hours of typing from garbled tapes and indecipherable chicken scratchings, and to Jim Linville for his essays, "Sail Cloth" and "Sail Care," which first appeared in *Yacht Racing and Cruising Magazine*.

To Gary Storch, the sailmaker, for his many hours of patient explanation, a big *danke schön*.

TABLE OF CONTENTS

SECTION I: COCKPIT

SECTION II: ON DECK

SECTION III: MAST AND RIGGING

SECTION IV: SAFETY

SECTION V: GROUND TACKLE

SECTION VI: BIBELOTS

SECTION VII: CANVAS AND SAILS

SECTION VIII: TOOLS

cockpit

COCKPIT BILGE PUMP

You will probably have noticed by now that if you install half of the items suggested in this chapter into the average cockpit, the crew will have to dangle over the sides for lack of room. But, if you have room for only one item in your thimble-sized foot soaker, *this* is the one it should be.

Every yacht should have two bilge pumps, just in case one gets jammed with whatever grotesque things bilge pumps get jammed with, and of the two, one should certainly be in the cockpit. One never knows when one will have to single-hand the boat because of illness or injury or volition, so early preparation would be a nice idea.

One of the best pumps for this type of work is a medium size diaphragm pump like the Whale Ten. Diaphragm pumps are very reliable machines and easily maintained and serviced, and this particular model has the spectacular quality of movable brackets which can be turned 90° so they can be installed very serviceably regardless how your structural supports are positioned. The Whale Ten is designed specifically for flush mounting and has a tidy cover plate that protrudes no more than 1/4" from the cockpit wall.

Location should be carefully thought out. It should be placed close enough to the helmsman that he can work it without releasing the helm, yet far enough away so that someone else can work the pump without getting in the helmsman's way. When finding a location, don't forget to allow for unobstructed movement of the handle. An up and down movement is preferable. Pumping is made much easier if the one stroke (down) can be accomplished by simply applying weight. The body of the pump will, of course, be belowdecks. Total and quick access to all its parts are mandatory. Remember to allow space for hands and tools. Some sort of light, either natural or artificial, should be provided since pump removal and cleaning will require two hands. The entire servicing can be accomplished in minutes assuming that the above hints have been followed. If not, your boat might just sink like a rock.

THE FINELY FITTED YACHT

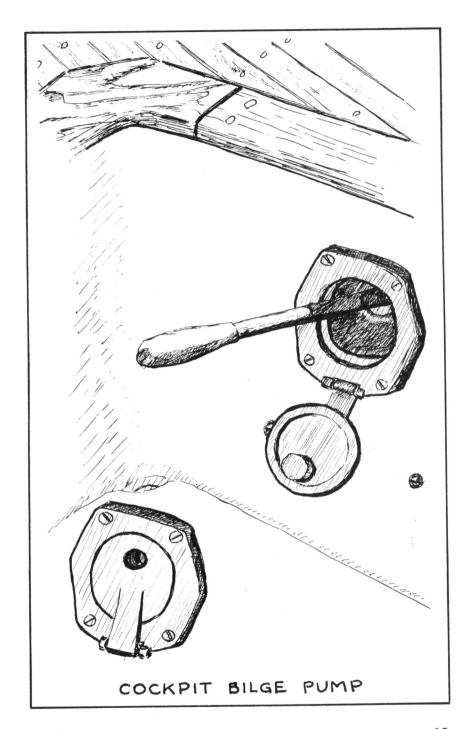

COCKPIT BILGE PUMP

THRONES FOR THE HELMSMAN

I have always advocated the use of tillers on small yachts, arguing that wheel systems are too involved and vulnerable to perform such a basically artless task, and now, my case has been buttressed unshakably, for as it turns out, not only do you need gears and levers and chains and cables to sustain a wheel, but you also need abstruse butt-supports to humour the helmsman (see photo).

The one advantage that these thrones have is that they can be nicely incorporated into small storage areas which are most valuable in any cockpit. The angular one is from *Nightingale*, a lovely little ketch from Newport Beach, while the curved one can be found on the Cheoy Lee 41's. (By the way, notice the nice compromise on its steering wheel that incorporates the beauty of a traditional wood wheel with the smooth and safer function of the modern destroyer type.)

The Angular Seat

This is made of solid 13/16″ teak with let-in corners. It's secured to the deck by an interior run of cleat stock. Alternately, you could screw into the teak base itself from below by putting the box into place, scribing its outline onto the deck, then drilling the pilot holes from above. The ideal height for the seat would be such that allows the helmsman unobstructed vision over the cabin top. The lid is also solid teak.

Because of its cost, the amount of teak used should be cut to a minimum. This can be done by making the basic lid of a piece of 1/2″ plywood, then covering it with 1/2″ or 3/8″ teak. Great care must be taken when countersinking and screwing down these pieces, for their thinness makes them very prone to splitting. Use flat head screws carefully, and try to leave as much space above them as possible so the plug will have adequate seating. Use resorcinol glue for both the teak-to-plywood and teak-to-teak adhesion. Trim out to cover the plywood's edge with 1/2″ × 1″ wide trim having 3/8″ bullnosed edges. The shallow frame part of the lid will act as a strong back on the plywood and keep it from warping. The two hefty handholds on either side (see "Grabrails") will actually act as a sort of coaming to keep the helmsman from sliding away on a heel.

The backrest is a solid piece of teak supported by a pair of galvanized pipes in through-bolted bases.

THE FINELY FITTED YACHT

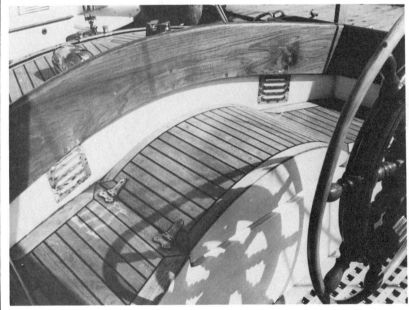

THRONES

The Curved Seat

This is by far the most comfortable seat for a helmsman when driving windward. Its fabrication is uncomplicated, especially if one is willing to forget the idea of a locker beneath it. The width of the seat will need to be at least 20″ if a rise of 4″ is to be achieved. A lesser rise will be too gentle to be of much help. Conversely, a much steeper rise will yield the sensation of sitting on Mount Everest. In any event, the overall height must be carefully watched to make sure you don't end up with the helmsman's feet dangling helplessly in the air. Cut the front and back curved pieces from 2″ × 6″ fir stock (or teak if you can afford it) to the shape decided upon, and let in the inside edge of the curves as shown 1/2″ high and 3/4″ deep, to provide a shoulder for the plywood seat base to fit into. The plywood itself will have to be laminated, for it's impossible to bend a 2′ long piece of 1/2″ plywood to form a 4″ deep arc. So start by securing the fir pieces to the existing seat much as explained in the "Angular Seat," then lay in the first piece of 1/4″ plywood, glue, and screw it to the shoulders. Cover the first piece with waterproof plastic resin, lay your next 1/4″ piece over it, and screw it down into the shoulders. In both cases, do a dry run first so you can mark in the bevels that will be required at the ends of each plywood to form a suitable fit with the seat. Now, lay 1/2″ thick teak stock milled to 1¾″ wide strips (anything wider will rock on the curve) over the plywood, glue, screw and plug. Use the same precautions and the same glue as described for the angular seat.

Under no circumstance should you use teak that's less than 1/2″ thick, for this seat must not be varnished or it will turn into a uselessly slippery slide. Without varnish, however, the teak will have to be cleaned periodically, and this cleaning will result in the eventual erosion of the wood to the point where the frighteningly frail teak plugs (frail because of the thinness of the teak stock which has to house a screw head with a shoulder below and a plug above) will unanimously crack and pop out. Sure, you can pull the screws, countersink, deepen, and re-plug, but you can only do that so often before you come through the bottom.

At any rate, if you find you're dissatisfied with the results, grab a chainsaw, trim off a few things, then install a tiller and have a good time.

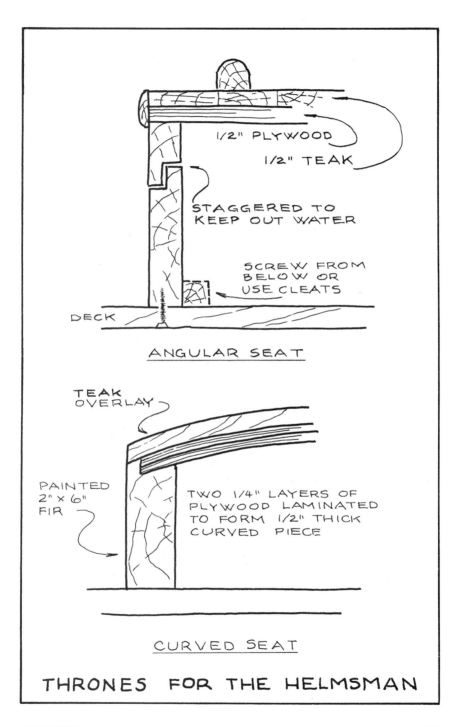

1/2" PLYWOOD

1/2" TEAK

STAGGERED TO
KEEP OUT WATER

SCREW FROM
BELOW OR
USE CLEATS

DECK

ANGULAR SEAT

TEAK
OVERLAY

PAINTED
2" x 6"
FIR

TWO 1/4" LAYERS OF
PLYWOOD LAMINATED
TO FORM 1/2" THICK
CURVED PIECE

CURVED SEAT

THRONES FOR THE HELMSMAN

COCKPIT INSTRUMENT COVER

Many valiant attempts have been made by manufacturers and individuals alike to construct some sort of opening instrument panel cover that will be waterproof and still leave access to switches within, yet I have never seen one that worked. The best solution seems to be to put things needing constant handling into an opening portlight (see that section) and seal all the *read-out* instruments under a waterproof plexiglass cover. Crowd all your instruments into as tidy an area as possible. Be sure to include here the oil pressure sound alarm, for as well as providing protection, the plexiglass will somewhat muffle that shrill, nerve-wracking little sound.

For the frame, use 3/4″ X 3/4″ remnants that any good plastics place will have available. If you have any instruments with faces that protrude from the cockpit wall more than 3/4″, you have to make your frame to suit.

The cut plexiglass frame can be adhered with plexiglass solvent to a sheet of 1/8″ thick plexiglass which is to be the protective cover. This will create a completely waterproof unit. Radius all corners and sand all edges. Caulk and screw the cover into place. Don't forget to put a drop of caulking compound into each screw hole. The screws should be spaced no farther apart than 3″, for the plexiglass will want to work with temperature variations, causing seal breaks, causing leaks.

Next, breather holes must be drilled to keep any moisture that ventures in from settling and staying. One 1/8″ hole just inside each corner should suffice nicely. The holes should be drilled from inside, that is, through the cockpit face itself. The humidity is bound to be less belowdecks, unless of course you're the proud owner of a six-ton sieve.

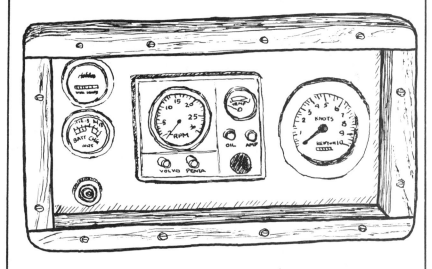

COCKPIT INSTRUMENT COVER

PORTLIGHT FOR COCKPIT SWITCHES

An endless array of new production boats, as well as limited edition beauties, appear with exposed ignition switches in the cockpit. These, without variation, take on water, which at best causes a temporary short, at worst, after a two-week cruise with the key always in place, freezes the key irremovably. A simple solution exists — that of installing an opening portlight in the side of the cockpit. Besides protecting the ignition, it will also provide a quick access, all weather home for essential switches which are best next to the helmsman. A switch for the spreader lights would enable the helmsman a quick glance at the sails at night, or allow verification of deck conditions without having to disturb the crew down below. A switch for the instrument panel light (preferably with a dimmer) would also be most handy here. If the portlight is well located and the switches mentioned are mounted inside on a small sheet of plexiglass, badly needed light can be supplied to the engine room or stowage area beneath the cockpit.

Locate the portlight out of the way of legs and install it inside out (dogs accessible to cockpit). Be sure the hinge is on top so the natural position of the port will be *closed*. The sleeve of the portlight should be long to provide adequate space for the keys and switches. Try to crowd everything on as small a piece of 1/4" plexiglass as you can, leaving open as large an area as possible for belowdecks ventilation. Cut the plexiglass to the outside diameter of the portlight ring and attach it with the same through-bolts that hold the portlight in place. Bed everything in polysulfide.

Replace the usual cotter pins in the hinge rod with rings to leave as much skin as possible on legs and knuckles.

Once you've got it installed, you'll never understand how you could have ever lived without it.

THE FINELY FITTED YACHT

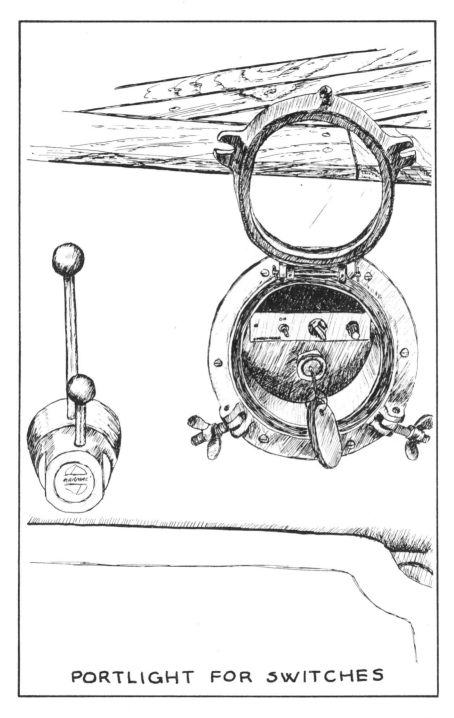

PORTLIGHT FOR SWITCHES

COCKPIT 23

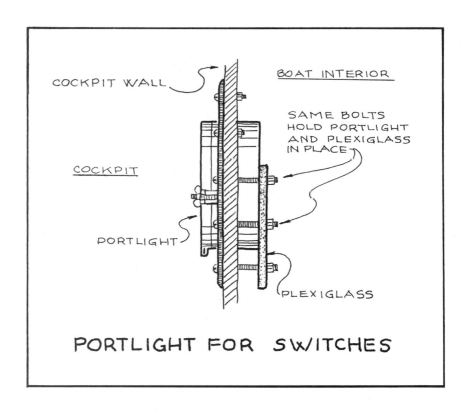

COCKPIT WALL

BOAT INTERIOR

SAME BOLTS
HOLD PORTLIGHT
AND PLEXIGLASS
IN PLACE

COCKPIT

PORTLIGHT

PLEXIGLASS

PORTLIGHT FOR SWITCHES

WHEEL AND COMPASS GUARD

Spoke-handled ship's wheels have a nasty habit of clouting a relaxed cockpit crew in the elbows and knees. Since a wheel of this sort is quite often accompanied by a binnacle compass which needs protection from falling bodies and winch handles, installation of a multi-purpose steel guard like the one in the photo would seem to be a very good idea.

In addition to the above functions, it makes an excellent handhold for the helmsman in broken seas, as well as giving the crew in the foreward part of the cockpit a good leaning and bracing place, and a handhold.

It should be fabricated of 1″ diameter stainless pipe and, of course, it will have to be bent to the proper radius by a metal shop. To furnish them with sufficient information, give them: a) the diameter of your wheel (handles included), b) the width of your cockpit, c) the depth of your cockpit, d) the distance from the cockpit sole to the top of a handle at 12 o'clock, and e) the amount of space you would like between the top of the wheel and the bottom of the guard. Have them run the straight pieces that make up the feet of the guard clear to the cockpit sole. Drill at least three holes in each, and bolt through the cockpit sides with 3/8″ bolts.

COCKPIT GLASS LINER STOWAGE

I took a sampling at some boat shows and found the following engineering oversight on many fiberglass production boats. Although great pains have been gone to, to build comfortable cockpit coamings with wide enough tops for winch mounts, most of this lovely hollow space is unused. From below, it's merely a dead air area in either the engine room or quarter berth, and while it goes begging, genoa and mainsheets lie about in the cockpit hopelessly entwined. Dumb. These areas should have access cut to them from above and should be sealed off from below, and used as a perfect place for reams of sheets to keep them from tangling around ankles and engine controls.

The cutting should be done by drilling a 1/2″ hole within the surface to be cut away, and then with a very sharp hacksaw blade in a saber saw, the whole piece should be removed. Do not leave the hole too large or too close to anything structural like a cleat, or you'll weaken the whole arrangement. The saw must be sharp and have very fine teeth, or great bits of gelcoat will chip away and necessitate frustrating repairs. Next, with 100 grit sandpaper, round all new edges thoroughly or the above-mentioned chipping will occur on first contact. The insides of the edges should be done as well to save lines and skin from catching. Next, rough cut pieces of plywood to act as temporary sides and bottoms of the new space. Put judicious amounts of mold release wax on these, for they will be removed as soon as the fiberglass has set up in the pocket. You'll see why in a moment. Wedge, or if need be, tack these into place. Using two layers of mat with a layer of cloth between, lay up the new sides and bottom of the pocket. Be sure to seal off all corners and holes. Overlap generously onto the existing glass. (If the underdeck was painted, the paint has to be removed with paint remover before bonding.) Work all loose strands flat while the resin is still soft. When it has set up, remove the plywood baffles. Put a couple of coats of clear gelcoat over the outside of the pocket. For drainage, drill two 1/4″ holes in the face of the liner as close to the bottom of the low spot of the pocket as possible. Test with a cup of water to determine this. You now have: a) a perfect place to heave your mass of sheets, and b) a lovely source of natural light to brighten up some dingy belowdecks area.

COMPASS GUARD

The compass guard is nearly a must in most yachts, for anxious winch handles are apt to be flying about. The notion that one doesn't require a guard because one usually uses great care can be compared to leaving the life ring on shore because you're not falling overboard today anyway. Loss of the compass is not only a very costly bit of misjudgement, but can cause severe discomfort on a long ocean passage.

The most desirable guard is, of course, a second transparent shield which would permit an unrestricted view of the compass card at all times. This is simplest to adapt to a vertically mounted compass. The sides can be left open for cleaning access, the upper part of the face can be made from 1/8" plexiglass to limit light refraction as much as possible, and the lower part can be of 1/2" plexiglass. It should be noted that the lower part exists not to protect the compass per se, but to avoid having a protruding, very kickable blade of plexiglass exposed which would be the case if the top were simply extended to the bottom of the compass. The point where the faces meet should be rounded as much as possible, hence the need for using 1/2" thick glass on the lower face. Attachment to the bulkhead can be made by cutting 1/2" × 1/2" plexiglass on a bevel and using the two pieces as you would cleat stock. See drawing.

Another type of guard can be made of small stainless or brass tubing. The "T" shape indicated in the illustration is the simplest to use, requiring only one weld. The ends of the tubes can be flattened with a hammer, rounded, then drilled to accommodate attaching screws. No flat metal stock should be used as a substitute for the tubing for unavoidable sharp edges will result. The horizontal or main part of the guard must be so designed that it will fall well under the compass card to avoid any possible visual interference.

For horizontally mounted compasses, the solution would involve fabricating a shallow all-plexiglass or plexiglass-teak combination box. Again, leave access for cleaning and ventilation to avoid condensation.

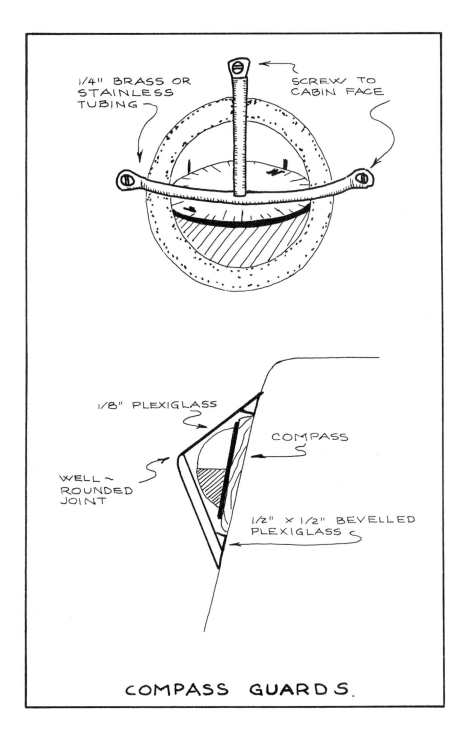

1/4" BRASS OR STAINLESS TUBING

SCREW TO CABIN FACE

1/8" PLEXIGLASS

COMPASS

WELL~ ROUNDED JOINT

1/2" × 1/2" BEVELLED PLEXIGLASS

COMPASS GUARDS.

COCKPIT STOWAGE BOX

If no other way exists to increase stowage in the cockpit, then, as a final solution, a wood box can be built and fitted into a little-used area of the cockpit — like aft just under the tiller or foreward where it can act as a step to the bridge deck. The box can be a conservative size, say 8″ X 20″, so it will rob the cockpit of as little space as possible. Only solid 13/16″ teak or mahogany should be used for all parts except the bottom, where a piece of 3/8″ plywood will suffice. The height of the box should be no more than 16″, otherwise, it will become nothing but another garbage bin. If kept small and well organized, it will be a perfect place for a flashlight, engine and boat keys, a thermos for the helmsman, winch handles, a bilge pump handle, fire extinguisher, etc.

Cut your sides and your front to size. Cut drain patterns in the bottoms of all three pieces, for sooner or later, water will get under the box and somehow it must get out. Cut the drain patterns at least 1½″ high so the space beneath them can be cleaned and lost things retrieved. If you have a dovetail jig, by all means use it; if not, use a piece of cleat stock in the corners. Merely butting will not suffice here, since bodies will be flying and giant feet stomping, always in the wrong places. Put cleat stock along the aft edge of the sides to act as mounting pieces onto the cockpit walls, eliminating the need for a solid back to the box. If you have a removable cockpit sole, fabricate a permanent back onto which the hinges for the lid can be screwed, then the box can be mounted by means of the wing nuts and bolts inserted on the belowdecks side of the cockpit walls. In this way, removal will be quick and non-destructive.

Assemble the sides and bottom using resorcinol glue, screws, and plugs. If installing a backless box, cut the bottom 1/4″ short of the cockpit wall, for the lid will be hinged from the wall, and water will inevitably be draining down same; so cut the bottom short and let it drain in peace. Put caulking under the legs of the box and install with 1″ sheet metal pan heads.

The lid can be fabricated from a single piece of 13/16″ teak, overhanging the box by about 3/4″ front and sides. Bullnose all around and, about 3/8″ from all the edges, cut a shallow 1/8″ drip groove along the bottom. Nothing will keep all the water out, but this will help a bit. Install two strong backs to prevent warping. Attach the box to the cockpit wall with brass or stainless butt hinges.

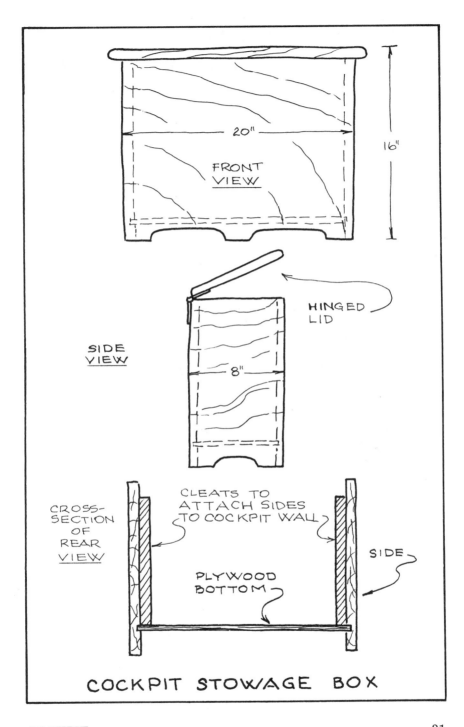

20"

16"

FRONT
VIEW

SIDE
VIEW

8"

HINGED
LID

CROSS-
SECTION
OF
REAR
VIEW

CLEATS TO
ATTACH SIDES
TO COCKPIT WALL

PLYWOOD
BOTTOM

SIDE

COCKPIT STOWAGE BOX

SLATTED COCKPIT SEATS

Many fiberglass, steel, and cement boats have very cold, very slippery, cockpit seats made of the above materials. Since cushions are not always practical, especially in foul weather when things get the most slippery, a very fine solution is the use of fixed or hinged (depending on whether a locker lid makes up the seat or not) teak slats. These are widely used from the Dutch Trintella line of yachts to *Wanderer IV*.

They are no more complicated than they sound to construct, and they add much warmth and friction in exchange for a handful of dollars. Rip 13/16″ teak into 2″ wide slats, and bullnose the top edges. You will be leaving 1/2″ spaces between the slats, so calculate the number you'll need accordingly. If you come up with an odd measurement that would require your ripping a slat to half width, don't. Instead, either increase or decrease your spacing.

Next, from the same stock, rip 1½″ pieces that will act as ribs to which the slats will be screwed. Bullnose the *bottoms* of these. You will need one rib at each end and one about every 12″. Assemble, using a 1/2″ plywood spacer, resorcinol glue, and slightly countersunk 1″ pan heads, drilling and screwing from the *ribs*, of course, so the screw heads won't show. There is no need to plug them here, just be sure they're deep enough so they won't act as pivots. If you are hinging the seat, let in butt hinges about 24″ apart, and attach to the cockpit coaming.

If you are installing the slats permanently, just run a bead of caulking on each rib and drop them into place. This is no place to get carried away with caulking. If you do, you will have the stuff squishing out all over, and cleaning it up between the slats will be no small task. Two 1″ pan-head screws through *each rib only* should be enough to hold in any circumstance.

I once saw an attempt to simplify this slat operation by eliminating the ribs and screwing the slats directly onto the tops of the seats. Unbelievable. The space between the slats became a holding ground for water, crumbs, bugs, and dirt, all of which congealed into a kind of greenish goo. I, as obedient humble crew, was obligated to sit atop it all with my clean white tennis shorts. I burnt them the next day.

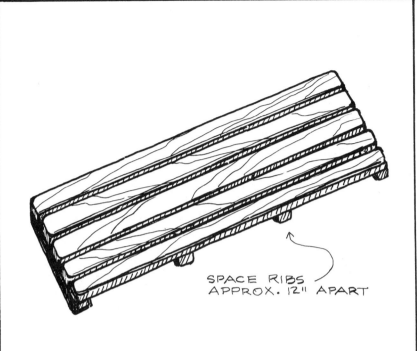

SPACE RIBS
APPROX. 12" APART

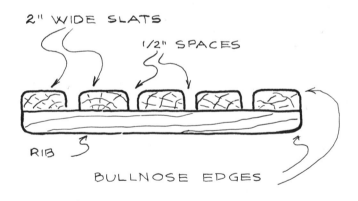

2" WIDE SLATS

1/2" SPACES

RIB

BULLNOSE EDGES

SLATTED COCKPIT SEATS

SIMPLE BOOM CRUTCH

Probably no two boats exist with similar boom gallows, and that's quite as it should be. Most are masterpieces of design, incorporating holders for life rings, davits for dinghies, bases for ship's bells, and brackets for outboards, but if you want to make a very functional removable boom crutch without the trimmings, here it is. It will fit any boat with a raised cabin. It consists of two brass pipes, one of slightly greater diameter than the other, to allow a telescoping assembly, and a hefty head piece to house the boom.

First, secure brass pipes of about 1½" diameter for one, slightly less or more for the other. The length of the larger piece will be determined by the height of your cabin; the lower end being as close to the deck as possible, the upper end being about 2" below the cabintop, so it will not be a protruding weapon when the crutch part of the pipe is removed. Through-bolt these to the face of the cabin about 3" from either end with 1/4" round head bolts, making certain that you do not distort the walls of the tubing with undue pressure. If you do, you will never be able to insert the removable pipe.

If your deckhouse face slopes, as most do, cut a teak shim block about 3" square, to achieve perpendicularity. To be sure the pipe sits on the block snugly, file a hollow seat 1/4" deep with a shoe rasp.

The length of the pipe that fits into the crutch should be measured from the boom when it's in a resting position. It should be cut to reach the top of the fixed pipe, plus 6". The last 6" will be the part to slip into the fixed piece. Next, you will have to cut a slot in the removable tube to accommodate the top bolt. Cut it with a hacksaw and then bend it out until it breaks.

For the wooden head, cut a 6" square piece out of 2½" teak stock, and shape it as in the illustration. The star is optional. To affix it to the tube, drill a 2" deep hole to fit your tubing, clean the hole and tubing, and apply a nice coat of thickened epoxy to both, and unite. Perform this last step with the tubing firmly in place; you can then align the head perfectly by actually setting the boom in it to determine the most ideal angle. If you try to do this last step on some distant work bench, you'll find the head piece permanently askew, correctable only by chopping down the mast and planting it on your starboard caprail. Weird.

THE FINELY FITTED YACHT

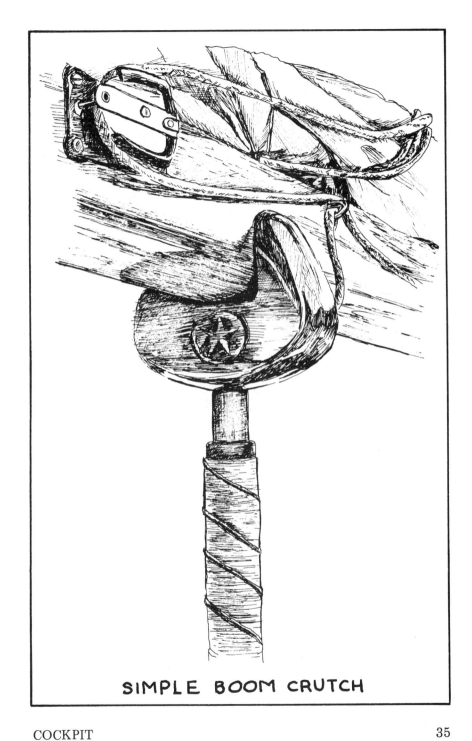

SIMPLE BOOM CRUTCH

COCKPIT TABLE

In spite of what you may have been told, beer cans jammed into cockpit scuppers, salami resting on hairy knees, and coffee cups squeezed between quivering thighs, is not the most civilized way of conducting lunch above decks. An improvement is a portable wood cockpit tray which can be taken below to be loaded up with goodies, then can be fixed firmly in the cockpit with the simplest of attachments.

The tray should accommodate four mugs; some people advocate four *cans*, although I've yet to see one of them sip coffee or tea from a Coors can. It should have separate areas for two small plates or containers for food, and one small space for serviettes and cutlery. The whole thing need be no larger than $10'' \times 20''$.

A $3/8''$ piece of plywood cut to the above dimensions is the starting point. Surround this on all sides by searails. The aft and foreward searail can be solid, but the two short ones on the ends should be the hand-holed variety (see "Searails"). The corners can be enclosed, for the tray is portable and can be turned upside down for cleaning. Glue, screw, and plug.

The internal partitions may be made of solid stock or plywood. Cut two pieces of $3/8''$ plywood to a width of the diameter of your favourite mugs plus $1''$, and a length of the *interior width* of the tray. With a hole saw, cut your holes, leaving at least $1/2''$ of wood all around. Next, from $3/4''$ solid stock, cut four $1\frac{1}{2}''$ wide pieces, whose lengths are equal to the width of your mug-hold inserts. Glue and screw these to the aft and foreward searails, and glue and screw the mug insert onto them. Note: do not enclose the space you've just created below the mug holders. If you do, and anything spills or sticks in there, cleaning it out will be a horror show. Repeat the above on the other side.

Next, cut another piece of $3/8''$ plywood that will fit into the remaining central space. Scribe onto it the outlines of the containers or plates you will be most often using, cut them out with a jigsaw, and glue the plywood directly onto the inside of the tray bottom.

Now, purchase two sets of dinghy gudgeons and pintles, attach the pintles to the aft searail of the tray about $3''$ in from the ends, and attach the gudgeons onto the aft or foreward face of the cockpit. Slip the tray in place and bon appetit. If this doesn't beat stuffing pepperoni in your pant cuffs, I don't know what does.

THE FINELY FITTED YACHT

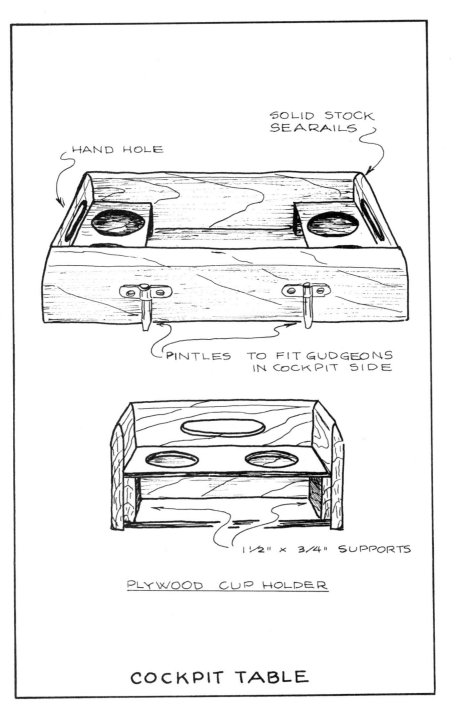

HAND HOLE

SOLID STOCK SEARAILS

PINTLES TO FIT GUDGEONS IN COCKPIT SIDE

1½" × ¾" SUPPORTS

PLYWOOD CUP HOLDER

COCKPIT TABLE

WHEEL WRAPPINGS

The slick steel wheels of modern yachts look very fast and racy, but can become frighteningly slippery when covered by drops of rain, or the sweat of fear. In northern climates, they can also be inhospitably cold for the hands.

To overcome the above traumas,you can do one of two things: wear gloves, or put a fine whipping of cotton twine around the wheel. The first solution is more practical,but does pathetically little to enhance the beauty of the wheel.

Begin by laying about 4″ of the end of a ball of cotton line along the wheel, then proceed by taking the ball around the rim and tying a series of half hitches. Continue each half hitch the same way by passing the working end through the loops from right to left. If you make all your hitches the same,you will develop a nice spiral pattern because each knot (where the line passes over itself) will fall automatically in order.

To finish off the line at each spoke, leave the last hitches fairly loose,then pass the line back through them, draw it tight,and trim. Continue on to the next arc of the wheel.

An alternate to the above is the straight whipping, where the line is passed around the wheel's rim without the half hitches. This is just as functional, although somewhat less decorative.

To mark the set of the wheel at the point where the rudder is dead fore and aft, fit a Turk's-head over the rim. If you say that's too much bother and why not just wrap a piece of electrician's tape over it, then you're probably the kind of person who puts ketchup on his escargot.

COCKPIT

WINCH HANDLE HOLDERS

For instant mounting, little maintenance, and general all around practicality, one is hard pressed to recommend anything but the soft molded plastic winch handle pockets available at your ship's chandlery, with the exception of the blatantly obvious solution in the photo. Instead of spending about $15 for a pair of white molded beasties (one at the mast and one at the cockpit), one can simply purchase a length of soft plastic tubing with an ID of about 2½" and simply cut it as shown. Total cost for two will come to a whole dollar. Do cut the top as shown to enable the handle to slide into the most accessible position. Round off the edges with a knife or file, for sharp edges can cause nasty paper cut-like wounds. Besides the low cost, these units have the unquestionable advantage of having their bottoms completely open, making the entire tube accessible and cleanable. The store-bought ones have a joke of a drain hole which plugs up with the first available nasty goo, forming an inaccessible damp pit where all sorts of slithering, slimy things propagate.

One caution. I have seen some people use aluminum tubing or hard PVC tubing for the holders. This is a mistake. Their hard edges will become shin hunters of the first magnitude.

COCKPIT CUTOUT

Vast unused space can be found between the solid molded walls of most fiberglass cockpits as well as many old plywood ones. Aside from being inaccessible from the outside, these areas are usually barely accessible from within. Such a condition is ideal for a cutout box for winch handles. The length of the opening you cut should be just less than the length of your handle and the height should be 4''. In solid fiberglass or plywood, the drilled hole and jigsaw method should be used. Pencil in the cutout marking 1'' radius corners, and drill a 1/2'' hole anywhere within it. Through this, insert your jigsaw blade and cut away. Make the cut as perfect as possible. Now construct a box from 1/2'' plywood. Make the interior measurements 6'' high, 5'' deep and 3'' longer than your handle. Slope the bottom 10° for drainage. You'll notice that the box will be considerably larger than the opening, and so it must be so that the lip on the bottom (2'' high) and a little at each side can act to keep the handle in place. Butt and glue and screw all joints. Trim the perimeter of the front of the box with 3/4'' cleat stock. You will be using this to attach the box to the cockpit wall. Fiberglass the entire inside with cloth and matt tape to make the box waterproof. Fasten it to the cockpit side with #10 R.H.S.M. screws. Use a very generous uninterrupted bead of polysulfide between the cleat stock and the cockpit and screw tightly. Drill a small 1/4'' drain hole in the cockpit wall just above the sloped floor for drainage. In a plywood cockpit, this hole should have a light copper tubing inserted and bedded in polysulfide to prevent water from seeping between the veneer laminates and causing dry rot.

Trim in teak. Bed the teak trim solidly to prevent any water retention.

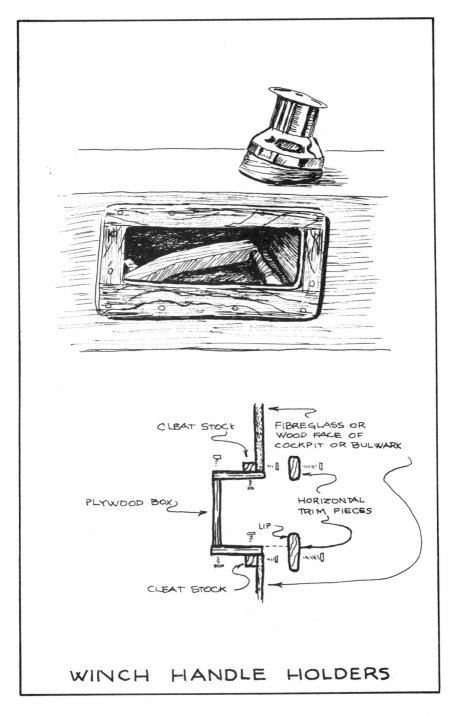

CLEAT STOCK

FIBREGLASS OR WOOD FACE OF COCKPIT OR BULWARK

PLYWOOD BOX

HORIZONTAL TRIM PIECES

LIP

CLEAT STOCK

WINCH HANDLE HOLDERS

COCKPIT

COCKPIT COAMING

In many vessels (*Warm Rain* included), the seating accommodations in the cockpit are considerably less than luxurious. Even if a coaming of some sort does exist, it's usually just high enough to torture the small of your back. *Scorpio*, a lovely teak ketch from Venezuela, has had a beautifully designed and fabricated extension installed above the original coaming. Aside from enhancing the yacht's appearance, it has created a safer and infinitely more comfortable cockpit. Even a quick glance at the photo, however, will tell you that this is a major undertaking, so unless you have access to a steambox and have a goodly collection of clamps, don't even begin.

The material required will be a single piece of 1″ teak, or mahogany stock, about 4″ wide and as long as you desire to make it. Now, find the thinnest blade you can for your table saw, or alternately, take your piece of wood into a furniture or door maker and have him rip the 1″ stock down to 1/8″ thick by 4″, wide strips. Next, carefully measure off the cockpit coaming, curves and all, or better still, make a paper pattern of it. Using this pattern, set up a series of blocks on a workbench or a piece of old plywood. Nothing elaborate needs to be done here; just use pieces of 2 × 4 and screw them down temporarily per diagram. Ten-inch blocks will do quite nicely, unless you want to run two full length pieces for the long stretches. The space between the inboard and outboard blocks should be about 1/8″ more than the total thickness of your planks. When your blocks are secure, gather up all the clamps you have (the wood handscrews are the best for this purpose). It would be good to place one every 6″-8″. Steam a 16″ area of a plank where your curves are to be, then lay it out, and brush glue over its surface. Be sure you use resorcinol glue. Teak is impossible to laminate with anything else. Place the plank into the blocks, then quickly glue up both sides of the next plank and slip it inside of the first one. You'll find the use of discardable rubber gloves most helpful here. If you have a friend who could help to clamp and to hold, so much the better. When you have all the planks in place, use a mallet to hammer them all down as evenly as possible, and clamp as suggested. If you're not using clamps with wood jaws, slip wood pads (scrap plywood about 2″ × 3″ is fine) between the metal and the teak to prevent pressure marks. When all the clamps are set, wipe off all excess glue with a damp cloth. Allow it to set overnight. In the morning, trim the edges off with a minimal setting on your table saw and sand thoroughly. Varnish or oil. Next, have a shop make up three stainless or bronze brackets. If your cockpit coaming is sloped, have them bend the bracket to suit. Through-bolt, using carriage bolts inboard and cap nuts outboard. Bed your bolts in a caulking compound. Now, just sit back and relax. Slouch if you like.

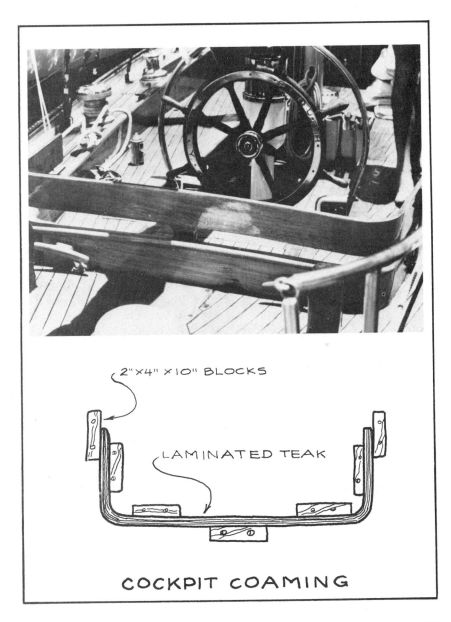

2" X 4" X 10" BLOCKS

LAMINATED TEAK

COCKPIT COAMING

TEAK COCKPIT GRATES

A cockpit grate or, at least, cockpit slats are mandatory in many of the modern yachts whose cockpit soles, whether all fiberglass or steel, or glass over wood, are often too inadequately textured to be sufficiently effective as a non-skid surface when substantial amounts of water are taken on board. Besides, grates look pretty.

This grate differs vastly in complexity from the lighter construction stowage-grates. It requires two interlocking sets of dadoed 3/4" X 3/4" stock, glued and screwed at every joint, as well as a substantial framework (tapered adequately along the sides to suit the cockpit), which will have to be attached to the end of each strip with the use of dowels.

First measure the cockpit to establish how many and what length of each dadoed strip you'll need. Three vital points must be taken into consideration:

(a) The grating grid itself must end up having perfectly parallel sides. All tapering and fitting adjustments will be made to the solid surrounding frame.

(b) The surrounding frame should be made to be at least 2½" wide at the narrowest point, meaning that in a severely tapering cockpit, you may end up with a 5"-7" frame piece on the beamier part of the cockpit.

(c) The arrangement of the grate grid should be calculated so that a full space always adjoins the frame (see diagram). This will be needed so that each dowel will have an undadoed full 3/4" X 3/4" stock end to go into.

Now, with the number of short and long pieces determined, select 3/4" teak boards so that the least amount of waste will be necessary, i.e. the length should equal the combined lengths of one short plus one long or two shorts and two long, etc.

Next, divide the length of your board into 1½" intervals with a short and exact mark, then set your 3/4" wide dado blades to remove half thickness (3/8"). Do a test run on a scrap piece of wood to verify the settings. The dadoing can be performed on either a table saw or radial arm saw. The radial arm has the advantage of a longer table and non-moving board, but if care is used, a table saw will do the work just as well. Begin dadoing at the first mark and continue for the length of the board.

Next, set a single carbide blade for a 3/4" wide cut and rip your grate slats. Be sure to use a good stiff blade to guarantee a perfectly straight and vertical cut. After every three or four cuts, recheck the

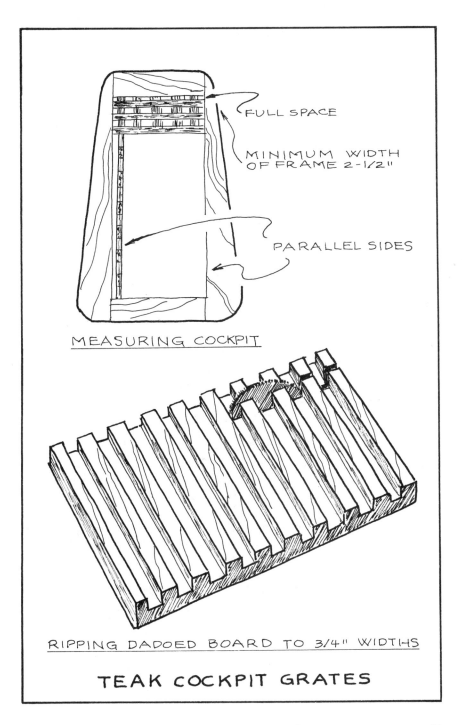

FULL SPACE

MINIMUM WIDTH
OF FRAME 2-1/2"

PARALLEL SIDES

MEASURING COCKPIT

RIPPING DADOED BOARD TO 3/4" WIDTHS

TEAK COCKPIT GRATES

blade settings by fitting a couple of the cut stock together. Now, cut your strips to length making sure you end up with a full 3/4″ X 3/4″ block at each end.

Next, take your athwartship pieces, turn them dadoed side down, and with an appropriate drill bit and countersink, drill holes *above* each gap to fit a #6 F.H. screw. Now, brush a bit of resorcinol in the dadoed areas — very little indeed or the stuff will squeeze out, and: a) stain the wood, and b) necessitate your scraping excess glue out of a half million little square holes — and assemble the entire grate with screw holes up. Pop in your screws, set them gently with a hammer, then screw down. Use caution; remember that the little wedge-shaped shoulders of screws can split wood. Plug each hole using resorcinol glue, and let it set for a few hours.

While you wait, cut out your frames leaving a good 1/8″ all the way around to facilitate removal. If you have a lip of any kind around your cockpit seats, you'll have to allot for that with more perimeter space. Make the fore-and-aft pieces of the frame full length, fitting the athwartships ones in between.

Run a light bullnose of 1/4″ radius around both upper and lower edges of the outside of the grate to prevent splintering.

Next, with a chisel, remove the bulk of the plug heads (see "Detailing"), then belt-sand off the rest.

To attach the frames to the grate grid, set all the pieces in place, and using a small square, draw a line from the center of the end of each grid piece right onto the frame in that position, and also a couple of marks joining the ends of the frames to each other. These marks are for centering your dowel holes. Code all your pieces for easier identification.

Now, clamp each of your pieces (frames and each grate side) one at a time, to a workbench, and, using the doweling jig (see "Tools") with a piece of tape on your drill bit as governor, drill each hole to a depth of a half inch plus a hair. Be sure your jig is perfectly centred on the lines you've drawn. Drill all holes in all frames and the grate, then, using 1″ dowels dipped in resorcinol glue, assemble. The fastest method is to fill one piece with dowels, drive them to seat with a mallet, then tap the whole thing in place into the corresponding piece. Bar clamp the whole grate firmly, using two bar clamps on top to clamp the ends and two on the bottom to clamp the sides. Allow it to set overnight. Then fit it into place and do final adjustments.

Some people like to elevate their grates to facilitate drainage. To do this, rip runners to 3/8″ height from 3/4″ wide stock to the length (minus 2″) of your grate and secure it to the grate on either side plus every eighth fore and aft grate strip.

THE FINELY FITTED YACHT

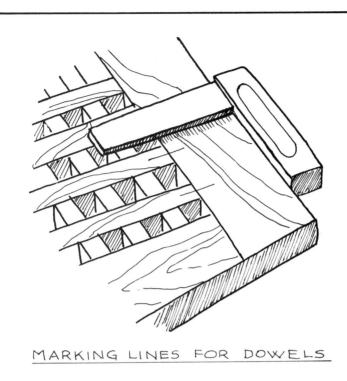

MARKING LINES FOR DOWELS

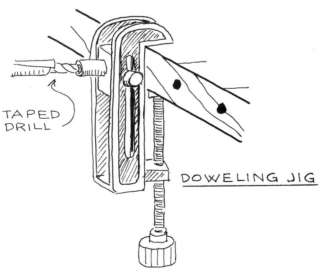

TAPED
DRILL

DOWELING JIG

TEAK COCKPIT GRATES

on deck

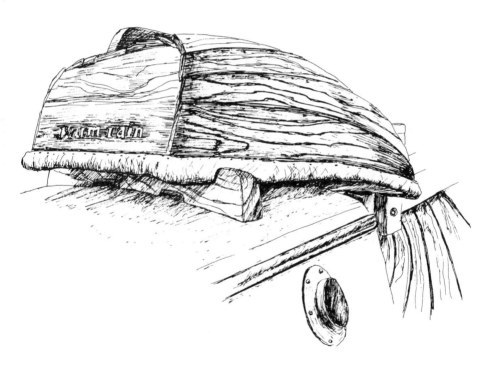

SKYLIGHTS

I can say without exaggeration, that the greatest single interior change *Warm Rain* underwent, was when we cut a 21" X 20" hole in the coachroof of the salon. Until then, the most pleasant places aboard were the forepeak, with four portlights and a deadlight in the foreward hatch, and the galley area where light poured in through the open companionway hatch. The salon, up to that point, was a rather gloomy place with a pair of settees. The hole in the coachroof changed all that. With ample light, the nooks and crannies were brought to life, the beautiful grains in the teak tongue-and-groove were finally visible, and the settees became great places to read or visit or just watch the sky.

We proceeded to weatherproof the hole with a traditionally shaped, but vastly redesigned, skylight, which then added as much life to the topsides as the hole in the roof did belowdecks. The major aspect of the redesign was to make the entire skylight one piece, eliminating the traditional hinged wings which on many yachts leak so ferociously. The skylight now functions very much like a foreward hatch, with a pair of cast hinges, and a thread-lock.

The glass in the skylight is tempered, which makes it very resilient to blows from dropped winch handles. Tempered glass was chosen over plexiglass, because the latter will scratch and become quite unsightly regardless of how careful one is with it. If you don't mind a few scratches, by all means go ahead and use it, for it is much less trouble to fabricate (you can cut it with a jigsaw as long as the protective paper coating is still on it), and it's truly unbreakable once you get into 1/2" thickness, which is what you need for a skylight of any size. With the plexiglass, you obviate the need for protective bars which do look handsome, but are rather a pain to install. For all that, you can actually bypass the gabled skylight and construct a slightly curved one to match the camber of your coachroof, using only a single piece of plexiglass and an elegant, but simple, frame of four pieces of teak (see photo). The time saved on such a simplified version could easily add up to 40%.

Whichever you choose, design the skylight to be as low as possible for both aesthetic and practical reasons.

The following design and construction methods will be interchangeable up to the coamings, after that, each skylight will be covered separately.

Warm Rain's skylight.

Hatch type skylight.

Building the Hole

There is, of course, no particular size the opening of a skylight should be, but I've always thought that 22″ × 22″ is a good size, for it allows a body or sailbags to pass through. For more light and more air, a skylight as large as 36″ × 22″ could be built using four separate pieces of glass in a much reinforced frame,as was on *Nightingale* (see photo). When measuring for the cutout, remember you'll be losing 1½″ in both directions to coamings. Putting the skylight between two deckbeams is most advisable. Once you begin to tamper with structural beams, the reinforcement required to replace them will become discouragingly complicated. Check to make sure you won't be cutting into wires, then drill a 1/2″ hole anywhere within the perimeter of the skylight, stick your jigsaw blade through the hole and cut away. Make your cuts as true as possible to avoid any potential gaps and subsequent leaks. Next, from 13/16″ stock,cut four pieces for your inside coaming, to a width 2″ greater than the thickness of your coachroof. Wipe the sides of your opening thoroughly and lay a generous bead of caulking (Dolfinite will do) all the way around the edges and install the four pieces, one at a time, so their lower edges come flush with the inside of the coachroof (see diagram). Countersink and screw the frames to the coachroof,making sure you screw right into the centre of the plywood core. Brush a bit of resorcinol onto the ends of the frames that will butt against the other frame pieces and screw them to each other as well.

Trim out the coachroof-to-coaming interior joint as in Diagram B. You will next have to install the outside coamings as in Diagram A. Both pieces can be cut from 13/16″ stock; the lower one to a width of 1″, the higher one to a width of 2″. Cut the corners to 45°. Screw both of them directly into the coachroof, leaving a 3/4″ gap between the outside and inside coamings. Use generous amounts of bedding compound on coaming-to-coachroof joints and a bit of resorcinol on coaming-to-coaming joints. Lightly round all edges with sandpaper to prevent splintering.

The coamings are now complete. The only thing left to do is to build the skylight itself.

The Flat Plexiglass Skylight

Mill the frame for the hatch as shown in Diagram C. Lap and screw, dovetail, or cut on 45°, and dowel the corners. When together, make some very exact interior measurements for the plexiglass and cut it to size with a good hacksaw blade in your jigsaw. An ordinary blade would make too rough a cut. Very slightly round the outside edge with sandpaper and dry-fit it into place. Drill countersunk holes

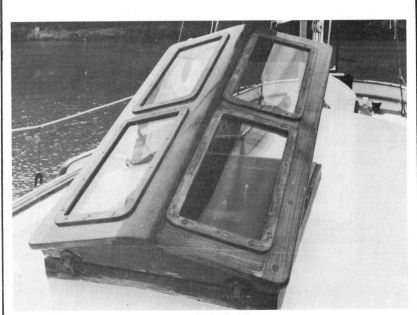

Nightingale's **skylight.**

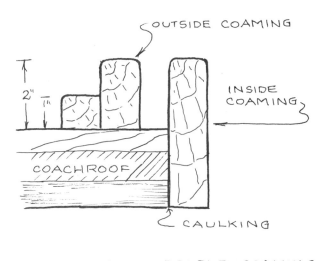

OUTSIDE COAMING

INSIDE COAMING

2"

COACHROOF

CAULKING

DIAGRAM A — DOUBLE COAMING

SKYLIGHTS

for 1″ #10 F.H.S.M. screws every 4″ into the plexiglass. Countersink so the screw head will come flush with the surface of the plexiglass. Run a bead of silicone sealer around the 1/2″ rabbet, set the plexiglass in place, and screw it down. Don't try to wipe off the excess sealer now; you'll just smear it and make a mess. Wait until it's dry, then you can easily scrape it off with your fingernails.

The Gabled Skylight

First, determine the amount of rise you'll want. Something like Diagram E is a pleasant amount. Cut your foreward and aft frame pieces from 13/16″ stock. Skip the rabbet. Cut your side log frames from 1½″ stock, and rabbet the bottom, and slope the top to the angle of your end (foreward and aft) pieces (Diagram D). Butt them and glue and screw. No need to get fancy here.

Next, from 13/16″ stock, cut 3½″ wide pieces. Cut three long ones to overhang the frame by 1″. Remember to allow for a 1/2″ rabbet at both ends of each of the short pieces; see Diagram F where they lap into the long pieces. Run the 1/2″ rabbets the full length along the inboard edges of the outside long pieces and on *both* edges of the central long piece. The angle of its rabbet will have to be adjusted to the gable of the skylight. Run the 1/2″ gable on the inside edges of the four short pieces, as well as their ends, as previously mentioned. Set them all in place, glue them, and screw them to the frames, i.e., glue and screw Diagram F into Diagram E and D. Whew!

Now comes the easy part. Measure in your glass (or plexiglass) areas, then install the plexiglass, as in the flat plexiglass skylight. If you'd rather use tempered glass with a little tinting in it, just take your measurements to a glass shop and have them fabricate the pieces for you. Be sure your measurements are exact because after the glass is tempered, it *cannot* be cut. Now, just run the silicone around the rabbet and press the glass into place.

If you want the brass rods running fore and aft as in photo, fabricate four identical end pieces as in Diagram G. Cut your rods to the *same* length as the glass. Assemble with the rod supports, and screw the supports into the frame, one screw per end, with #8 screws. Use glue. If you've done everything properly, your rod supports will overhang the glass by 1/4″ at either end, just in case the silicone fails. Don't hold your breath.

If possible, double hinge the hatch (a set both foreward and aft). To hold the hatch open, use a chopstick. I do.

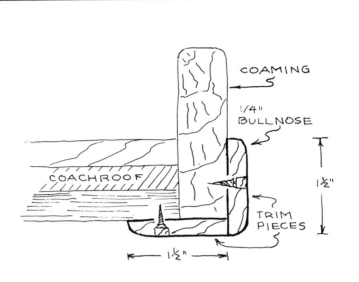

COAMING

1/4" BULLNOSE

COACHROOF

1½"

TRIM PIECES

1½"

DIAGRAM B - INTERIOR TRIM

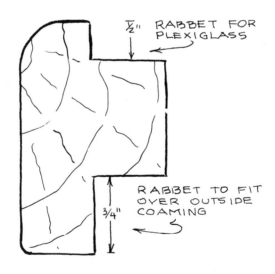

$\frac{1}{2}$" RABBET FOR PLEXIGLASS

RABBET TO FIT OVER OUTSIDE COAMING

3/4"

DIAGRAM C
SIDE LOG FRAME - FLAT SKYLIGHT

SKYLIGHTS

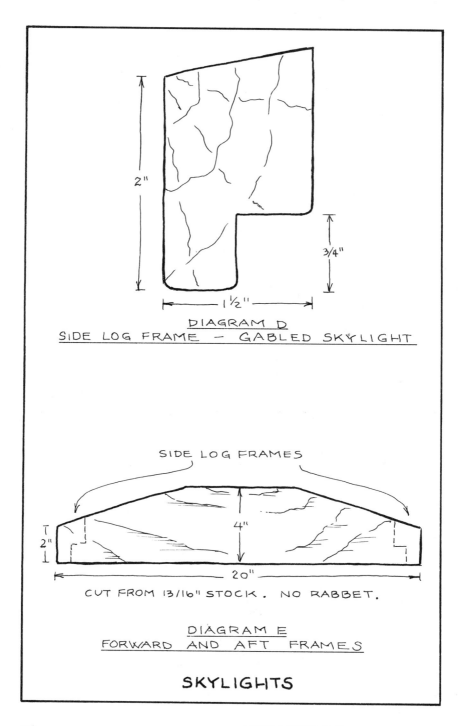

DIAGRAM D
SIDE LOG FRAME — GABLED SKYLIGHT

SIDE LOG FRAMES

CUT FROM 13/16" STOCK. NO RABBET.

DIAGRAM E
FORWARD AND AFT FRAMES

SKYLIGHTS

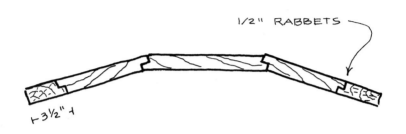

1/2" RABBETS

⊢ 3½" ⊣

DIAGRAM F
END VIEW OF GLASS FRAME

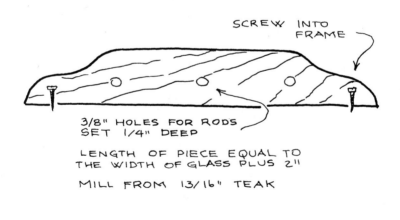

SCREW INTO
FRAME

3/8" HOLES FOR RODS
SET 1/4" DEEP

LENGTH OF PIECE EQUAL TO
THE WIDTH OF GLASS PLUS 2"

MILL FROM 13/16" TEAK

DIAGRAM G - ROD SUPPORTS

SKYLIGHTS

DORADE VENTS

If you've sworn to have no teak at all on your boat, please relent and sacrifice an hour's maintenance annually and make yourself a beautifully varnished teak dorade box with a glistening brass or stainless cowl that has its inside painted the same colour as your sheer stripe. Once it has funneled the cooling air below and teased the eyes above, you'll send me letters of thanks. (Post cards will do.)

The best throat diameter is $3''$ and up, the problem of course being that monstrous vents will require monstrous boxes. In spite of what you frequently hear, "bigger" in the box itself is not at all "better". Commonly thrown about formulas, such as box height must be twice the diameter of the throat, are naïve. Surface areas must be discussed here and not heights. The box as shown in the diagram should have air passage capacity equal to the number of square inches available in the throat, e.g., $3'' \times \pi r^2$ is equal to the surface area that must be provided as an opening in the box. This, of course, is not only designated by the height and width of the box, but also by the height of the baffles inside it. To make a box with greater area capacity than the throat would be damaging to the system, for it would provide an expansion space where the air can eddy and disrupt the flow into the cabin.

The box should be made of $3/4''$ solid teak with butted ends glued and screwed. Semi-circular drain holes should be cut on either side just below the cowl in case water finds its way into it.

The lid of the box has also been a matter for controversy, with many people advocating the use of $3/4''$ plexiglass instead of solid teak to allow more light belowdecks. This seems initially quite a pleasant idea, but just as successful a system can be achieved without depriving the yacht of a lovely teak box lid. Into the foreward part of the box just above the vent hole in the coachroof (same diameter as the throat of the vent), a similar hole can be cut and a bronze ringed deadlight inserted. Since the hole in the coachroof is only of $3''$ diameter anyway, plasticizing the entire lid of the box for light would be quite redundant.

For tropical use, one should consider a second threaded ring (the same one the cowl usually sits in) instead of a dead light. Now, a $3/4''$ piece of plexiglass can be cut to act as a plug in the ring. It would have to be taken to a machine shop to have appropriate threads cut into it.

The inside base of the box should be lined with cleat stock. The whole thing should then be bedded in Dolphinite or polysulfide and

DORADE BOX

the cleat stock drilled and screwed to the deck. One last thing before you install the lid. Futile attempts of all sorts have been made to install adequate circular mosquito nets into the deckhouse hole after the system has been built. Thoughtless and regrettable. Now is the time to act. Acquire a fine brass screen, and using Monel staples or light tacks, attach it over the inside of the hole *on the lid*. You'll now be permanently bug-proofed.

Here, perhaps, a word on the type of cowl to be used. Cowls range from soft squishy plastic to cast bronze you couldn't dent with a hammer. Advantages of the soft plastic ones are obvious: they are less likely to foul lines, they cause less damage to falling bodies, and they are inexpensive. But boy, are they ugly! They oxidize and stain rapidly and very little can be done to bring them back to life. The heavy stainless or bronze ones come with solidly cast rings into which fit solidly cast plugs for winter sailing when even a breath belowdecks is too much.

A point here about installing the threaded ring. When marking the screw holes for it, be sure the cowl is in it tightly. Have the cowl face forward and now mark the holes and drill.

To add a finishing touch to thick cabin tops made up of fiberglass, plywood, and insulation — all of which are visible belowdecks once the hole is cut, a thin sleeve of light gauge brass or copper should be formed into a ring and held in place inside the hole with three or four brass tacks. This will provide that slight accent that differentiates the master from the hacker.

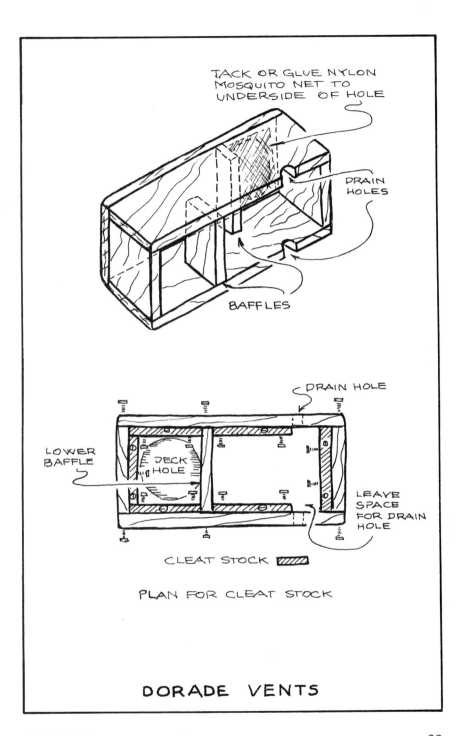

TACK OR GLUE NYLON
MOSQUITO NET TO
UNDERSIDE OF HOLE

DRAIN
HOLES

BAFFLES

DRAIN HOLE

LOWER
BAFFLE

DECK
HOLE

LEAVE
SPACE
FOR DRAIN
HOLE

CLEAT STOCK

PLAN FOR CLEAT STOCK

DORADE VENTS

SIMPLE BOOM GALLOWS

The range of potentially functional gallow designs is so great, that I feel it would be futile to even begin discussing it, especially because most make use of complex steel fabrication, incorporating them into stanchions, or davits, or stern pulpits.

One very fine traditional set, using a very simple concept, that can be adapted to most yachts, whether on the aft deck or the coachroof, has been given rebirth by the nautical hardware firm of Merriman-Holbrook. The set consists of two corner fittings and two bases. Both can be slipped into brass pipes that make up the uprights. The bases should be bolted through the deck or cabin top and backed up belowdecks with either a single plate of the same diameter (1/8″ thickness is fine) or a set of washers. The single plate is, of course, the preferred alternative since it gives the most aesthetic finish and the most even reinforcement as well.

The location of the gallows will have to be decided in order to establish the length of the wood cross member. The coachroof just at the companionway hatch has been a favourite of many yachtsmen, for there the uprights can be made quite short and, consequently, quite stable. The obvious drawback of this arrangement is that the wooden cross member interferes with forward vision.

Most yachts have the gallows on the aft deck and this, indeed, is a great friend for the helmsman or night watch to lean against or hold on to. The problem, of course, is how to secure the gallows in this position since the height of the uprights will often reach a rather wobbly four feet. The cleanest and most functional solution I have seen was the use of guy wires (see diagram). The wires used were sheathed stainless, the same as used for the lifelines, with a single turnbuckle in each piece for aligning and tensioning the gallows. Since the sloped aftmost wire is pinched in at the stern (especially so on double enders and canoe sterns), a very stable guy system is established. Padeyes or eyebolts can be used aft for the wire bases.

The wooden cross member is most easily made up of a single piece of 1½″ teak cut to the shape in the illustration. It should have three nests for the boom to facilitate aft deck traffic, regardless of whether the yacht is docked port-to or starboard-to. For the most even job, cut the nests with a hole saw with a radius equal to 1/4″ more than the beam. Bullnose all edges. To protect the boom's paint or varnish, line the nest with a piece of leather and tack its edges with brass tacks to the foreward and aft face of the cross member.

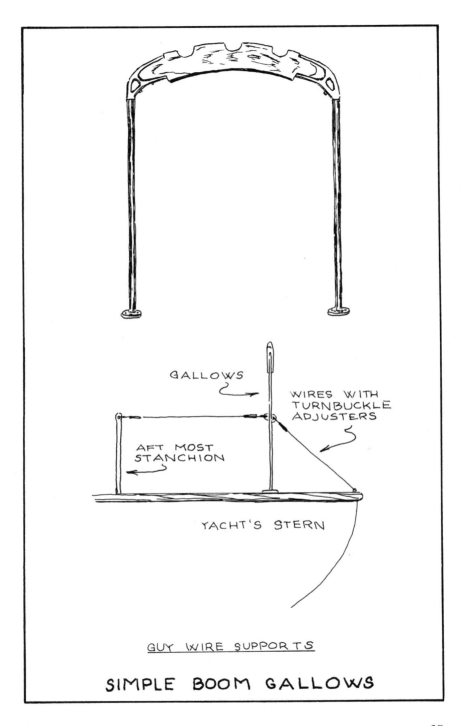

GALLOWS

WIRES WITH
TURNBUCKLE
ADJUSTERS

AFT MOST
STANCHION

YACHT'S STERN

GUY WIRE SUPPORTS

SIMPLE BOOM GALLOWS

GRABRAILS

Since grabrails are, in most cases, a matter of life and death, or at least a good lengthy swim, their installation should be one of the first major undertakings. When the dust clears after all arguments, only two sensible alternatives remain. One is the traditional looped wooden rails, and the other,the brass eye with rope line rails. A third variety, a solid rail with a concave detail for grip, has many supporters, but this seems to me sadly inadequate, for although it is undeniable that a ready hold can be gained in any given spot, that hold is tenuous at best, being literally of the hanging-by-the-fingernails variety.

Looped Rails

The first thing to do is determine the placement and length of your rail. Running parallel to the cabinsides, about 6″ inboard from the edge, is ideal. If you have good thick laminates in your cabintop (for example, 1/2″ plywood core with 1/8″ glass on either side),you need no precautions, for you can simply screw into the cabintop with #14 sheet metal screws. If your cabintop is of a weaker construction, or has a foam or balsa core, you will have to through-bolt, in which case you better be certain there are no fittings or fixtures belowdeck that would impede your work.

Milling should be from 1″ solid stock, to a width of 2½″. Fabricate a single loop jig out of 1/8″ plywood, and use this as a pattern to guarantee that all your loops will be identical. The loops should be on 10″ centres with the footings between at least 2″ to make a solid base.

Divide the 2½″ width evenly between wood and space. Be sure not to taper the tip of the last loop too drastically, for it will become frail, and splinter with changes in the weather. Once cut, bullnose the loops and the top of the rail with a 3/8″ router bit. Next, pre-drill your grabrail, and countersink to a depth of 1/2″. The size of your drill bit will depend on whether you screw or through-bolt. If screwing, use #14 PHSM screws; if through-bolting, use stainless steel round heads. Try to calculate the exact bolt length needed, allowing 1/4″ to protrude belowdecks, for then you will be able to use cap nuts, which look much more pleasing than a regular nut which has a bit of the bolt sticking through. In neither case should you use flat heads, for these have wedge-shaped shoulders and wedges split wood, and if you want to split wood, get a job in a shingle mill.

Next, using the rail as a guide, drill your first hole and screw it gently to the deck. This is a dry run; do not use caulking. Drill and screw the entire rail into place, then remove all screws and clean the drilled out rubble between the rail and deck. Place a good ring of caulking around each hole and re-insert screws. If you're through-bolting, you'll need a person belowdecks to place washers and nuts. Tell him to tighten gently. Remove any excess bedding compound with a wooden scraper. Plug, making sure you use resorcinol glue. Let set overnight before you lop off the heads of the plugs.

Brass Eye and Line

The most difficult part of using this method is finding the looped brass fittings. Once found, they should be screwed or through-bolted to the deck with the same precautions as above, on 20″-24″ centres. A good length of 1″ dacron should then be secured and spliced and whipped, as in the photo, onto the fore-most and aft-most fitting. Do not use poly line, for it becomes a bit too hard with weather, and much too rough on the hands.

As seen in the photo, this makes for extremely attractive and almost flawlessly functional, grabrails. Upkeep is non-existent, initial expenditure of time and money minimal. The one major drawback is that it cannot be used as a foot brace while fumbling around the mast or boom, but then you can't have everything.

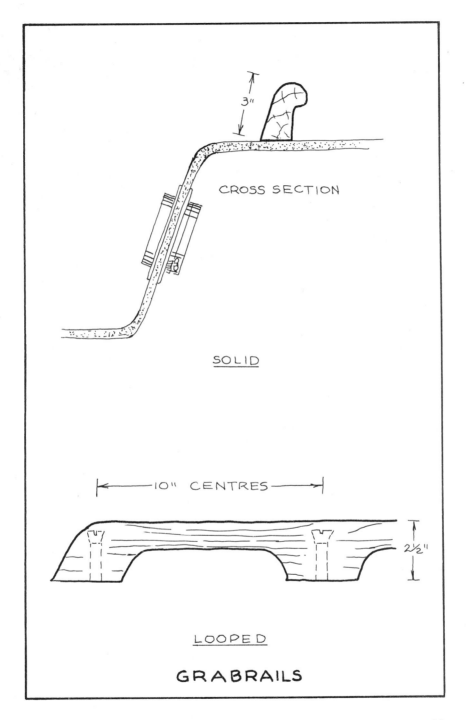

3"

CROSS SECTION

SOLID

10" CENTRES

2½"

LOOPED

GRABRAILS

DECKHOUSE STEP

On many motor sailors and power yachts, the height of the cabin makes commuting from deck to cabin top rather treacherous. A cabin side step on the cabin's aft face (not on the narrow side deck where it could endanger shins and knees) can be of great help.

The location of the step in the photograph is not the most ideal since it protrudes past the corner of the cabin.

The step and the support should be of 13/16" teak. A piece 6" wide and 12" long will be enough for both. Cut the piece into two 6" long portions. The depth of the step can be left at 6" if space on the aft deck allows, but 4" is quite serviceable and 3" is better than nothing. Two inches isn't.

Fit the knee support against the cabin side. With the aid of a small level, scribe a horizontal line onto it and cut it. Eyeball in the curved shape of the knee, then scribe, and cut, and bullnose the curved edges. Next, place the knee in position on the cabin (usually at the halfway point between the deck and cabin top) and after making sure it doesn't rock either vertically or horizontally, scribe a line around it onto the cabin. Now, go below and measure in the location, and make sure that when you drill through from the outside, you will be doing so in an unobstructed area. Drill two holes 2" apart in the area you scribed. The hole should be for #10 S.M. screws.

Next, ask a friend to hold the knee in place, then go below, and using the holes you've just drilled as guides, drill into the knee to a depth of 1¼" to 1½", then clean the knee and cabin surface and cover one or the other with bedding compound. Now, ask the friend to hold the knee most securely and very exactly in place, then, from below, insert your screws, choosing such a length that will allow 1½" deep penetration into the knee.

When the knee is installed, lay the piece for the step on top of it, and scribe the edge parallel to the house. Bullnose all non-contact edges. Cut and refit just to check, then install in identical fashion, but adding a bead of resorcinol glue and a couple of 1" # 10 P.H.S.M. screws to fix the step onto the knee. Plug all screw holes.

If you elect to varnish it, sprinkle a bit of very fine silicone, for friction, on the stepping surface while the second coat is still tacky, then brush off all excess silicone and go on with successive coats.

THE FINELY FITTED YACHT

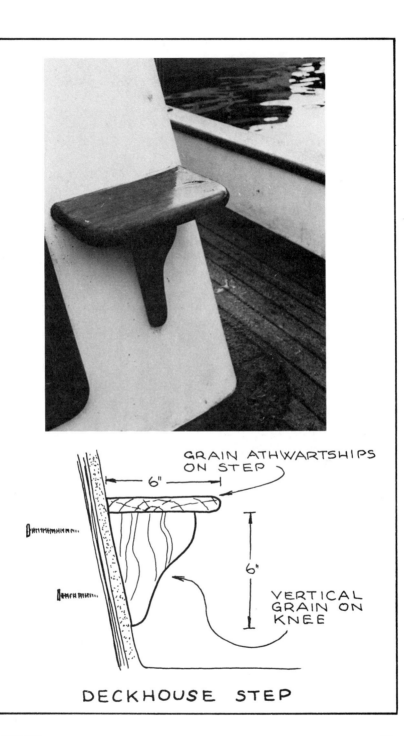

GRAIN ATHWARTSHIPS
ON STEP

6"

6"

VERTICAL
GRAIN ON
KNEE

DECKHOUSE STEP

TEAK TURTLE HATCH

This is a very practical item on most vessels, for not only does it keep the main hatch totally dry when driving hard to windward, but it also makes for a good base for the mainsheet travellers and dinghy chocks. Furthermore, it provides a good firm place to stand when reefing or wrapping up the main sail; the main hatch on its own tends to slide when stepped upon.

The turtle hatch should, if possible, reflect the look of the main hatch in both material and construction, although there is basically nothing profane about mating a teak hatch with a fiberglass turtle hatch, or vice versa.

In most cases, the simplest method of installation will call for bolting the turtle hatch directly to the deck and if this is indeed feasible, then you will be involved, basically, with building a three-sided, bottomless box.

The three sides should be milled from 1¾" stock, cut to a width 2" greater than the overall height of the side of your hatch (see diagram). This is to allow for a 1" rabbet into the inboard top edge, into which the top can be laid, plus some sort of an aft piece to support the aft edge of the top, plus about 1/4" clearance between the hatch and the turtle hatch to avoid binding.

Run the rabbet clear along the side pieces but terminate it 7/8" from the forward end so the rabbet ends will not interfere with the dovetailing or lapping of the frames. For dovetailing, use a dovetail jig (see "Tool" section) and for lapping, use common sense and Diagram A. Assemble the frame with resorcinol glue and clamps.

Since most hatches (and consequently turtle hatches as well) have some sort of a camber, the 1/2" layer of plywood, which is to be the foundation layer of the top, will have to be made up of two 1/4" sheets. This is to avoid having to force-bend a 1/2" piece into place. So, lay in your first 1/4" plywood and glue it (resorcinol glue) to the frames, slipping in a screw every 8" and carefully countersinking it just below the plywood's surface. Next, cover the first layer of plywood with glue and lay in the second layer. Screw this into the frame at 8" intervals, but staggered between the screws holding down the first layer. Next, rip teak to a 1/2" thickness and 2" width (or the width of the hatch slats if they are teak). A width greater than 2" will require that you double screw each piece (two screws side by side) or the edges will forever curl up. Unless you must have a caulked turtle hatch to match your main hatch, just butt the slats

TEAK TURTLE HATCH

side by side as tight as you can. Use resorcinol glue and very carefully countersunk and most carefully tightened #8 flat heads. Plug, sand and varnish or oil.

Next, saturate the underside of the turtle hatch (the plywood) with a good wood preservative like Cuprinol to prevent any mildew from forming. Remember, you won't have any access to this surface once the hatch is screwed down.

Lastly, to install, set the turtle hatch in place, pencil in its outline and drill pilot holes right through the deck. Now clean both the deck and the bottom of the turtle hatch thoroughly, then run two beads of polysulfide around the hatch frame and put it back over the holes. Ask a friend to sit on the turtle hatch and not move while you run below and secure it in place by running #10 or #12 pan head screws into it through the cabin top. Be sure to use screws of such a length that will penetrate at least 1½" into the hatch frame. Space them about 6" apart.

Clean off the excess caulking and enjoy.

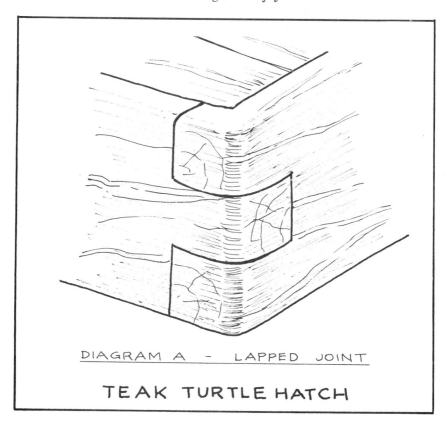

DIAGRAM A - LAPPED JOINT

TEAK TURTLE HATCH

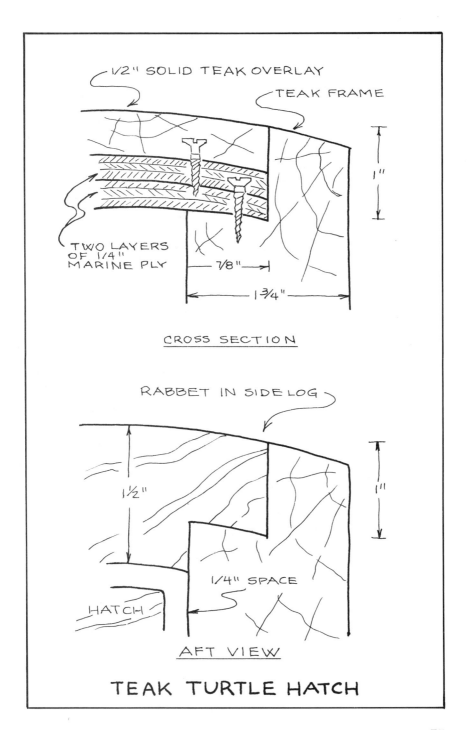

1/2" SOLID TEAK OVERLAY

TEAK FRAME

1"

TWO LAYERS
OF 1/4"
MARINE PLY

7/8"

1 3/4"

CROSS SECTION

RABBET IN SIDE LOG

1 1/2"

1"

1/4" SPACE

HATCH

AFT VIEW

TEAK TURTLE HATCH

KEVEL

This is most practical for those with pirate-phobia, although it can be a useful tidbit aboard most vessels with bulwarks. As shown in the diagram, it has its own enclosed fairlead. To determine the size of the kevel to be made, one would be well advised to obtain a cast or spun hawse pipe fairlead first. Then, from 1″ stock, cut the kevel to the shape shown, being sure to leave at least 1″ around the hawse pipe.

For a typical 12″ kevel, the horns (past the point of fastening) should be 3″ long. Drill 3/8″ holes for mounting bolts. Bullnose all edges. To mount, cut vertical spacers from 1″ stock to fit snugly between the cap rail and the deck. If required by the cap rail overhang, taper the spacers to fit snugly. Bed the verticals in beads of caulking, set them in place, and, using the kevel as a pattern, drill the mounting holes. There is no need to fasten the verticals separately to the bulwark, for the kevel mounting bolts should be enough.

Mounting should be done with 3/8″ carriage bolts to minimize head exposure and, for the same reason, cap nuts should be used or nylon bushinged lock nuts. Any protruding bolt end should be trimmed flush with the nut with a hack saw.

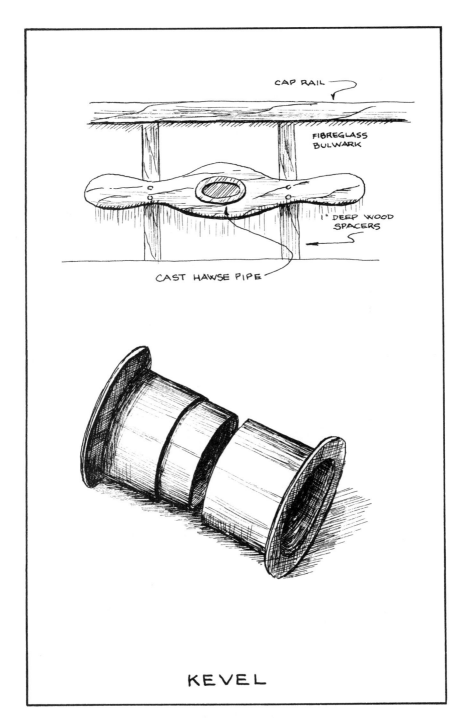

CAP RAIL

FIBREGLASS
BULWARK

1" DEEP WOOD
SPACERS

CAST HAWSE PIPE

KEVEL

WOOD CLEATS

Good wood cleats can last as long as bronze or alloy ones and are infinitely easier for the average sailor to fabricate. Cleats should be very hefty, made of oak or teak, and extremely well-rounded to avoid chafe at all points. The dimensions given in the diagram are for a 10″ long cleat. They can be adjusted proportionately for any cleat.

Draw the profile of the cleat onto a piece of 1¾″ stock, drill the 1/2″ holes to give a nice smooth bite, then cut out around the holes with a jig or band saw. Next, holding the cleat in a vise, drill the 3/8″ bolt holes. Bevel the sides on a table saw (see end view diagram), then settle down with a little shoe rasp and start forming, shaping, and rounding. Bullnose all edges and round the throat. Finish with sandpaper, then oil. Varnishing cleats that are used with any frequency is rather futile, since a line will eat the varnish off in little time.

When the cleat is finished, ascertain that the base is clean and even (as is the surface upon which it is to be installed), then, using the cleat holes as guides, drill the mounting surface, wipe it clean, then coat both the cleat and mounting surface with polysulfide bedding compound (squirt a little into the holes just to be sure), and then bolt it into place. The best underdeck reinforcement is, of course, a single steel plate with two holes. Lacking this, utilize the largest washers you can get your hands on. Use nylon bushinged lock nuts, or a dab of polysulfide on a common nut, to avoid its working loose. Check the nuts once a year just to be sure.

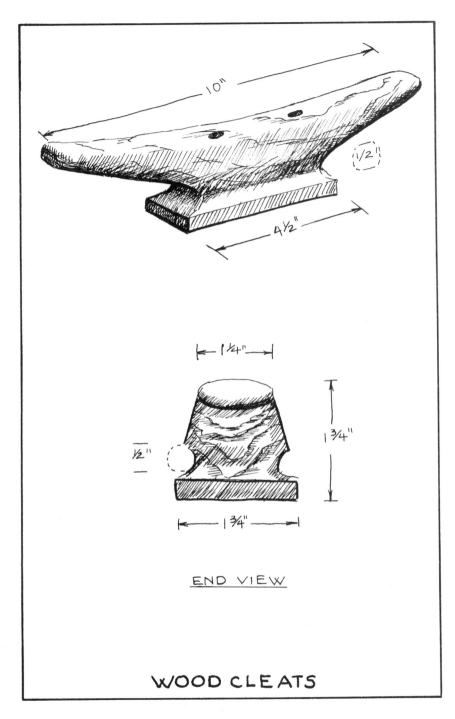

10"

½"

4½"

1¼"

½"

1¾"

1¾"

END VIEW

WOOD CLEATS

RECAULKING OLD TEAK DECKS

On mature yachts, the seam caulking of teak decks will have to be redone eventually. The manufacturers of "black death", Grove Caulking, suggest a thorough study of procedure before beginning.

Preparation

Old deck seams require careful preparation to achieve years of protection. The old caulking compound, which must be removed, may be hardened or gummy. In either case, it should be taken down to the cotton in a "V" seam, and to the wood in a rabbetted seam. All traces of the old material should be cleaned from seam edges as well.

For hundreds of years, shipwrights have used a variety of simple, handmade tools for removing seam compounds. In the amateur's hand, these "reefing" tools are far superior to power equipment for there is less chance of damaging adjacent wood surfaces.

The tail of an old file may be heated, bent at a 90° angle, and ground to sharpness along the edges to the shape of the seam (Diagram B) or an old, good quality steel screwdriver may be similarly adapted. Linoleum knives are often used also.

Bear down on the tool while pulling it toward yourself, working to the bottom of the seam in the process. After the bulk of old material has been thusly "reefed", the tool is carefully pulled along both seam edges to scrape away crusted material. This is important, as the new bond really starts in that area (Diagram C). Be sure all burrs and splinters along the seam edges are removed also. Sliding a rasp along the seam grooves does this easily.

Electric power tools can be adapted for seam reefing without too much difficulty. The face plate on a router or circular saw can be altered by drilling, tapping and inserting small studs of desired seam width, behind cutting bit or blade. By hand reefing a few inches, the blade and studs may then be inserted into groove. The blade then cuts out old material while the studs act as a guide. Considerable time may be saved by this method but more care must be exercised to avoid damage to planks. Hull seams can be reefed in this manner as well.

Carefully search lapped seams for wood deterioration and repair as necessary. Renew slack cotton caulking as necessary, but leave at least 1/4″ for the Deck Caulk. Check for loose plugs and renew as necessary. If refastening is needed, now is the time to do it. Seams

THE FINELY FITTED YACHT

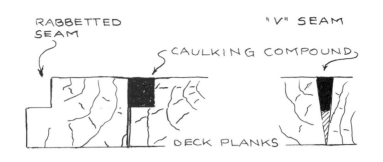

RABBETTED SEAM

"V" SEAM

CAULKING COMPOUND

DECK PLANKS

DIAGRAM A

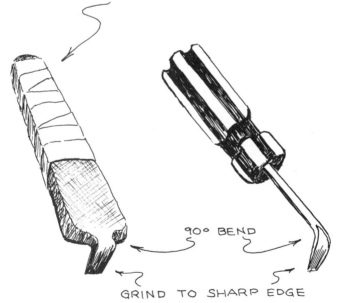

WRAP FILE WITH TAPE TO HOLD COMFORTABLY

90° BEND

GRIND TO SHARP EDGE

DIAGRAM B

RECAULKING OLD TEAK DECKS

should be thoroughly vacuumed to insure dust and debris-free surfaces. The worst is now over!

Caulking

Fill your cartridge and caulk the seams from the bottom up. Be sure to leave excess for sanding later (Diagram D). If decks will not be sanded, however, seams may be masked, then caulked. When applying to masked seams, leave a slight excess above the deck surface. Then, hold a putty knife almost horizontally and pull it along the filled seam with a slight downward pressure. This will allow a slight extrusion of material behind the blade so a slight convex surface will be left. This usually creates enough excess to compensate for minor shrinkage during the curing process. Deck Caulk starts its cure or "tacks up" quickly after application, permitting immediate removal of the masking tape. While masking and filling is satisfactory, the results will by no means approximate the "newness" you will have created by filling and sanding.

DIAGRAM C

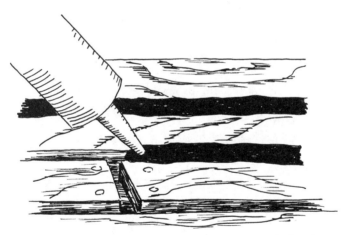

ALLOW CAULKING TO OVERFLOW

DIAGRAM D

RECAULKING OLD TEAK DECKS

DINGHY CHOCKS

The initial decision apart from "where" to stow the beastly dinghy is whether to stow it upside down or right side up. You may think that pondering this is a rather prosaic expenditure of time, but I assure you that the following considerations are of great value:

(a) Visibility — an upright dinghy is of course broader at the top; it therefore blocks out, on the average, about 30% of forward vision.

(b) Readiness — an upright dinghy is a most inviting stowage box collecting everything from fenders to apple cores, which require relocating before the dinghy can be used. Of course a beautifully fabricated cover will obviate this problem, but then time will be required to remove (and later put neatly back in place) the cover itself. The "upright" undeniably has the one advantage of not requiring flipping; an operation that is oftentimes awkward and strenuous.

(c) Protection — I've found the upside down dinghy on the foredeck of *Warm Rain* an invaluable friend. On rainy nights when portlights must be kept closed, the forepeak hatch, which is below the dinghy, can be left open to let in great quantities of fresh air. During rough days, the dinghy becomes a reassuring leaning place when headsails need to be changed. If you have a slow, manual windlass like we have, then you'll find the dinghy a lovely seat from which to contemplate the scenery while you relentlessly haul in 200 fathoms of chain. For the efficiency-minded sailor, the foredeck dinghy becomes a "sail weight," under which a headsail can be temporarily jammed while the other is being hanked into place. The removed sail can then be bagged after the new one is aloft.

A dinghy on the foredeck blocks a smaller area of your vision than a dinghy amidships, but it is of course more vulnerable to large headseas.

After pondering the above, the choice is obvious: all dinghies should be stored in torpedo tubes. If you haven't one on your current vessel, here's a dinghy chock to tide you over. I have always been a firm believer in simplicity, so I feel the one-piece chock in the illustration the most sensible.

Rough cut a 4″ wide piece of 1½″ teak, oak or mahogany to length, allowing 4″ to overhang the dinghy's bulwarks on either side. Lay it on the cabin top where it is to live, and scribe the cabin's crown onto it and cut. Scribe and cut the upper edge to match. Next put it back in place, and put the dinghy on top of it and mark in the

THE FINELY FITTED YACHT

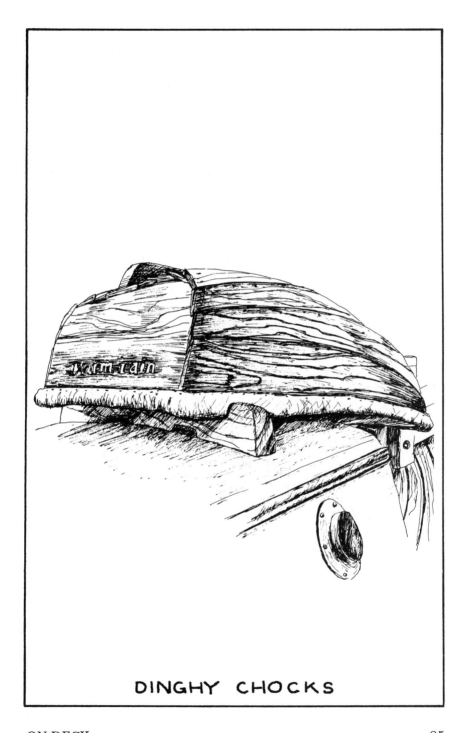

DINGHY CHOCKS

cutouts in which the dinghy will rest. Allow 1/4″ on either side, to make placement and removal easier, then cut to a depth of 1″. The inch will be enough to keep it snugly in place. On the lower side cut two drain spaces about 3/4″ deep and 3″ long. Bullnose all upper edges. Next, fit the bottom edge of the chock to the cabin top to perfection, then bed in polysulfide and, with two carriage bolts, bolt it to the cabin top as shown. On the forward face of the chock overhang, install a 3/8″ shaft padeye (diamond base will provide the best screw configuration for this application) to act as the aft tie downs for the hold-down straps. For fabrication of same, see "Canvas" section.

If your dinghy has a pram bow, and you're using the half-round rubber bumper along its bulwarks, you can bypass a forward chock and let the bow rest happily on the deck or bowsprit end. The chock and the hold-downs should prevent most fore and aft movement of the dinghy, but since you have a painter anyway, you may as well use it and tie it firmly to a samson post or bow cleat or something.

About a third of the way aft of the dingy's bow (or wherever they'll be most out of the way) install two eyebolts to act as bases for the forward ends of the hold-downs.

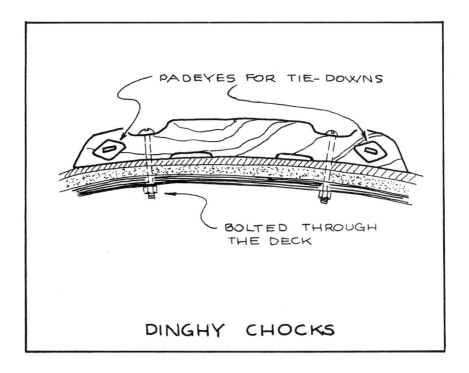

PADEYES FOR TIE- DOWNS

BOLTED THROUGH THE DECK

DINGHY CHOCKS

THE FINELY FITTED YACHT

TEAK DECKS

Teak decks are the epitome of decadence on a fiberglass boat, application or exclusion of which can be decided only after lengthy deliberation between you and your ego. I have always thought it would require a babbling moron to take a perfectly solid non-skid, waterproof and rot-proof fiberglass deck, spend $900 on teak and fasteners, then drill a thousand holes to hold the wood down, then spend $300 on caulking and bedding compounds to seal and waterproof the thousand holes he has just drilled.

Needless to say, we put teak decks on our boat at the expense of almost 200 hours of screamingly frustrating labor. But they are beautiful and they are non-skid and we do love them and I wouldn't trade them for a brand new Porsche . . . well, maybe a silver one. Here's how it's done.

Type Of Deck and Wood Selection

Try to pick the straightest, least knotty pieces of wood you can find. The longer, the better. If need be, shop around for long clean pieces. One of the worst jobs in doing the decks is butting ends together, so try to avoid too many joints. Knots look beautiful down below if oiled or varnished, but topsides they'll just weather and pop out, or if you are bending your planks, they'll surely snap in two at the knot.

If you do have to have joints, be sure to place them in the area of least curvature. Even if your planking is milled as narrow as an inch and three-quarter it will be almost impossible to bend the last foot of teak, so try to get your joints to stagger and try to put them amidship where the curvature of the deck is at its least.

Predetermine the width of the planking you intend to use. If you are running your decking straight fore and aft without bending, the width of your planks can be unlimited. Running them in this fashion is a traditional procedure and it is very simple to do, but only if your cabin sides themselves are uncurved or only slightly curved. If their curve is drastic, an attempt at straight decking can only result in a myriad of short, unsightly, slivery pieces. If you intend to have a curved deck with either a king plank or herringbone foredeck, using planking wider than two inches will lead to grave problems during bending unless the boat is of great length and very slight of beam. If it is, perhaps you could push the width of the decking to 2-3/8" or to 2½". I mention this tradeoff here because it's good to know your intended plank width before you buy your teak stock so that you will select only those widths which will lend themselves economically to your purpose.

The thickness of the stock should not fall below 3/4″. Anything thinner will be very difficult to plug as well as be more inclined to warp and crack with constant weathering. If the plug thickness ends up being less than 1/4″, the plug is guaranteed to crack and pop out before the year is over.

Milling

Whether you use straight decks or curved ones, you should mill a caulk groove into the edge of each plank. You will need this groove into which to pour polysulphide sealant after your deck is laid. The caulking not only seals the deck and keeps water from entering into the plywood core through the screw holes, but it also remains flexible to allow the decks to shrink and swell without causing the wood to buckle or crack. The caulking groove need not exceed 1/4″ X 1/4″. I have seen some teak decks without grooves, but I have never known how they survive. The grooves can be milled into the planks with either a dado or two cuts of a table saw.

Covering Boards

To determine the shape of the covering boards, you will have to scribe them to fit the cabin and/or your bulwarks. To be sure that you don't waste expensive teak, cut templates for each board out of 1/8″ thick veneer. The length and width of each board will be dictated by economy. The wider and longer you make your covering boards, the more scrap you will have. Boards 3½″ wide look wide enough to seem intentionally different from the 2″ planking and yet are narrow enough to be fairly economical. The length of each board will depend on how drastically curved your cabin sides or your bulwarks are. If they are curved as much as ours, the boards cannot economically exceed five feet.

Making and fitting covering boards will probably be the single most time-consuming task in your decking. They should be cut with a band saw (if one is not available a saber saw will do) out of wide planking. I managed to cut ours on a table saw; if you set your blade at a height barely sufficient to cut through your wood and no more, you will be able to do it too if you concentrate.

A side note: if you want teak decks, I think it practical to mill and lay them before you do any small projects. The amount of large scraps from milling the decks is phenomenal, and all this scrap can be utilized for corner trim, searails, etc.

If you have an extremely small radius at your cabin-side-to-deck or deck-to-bulwark turns, fitting the boards flush against the cabin or bulwark will be simple. If, however, you have a substantial radius, you must choose one of two alternatives. You can: a) begin your decking at a distance from the vertical side where the curve will have no consequence, or b) hand plane the bottom edge of the covering boards to accommodate the radius in the fiberglass. The joints for the covering boards can be made using any number of traditional scarfs. The structural integrity is virtually identical; thus, your choice will have to be based on taste alone.

Do not mill caulk grooves into the covering boards. For the long sides,you can use the groove in the first plank; as for the scarfs, it is preferred that you bed and screw the boards down in their final position first, then belatedly chisel in the grooves. This way, if your butting or alignment is not perfect (and they never will be even though the screw holes have been dry fitted), you will be able to cheat a little and chisel a nice parallel-sided caulk groove.

The King Plank

I am not sure that a single logical argument exists in favour of a king plank except that it is pretty. To do one is time consuming and painstaking. If you can get the pattern for it from someone with a sister ship you will be far ahead; but if not, you will spend many hours drawing in the lines and routing them out.

The fastest procedure involves laying the planks with roughly hacked off ends. The angle at the ends is irrelevant and the fit unimportant for the ends will later be overlapped by the king plank. Once the planks are all down, make a pattern out of thin veneer or cardboard for the king plank. The width of the plank and the angles you use will be of your own choosing. Cut out the king plank from a solid piece of teak, lay it over the deck, and draw its shape onto the over-long planks. Now take the router and set it exactly to the depth of your teak decking. If anything, leave it 1/32" shallower, because then you can easily penetrate the last bit of wood with an old chisel and remove the excess. This way you won't have your expensive router bit dulled by the fiberglass.

Now you can drop in your king plank and see how it fits. Don't worry about it being in perfect alignment. As long as your mistake is no greater than a sixteenth of an inch,you will be able to correct it when you rout in the caulking groove between the king plank and the other planks.

Herringboning

This method is less demanding. It is quicker than a king plank, because it involves only the first stage in laying the deck. You must use more caution, however, in scribing your angles on the end of each plank to make certain you don't wander too far off the centre line. But again, remember that a one-sixteenth or even a three-thirty-second mistake is allowable. You will then only have to rout in a centre line caulking-groove to notch out the mistakes and complete the job.

An absolutely vital note, whichever method you employ, is to have the straight bit for your router sharpened just before you start working on your teak decks. If you can get a carbide-tip bit, so much the better; whatever else you may have heard, teak is a brittle wood and prone to chipping if anything but the sharpest of tools is used.

Deck Laying

The first step in laying a deck should be shaping and fitting the covering boards. Dry fitting should include the placement of each board into its final position and putting at least a few screws into their final places.

When it seems you have done everything you can to make the covering boards fit perfectly, take out the screws you have just put in and lift up the covering boards. You will find little mounds of white fiberglass powder surrounding the mouth of every hole. Some of the powder will have stuck around the screw hole on the wood too. This powder must be wiped off completely or the board won't set evenly and may teeter over the little mound, eventually causing it to crack. This procedure of dry fitting and cleaning off the dust mounds should be observed with every teak-to-glass joining to guarantee better joints. Once the dust has cleared,you can permanently install the boards.

The first step in installation is to lay two unbroken beads of black polysulphide about one inch from either end of the plank onto the fiberglass. Many people have used Dolphinite as the bedding compound, but Dolphinite has the tendency to expand and ooze oil in very hot climates even a few months after laying. I've heard of some decks buckling because of the expansion. Even if buckling doesn't occur, the seam-caulking may be pushed away from the wood, allowing water to penetrate.

At any rate, lay down two beads of polysulphide, and just for safety, pop a drop into each screw hole. If you think that's being over-anxious, just try not doing it and see how you sleep at night. I

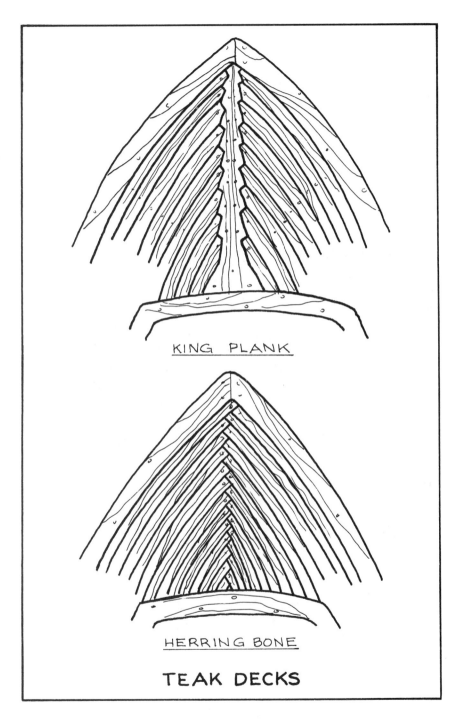

KING PLANK

HERRING BONE

TEAK DECKS

didn't do it originally, only to end up four days later taking every fastener out of the deck, screw by screw, and popping in a belated drop of sealer, then putting the screws back in. That's being over-anxious.

Once the covering boards are in their final place, the fun begins. Use your table saw to cut about ten pieces of 3/4″ thick by 4″ X 4″ plywood blocks. Now gather up all the oak, ash, and teak scraps you have and cut them into wedges ranging from 4″ X 10″ to 1/2″ X 5″.

The harder the wood you use, the better, because you will be smashing these blocks with a hammer and you will want the wedges to last as long as possible under this onslaught.

Wedging teak planking to form curves.

Next, establish the athwartship points where you will be putting screws into the planks. The screws should be no more than 12″ apart; if the bends are radical, use closer centres. At these 12 or whatever inch points draw a straight pencil line athwartships on the fiberglass. Nothing looks prettier than perfectly lined up plugs, and the pencil lines will help you prettify.

Now get your first plank, cut it to length, then take the 3/4″ ply blocks you have just cut and screw them into the deck 4″ or 5″ from the covering boards and about 12″ apart. Use one screw only and use it in the centre of the block so that the block can swivel when you insert different shaped wedges. Drive in this one screw deep, or the force of the wedges will cause the screw to bend, and it is almost impossible to pull a crippled screw out of fiberglass.

Now lay double seams of caulking down the length of the deck where the first plank will go. Spread it evenly and thickly. Be sure to put a bead right next to the covering board to seal the edges. Don't scrimp. It's easier to wipe off the mess that squeezes out than to try to fill the voids under a screwed down deck. Also, have a couple of rolls of paper towels ready along with a can of acetone to wipe the goo from your hands, tools, and your left ear lobe. Rags are passable, but too frequently, you'll end up wiping old goo onto your hands, instead of wiping the new goo off; so, use paper towels and throw them away. It's only money.

Now, summon the bulkiest friend you have and secure his loyalty for the next four days. You will need every ounce he carries. The longer his reach, the better.

With a screw gun and drill motor, some 1″ pan head sheet metal screws (remember flat heads split wood) and a couple of hammers, you will be set. You will also need about 30 tubes of polysulphide. Have them handy, for it's very ulcerizing to run out when you're raring to keep going.

Now, with the goo spread evenly and with the large friend hanging onto the other end of your plank, bend the plank and place it behind the blocks. Once it's down behind the blocks, don't ever take your weight off it. Be sure to hold down both ends and both centres, and tell chubby not to lose his balance or the plank will spring up like a steel coil and smash his face in.

Now comes the critical point. Insert wedges between each block and the plank; begin to tap each wedge gently and evenly, one tap each at a time. Give your helper a hammer too, but tell him to be gentle and never to take his weight off the plank. As the plank is stressed more and more, the more vital this constant pressure becomes, because the greater the tension,the greater the tendency of the plank to spring up and smash in the aforementioned face.

Be certain, also, that all wedges *advance* evenly. If one proceeds or lags behind the others by too much, the plank will crack and literally explode. Teak shatters in the most frightening fashion, taking its toll of skin and blood as it does. Try to keep the leading edge of the plank somewhat off the fiberglass. If the plank is squeezed down completely tight, you will be scraping off all of the preciously spread polysulphide; so, keep hammering gently until the plank is butted tight against the covering board.

Once in place, screw it down and screw it down tightly immediately. Drill your countersink holes about halfway through the 3/4″ plank. If you drill any less,you will not have a deep enough hole for your plug; as mentioned before, if the plug is less than 1/4″, it is guaranteed to crack and pop out very shortly.

If,by some chance,you hear a nasty cracking sound before you wedge the plank into place, don't start bashing in the nearest portlight in anguish. As a matter of fact don't even move. Take a bit of resorcinol glue (which you should have sitting around ready mixed) and pour it generously into the obviously cracked wood. Now hammer the wedges home and, as if nothing has happened, screw the plank into place. You may have to disturb the straight line of the plugs and put a couple of screws out of sequence to make sure the crack won't open up. Wipe off the excess resorcinol glue and try to forget about it. You may now get off the plank.

Move your blocks back about two inches, screw them down, and start the whole process over again. Some people advocate not cutting the planks to length until they are laid in their final place. This idea is probably very good, for then you won't have to worry about ending the planks in exactly the right location. While you are attempting to bend them,it's almost an impossibility anyway.

On the other hand, it's simple to set in a board, set it and screw it, then just whack the end off with a good sharp chisel. Use only the sharpest chisel or you will split the teak. Don't try to hack the whole end off in one oafish blow. Penetrate no more than 1/8″ per blow; then chisel out the groove and do the next vertical penetration. Don't use this chisel to go right to the fiberglass. Nothing can ruin a good chisel quicker than a few blows at a steel-hard deck. Have a duller chisel at hand to cut through the last 1/16″.

Other Things

There are a few problem items with teak decks, like nibbing, which I prefer to making wedges, where the sheer line no longer

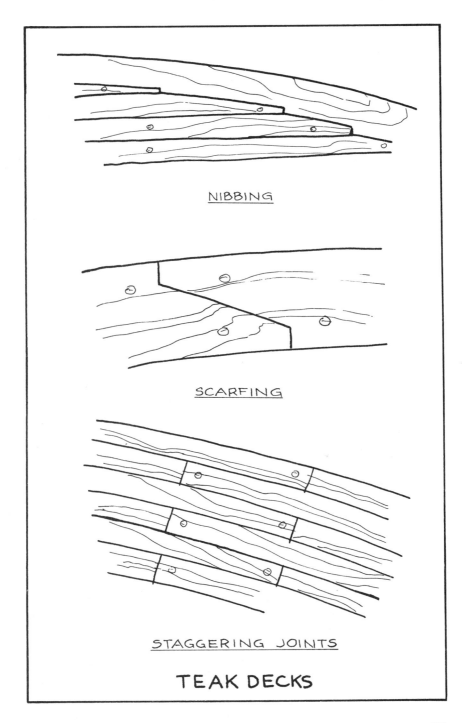

NIBBING

SCARFING

STAGGERING JOINTS

TEAK DECKS

parallels the cabin sides. Nibs can be angled and lengthened to taste. Other problems like corners, deck fills, cockpit trim, etc. are shown in the photographs.

Once you have finished laying the deck, the fun is just beginning. Your next job is to plug the 1,000 screw holes. Make sure you align grains of the plugs and tap them in good and deep. It is preferable to use a clear epoxy glue on the plugs instead of resorcinol, for resorcinol is a very dark red colour which leaves a very dark brown ring around the plug, no matter how great your care.

Now go back, and with a chisel whack off the tops of the plugs. Don't bother to get them flush at this time. Just get rid of the bulk, so that if someone kicks one, it won't break off and require replacement.

Caulking

Get the most powerful vacuum cleaner you can find and clean all the scrap and dust from the caulking grooves. Make sure you unlodge every piece of junk you find.

Now go shopping and take a lot of money. For a 30′ boat, you will need about three gallons of "Detco" two-part polysulphide. About 1/2 pint of hardener comes with each 3/4 gallon kit, and each 3/4 gallon kit costs about $65. You will also need to buy about 40 empty caulking cartridges, a quart of Detco teak primer, a gallon of acetone, and a lot of paper towels.

Caulk seams to overflowing.

The one item you may have difficulty finding is the empty cartridges. I did, and when I found them I was so happy that the atrocious price of 55¢ each (for an empty cartridge??!!) gave me heart failure for no more than 49 seconds. You will get used to highway robbery like this throughout your boating career. At any rate, secure about 40 of these tubes early and have them ready.

Now, using a small acid brush, primer all the immaculate caulking grooves thoroughly. Don't worry about getting primer on top of the teak deck itself. It will be sanded.

Caulk right away. To be economical time-wise, you will have to mix a gallon of caulking a a time. Mix in the catalyst thoroughly. This is a demanding task, because the polysulphide is as thick as tar. Fortunately, the catalyst is a light brown colour, so its path is easily traceable.

Stir the catalyst in completely, but *slowly*, or you will trap a jillion air bubbles which will stay in the thick caulking compound. They will be transferred and trapped in the caulking grooves only to pop when you are sanding the hardened caulking. Once you sand off the top of the bubble, you will be left with gaping holes which you will have to open, clean out, and fill with more "black death." To this end save a quarter of a gallon of polysulphide and a bit of hardener. You will need almost that much for repair work.

Don't be afraid to let the polysulphide fill the grooves to overflowing. When it hardens, it will shrink and settle. It is a lot easier to cut off the excess than to fill the voids. Once the poly has gone off, trim off the overflow rubber with a sharp chisel. Then get a belt sander and about four 50 grit sanding belts (anything finer will have its pores filled in no time) and grind the caulking right down to the wood. If you find any air holes in the seams, fill them now.

You will find if you curve your decks that the edges of some drastically curved planks will have a tendency to turn slightly upward, necessitating very extensive belt sanding to bring it to an even level. After you have leveled the deck with the 50, use the 80 grit paper to get out the cross-grain gouges, and finish off with 100. Then oil or let bleach or whatever you like.

You can see from the foregoing that laying a teak deck is not something you can leave for a dull Sunday afternoon. It does take time (as mentioned, approximately 160 hours) and quite a bit of money to do a satisfactory, lasting job. If you can afford it, by all means don't hesitate, for there are very few sights to a sailor quite as heartwarming and satisfying as the sight of a freshly scrubbed, bright teak deck. .... Anyway, it's probably the best non-skid you can find.

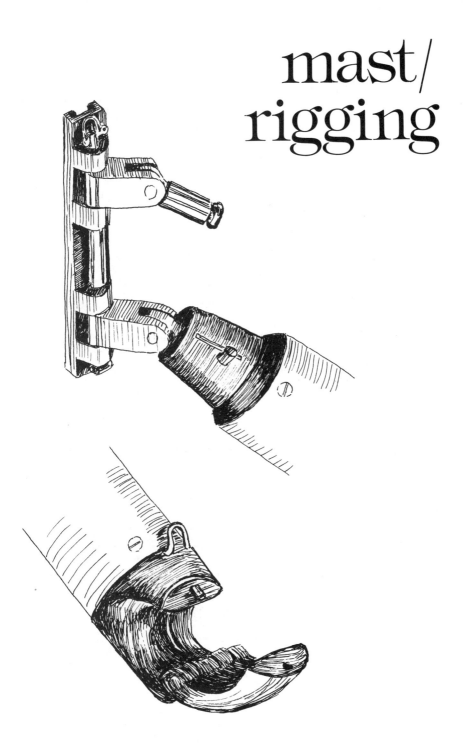

mast/
rigging

MAST STEPS

Personally, I think mast steps are a terrific thing, but only on other people's boats. I find that I have more than a sufficient number of things on my mast, as it is, to snag halyards. The old cast bronze steps one finds on some yachts seem to be the most harmless, offering little chance for a snag, but even less chance for a good footing. Since your feet literally perch on a tiny foothold, your knees automatically clutch the mast with all their might, so that by the time you reach the spreaders, gangrene will have devoured your lower limbs. The new stainless loop steps have the advantage of providing secure footing, but because they are cut from light gauge strapping, they cut into your hands so effectively that you are periodically tempted to let go, and let the corpse fall where it may.

The aluminum rungs are of the same basic design, but being cleverly extruded from tubular material, have the advantage of offering more surface and fewer sharp edges. So take your pick. Whichever you choose, be forewarned that the only thing harder than climbing mast steps, is installing them, unless you pull the mast and set up your little side-show on the dock. Dangling forlorn from the bosun's chair, trying desperately to drill true holes, then tap truer threads for machine screws, is not for the faint of heart. But if you must do it, drill and tap with great accuracy and care. Drill just barely through the mast wall, otherwise, you might be stripping the casing off wires within. Tap true, and use the shortest screws possible. If you can find 1/4" machine screws of about 3/8" length, terrific, for then you won't have about a hundred long bolt stems inside your mast for your wires to chafe against. In a wood mast, you will, of course, be using bronze or stainless steel wood screws. In either mast, the steps and screws must be thoroughly bedded in polysulfide or corrosion/rot will be a guaranteed result.

When measuring for steps, be as ascetic as possible; for the fewer holes, the less work; the fewer holes, the less weakening; and the fewer steps, the fewer snagged halyards. If you have average legs, one step every 14" (alternate sides of the mast) will be ample.

Before you drill the first hole, have a drink and think it over, then take the steps back to the chandlery, buy a good bosun's chair with the refund, and spend the rest on the ladies. *Sic transit gloria mundi.*

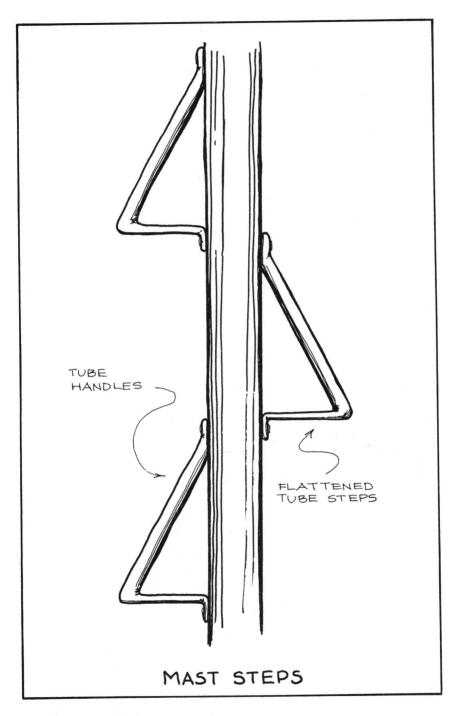

TUBE
HANDLES

FLATTENED
TUBE STEPS

MAST STEPS

THE PROPER MAST STEPS

Now that you've rested up after a night with the ladies, you are emotionally cleansed to the degree where you can undertake some serious mast step construction. Up to the spreaders, ratlines of rope should be installed, as described in that section. From the spreaders up, your new project begins.

To be succinct, it's a long and narrow rope ladder with 13/16″ teak rungs. A lovely advantage of this ladder is that it stows in a conservative amount of space, and since it is stowed, it's out of the way of halyards and wind. The flat steps make for relatively good footing, and the rope sides make for excellent hand holds. The ladder will be hoisted by a halyard to the masthead, and it will be held taut by having the lower end tied to the halyard's other end and it, in turn, made fast to a mast base cleat. As can be seen in the illustration, the rungs are cut to hug the mast and eliminate that leaf-on-the-vine feeling. The rungs should be patterned to fit the *foreward* part of the mast (unless you have cutter rig with an obtrusive forestay), for the most likely mast emergency requiring the ladder will involve the mainsail with a jammed or broken track, which will obstruct the sail and keep it from coming down. In such a case, a ladder fitted for the aft face of the mast would be of precious little value. If you do have a cutter rig, and have to run the ladder aft anyway, it would behoove you to attach a slide on every second step, and run the slides in the track for added security.

The line used for the sides should be 5/16″ three strand. It will be run on the aft, as well as the foreward, part of each side of each run for maximum stability. If only a single line were to be used on each side, the steps would pivot and make a nerve-wracking operation into an almost unbearable one.

The rungs should be cut 6″ deep and 6″ wide, with the wood grain running athwartships. I once had an acquaintance who tried to do otherwise, only to find his cedar rung split in half as soon as weight was applied. Radius all corners well, especially the pointed ones nearest the mast, to reduce any chance of splintering. A note on materials. Teak is the ideal wood to use, but since the ladder will be exposed to weather only infrequently, any good short-grained wood like ash, oak, or mahogany can be used. Do try to stay away from soft woods, like fir and cedar, for although they are lighter and less expensive, they tend to split as they dry with the years, and may cause a descent from the mast at a rather breathtaking speed.

Once the rungs are cut, mark your holes at least 3/4″ in from any edges, and drill a 1/8″ pilot. To prevent breaking out and

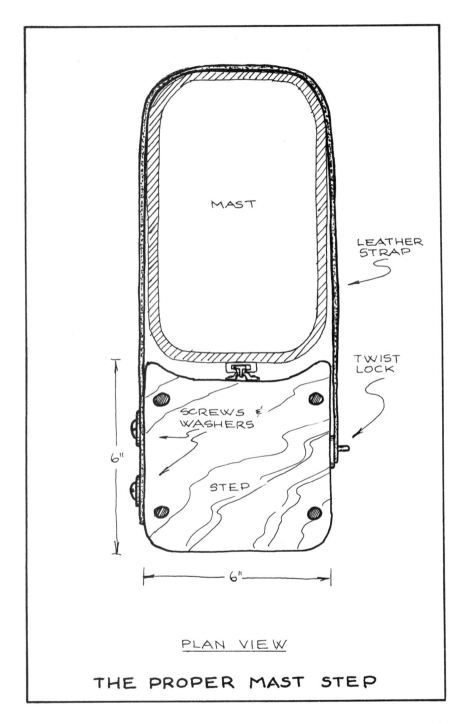

MAST

LEATHER
STRAP

TWIST
LOCK

SCREWS &
WASHERS

STEP

6"

6"

PLAN VIEW

THE PROPER MAST STEP

MAST AND RIGGING   103

splintering on the other side, drill with caution, especially when your drill bit is about to come through. To further prevent said splintering, drill your 5/16" hole from each side, meeting in the middle, then ream thoroughly to make sure no ridges are left within to cause chafe on the lines. Round the edges of the holes with sandpaper. Next, ascertain the total length of your ladder, and cut a single piece of line about four times that length plus a few feet for mistakes. Weave your line through a hole of the lowest run, then through a matching hole in the rung above, and so on. Above the top rung, leave a loop of two-foot length, and begin a descent of the rungs on the opposite side. If done properly, you will have four lines parallel, with crossovers under the bottom rung and in the two loops over the top rung. Only two knots will be utilized, thereby cutting the possibility of failure to a minimum. Both will be under the first rung, so if the knot fails, you will fall only half the height of the mast. Terrific consolation, yes?

Next, bring the two lines on one side (port or starboard) together, as close above and below each rung as possible, and secure them to each other with round seizings. See diagram. Do these seizings as if your life depended on them. Seize the tips of the two loops together above the last rung as well. In the bottom rung, through-bolt a swivel ring, with the ring beneath and countersunk nut on top. The downhaul end of the halyard will be attached to this.

Next, cut three lengths of 3/4" wide leather strapping, the length of which should be determined by measuring from the centre of a side of a rung, then around the mast, back to the centre of the other side. Fix one end of the strap to one side of the rung with two screws and finishing washers. On the other end, affix a metal loop for a twist lock. Fix the twist lock itself to the centre of the side of the rung, determining the exact position by holding the rung in place on the mast. Repeat this procedure with the centre and topmost rungs as well. The straps will be activated to hold the ladder firmly against the mast. Oh yes, don't forget to unsnap these on the way down.

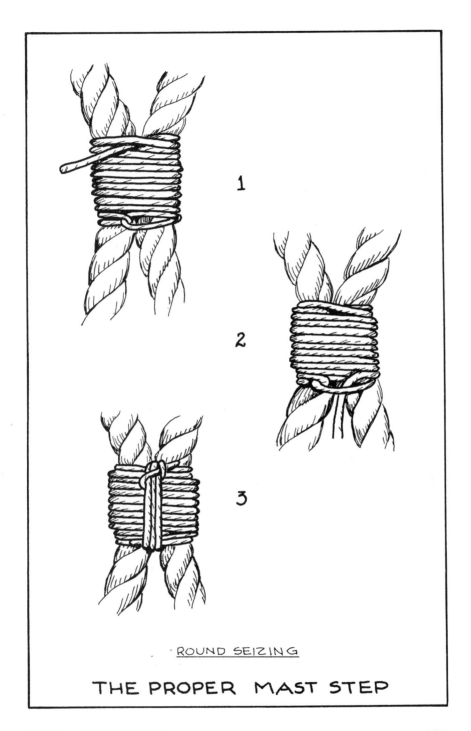

1

2

3

ROUND SEIZING

THE PROPER MAST STEP

RATLINES

I dislike mast steps for the reasons mentioned in that section, but ratlines have always appealed to me, first for their appearance and second for their usefulness. It is of course true that they will carry you only to the spreaders, but that to me seems a very nice spot to go, to look out for reefs, logs or rocks, or just to sit and relax and hug your favourite mast.

Wood Ratlines

These can be fabricated in much the same way as the rails for the in-shroud belaying pins, but of course the stock used can be scaled down to 13/16" laid on edge. One and one-half inch width will be plenty. A great problem with wood ratlines is that they protrude past the shrouds and chafe the mainsail on a run. Since they are also more difficult to make than rope ratlines, I see little reason for their use except that, because of their rigidity, they do add that feeling of security lacking in the limp ropes.

Rope Ratlines

Susan and Eric Hiscock have used theirs on *Wanderer IV* for some years, and feel that they have served very well with minimal maintenance.

The ratlines can be spaced anywhere from 12" to 18" apart depending on the length of your legs and your skill with seizing and splicing. If you're not very handy, make them as few and far between as possible. Three-strand rope will have to be used for the rungs so neat eyes can be spliced into their ends. Hervey Garret Smith advocates splicing the eyes so they barely meet the shrouds but some people prefer to make the rung somewhat longer to create a built-in sage in the rope to act as a safe "crotch" for the feet. Whichever you decide, splice all your eyes neatly, then using racking seizings, fix them to the shrouds.

When I discovered a black tarrish compound peeking out between the seizings, I asked Eric Hiscock if that was a special compound he used to prevent the rungs from slipping down. He said, "Quite." And his eyes sparkled mischievously. "Friction tape."

MAST AND RIGGING 107

SPREADER TIP GUARDS

Many people contend that because they don't own large head sails which sheet flat against spreader ends, they have no need for tip guards. Quite false. Sooner or later the main sail will make its way out there on a sloppy day with the boom well out, and it only has to happen once in a rolling sea and rip; a lovely new main sail goes back to the sailmakers. Many fine commercial tip guards are on the market, ranging from the old-fashioned "T" shaped wire hugger to the new above-the-spreader wheel. The former has many varieties, most of them having an identical flaw, that of pressing too tightly around a spreader creating a non-venting space where water settles and rots wood or corrodes aluminum. The wheel, on the other hand, sits above the spreader on a spacer, and although it looks rather unsightly, it does avoid the above-mentioned problem. But a pair costs about $15, which seems silly, because if you want something unsightly up there, you can use old tennis balls that are usually free. A more aesthetic, more economical solution exists. Small bits of sheepskin can be quickly cut and wrapped around the shroud above and below the spreaders. A scrap piece bought for about $3 will last for years on spreaders and other chafing areas. The one terrible drawback of sheepskin is that it creates the same rot and corrosion encouraging condition as the old rubber case, so care must be taken that they are kept away from the spreader itself, at all times. If they get soggy and filthy, they can be removed and replaced, using care to allow the spreader to vent.

In tropical areas with much rain, the greatest invention is still the wheel.

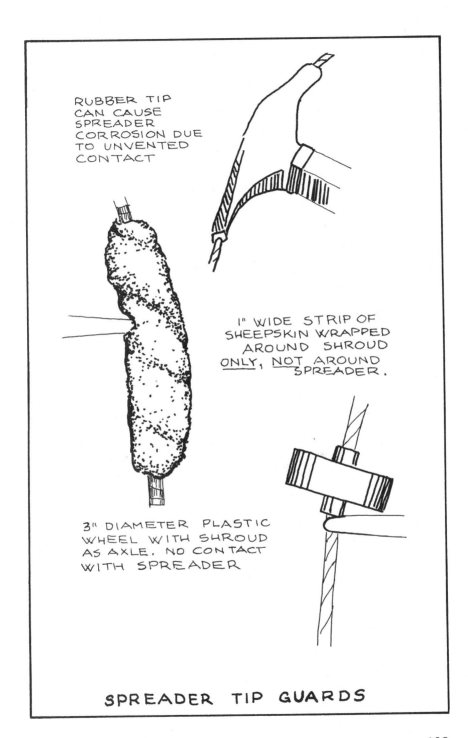

RUBBER TIP CAN CAUSE SPREADER CORROSION DUE TO UNVENTED CONTACT

1" WIDE STRIP OF SHEEPSKIN WRAPPED AROUND SHROUD ONLY, NOT AROUND SPREADER.

3" DIAMETER PLASTIC WHEEL WITH SHROUD AS AXLE. NO CONTACT WITH SPREADER

SPREADER TIP GUARDS

REACHING POLE

Far too often, far too many people end up using their engines in light breezes or rolling seas for lack of a reaching pole. The excuse given by most is the prohibitive cost of these beasts, and that is, of course, true, but only in a myopic sort of way. Now that diesel is edging its way to a dollar a gallon, a good pole would pay for itself in a couple of years, and just think of the pleasure you'll have had, the eardrums you'll have saved, and the vibrations you'll have avoided.

I shall try to avoid a lengthy discussion on end fittings, suffice it to say that in this case, the more expensive the better. Of inboard fittings, the best is a socket end which locks onto a mast toggle which, in turn, is attached to a mast car; the worst is Gertrude clutching the boat hook under her arm. A socket/car arrangement is about $150, whereas the hospital bill for Gertrude can be limitless. The socket pin is in all ways superior to the piston-lock, because the former can effortlessly swivel 360°, while the latter can bind and snap. Outboard ends range from $30 piston ends to the spring-jaw type racing end at $160. We bought the latter. I must have been out of my mind.

It is basically difficult to save money on the fittings, but about $60 can be saved on the extrusion for the pole. All kinds of raves are made about the quality of extrusions to justify the price of $100 for a 15' pole of 3½" diameter, when a similar piece of tubing can be bought from any major irrigation firm for about $1.50 a foot. The things to watch for are: even wall thickness and absolutely no dents or dimples. The following tube-diameter-to-tube-wall ratios should also be insisted upon: 1" to 2" tube — .065" wall; 2½" to 3" — .085" wall; 3½" and up — .125" wall. A couple of thousandths either way will change nothing. The tube must, of course, fit snugly onto the fitting so it is best to take the fittings with you when you buy the tube. Assembly is done with four 1/4" machine screws at either end. The holes will have to be tapped. Coat the end fittings with polysulfide or silicone to prevent water from settling in and causing rapid corrosion. If you have an internal trip line, a Harken wire block fitting will be needed about 18" from the inboard end of the pole. Now, wrap and tape your end fittings and hustle the pole down to an auto body shop and have it primered and painted your favourite epoxy colour. Then just settle back and watch that genny pull and listen to the silence.

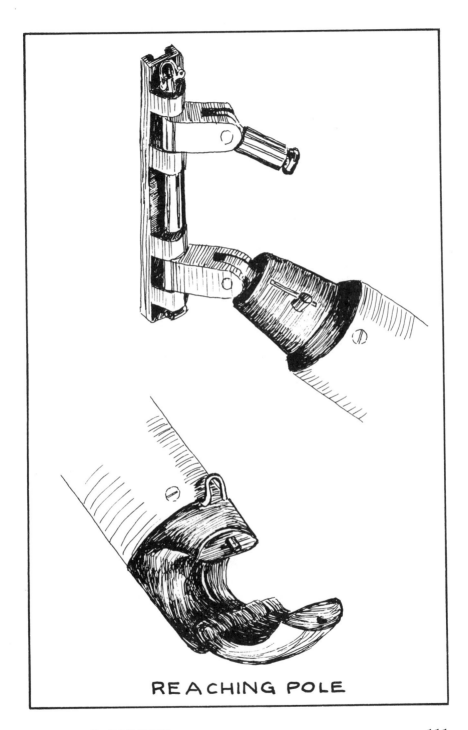

REACHING POLE

PIN RACK FOR MAST BASE

Apart from the fact that they remind you instantly of Captain Blood and pirates and parrots, and make you feel like you could be a kid again forever, I can't see a single good reason for having mast base pin racks. True, they are out of the way of sheets, unlike their shroud-mounted counterpart, but it is also true that, used in conjunction with a mast of any height, which according to somebody's law means halyards of at least twice the length, tensioning of the halyards will be almost impossible, so they will forever bang the mast.

Stock used should be 1″ for the rails and 1½″ for the uprights and pins. A 3″ width for the rail is adequate. When measuring for length (which, of course, depends on the dimensions of your mast), allow at least 2″ between the inboard edge of the rail and the mast. That, along with the extra clearance you'll gain from the narrower pins, will give you sufficient room for your knuckles to work around the lines. The rail ends will have to be lapped. Since most force on the rail will be upward, have the pieces aligned fore and aft, shorter on top than the ones aligned athwartships. This way you will not be pulling apart on the laminates, but rather pulling them together. If you can't quite follow the reasoning, don't worry about it, just do it. Use resorcinol glue and clamp them overnight. If you wish to fabricate fancy uprights, do it on a lathe, otherwise, just rip your 1½″ pieces to 1½″ squares (8″ in length will be plenty) and bullnose all edges with a 3/8″ bullnose. When your rails are set, bullnose them also, inside and out.

For size and kind of pins, see "Pin Rails in Shrouds." The one difference here is that the pins need not be fixed to the rails, and cast bronze pins can be freely used, since the rails are well inboard, considerably lessening the chances of a pin-overboard situation.

To affix the rack to the deck, you will have to drill an extremely straight 3/8″ hole down the center of each leg, at the allocated spot of each corner, as well as the deck. Use caulking on all joints and assemble with a length of 3/8″ all-thread and sizable washers and cap nuts, both above and belowdecks.

If you want to protect the edges, line them with a strip of brass as in photo.

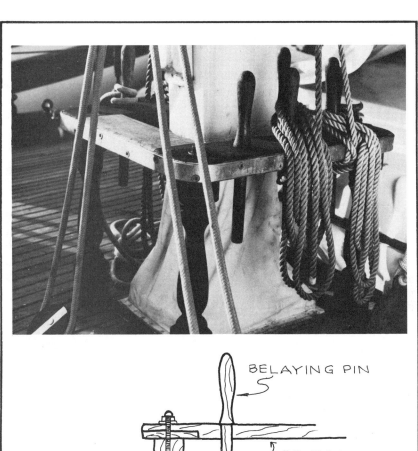

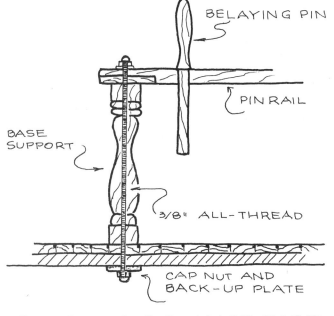

BELAYING PIN

PIN RAIL

BASE
SUPPORT

3/8" ALL-THREAD

CAP NUT AND
BACK-UP PLATE

PIN RACK FOR MAST BASE

MAST PULPITS

I am told that this is an essential piece of cruising equipment, without which one may fall overboard or worse. I have not been able to ascertain precisely what the "worse" could be, but it sounds comparable to a steady diet of gut-bomb burgers, so it must be avoided at all costs.

The one obviously positive feature of the contraption is that it makes for a perfect base for pinrails away from the standing rigging and pleasantly close to the mast where the most frequent need for them arises. It's a pretty looking piece of engineering,but one which will have to be fabricated almost entirely by a machine shop. The height should be designed to personal measurements, more specifically, the top should brace you half way up the back of the thighs for good balance and mobility, and still permit you to lean well back on a heel and use your weight to good advantage. The spread between the bases need be no more than 20″. One and one-half inch pipe should be utilized and bent from a single piece. A crossbar welded to two uprights would have two horrendously sharp corners resulting in charley horses the size of an average Clydesdale. Have 3″ diameter base plates with four 1/4″ holes in them welded onto the legs. Get a second set of these plates with matched mounting holes to use as backup plates belowdecks. Individual washers will not provide the strength of a single plate. About two-thirds from the bottom of the pulpit, have two 2″ X 2″ flanges welded. Upon these,you can mount the pinrails. For construction of these, please consult "Belaying Pin Rack." Bypassing the pinrails would be quite acceptable here, for the horizontal piece of the pipe could be used to secure the halyards, although tying and untying them would require a bit more time than using belaying pins.

Mounting the pulpit about 20″ outboard of the mast would seem a good compromise, allowing unhindered mobility, but still providing reassuring support. This last measurement is flexible with personal preference and should be decided upon only after a friend holds the boat hook behind your thighs and you go through your basic mast related eccentricities on different angles of heel.

MAST PULPITS

RADAR REFLECTOR

It's odd that so many people are willing to part with ten precious dollars for three hunks of aluminum with slits.

The cost for a piece of salvaged light gauge 12″ × 36″ aluminum should not run more than about 90¢. Nor is the project labor intensive. The two vertical pieces are identical, thus can be shaped at the same time by laying one on top the other. Use a couple of C-clamps or a vise to hold them together while fabricating.

You will find that you will need two side-by-side cuts to make the slits, but don't panic, remember aluminum is soft and the hacksaw blade in a saber saw will go through it as if it were butter. To remove the slit piece, simply bend it back and forth a few times; it will break off quite willingly. If you're fussy, clean up the crotch with a fine file.

Cutting the horizontal piece requires a bit more finesse, in that you'll have to drill a series of 1/8″ holes as close to each other as possible, then join them together by gently maneuvering the drill bit back and forth until it erodes the thin partitions. Now slip in your hacksaw blade and cut away.

Clean off all rough edges, then drill the four holes in each vertical plate — 1/8″ holes will do nicely. You will just be running light bits of wire through them to hold the pieces together.

The beauty of the thing is its stowability. By pulling out the bits of wire, the pieces can be collapsed and stowed anywhere. When needed, they can be assembled in a minute and run up to the spreaders on a burgee halyard. When doing this, one would do well to tie both top and bottom of the reflector to the halyard to make it as stable as possible. It sure beats yanking your pots and pans aloft in the fog.

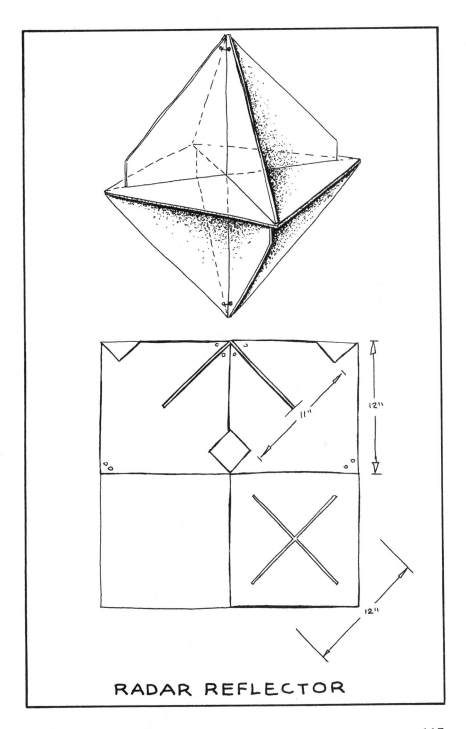

RADAR REFLECTOR

BAGGY WRINKLES

I'm not sure why baggy wrinkles carry as much connotation of romantic voyages as they do, but apart from this quite sufficient reason for their existence, they constitute some of the most functional chafing gear ever conceived. In their most limited use, they make perfect spreader ends where sails would otherwise become victims of stitch chafing and cloth tearing. On a larger scale application, four or five 10″ lengths spaced evenly over the upper half of the aft lower shroud will prevent general chafing when the main lies hard against a shroud on a run. It is true, of course, that the use of vangs can largely reduce the pumping action of the boom which comes upon every roll of a running yacht, but *largely* doesn't mean *completely*, and if the baggy wrinkles add only another year or two to the life of a main, I feel they have done their duty. A 400-square-foot main at $3.00 a foot buys a lot of bananas. Some people claim that baggy wrinkles cause too much windage aloft, but then, so does the mast and if you were to discard *it*, you'd have nothing to hold up your shrouds.

The best material to use is old synthetic ropes. Organic ones, like hemp, can be rather stiff and tend to retain moisture for an excessive period of time. The moisture has little bearing on chafe gear used on shrouds, but at the ends of spreaders, it can cause corrosion in aluminum and rot in wood.

Peel the old rope apart into individual strands and cut them into lengths of 3″ to 6″ depending on how baggy you like your wrinkles. Next, sit up on deck on a fine sunny day and halve a piece of 10′ line over a stanchion, tying the two loose ends behind you a few inches apart so your fingers will have room to work between them; then take an individual strand you've just cut and lay it under the two lines. Bring the two ends over and down in between them and slide the strand down within a few inches of the stanchion. Proceed in a similar fashion until you have finished the length you wanted, remembering that on a quarter-inch shroud, three to four feet are required to make up one foot of finished baggy wrinkle. Now, knot the two pieces of line. If you choose, you can trim the ends of the strands to even lengths, or be adventuresome and leave them rough. Now, wrap the baggy wrinkle around the shroud, strand ends out, and tie top and bottom with your leftover line.

They make beautiful silhouettes in the sunset.

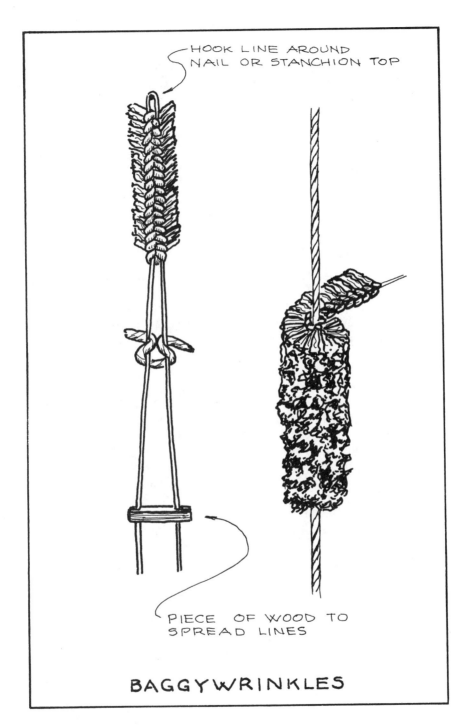

HOOK LINE AROUND
NAIL OR STANCHION TOP

PIECE OF WOOD TO
SPREAD LINES

BAGGYWRINKLES

VANGS

A skipper sailing his vessel on a run or a reach without the aid of a vang, is not only losing efficiency and chafing his sails unnecessarily, but in an active sea, he's begging for a scalping.

If a sail has slugs in its foot, the only equipment required will be a piece of rope, a place to tie it to, and a rubber snubber. The snubber I feel to be a mandatory part, for without it, unnecessary loading will be put upon the middle of the boom. On a violent roll, booms have been known to break because of poorly assembled and handled vangs, vangs that did not have a rubber snubber to absorb the shock of the crew's mistake. The snubber can be slipped through the slot between the sail and boom (see diagram), then the length of line run through its bronze loops, while the line's outboard end can be made fast to a padeye, eyebolt or stanchion base. *Warm Rain* has her stanchions bolted through the bulwarks with 3/8" carriage bolts so to facilitate a footing for the vang, we simply used a longer bolt and slipped a 1/4" thick stainless steel tang over its end, thus avoiding the need for additional holes in either deck or bulwark. To accelerate engagement and removal of the vang, the lower end of the line can be fitted with a snap shackle. The rubber snubber will usually yield sufficiently under manhandling so that the line will slack, enabling the shackle to be disengaged.

A problem does arise, however, when the crew sits back and enjoys the exhilaration of the run too much to notice the freshening of the wind. Attempts to disengage the vang will become difficult as knots tighten and lines strain. To prepare for such an occasion, *Warm Rain* has been fitted with a fine (and expensive) block system. The lower one is a becketed fiddle block with a cam cleat and built-in snap shackle, the upper is a single sheaved fiddle block with a snap shackle. With ample line and the cam cleat, very rapid adjustments and releases can be executed even by the least muscular of crews. To stow out of the way, the block is snap shackled to the foremost mainsheet boom bail and the line hauled tight.

On vessels with boltropes instead of slugs on the main, a boom bail will have to be fitted. Generally, a good location is six to eight feet aft of the mast. On all but the smallest of craft, a bail with a three-bolt hole pad should be used to lessen the possibility of its being torn out.

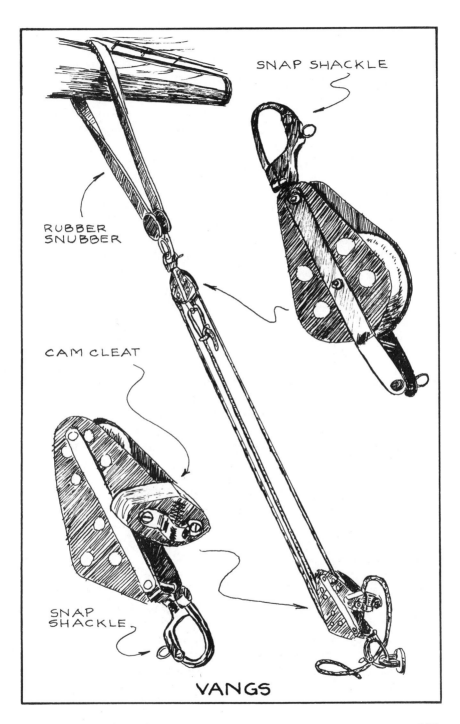

SNAP SHACKLE

RUBBER SNUBBER

CAM CLEAT

SNAP SHACKLE

VANGS

MAST AND RIGGING

MAINSHEET TRAVELLER BRIDGE

The overall trend in modern yachts has been to move the mainsheet traveller off the bridgedeck and onto the cabin top in the region of the main hatch. Although this method lacks the classic simplicity of its bridgedeck cousin, which usually consisted of a piece of aluminum or stainless track simply bolted through the deck, it does have some major points on its side. First, it removes the whole apparatus from the heavy traffic of the companionway mouth where the mainsheet forever tangles around arms and legs. Second, it makes fairleading to a winch quite simple. Indeed on a cutter, one can simply lead the sheet to the leeward staysail winch, although if the approach angle is too steep, jamming can easily occur. Third, because the arc travelled by the boom becomes smaller the closer you get to the mast, and because the traveller on the cabin top is at least 15″ higher thus much closer to the boom, considerably less line will be required to operate the traveller, although one will have to use a bit more muscle. Fourth and last, with a bridgedeck traveller, it's almost impossible to avoid mainsheet chafe on the aft cabin corners when the yacht is generously boomed out on a run. With the cabin top version this problem is averted.

But. You can't just take a piece of track and bolt it simple-mindedly through the cabin top, for quite often hatches and grabrails will be in the way, necessitating construction of a bridge. As you can see from the illustration, the fabrication of the bridge is fairly straightforward, involving only four blocks for support and a laminated span, but the difficulty arises in securing the bridge to the cabin top. More about that later.

First, establish the fore and aft location of the bridge, remembering that any distance less than 7′ from the average mast, will decrease your leverage to where tremendous forces will be acting on both bridge and gear. The most ideal positioning would of course be directly over a deck beam which would help distribute all forces over the entire width of the cabin top.

Second, establish the length of your bridge. In most instances a three to two ratio can be used as rule of thumb, i.e. at a point 7½′ from the mast, a 5′ track would be the maximum needed. Common sense factors like positioning between grabrails etc. should also be taken into consideration. Once the length has been determined, rip teak and mahogany, or teak and ash, or any decent hardwood for that matter into 1/2″ thick by 2½″ wide pieces. Your final product will be 2″ wide when finished, but the spilled glue, and some slippage

THE FINELY FITTED YACHT

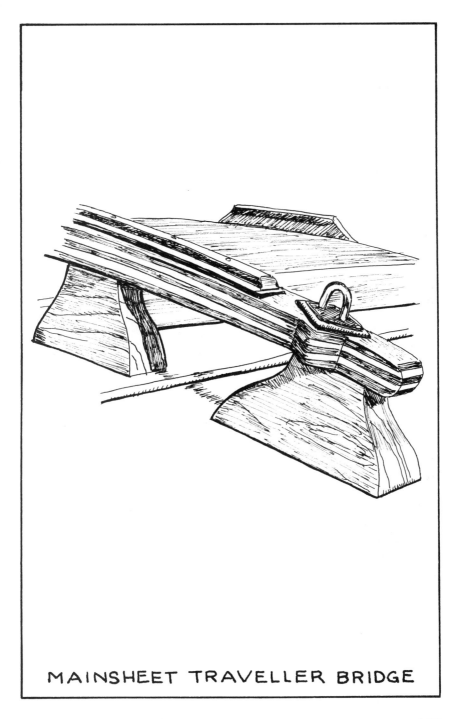

MAINSHEET TRAVELLER BRIDGE

MAST AND RIGGING

of the laminates during clamping, will require that you trim off 1/4″ on either side.

Next, determine the camber of the cabin top by running a horizontal string from one proposed end of the bridge to the other (points "X" on diagram) on the aft edge of the cabin, and measuring the two points "W" and "Y". Transpose those measurements to a workbench and cut blocks from scrap material, on top of which the laminates can be clamped (see illustration) to establish the proper curve. Use resorcinol glue and as many clamps as necessary to insure that all laminates make contact at all points. Let set overnight.

Meanwhile, cut at least four blocks to act as supports. Your blocks can be shaped to your personal taste, but remember that any variety of a truncated pyramid will provide much more stability than just a squared block of wood whose fore and aft dimensions simply equal that of the span itself. Since the blocks will be subject to much weathering and strain, teak would be the best choice for material.

When the resorcinol has set on the laminates, run them through the table saw to trim the fore-mentioned 1/4″ from each side, sand the edges lightly, and get the whole rig on deck. From below decks, drill through the deck beam that's to act as backup to the bridge as perpendicularily *to the beam* at that point as you can. Remember, that's right angles to the beam, not to the cabin sole or anything else. Drill a single 3/8″ hole for each block, then have a friend centre the blocks above each hole and drill again, this time right through the block, and, lastly, repeat with the span in place. Countersink the span to let in a 1½″ washer and the head of a bolt. Below decks the aesthetically cleanest thing to do would be to run a 1½″ wide brass strip (an 1/8″ thickness is ample) along the length of the deck beam and tighten the bolts down with bronze cap nuts.

Finally, the track can be installed on the span. Here you can either use 1¾″ #14 F.H. sheet metal screws or you can through-bolt. The latter is of course the more structurally sound thing to do.

Be sure to use ample bedding compound (Dolfinite is the easiest to clean up from teak) between the track and span.

A last word. If you use the flat genoa-track-type track, under no circumstances should you use plastic track ends. If the track car ever slides over with any power at all, the plastic end can shatter and the car can fly off the track. I'd like to see anyone sail a 40 footer in a blow with an ungeared mainsheet in his hand.

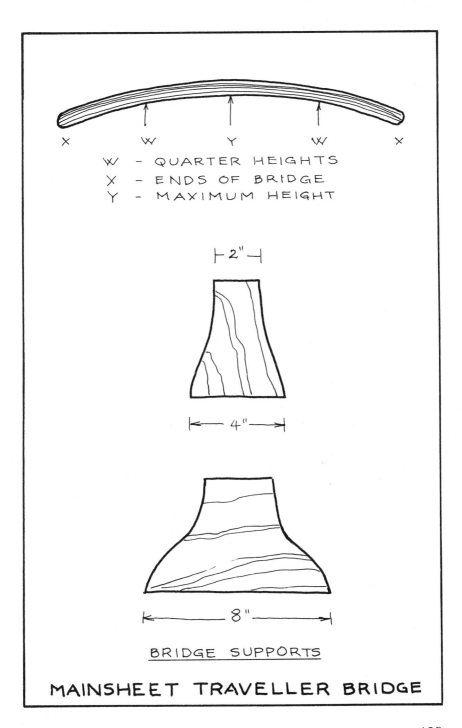

X   W   Y   W   X

W – QUARTER HEIGHTS
X – ENDS OF BRIDGE
Y – MAXIMUM HEIGHT

⊢ 2" ⊣

|← 4" →|

|← 8" →|

BRIDGE SUPPORTS

MAINSHEET TRAVELLER BRIDGE

IN-SHROUD PINRAILS

Aside from adding character to most yachts, pinrails provide marvelous places for stowing halyards. Carefully designed and fabricated, they can be of great value; shoddily assembled and mounted, they will endlessly foul sheets and nerves.

The size of your vessel (distance between lower shrouds) will determine the length of the rail, but simple general guidelines are available. The rail should fit between the shrouds 30″-35″ off the deck, depending on whether you're Mickey Rooney or John Wayne.

Use 1¾″ stock ripped to 3″ in width. This width should not be compromised, for every bit of it will be needed as mounting support. I'll explain later. The rail should overhang the shrouds, on either end, by 1½″. Cut a groove in each end to the exact thickness of your shroud, to a depth of 1½″, and no more. Perform this with two cuts of your bandsaw. To get the proper angle, clamp a piece of wood across the bandsaw table (in front of the blade) with two C-clamps. This piece will act as a fixed guide. That the ungrooved part of the rail be equal to the distance between the shrouds is mandatory, for it is this length of the rail that will keep it from riding upwards when tensioned by halyards.

Next, scribe and cut a curve from the bottom to the top of the rail at the point where the shroud runs through it. The scribed area should be shaped as in the diagram — very fine at the bottom and wider at the top. Near the top, it should incorporate the full 1½″ overhang of the rail. You are now ready for the pins.

For these, either wood or bronze can be used. If you can rustle up an old set of bronze ones, great; if not, a wood or metal shop can turn out a set for you. The number of pins to be used should be carefully contemplated. Pins should be set no less than 5″ apart, otherwise lines will foul and knuckles bruise. A good pinlength, of either material, is 8″-10″. The shank diameter should be 1/2″ for bronze and 3/4″ for wood.

The pins can be made to be either permanently fixed or removable. If removable, the base of the pin's grip should be clearly flared, to prevent the pin from wedging in the hole, inhibiting quick removal and line release, which is the only reason for having removable pins in the first place. If your pins are stationary (glued or side-screwed) the flaring is not important. One word on removable pins: as quick as they are to operate, as handy as they are for cracking nuts and skulls with, they do have a nasty habit of jumping overboard. Remember, bronze does *not* float!

THE FINELY FITTED YACHT

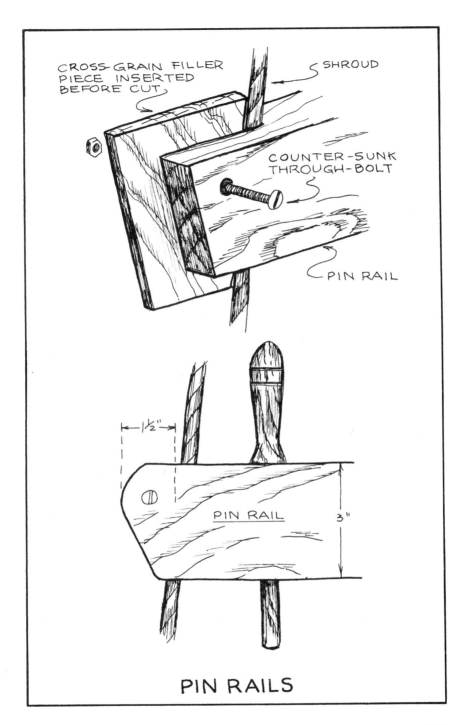

CROSS-GRAIN FILLER
PIECE INSERTED
BEFORE CUT

SHROUD

COUNTER-SUNK
THROUGH-BOLT

PIN RAIL

1½"

PIN RAIL

3"

PIN RAILS

Once you have drilled the holes for your pins, you will be ready to mount the rail. Fit it into place and insert into each slotted overhang a piece of wood (fitting very snugly), filling up the entire slot right to the shroud. This piece should run crossgrain to the rail to help prevent cracking or splitting. It should overhang the rail everywhere. Remove the piece, cover both its sides with resorcinol glue, and slip it back into place. Drill a 1/4″ hole through the center of the widest part of the overhang, countersink from both sides to a depth of about 1/4″, and through-bolt. When the glue has set, jigsaw off the excess stock. To make sure you don't nick the shrouds, slip a piece of tin between the shroud and excess wood to act as a stop.

You can, of course, follow a safer procedure by trimming *before* gluing, or even shaping, of the rail's end. To do this, rough-fit the rail and the filler, drill the 1/4″ hole, remove the rail from the shrouds, and fit the bolt to hold filler piece firmly in place. Now, shape the rail (with filler piece in it) with a jigsaw, on a nice solid surface, such as a work bench. Sand and detail, then reassemble, and glue and bolt into the shrouds.

Whichever way you did it, you're done. The rail will slip neither up, nor down.

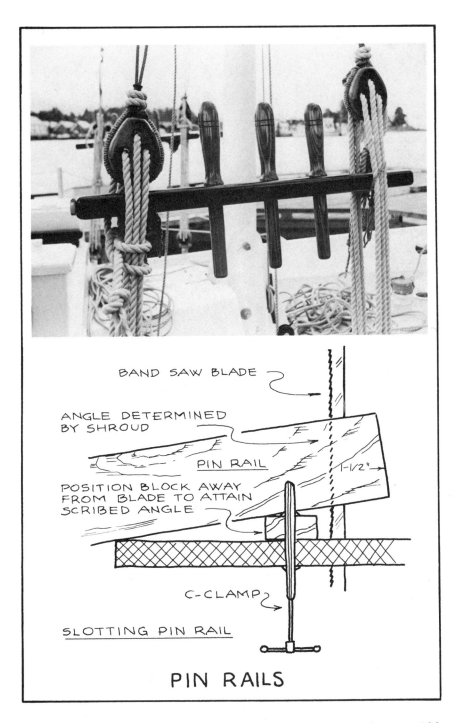

BAND SAW BLADE

ANGLE DETERMINED
BY SHROUD

PIN RAIL

POSITION BLOCK AWAY
FROM BLADE TO ATTAIN
SCRIBED ANGLE

1-1/2"

C-CLAMP

SLOTTING PIN RAIL

PIN RAILS

safety

BOATHOOKS

Much too frequently I have seen injuries to both yacht and limb for lack of a simple,but sturdy,boathook. In today's harbours, where the numbers of both vessels and half-wits is on an irreversible upsurge, a proper boathook should be considered a tool of basic self defense. The collapsible aluminum backscratchers have only one positive point in that they are light, so that when you're standing with smashed caprail and crumpled little boathook, you can take it and heave it a long long way.

Even sadder than crushed caprails are crushed hands and feet that have been thrust between yacht and piling, or yacht and yacht in last minute,helpless desperation. None of the above would have occurred had a good boathook been well used.

The Pole

The best poles are of spruce. Granted they are heavier than aluminum, but they do have two major advantages in that: a) when wet they are less slippery,and b) if dropped overboard they will not fill with water and sink as their aluminum counterparts some-times do.

The traditional diameter of 1¼" seems to be one easily handled by most hands. The length is another problem. We have on *Warm Rain* one that's just over 10' long,and I must say I have needed every inch of it plus some on numerous occasions, ranging from peeling kelp from the self steering vane, to taking accurate soundings in very shoal bays. Many will argue that a pole of such length and weight is unwieldly and impractical, but to those I say that most poles can be easily handled by anyone after a few practice runs. Everyone has man-overboard drills and abandon-ship drills, the need for which occurs much less frequently than maneuvering in close quarters, so why not have "half-wit abeam" drills as well.

The Tip

The ideal boathook tip, I feel, is one with a hook and a spike. The spike will get firm footing on wet rocks or slippery pilings, while the hook of course will grab mooring lines and fallen caps. The fear that a spike will gouge another boat's hull or brightwork can be eliminated if proper use of a pole is learned. Both the rigging and lifelines of most boats are very strong points and one can, with a bit of finesse,snare either in the crotch of the pole between the hook and the spike. Lifelines are especially handy, for the pole can be slipped along them as the vessel progresses.

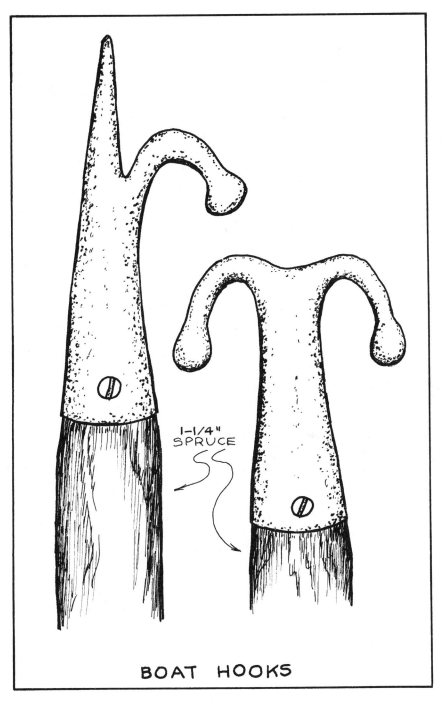

1-1/4"
SPRUCE

BOAT HOOKS

NAVIGATION LIGHT BOXES

A little bit of character doesn't hurt any yacht, and if it can be derived from a functional piece of equipment, so much the better. Wood navigation-light boxes can be made very easily, and, if well situated so they do not interfere with any running rigging, they can be a feast to the eyes for years to come. They have traditionally served as home to kerosene lamps, one green, one red, but they look just as good if any of a variety of handsome electrical fixtures are installed upon them. Traditionally, they were installed in the shrouds, but I feel that this is a somewhat treacherous location for they're in the way of genoa sheets. At any rate, a teak navigation-light box is the perfect thing to carry the yacht's name smartly engraved. Not only does this look handsome, but the light emanating from the lamps may just be enough to illuminate the yacht's name. Of what conceivable advantage that could be I'm hard pressed to imagine, but it sounds good.

Four-inch wide 13/16" teak stock is ample here. The sides and the ends can be cut to a 4" radius to reduce bulk and the look of severity. The bottom piece can be cut away drastically (see diagram) retaining bulk only aft, and that only to house the lamp. Butt the three pieces together and glue, screw and plug. If you had thoughts of carving the boat's name into the box, you would be wise to do so before assembly just to give your hands a bit more room to work.

I have seen very smart installations on bow pulpits (where wires can be run relatively inobtrusively along the pulpit frame) but the most imaginative implementation I've seen, was the incorporation of the light box into the base of a dorade vent (see diagram). This method obviates the need for the one long side, requiring only a narrow base and a back. The most convenient thing with this method is that the wires can be run out through the dorade box so they'll remain at all times hidden from sight and weather.

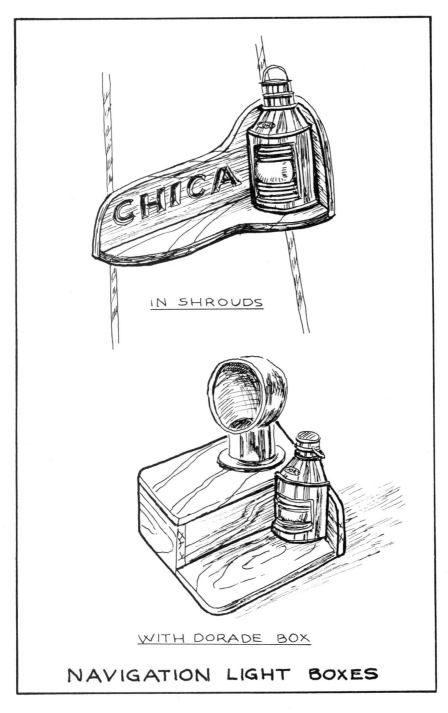

IN SHROUDS

WITH DORADE BOX

NAVIGATION LIGHT BOXES

BOW NETS

On most cruising boats, especially ones with bowsprits, bow nets are an almost indispensible item. They are a great help in keeping lowered headsails and headsail handlers out of the water. On *Warm Rain,* they also serve to hold in dinghy oars and boat hooks.

Some beautiful handcrafted nets have appeared over the years (*Warm Rain's* was fabricated by dear Candace in about three days), but the most utile, least expensive, and least time consuming nets are those cast away by fishboats. The very fine herring nets are, of course, of little or no use, but the old woven hemp and the newer acrylic nets with substantial strands, make perfect boat netting.

The cleanest method of installation utilizes a single line reeved, or really stitched, over the bow pulpit for the top, while a similar line can be reeved through small padeyes attached every 8″ or so to the sides of the bowsprit platform. This single line method enables one to remove the net with ease for washing, varnishing, etc.

Acrylic nets should be cut with a hot-knife to seal the strands and prevent them from unravelling.

Normally bow nets terminate at the first set of stanchions, but I've seen numerous cruisers with small children or dogs (sigh) run netting completely around their boats. If this procedure is to be followed, one must cut lead holes in the netting for genoa sheets. To avoid the tearing or chafing of the net, a frame of dacron tape should be sewn around the holes.

I have found bow nets most useful when used in combination with shock cords to hold down folded sails. The shock cord can be hooked into any loop of the net, hastening all foredeck activities by eliminating the need to search out and snare miniature padeyes hidden somewhere beneath 500 square feet of genoa.

Nets not only help to keep sails and people aboard, but they make dandy stowage places for oars and boathooks.

RUDDER STEP

This is beneficial only to vessels with aft hung rudders, but for them it is of such great value that it can be called *vital*. On a mundane level, it serves very well in replacing the boarding ladder which is, at the best of times, awkward to stow. It will not have the charm and comfort of a craftily made teak ladder, but it doesn't take ten hours to make either. The vital aspect comes in life saving. It's all fine and well to have magnificent life rings and man overboard poles and strobe lights, but getting the man back on board should be given some thought as well. Almost anyone can help himself to some degree given at least a footing of sorts, and it is exactly this footing that the rudder steps provide.

In its simplest form, it can be made from a teak block cut to a modified wedge shape, with the fore and aft parts beveled to reduce drag, and the outboard face cut to a wedge, to halve the possibility of it being torn off in case a stern plunges in heavy seas. Two through-bolts per step should be used for mounting. It is mandatory that the rudder be pre-drilled, cleaned, and the holes and the step sopped in polysulfide, otherwise headaches will forever be caused by leakage. Because salt water will tend to dry out the blocks, they should be well oiled at least twice a year.

As a substitute, the old bronze mast steps can be used, one on each side. When selecting them, care must be taken to choose the one that has the most holes, to reduce resistance as much as possible. Where you can find these nowadays is beyond me.

Whichever steps are utilized, one should be installed just above the boot stripe and the other about 14" higher.

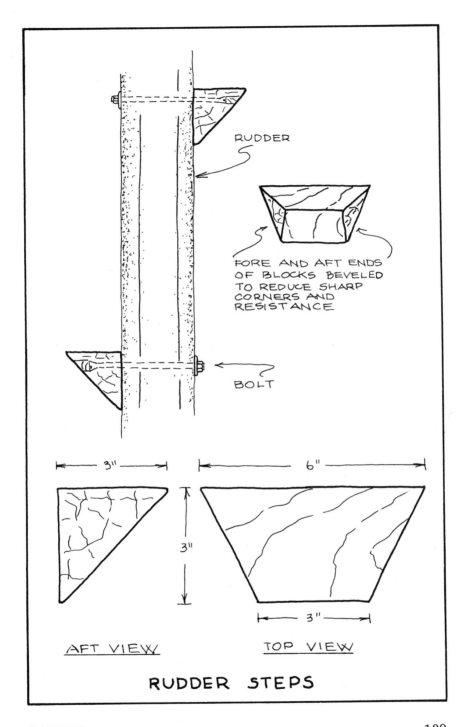

RUDDER

FORE AND AFT ENDS
OF BLOCKS BEVELED
TO REDUCE SHARP
CORNERS AND
RESISTANCE

BOLT

3"

6"

3"

3"

AFT VIEW

TOP VIEW

RUDDER STEPS

LIFE RAFT STOWAGE

A life raft should be totally accessible and quickly releasable. Its ideal location has always been a matter of debate, some advocating as a matter of primary importance, proximity to the cockpit, others, proximity to the stern, to keep it on deck in storms. Still others advocate keeping all areas around and above the raft completely clear to prevent the possibility of its wedging or entrapment when half inflated.

Wherever you do put it, think it out well, then proceed to secure it with the help of the following chocks:

From 13/16″ stock, cut four triangles with 3″ legs. Round all three corners to prevent splitting. Using one of these as patterns cut four "L's". The radius of the "L's" crotch should be determined by the corners of your life raft cannister. With resorcinol glue and 1″ #10 P.H.S.M. screws (drilled and inserted from the triangle into the "L" to obviate the need for plugging), assemble the two pieces as shown. Bullnose all upper edges. The triangles will serve to elevate the cannister off the deck, preventing accumulation of moisture and dirt beneath it.

Now, install the chocks with two screws each into the cabin top, not forgetting to use polysulfide generously for bedding. Plug the screwholes using resorcinol glue on your plugs.

Since the cannister will have about equal forces on it athwart-ships as fore and aft, a cross system of securing would be most advisable. Many cannisters come with hold-down gear. If yours doesn't, fabricate your own. This requires four 2½″ open padeyes, one on each side of the cannister. Mark the locations for the padeyes, and drill the screw holes and install the padeyes dry. Now, acquire good quality 2″ dacron strapping, and cut four pieces for straps. To determine the length, measure from the inside of the padeye to within 2″ of the center of the cannister. Add on twice four inches for the fold-under loops at each end. Now, for optimum strength, sew the folds in the pattern shown, leaving 1″ loops at either end. Slip a padeye through each loop, and screw the pads firmly onto the deck. You will notice a 4″ square space formed by the apparently short straps in the center of the cannister, and so it should be, for now you can run a 5/16″ lanyard through the loops to join them. Just pull the lanyard tight and make it fast with a perfect bowline. This will provide an instant, one-knot release.

Just pray that you'll never have to untie it.

Chocks can be large and bulky, as above, or just corners, as below.

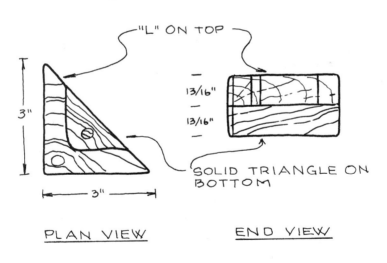

"L" ON TOP

3"

3"

13/16"

13/16"

SOLID TRIANGLE ON BOTTOM

PLAN VIEW

END VIEW

LIFE RAFT STOWAGE

MAN OVERBOARD POLE

The marine industry has a nasty habit of occasionally over-pricing items, and the man overboard pole seems to be a jewel in their high cost crown of lifesaving devices. It retailed, at time of writing, for about $90, which is somewhat prohibitive for a glorified fishing pole which can be made for a total cost of $10 and two hours work.

For the basic pole, use either a fine 10' bamboo pole or a hefty but cheap 1/2" ID CPVC pipe. CPVC is a hard, yet flexible, product used for indoor plumbing. It costs less than copper pipe and is available in lengths of 10' which is what's needed here, and comes in orange, beige and blue. Next, secure a block of rigid urethane foam about 4" X 4" X 12". Round the edges and corners neatly with a file to make them less fragile. For the tapered bamboo pole, measure the diameter of the pole two feet from the wide end and drill a vertical hole through the centre of the foam, having a diameter of 1/16" less than your newly acquired measurement. Slide the foam down from the thin end til it fits snugly. Next, using light fiberglass mat, bond over the whole foam and over a few inches of the pole directly above and below it. Be sure there are no leaks. Trim the ends of the wet mat on the pole with a razor blade before the resin sets. Paint it a bright non-gloss color. (Non-gloss will hide the flaws in the fiberglassing.)

Alternate flotation can be gotten from two float beads of cork or wood, the type that fishermen use on their nets. They may have to be reamed with a round file or drill to fit. Use 1/4" stainless steel bolts drilled through each float and the pole as well to hold the rig together.

Now for the counterweight. The bottom end of the pole must be heavily weighted to maintain verticality while in the water. Procure two pounds of lead shot from your local gun shop, and after having cleaned out the bottom 20"-25" of your bamboo pole with a long drill bit, or of your CPVC tube with an acetoned cloth and a stick, mix the shot into a batch of resin. Stir and stuff the mush into the pole. Fill it flush. A rubber end from a crutch makes a nice, safe cap.

For the top of the pole, sew and affix a red and yellow flag 12" square, red triangle top right, yellow triangle bottom left. This is the international signal for the letter "O" and "man overboard".

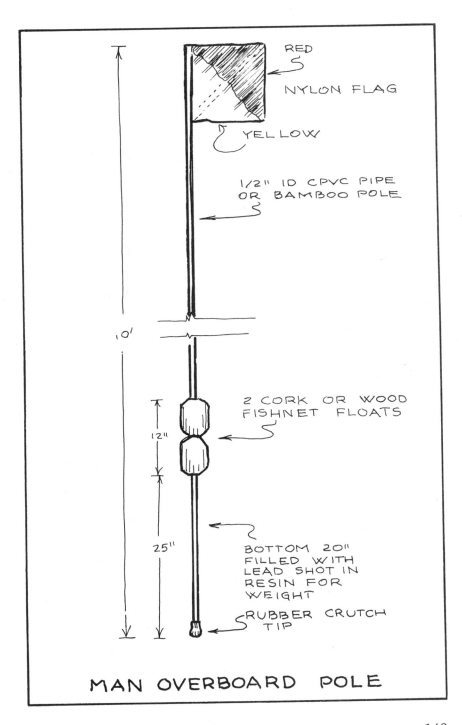

RED

NYLON FLAG

YELLOW

1/2" ID CPVC PIPE OR BAMBOO POLE

10'

2 CORK OR WOOD FISHNET FLOATS

12"

25"

BOTTOM 20" FILLED WITH LEAD SHOT IN RESIN FOR WEIGHT

RUBBER CRUTCH TIP

MAN OVERBOARD POLE

SAFETY

MAN OVERBOARD POLE STOWAGE

Whether the pole is purchased or self-fabricated, proper stowage arrangements must be made to make it readily accessible in case of emergency. Since most yachts, at most times, travel forward, leaving the person overboard behind, the aft section of the vessel makes for an ideal stowage area. To be more specific, the backstay with two small attachments makes for a very secure support.

The base of the pole can be rested in a length of white PVC tube of 10″ height that has a diameter large enough to allow for a quick draw. Some people advocate the use of metal flag pole fittings, but I find these a little too shallow to be relied upon. The tube can be fastened to the backstay with rope lashings top and bottom. To keep these from wandering about vertically, file deep notches in the areas which they are to occupy. Stainless steel hose clamps make adequate substitutes, but they do look rather unsanitary, reminding one of radiators and sewage pipes.

At the top end, a narrow sleeve of canvas will house the pole and protect the flag from the sun. A length of 16″ will suffice. To fabricate, cut a piece of canvas to 18″ × 8″, double fold all edges and hem. Fit snaps at 4″ intervals along the long edge, and one snap in the middle of the long end. This will be the top of the sleeve and will keep it from slithering down the backstay. Stitch 1″ of the top corner shut to keep the flag and pole inside, otherwise the flag will forever protrude and get sun bleached and ugly. Be sure the sleeve fits snugly, but not snugly enough to impede sliding the pole up the backstay, which is what you must do to remove it from the tube base.

Some yachtsmen prefer having the pole slung into brackets or hung from snapped canvas straps from the lifelines. This often results in unscheduled man overboard pole overboard practices, which is not at all a bad idea since very few people have adequate manners to fall overboard at the properly scheduled times anyway.

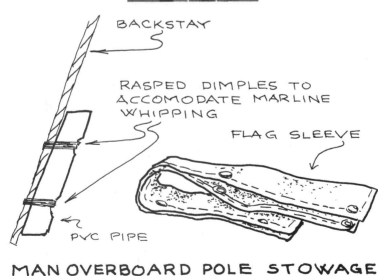

BACKSTAY

RASPED DIMPLES TO
ACCOMODATE MARLINE
WHIPPING

FLAG SLEEVE

PVC PIPE

MAN OVERBOARD POLE STOWAGE

MAN OVERBOARD SYSTEM

The advent of Hank Searl's novel *Overboard* emptied chandlery shelves of most safety systems and probably just as well, for with a little patience and ingenuity, one can duplicate a system which retails for $250 for about $90. The two items too difficult to build at home are the strobe light and the whistle. I have doubts whether one can produce the horseshoe buoy for any less than they sell for on sale (about $25), but everything else can be done by even the clumsiest among us.

The Strobe Light

I dislike absolute remarks, but consensus has it that the most functional and reliable distress strobe light is the ACR model 565. This is a self-activating unit which is stored upside down, righted immediately as it hits the water by its own counterweight, and activated by gravity, i.e. the battery's own weight causes contact. It puts out about 250,000 peak lumens per flash which is visible for about 15 miles on a clear night. It operates on the one battery non-stop for about 40 hours and costs about $1.40 per hour. Not a bad rate for saving a life.

The Overboard Pole

A good size overboard pole with flag is another integral part of the system. It can be constructed at a cost of about $10. (See "Overboard Pole" for details.) If built to a proper length of 11 to 15 feet and equipped with the prescribed flag, it can be seen at great distances from the deck of a boat in all but the wildest seas, long after the head of the swimmer has become invisible.

Dye Marker

A small plastic bottle of highly concentrated fluorescent dye (available at commercial art stores) should be tied to the buoy. There's no need to get excessive and weigh down the thing with a five gallon jerry can, for one pint will cover a tremendous area that will catch and reflect sun and searchlights from a goodly distance. How you wash it out of your sock I just don't know. Sealed plastic bags of it made to navy specs are available at most surplus stores.

Horseshoe Buoy

As mentioned, these are hard to beat for value. They are made of dense closed-cell (waterproof) foam core with a vinyl plastic cover,

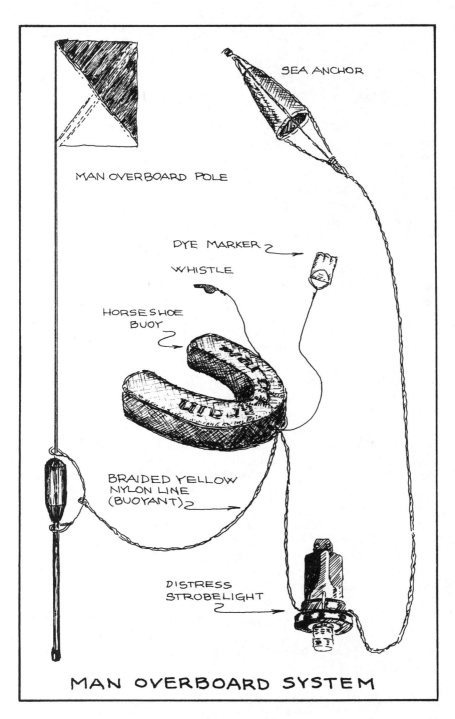

SEA ANCHOR

MAN OVERBOARD POLE

DYE MARKER

WHISTLE

HORSESHOE
BUOY

BRAIDED YELLOW
NYLON LINE
(BUOYANT)

DISTRESS
STROBELIGHT

MAN OVERBOARD SYSTEM

zippers, etc. They are U.S. Coast Guard approved and should be aboard.

Plastic Whistles

If the strobe fails and the fog is too dense to see the flag or dye, a plastic whistle might just be enough to attract attention. Since sound travels extremely well over water even in fog, this little 90¢ item might be one of the most important pieces of the whole rig.

Drogue

Once the fallen crew member is out of sight of the boat, he can easily become permanently lost because even though the crew marked course and time perfectly, by the time they return, the wind could have blown the entire rig of buoy and pole completely out of reach of the man. A small drogue of about 12″ diameter, made from scrap nylon (spinnaker material) and attached to the rest of the system, will prevent such costly drift.

Quick Launcher

Speed is of utmost importance in ocean rescue, as aptly demonstrated by an experience Candace had on a voyage from Hawaii to Newport Beach. As they sat forlornly with sails slapping and sun beating down in the Pacific High, Candace decided it was time for a swim. The boat seemed to be almost at a standstill, so over Candace went, big splash and all, and by the time she surfaced, the line trailing from stern was way out of reach, and after a bit of thrashing and a few shouts, the boat disappeared silently behind the huge Pacific swells, and there was ol' Candace, all alone, treading water, with four miles of ocean beneath her. Only some very quick action by the crew and a man in the spreaders brought dear Candace back aboard. Even the finest and most complete man-overboard system is completely useless if it's perched pertly on the yacht's stern, while the fallen crew bobs helplessly in the sunset.

To contain most of the gear aboard and then launch it quickly with the pull of a single lanyard, a canvas (or acrilan) case made to match your sail covers, etc. should be sewn (see Canvas section). And finally, to keep all the goodies from drifting all over the sea, a length of buoyant nylon line (discussions rage on whether this should be short, 30′, or long, 75′) should tie them all into a single chain so if the man overboard manages to grab anything at all, he'll have access to the whole thing.

BOWSPRIT PLATFORM

One hears endless tirades attacking old-fashioned ideas like bowsprits, terming them unnecessary, dangerous, and an extra expense when paying dock fees. Perhaps all that is true,but bowsprits do make room for large headsails on small boats, and they also evoke something akin to romantic thoughts, and the only real hindrance I find they have is that unless accompanied by a platform and pulpit, their presence will inhibit the use of sails. Off the coast of British Columbia, where islands dot the sea for 300 miles and beautiful anchorages abound, short 10-15 mile daily adventures are most desirable. But I have too often seen sailboats motoring along in a fine breeze, because the crew felt it too much of a task to unfurl their sails. This reasoning comes too frequently from yachtsmen with unprotected bowsprits. Doing a balancing act on a 5″ radius beam is no one's idea of relaxation, but I advocate not removal of bowsprits, but addition of platforms and pulpits.

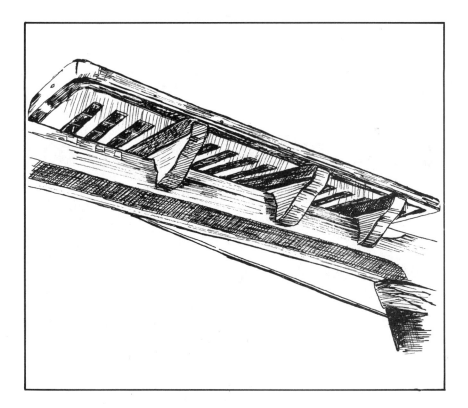

Two basic design theorems should be followed: make the platform strong, and make the platform light. The weight and solid surface should be as little as possible, for some platforms, once buried in a wave, never do come out alive. A grate-like solution seems to be the best. Simpler than grates are parallel teak slats 1½ " X 2" on edge, with spacers between (see photo). They should be resorcinol glued and screwed to each other. Space the screws four to six inches apart. Just gluing and clamping are enough, if that's what you prefer, since the whole platform will be through-bolted onto the bowsprit. These through-bolts will provide more than the necessary strength to hold the pieces together.

The overall width need be no more than 6" on either side for adequate foot support. The platforms will have to be wider if you plan to have them house anchor rollers, but even then one additional 2" piece on the outside will do nicely. The ideal method of attachment is using 1/2" or 3/8" all-thread every 24". This, of course, is run through from side to side, right through the bowsprit, and, hence, requires some very exact long distance drilling. Countersink spaces for lock nuts on either end. Bullnose all edges and round corners.

Beats tight-sprit walking all to hell, doesn't it?

Full grate platform.

Twin stemmed platform (A-frame) eliminates whisker stays.

Warm Rain's platform built from slats.

SAFETY HARNESS

For any offshore or serious coastal cruising, safety harnesses are mandatory, unless your fondest wish has always been to undertake a serious career as shark bait.

An attempt should be made to fabricate your own safety harness, for then, not only will you know how it is assembled, but you can also design it to your own measurements and needs. For the hardware, have a look at the best safety harness money can buy, and buy fittings at least as good.

The belt is the most important part of the harness. It has to be strong, for the line keeping you aboard will be attached to it, and it has to be wide, so the pressure will be well distributed over your back, instead of cutting viciously into vertebrae. Use heavy 2″ seatbelt material and, for extra stiffness, wrap it with two layers of heavy, but soft, dacron to make up a width of 3″. Cut the dacron so its ends come within 4″ of each other in the front (measure this while you're wearing a shirt and sweater to get a medium fit, somewhere between all out foul weather gear and bare skin). Have the seatbelt overlap itself by at least 16″, hanging past the dacron 8″ at one end and 12″ on the other.

Run a couple rows of stitching over the dacron ends to avoid fraying. Next, sew your buckle onto the 8″ free belt, folding the belt back over itself to house the buckle, as in the diagram. Of course, various buckles can be substituted; just be sure they're all brass or stainless, and not plated steel.

Now, using 1″ dacron tape, make up the shoulder pieces. Sew the long piece to the back and sew a short piece (with an adjusting buckle) to the front, just inside the dacron end, as shown. Try to determine what length of shoulder straps you'll be using so you won't have to have yards of tape trailing about. Cross the shoulder pieces in the back and sew them together to keep them from slipping off your shoulders.

Lastly, splice a 5′ length of braid to the triangular fitting, as in the diagram, and fit the line's other end to the best damn stainless snap hook you can buy — one that has at least 1,500 pounds breaking strength.

Two small points to make life easier: a) use different colour dacron wrapping for the belt for every member of the crew, so he can readily grab his own harness, made and adjusted to his own needs, and b) splice two braids with snap hooks to your fitting instead of one. This way, if you're clipped into, say, the lifelines, and you have to move about on deck, when you come to something like a stanchion, where you have to unclip to make progress, you can clip the spare snap hook to the next part of the lifeline past the stanchion, before you unclip the first one. Too many people with single snap hooks have fallen overboard just as they were making this transition.

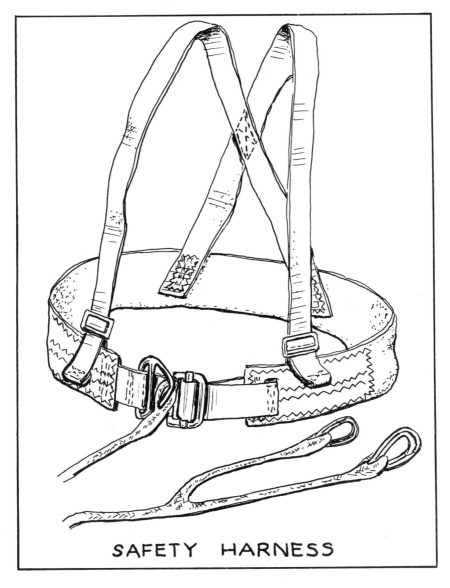

SAFETY HARNESS

ground
tackle

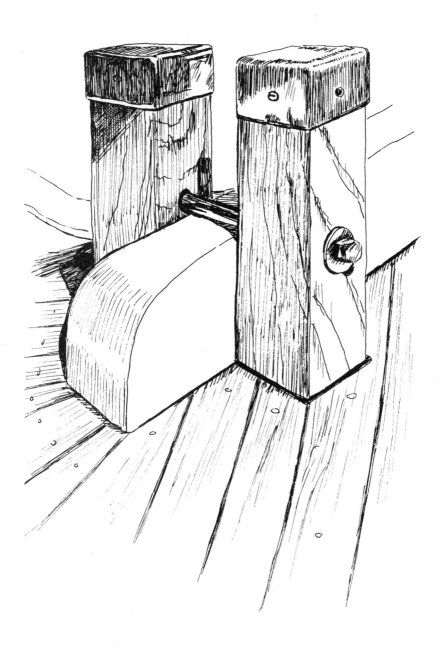

CHAIN PIPES

In many yachts, the mistake is made of leading chain directly through the deck pipe and stowing it immediately below in the bow. This is all fine if one's ground tackle consists of a 20 pound danforth and some line, but when one begins to use 200' or so of 5/16" chain, the weight quickly nears 220 pounds. If this can be lead aft even only two feet, 440' pounds of bow plunging, nose burying energy will have been moved, and that is well worth the effort on any yacht.

The way to achieve this is to lead the chain out of the chain locker aft beneath the V-berth in the fore peak. Most vessels have good space here for both line and chain.

The materials needed here, available from any plumber, consist of 4"diameter PVC pipe and some fittings. The 4" pipe is advisable because large eyes and shackles are often used and often these tangle and wedge themselves in small spaces. A PVC flange, one that can facilitate screws, will secure the pipe to the underdeck while a 45° elbow will take care of the bend and feeding through the bulkhead. The length of pipe should be such that the pipe outlet will come through the bulkhead as high beneath the V-berth and as far aft as possible. This measure is necessary to maximize the amount of space available for the chain beneath the pipe, for it can then drop merrily and stow itself without need for a guiding hand in the form of a crew in the forepeak.

Attach the deck fitting to the vertical pipe and then screw the fitting to underdeck. A 6" X 6" X 1¾" mahogany block should be fitted, screwed and glued onto the bulkhead where the pipe will come through. Drill the pilot hole from fore to aft at the desired angle in the bulkhead and block, and follow that with a 4½" hole saw. Insert pipe into the hole and cut it to the correct length and angle. Glue the elbow to both pieces of pipe. Screw the lower portion of the pipe to the block. If you wish to lead the chain farther aft, use another coupling and add on the desired length of pipe. Try to have the pipe outlet in the middle of the stowage area. If all chain is to be used, that is, no coil of rope will exist to provide bedding for the chain, thought should be given to lining wood or glass hulls with a webbed nylon padding to avoid direct chafe from cascading chain.

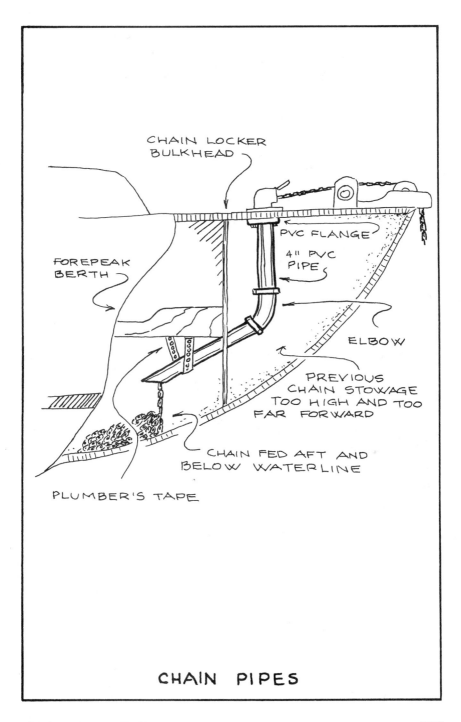

CHAIN LOCKER
BULKHEAD

PVC FLANGE

4" PVC
PIPE

FOREPEAK
BERTH

ELBOW

PREVIOUS
CHAIN STOWAGE
TOO HIGH AND TOO
FAR FORWARD

CHAIN FED AFT AND
BELOW WATERLINE

PLUMBER'S TAPE

CHAIN PIPES

DOCK LINES

I never cease to be amazed by the lack of reverence most people exhibit toward their dock lines. They are, after all, the yacht's only contact with dry land, and if well handled, they can assure most of us that our vessel will be found in roughly the same place some days hence, instead of having drifted off into or under something heavy. Although dock lines seem to be undemanding bits of rope, they do require at least minimal courtesies like proper handling and stowage.

No dock lines should be used without chafe guards. These can be made with a simple piece of leather of very substantial weight and sewn on wherever the line is in constant contact with hawse pipes or fair leads. They should be stitched on tightly and affixed to the line with two through stitches at either end. Make the chafe guards at least 8″ long to allow for variation of onboard attachment. Dock lines, as any lines on a proper yacht, should be whipped. Whipping is an extremely pleasant pastime, resulting in beautiful bits of craftsmanship in exchange for little effort.

The longest lasting and one of the most decorative whippings is the Palm and Needle Whip:

Cut a length of yarn and, using a regular sailing needle, anchor one end to the boat with two stitches. Lay on a number of turns snugly, then "thrust the needle through the middle of a strand and then worm the whipping back to the left side and thrust the needle through the next strand beyond. Now pull the twine up tightly and worm it back to the right side of the whipping, thrust the needle to the next strand and pull tight. Finally worm back to the left side again and again stitch through the strand and tighten." So says Hervey Garrett Smith, and he ought to know.

The stowage of dock lines on many vessels is a disgrace. They are heaved into dinghies, lashed onto dogs, or thrown into the lazarette among oily cans and dripping diesel containers, then hurriedly jerked and yanked out as the boat roars up to the dock. Sacrilege. Dock lines are the simplest things to stow. On the foredeck, they can be left on a samson post and coiled beautifully out of the way, while on the aft, they can remain on the mooring cleat and be coiled as well and used as a sitting pad, if one is lacking. In either case, they will be ready, obviating the need for stuffing the dog into the ice box while his leash is being used to lash the boat to the wharf.

THE FINELY FITTED YACHT

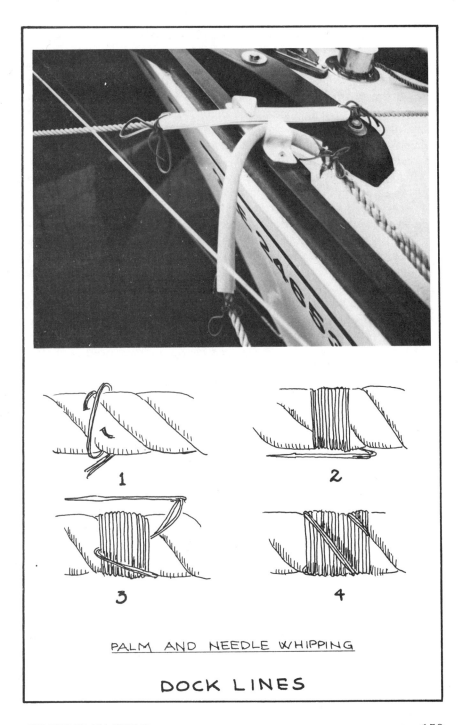

PALM AND NEEDLE WHIPPING

DOCK LINES

STERN ANCHOR CHAIN STOWAGE

Almost everyone accepts the need for stern anchor gear, but few people actually make a serious attempt to design and build proper stowage for it. Having chain and rope heaved into the bottom of the lazarette, with an avalanche of old paint cans and Hibachis and teddy bears atop it, is lunacy, when with very little forethought and minimal effort, accessible and safe stowage can be constructed.

Warm Rain, as most yachts, had a bottomless pit of a lazarette, holding everything and yielding nothing. As a first step, a shelf was built at about half depth and attached with the help of cleat stock to the lazarette bulkhead, and bonded with fiberglass mat and cloth tape to the hull. A tapered opening was cut into the bulkhead below the shelf, leaving 4" of the bulkhead intact on the sides and 15" on the bottom. We felt the hole necessary to inspect the chain or untangle it, if it was somehow caught below. A simple door was fabricated to fit over the hole to keep the chain from attacking the engine in rough seas. It was installed with a piano hinge at its bottom, and kept closed with the two brass tension snaps you see in the photo. The hull was lined with a piece of plastic cushioning, the kind people put over their rugs to save them from wear. This was installed because I didn't fancy the thought of the chain cascading down and grinding away the fiberglass. Next, a length of 3" plastic sewer pipe (the erudite call it PVC) was purchased, its length just sufficient to reach from the top of the lazarette hatch coaming to the bottom of the lazarette shelf. A hole was cut in the shelf, with a hole saw, to accommodate the pipe. It was placed into a corner of the lazarette coaming and secured to it by means of two 1" pan-head sheet metal screws. The coaming around was lined with very thin brass sheeting. All this is much easier than installing a deck pipe, especially if there is no room to accommodate one.

On the caprail, a bronze fairlead was installed, after the caprail surrounding it was also lined with the brass sheeting. A small Danforth stern anchor was stowed in the lazarette, made fast to the chain, and we lived happily ever after.

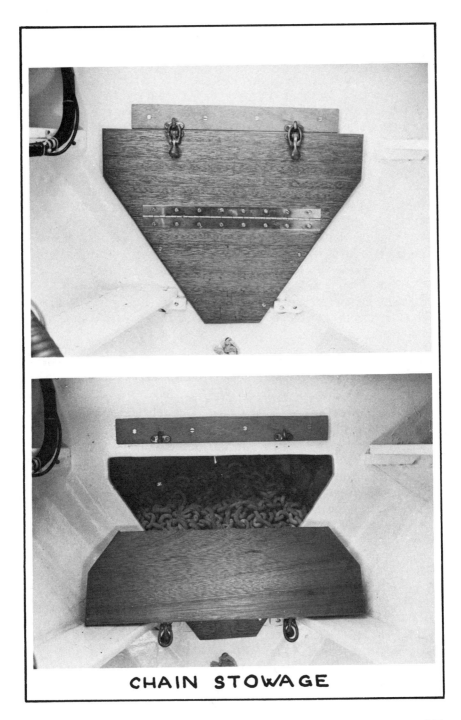

CHAIN STOWAGE

ANCHOR ROLLERS

I am endlessly amazed by people who come into anchorages, lift their anchor off the deck and dangle it over the side, scratching glossy paint or chipping gelcoat, all for want of a proper anchor roller. On any vessel with a bowsprit, the lack of an anchor roller is inexcusable, because installing one can be accomplished by the drilling of a single bolt. On other vessels where caprails and stem fittings must be designed around, the undertaking takes on larger, though not insurmountable, proportions.

Generally speaking, the ideal roller will be as large as conveniently possible. Large link chain simply snaps over small rollers, resulting in difficult chain hauling and a lot of noise. Care must be taken that the roller's jaws not be too narrow, or constant chain and rode jamming will occur. In recent years, the synthetic delrin rollers have endeared themselves to yachtsmen. They need no lubrication as their brass or stainless counterparts frequently do, but more importantly, they are almost noise free which the most considerate feel an important factor, especially if frequent late evening anchoring is the norm.

Attention should be paid to the height of the roller's shoulder, for too low a shoulder will often let the chain or line ride off and jam mercilessly in the most undesirable places.

On vessels without bowsprits, the problem is magnified by the fact that it's impossible to fit a large diameter wheel anywhere for lack of available support. Here, the major function of the roller must be to protect the topsides while the chain is being paid out, after which one must transfer the anchor rode into a substantial fairlead in which the rode can spend the night.

The location of such rollers should be close to the stem, otherwise, the shifting vessel will frequently override the rode and cause considerable chafe across the bow. I see no reason why the roller cannot be just off the centreline, giving only adequate clearance past the headstay fittings. A better idea is to have a roller on either side of the fitting, each being a specialist for either rope or chain. If you're lacking a windlass, the installation of a pawl will greatly facilitate hauling the anchor by holding, or more correctly, trapping the chain as it comes aboard.

If you steadfastly refuse to install a roller, would you at least please consent to a skookum fairlead so the next time you come into an anchorage, I won't have to turn away in horror while your caprail is viciously mulched by your chain.

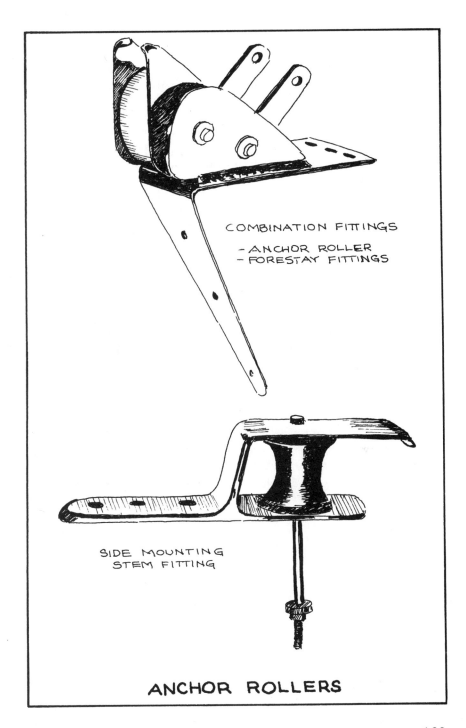

COMBINATION FITTINGS

- ANCHOR ROLLER
- FORESTAY FITTINGS

SIDE MOUNTING
STEM FITTING

ANCHOR ROLLERS

GROUND TACKLE

SAMSON POST

Far too often, one hears about a magnanimous gesture by a fellow sailor turning into a most embarrassing disaster that could have been avoided by the installation of a proper samson post for towing. Vessels under tow have had, for lack of a proper fitting, head stay stems, mooring cleats, and stanchions torn out when these were used as towing gear. The following bitt can be safely used on yachts up to seven tons if fabricated as shown and installed as suggested.

The heart of the bitt is a 1/4″ steel plate about 12″ square or tapered, if need be, to fit into the bow. Welded to this should be a 1/2″ plate about 4″ wide and 7″ high forming an upright, with arms protruding about 3″ on either side. A 3/4″ stainless rod can be used here welded to the top of the upright. The ends should be well rounded to minimize torn Achilles tendons.

Oak cheeks milled from 1½″ stock and cut with dimples, as shown, to accommodate heavy lines, should be fixed to either side of the upright. An oak cap from 13/16″ stock should be fitted over the cheeks to minimize weathering of exposed endgrain.

The base plate should be drilled with four 3/8″ holes in the corners for mounting. A 16″-square 1/8″ plate should be fitted below decks for support. If there is any doubt regarding the integrity of the foredeck, the entire foredeck surface belowdecks should be faced with 1/2″ plywood sandwiched between the deck and the back-up plate. The base plate must, of course, be bedded before being seated. Use polysulphide, and use it in the bolt holes as well, to prevent any possibility of moisture seeping into the deck bringing about dry-rot.

Of course, you should hope and pray that your rudder will never break, steering will never fail, and you won't have to be towed, but if doom does come, you won't have to get your boat torn apart while being rescued.

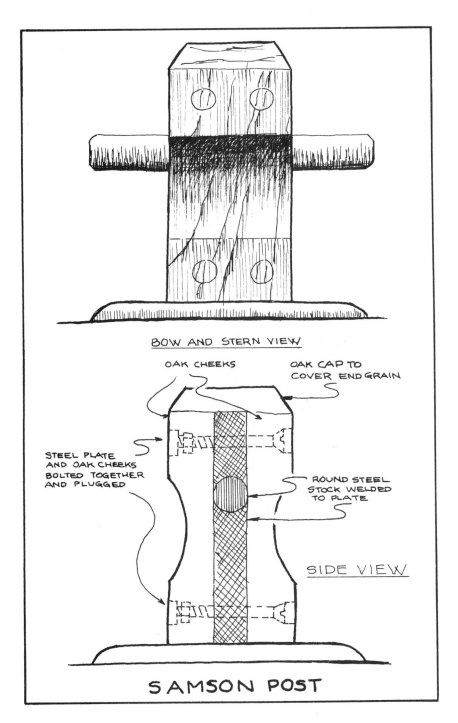

BOW AND STERN VIEW

OAK CHEEKS

OAK CAP TO COVER END GRAIN

STEEL PLATE AND OAK CHEEKS BOLTED TOGETHER AND PLUGGED

ROUND STEEL STOCK WELDED TO PLATE

SIDE VIEW

SAMSON POST

ALL-WOOD TOW BITT

If you have no aversion to cutting a hole in your foredeck, a single piece, all-wood, mooring bitt may be a nicer fitting to use than the metal/wood combination. For boats under five tons, a 3″ × 3″ piece of white oak is sufficient; for boats five to ten tons, 4″ × 4″ is fine; up to 15 tons use 6″ × 6″; over 15 tons get a stump. The above deck height can vary from 6″ to 12″ while below decks you'll go right to the hull.

First fabricate your partner as shown. The thickness of the partner will be determined by: a) the strength of your deck, and b) the displacement of your vessel. With an average deck strength, the best rule is to start with 1/2″ thickness of plywood for up to three tons, and add 1/4″ for each additional three tons. Whatever your thickness, the location of the bitt must be aft of the 2′ beam mark to provide for a partner of sufficient surface. Bond and screw it into place.

Next, form your bitt as shown, then measure for the deck hole to be cut, and cut it with the drilled hole and saber saw method. Do this very exactly. The snugger the fit, the better the hold. Next, rout a 1/4″ × 1/4″ groove around the hole for sealant. Slip the bitt into the hole, go below and establish its exact vertical location and mark the exact position of the base of the bitt accordingly. You will now have to fabricate two low bulkheads — 8″ to 12″ high is plenty — one directly forward and one directly aft of the bitt. Don't scrimp. Use 1″ plywood. Scribe these and fit them, then bond them into place. Double bond each bulkhead forward and aft with two layers of 6″ mat tape and one layer of 8″ cloth. To be sure you won't need any wedges you would do well to screw the bulkheads to the bitt temporarily. For wood boats the task is of course easier, for an existing floor can be reinforced by a step (see diagram) eliminating complicated bulkhead construction. Whether bulkhead or floor is used the bitt must be bolted to it for strength. Use 3/8″ to 1/2″ bolts with the largest washers you can find. Drill the bitt head for a Norman pin of 1/2″ diameter and round off the pin's ends with a file.

To protect the bitt, fit a fine gauge sheet of brass over its top and 1″ down the sides. Caulk beneath it and tack it in place.

If you've followed the above steps your bitt will never tear out; your boat might tear in half but the bitt will be okay.

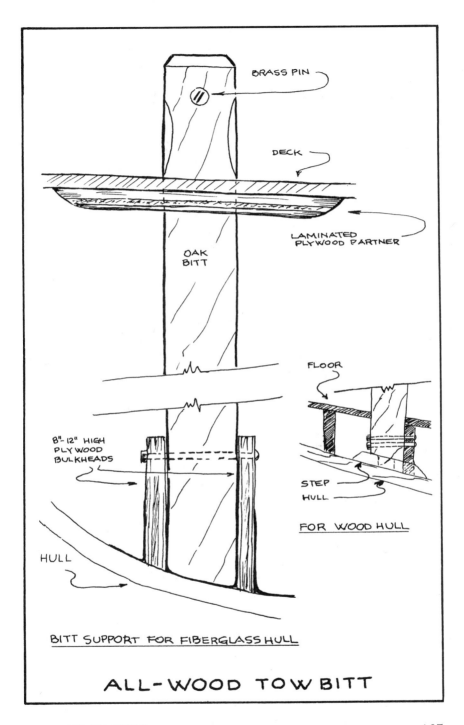

BRASS PIN

DECK

LAMINATED
PLYWOOD PARTNER

OAK
BITT

FLOOR

8"-12" HIGH
PLYWOOD
BULKHEADS

STEP
HULL

FOR WOOD HULL

HULL

BITT SUPPORT FOR FIBERGLASS HULL

ALL-WOOD TOW BITT

FOREDECK WELL

The best place to stow all ground tackle related gear is in a well in the foredeck. With the lid securely in place, the foredeck is cleared of all lines, chains and windlass, making sail changes an absolute dream. The molded well in the photo is in an *Ontario 30* but a fairly similar job can be done on any yacht if you don't mind taking a saw to your foredeck and doing some uncomfortably tight work in some very small spaces.

Because of the amount of reinforcing needed for an anchor windlass, I would not suggest incorporating it into the well. Rather, I see the well as a good place to stow anchors, chain and especially rope which otherwise has to be fed below decks or coiled and hidden away.

This simplified version will not have a flush fitting lid for one is just too demanding to install. Rather, it will have a very low profile hatch cover, with coamings to keep out the water.

The dimensions of the opening can vary with the individual yacht although I would strongly discourage cutting any opening with longer than 20" sides or wider than 24" aft side. The width of the front should of course narrow to allow the sides to follow the lines of the deck. Furthermore, a deck space of at least 8" should be left all around the opening so as not to endanger the hull to deck joint, and also to enable your hands plus some tools between the well wall and the hull.

Location of the well should be thoroughly considered keeping in mind that you will be taking about 14" of space directly below the deck in the forepeak. It would be most advantageous structurally to locate the well over the chain locker bulkhead, cutting a piece of the bulkhead out to make room, for then direct support can be returned to the deck by using this bulkhead as part of the foundation. If the yacht is not equipped with such a bulkhead, one would be well advised to make the aft wall of the well into a partial (upper) bulkhead by running it clear from hull to hull and attaching it there either to the frames of a wooden yacht, or bending it directly to the hull of a fiberglass yacht (see diagram).

Other than these precautions, roar on ahead. Measure out your opening and cut the deck most carefully with a saber saw. Reinforce the deck immediately with the 2" X 1¼" mahogany cleats (Diagram A). The cleats should be glued, clamped, and screwed to the underdecks after all old paint, etc. has been completely stripped

THE FINELY FITTED YACHT

GROUND TACKLE

away. Use epoxy glue and take particular care that neither your countersink drilling nor your screws come out topsides.

Next, determine the depth you will want your well to be. For rope and chain stowage, 10″ is deep enough; if you plan to keep a particular anchor in there, adjust the depth accordingly. Cut your sides from 1/2″ plywood to such a shape that the well sole will have a definite slope to it to facilitate drainage. Install all cleat stock onto your well sides as shown in diagrams, remembering to rip your vertical ones to angles that will make a perfect fit with both adjoining pieces. Now using 1″ #10 S.S. P.H.S.M. screws and epoxy glue, assemble the well in place. The order of assembly will depend on your belowdeck's limitations; do not, however, leave the well sole until the very last for you'll encounter an impossible situation if you do.

Once the well is together screwed and glued, lay strips of cleat stock cut to 45° along the bottom of the well (Diagram A) so the forthcoming fiberglass mat and roving will not have to make so drastic a turn. If they do, the chances of their cracking or delaminating will greatly increase. Glue the strips into place and, using 6″ fiberglass mat tape and 8″ fiberglass cloth tape (in that order), thoroughly seal off all joints of the well. (For directions on fiberglassing, see *From A Bare Hull*, pp. 265-70.) Be sure to work away all loose strands while the resin is still wet so they won't have a chance to become vicious porcupine quills when they harden. Next, clean out and primer the entire well, then cover with at least two coats of very durable enamel.

Now construct the coamings. Cut them from 13/16″ teak to a width that will allow the coaming to stick 1″ above the deck and 3/4″ below the heavy mahogany deck cleat. This lower overhang will form a drip lip, preventing water from seeping into the upper joints. To help the drip lip, cut a saw blade width groove to a depth of 1/8″ along the bottoms of all the coaming pieces. Bullnose all long edges. Now comes the tricky part. You will want to glue and screw the coaming to the heavy mahogany cleat, but *not* into the edge of the deck or you'll delaminate it. To add to the anxiety, you must lay a bead of caulking over the deck's edge where it will butt against the coaming. So, brush resorcinol glue onto your big cleat. Then, lay a thin bead of caulking on the deck edge above it (with caution), then screw the coamings in place. Remove excess caulking and glue.

Next, install your well drain. With a cup of water find the low spot in the well, and proceed to drill a hole for a 1/2″ plastic through-hull. Bed it thoroughly in white polysulfide and fit it with a

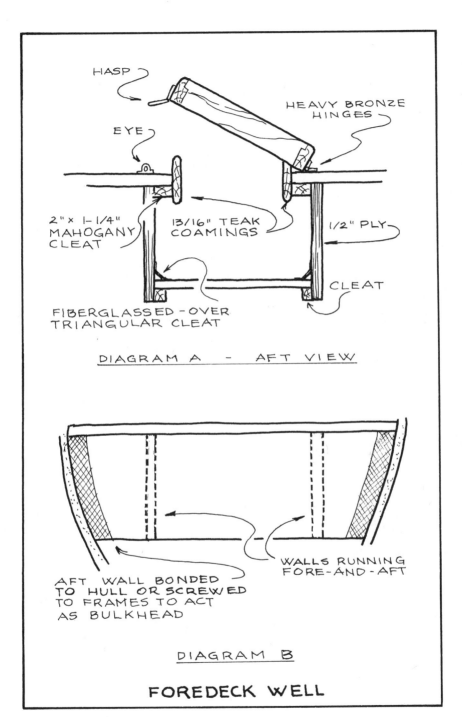

HASP

HEAVY BRONZE HINGES

EYE

2" x 1-1/4" MAHOGANY CLEAT

13/16" TEAK COAMINGS

1/2" PLY

CLEAT

FIBERGLASSED-OVER TRIANGULAR CLEAT

DIAGRAM A — AFT VIEW

WALLS RUNNING FORE-AND-AFT

AFT WALL BONDED TO HULL OR SCREWED TO FRAMES TO ACT AS BULKHEAD

DIAGRAM B

FOREDECK WELL

1/2" nylon hose. At a level just barely below the floor of the well, find a convenient spot on the hull for a 1/2" brass vent. Drill the hole for it and install it with the opening facing aft and down, that is, about 7:30 o'clock as you face that side of the yacht. Again, bed both inside and outside with polysulfide and tighten well.

The hatch will now have to be fabricated. Cut 1¾" stock to 2" width and mill a rabbet in one side 7/8" wide and 7/8" deep (see "Skylight") Carry the rabbet end to end on the two side frames, but terminate it at 7/8" from the ends of the aft and foreward pieces. All four frames must be cut to the hatch's over-all measurements because you'll be using lap joints, i.e. if your hatch is to measure 18" X 24", then your pieces will have to be 18" and 24" respectively.

For further hatch construction information see "Turtle Hatch" in this volume.

The hatch should be hinged on one side (the foreward end would be safest but then difficulties will be encountered paying out chain and line) with two very heavy bronze hinges. The opposite side of the hatch should be fitted with two hasps and twist-locks of a heavy duty kind. Always keep these securely locked.

Remember, you may just go to the well once too often.

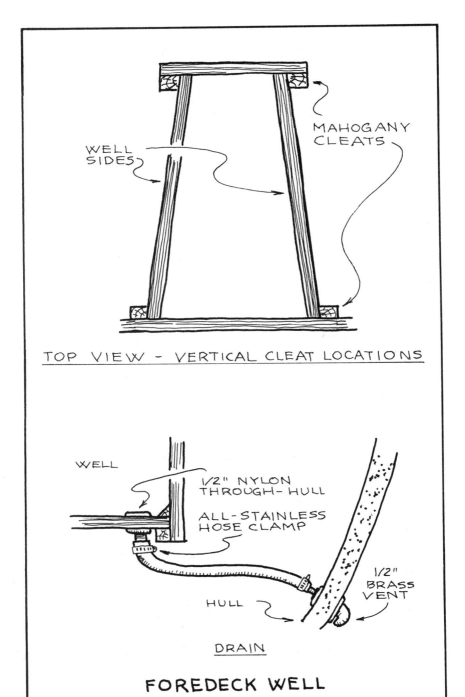

TOP VIEW - VERTICAL CLEAT LOCATIONS

MAHOGANY CLEATS

WELL SIDES

WELL

1/2" NYLON THROUGH-HULL

ALL-STAINLESS HOSE CLAMP

1/2" BRASS VENT

HULL

DRAIN

FOREDECK WELL

GROUND TACKLE

ANCHOR CHOCKS

To pretend for even a moment that a single best solution exists to stowing any anchor aboard, would demonstrate unforgivable shortsightedness. Too many different anchors and too many different boats exist for that. Basically, I feel that every attempt should be made to keep the anchor off the deck proper. If a bowsprit exists, the job will be simple, for then plow anchors can be left stowed on the anchor roller affixed to the side of the bowsprit with the stem of the fluke in tight against the roller, and the shank slung along the bowsprit and made fast to it with a short lanyard to keep the shank from banging about.

On a yacht without a bowsprit, accommodation for a CQR is still easily found on a self-stowing bow roller (see diagram).

If an off-centre roller is chosen, you can still atone by fabricating teak chocks that attach to the hull and keep the point of the fluke from gnawing away at the finish.

If you don't have any of the above facilities, you'll just have to bring the damned thing on deck and do what Captain Voss did aboard *Tilikum*, an Indian dugout canoe he sailed around the world in 1904-04, and just fabricate some chocks on deck and trip over them every chance you get.

With a CQR, the best solution is to get that monstrous fluke out of the way against the bulwark and run the shank fore and aft along same. You'll then need to hack out four small pads: two for the fluke, and one for each end of the shank.

Stowing Danforth-type anchors is a somewhat easier task, because they're lighter and have nice long stocks and a tripping palm, both of which are excellent things to hook into brackets of some sort. A most uncomplicated set is available at chandleries. It consists of two strips of stainless steel that clamp to the crosspiece of any stern or bow pulpit, and have notches into which the stock can snuggle. The shank is led down to the bow and made fast to avoid inadvertent anchorings.

Another bracket is available for Danforths, this for yachts without pulpits. It's a single piece design that clamps to a stanchion and holds the anchor securely in an upright position. Both of the above brackets facilitate quick releasing.

If you have neither pulpits nor stanchions, then you don't have to worry about having the anchor stowed and at the ready, because you'll probably fall overboard before you reach the harbour anyway.

CQR ANCHOR

SELF - STOWING ANCHOR ROLLER

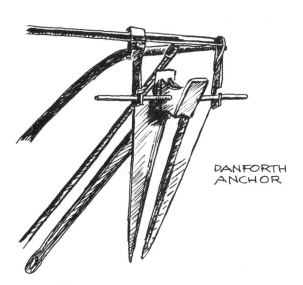

DANFORTH
ANCHOR

PULPIT MOUNTED ANCHOR HOLDER

ANCHOR CHOCKS

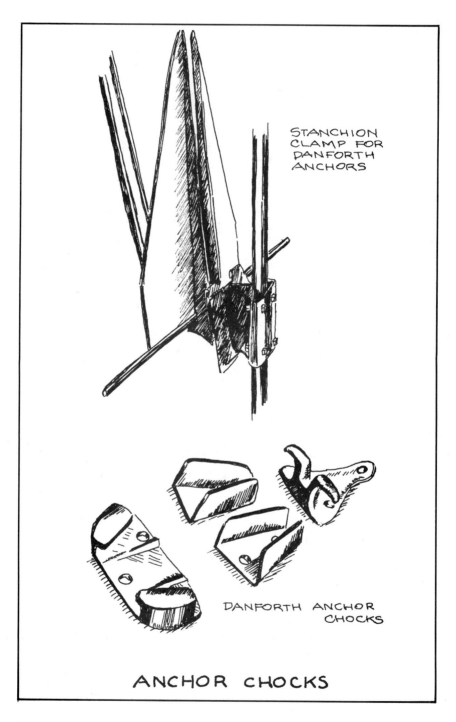

STANCHION
CLAMP FOR
DANFORTH
ANCHORS

DANFORTH ANCHOR
CHOCKS

ANCHOR CHOCKS

ANCHOR CHOCKS

GROUND TACKLE   177

Captain Voss' dugout canoe.

THE FINELY FITTED YACHT

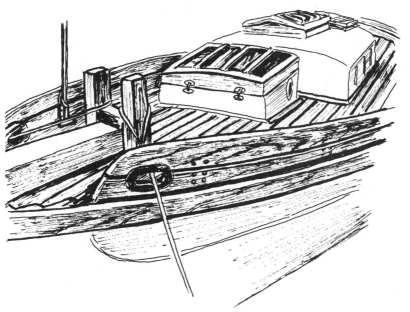

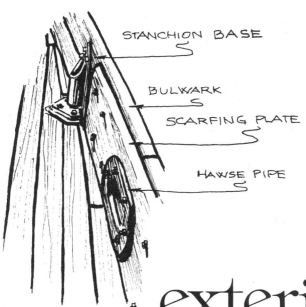

STANCHION BASE

BULWARK

SCARFING PLATE

HAWSE PIPE

exterior
bibelots

SOLAR BATTERY CHARGERS

After a few thousand years of civilization, we are finally giving thought to utilizing the power of the sun for something other than getting brown and growing turnips. We have discovered the phenomenon known as "photovoltaic effect" which allows the conversion of light into electrical energy without moving parts, with the use of silicon crystal based solar cells.

When exposed to sunlight, incoming units of light energy (photons) are absorbed by the electrons within the unit. This creates negative and positive charges which are attracted to their respective chemically treated type silicon of the cell. Consequently a photocurrent flows, voltage and electricity is produced. Thus a power source is created — a photovoltaic generator or a solar cell. It can keep the batteries charged while the boat is not in use, or it can trickle charge and help keep the battery level up during regular usage.

A typical 21″ × 21″ × 1″ unit can produce about 55 amp hours per week in an average U.S. location. In practice that means if you need to run your engine with a common 25 amp alternator (found on most two cylinder diesels) two hours a week to keep up your batteries for your radios and lights, then you can completely replace the engine use with a solar cell. Because silicon crystals are not yet mass produced, the cost of such a unit (about $500) would take about five years of constant boat use to pay for itself in gas or diesel at current oil prices (80¢/gal) but it sure wouldn't take long to pay off in silence.

The construction is of fiberglass and stabilized silicone rubber. Some makes, like the Solar Seamaster, are made especially for marine use and are completely submergible, hermetically sealed, and noncorrosive, without any exposed metal parts or external connections. The cells are protected by a removable 1/4″ thick plexiglass cover sturdy enough to walk on if needed.

Installation consists of gluing or screwing the panel to a cabin top or hatch cover, wherever it will get the most exposure (lazarette areas are ideal. See photo.) A single hole well caulked or a rubberized deck connector, will be needed to run the wires down to each battery terminal.

Since there are no moving parts the unit should last until the plexiglass breaks down, but even that can be simply replaced.

The whole thing seems like a very perfect idea; it's just a pity that Henry Ford hasn't gone into solar cell production.

THE FINELY FITTED YACHT

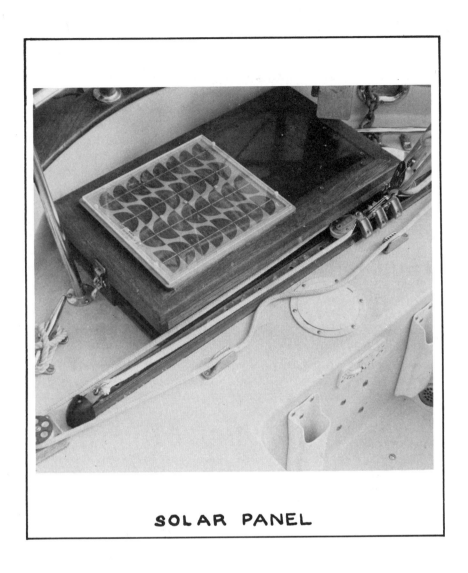

SOLAR PANEL

SOLAR WARM WATER TANKS

A very dear friend living aboard the cutter *Aepomene* in Puerto Vallarta had among his very clever inventions, a most ingenious one, that of solar warm water tanks. He had two fabricated and fitted far forward on the deckhouse, where they were out of the way. They contained enough warm water on most sunny days to provide two fine showers of nearly three quarts each. The tanks measured 2" X 20" X 10", were made of sturdy gauge aluminum (cheaper than stainless, easier to weld and drill, and a better conductor of heat), and painted a very flat black to help heat absorption. They had regular flush-fitting fills on the top and a small vent to allow water flow. At one point, he decided to increase the rate of flow from the tanks for a more dousing shower, so he had two bicycle tire nipples welded to the tanks and would daily pressurize each with a bicycle pump to have, in effect, pressurized water. Outlets were on the bottom and led through the coachroof into the cabin with 1/2" copper tubing.

Mounting on deck was achieved by two brackets at either end, tooled out of 1½" teak stock. These were routed to a 3/4" depth in the bottom half to snugly house the tanks, while the upper half was radiused on the corners and bullnosed. The brackets were screwed onto the cabin top after being bedded in Dolfinite. This is a completely serviceable, not unattractive invention that can solve the hygiene problem in any climate providing the sun is out. In the north, you may not be scalded, but you won't get icicles in the underarms either.

An improved version, that is, one producing warm water at a faster rate, would involve substitution of the tanks with a reconditioned auto air conditioning radiator. The numerous baffles of these vastly increase the exposed surface and can measurably decrease time required to heat the water within. The 1967 Cadillacs have had the smallest and most reliable ones. A plexiglass housing should be made to enclose the whole thing and create a nice greenhouse effect, that is, let in the sun and keep in the heat, as well as keep out cooling winds.

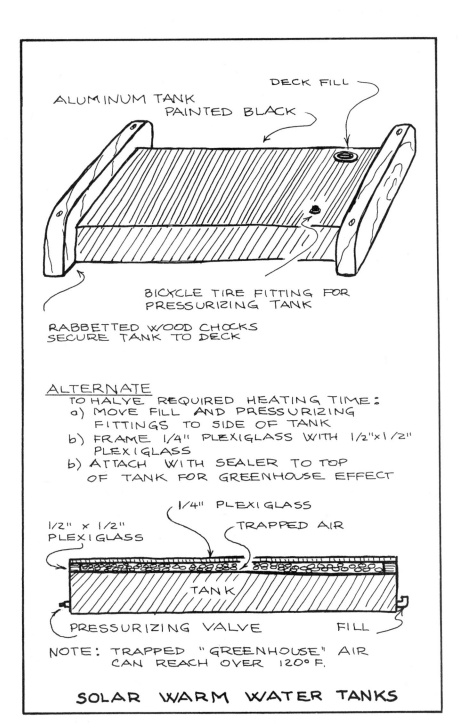

ALUMINUM TANK
PAINTED BLACK

DECK FILL

BICYCLE TIRE FITTING FOR
PRESSURIZING TANK

RABBETTED WOOD CHOCKS
SECURE TANK TO DECK

ALTERNATE
    TO HALVE REQUIRED HEATING TIME:
    a) MOVE FILL AND PRESSURIZING
        FITTINGS TO SIDE OF TANK
    b) FRAME 1/4" PLEXIGLASS WITH 1/2"x1/2"
        PLEXIGLASS
    b) ATTACH WITH SEALER TO TOP
        OF TANK FOR GREENHOUSE EFFECT

1/4" PLEXIGLASS

1/2" x 1/2"
PLEXIGLASS

TRAPPED AIR

TANK

PRESSURIZING VALVE

FILL

NOTE: TRAPPED "GREENHOUSE" AIR
    CAN REACH OVER 120° F.

SOLAR   WARM   WATER   TANKS

BIBELOTS

BOARDING LADDER

I shall not attempt to proselytise everyone to the use of a single type of boarding ladder, for I take immense pleasure in rowing around anchorages studying some of the most stupifying creations since the invention of gargoyles.

Apart from this selfish laissez faire, most boarding ladders should be left alone, for they do work. The simplest can be nothing more than a single piece of line with a couple of wood rungs, drilled and knot-held in place. From watching the owners utilize them, I have concluded that the two dollar and fifteen minute ladders work as well as the store bought $130 jewels.

The ladder to be discussed here is a homemade version of said jewel. First, purchase the hardware shown in the diagram, for you'll have to use measurements from these to cut out some of the wood parts. The whole set is available from H & L Marine.

For a four rung ladder that opens to 40″ and folds to 25″, with rung lengths of 14″ (clear) you will require seven lineal feet of 8″ wide and 1″ thick teak or mahogany. Cut the two 25″ lengths for the sides, and rip what's left (into 3″ wide pieces) for the rungs. Next, on 4½″ and 13½″ centres from the bottom, dado (half depth) the shape of your rungs.

Now, to cut the ladder into two pieces, begin by scribing a line 3″ from the edge of one of the sides all the way from one end to within 8″ from the other end. From this point, scribe a curve reverse to the top curve of the piece (the top curve having, of course, been derived from the shape of your mounting hooks). Next, cut very carefully along the line with a jigsaw remembering that both pieces are to be saved. Now, using this piece as a template, scribe in the opposite side of the ladder. Remember to have the dadoed surfaces facing each other when you're scribing, otherwise you'll end up with two left sides or two rights — whatever they'll be, they sure won't make a ladder.

Now scribe in the inboard cutout as shown. A 4″ high pad near the lower rung will act as a bumper against the hull, eliminating pinched toes between the hull and the rungs. The depth of the pad will of course depend on the hull curvature; one would be well advised to plan using the ladder amidships where this curve is the least drastic. Again, use one cut piece as a template to scribe the other.

The hand holds as shown are 1¼″ × 5″. These can be either routed or drilled-and-cut with a jigsaw. For the latter, drill the two

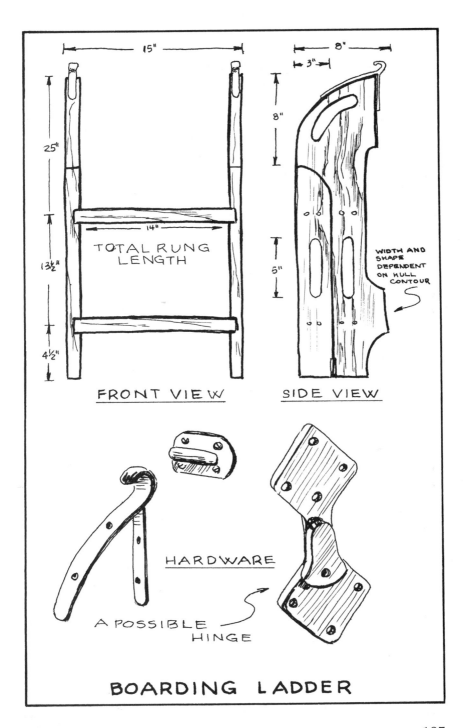

15"

25"

14"

TOTAL RUNG
LENGTH

13½"

4½"

FRONT VIEW

8"

3"

8"

5"

WIDTH AND
SHAPE
DEPENDENT
ON HULL
CONTOUR

SIDE VIEW

HARDWARE

A POSSIBLE
HINGE

BOARDING LADDER

hand hold ends with a 1¼″ butterfly bit, then join the holes with scribed curves and jigsaw out the rest.

Slightly bullnose all edges and sand thoroughly. Install the rungs with resorcinol glue. Glue, screw and plug. The whole unit is under too much strain to rely on glue alone. Wipe all excess glue now.

Install all hardware, then attach the padeyes to the hull with through-bolts or, if that's impossible because of limited interior access, use the most monstrous sheet metal screws that will fit. Bed them well.

Since, even folded, the ladder will occupy a space of almost 16″ X 25″ X 7½″, a good stowage space will have to be found. Hanging it from the underdeck in the forepeak seems to be ideal, with two padeyes housing the mounting hooks on the top, and a set of cabin hook-and-eye (eye on lower inboard rung, hook on underdeck) keeping it in place.

THE FINELY FITTED YACHT

The folding ladder can be used either doubled up (for boarding from a dinghy), or unfolded when required as a swim ladder.

BOARDING LADDER

ROPE BOARDING LADDER

A rope ladder is simple in every way imaginable: simple to make, to use, and to stow. The material should be either teak or mahogany. Some sailors advocate cedar, because it is light and inexpensive, but we're probably discussing three or four rungs maximum, and if you can't lift those with ease, you'd better stop right here in case you herniate flipping the pages.

To determine the number of rungs, measure the free board and divide by 10″. Amidships is best, where the hull is most vertical, because it eliminates the need to hang upside down after the ladder has swung under the hull's pinched ends. Add a rung for below the water, unless you're a flying fish.

Mill 13/16″ stock to 14″ × 4″ pieces, cutting out the hull-ward edge of each rung (see diagram) to prevent pinched toes. Two fine grooves, about 1/8″, can be cut the length of the surface to act as a non-skid.

Radius all corners, and bullnose all edges. Lay out hole patterns for the rope, 3″ in from all edges, and drill 3/8″ holes. If you can drill relatively vertically, just mark one step and lay it on top of the others (making sure you align all edges), then drill through as many as you can at once. If your drill bit isn't long enough to drill them all at once, use a rung already drilled as a template for undrilled ones, to save marking time.

The rungs can be held in position along the rope in one of three ways. One way is to tie knots beneath each rung. This is a hit and miss affair, but with a little juggling, it can be done.

The second is to have wood pegs cross-driven through the rope and the rung. Drill 1/4″ diameter holes and have them go past the inner edges of the rope holes by about 3/4″. Round off the edges of 1/4″ dowels, cover them with resorcinol, and drive them home. Trim off the ends.

The third method is to use marlin seizings; that is shown under the headings of "The Proper Mast Step."

Whichever you use, first cut 3/8″ line to four times the total length of the ladder. If you are using knots, add about four inches extra per rung (1″ per knot). A brass hook fastened onto the bulwark can hold the looped ends of the ladder line.

A word of caution: pull the ladder aboard every evening, or it will bang against the hull through the night.

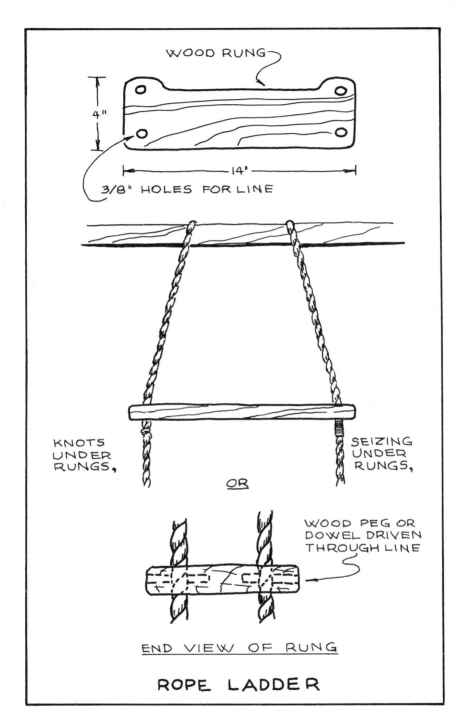

WOOD RUNG

4"

14"

3/8" HOLES FOR LINE

KNOTS UNDER RUNGS,

SEIZING UNDER RUNGS,

OR

WOOD PEG OR DOWEL DRIVEN THROUGH LINE

END VIEW OF RUNG

ROPE LADDER

THE DRAWBRIDGE

Anyone planning to cruise anywhere other than North America should equip his yacht with a drawbridge of sorts. The most common method of tying up from Papeete, to English Harbour, to Monte Carlo is the anchor-out, stern-to-the-seawall system which will usually mean a good healthy leap from ship to shore, unless one is willing to risk the yacht's transom and back down very close to the wall.

The simplest drawbridge consists of a long piece of $2'' \times 6''$, but these are usually too springy and insufficiently attached to the stern. Constructing a fine drawbridge is straight forward. It should be made of red cedar and mahogany, the first to cut down on the weight, the second to give strength. A plank $12''$ in width and $5'$ to $7'$ in length should suffice on all but the most inebriated occasions.

To start with, construct a ladder from $1'' \times 3''$ mahogany stock. Let in all the rungs to $1/2''$ depth and glue and screw them in place. Space the rungs on no more than $12''$ centres. Next, rip some $1''$ cedar stock into $2''$ widths and glue and screw (or nail) to the rungs and to the frame. Just inside the last rungs on either end of the plank, drill holes and insert brass or stainless bushings with $3/4''$ ID's into the sides of the frames, then run a piece of $3/4''$ all-thread right through. The all-thread should be of such a length that it protrudes two inches past each side. Lock the all-thread into that position with a washer and locknut. Now, halve a piece of a $20''$ length stainless wire, slip a $4''$ length of good nylon hose over it, and splice a thimble onto each end. Slip the thimbles over the all-thread and lock them there with large washers on either side and a locknut on the outer end.

The stainless wire harness will be supported by a halyard. Together they hold up the outboard end of the plank. The inboard end will have to be secured by slipping the all-thread into eyebolts or whatever type of fitting can be adapted to the specific yacht. The one in the photo had the plank permanently hinged to the aft pulpit where it could be drawn up vertically to stow. Two stabilizing whisker stays will have to be run from the outboard end of the plank to the beamiest points of the stern (see photo). Any old dacron line will serve nicely; if you want to have it really tight, put it over the sheet winch and haul.

To avoid erosion of the outboard end of the plank by its rubbing against seawalls, fit it with metal skids or a set of plastic wheels (see photo).

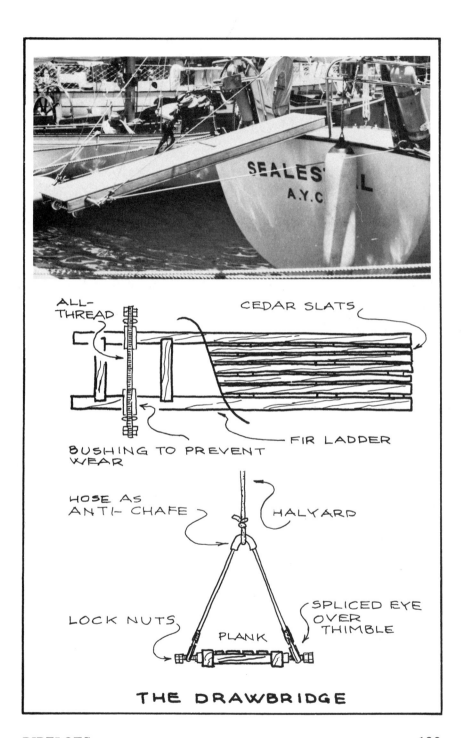

ALL-THREAD

CEDAR SLATS

BUSHING TO PREVENT WEAR

FIR LADDER

HOSE AS ANTI-CHAFE

HALYARD

LOCK NUTS

PLANK

SPLICED EYE OVER THIMBLE

THE DRAWBRIDGE

ADD-ON BULWARKS

Once in a while, a totally new and ingenious concept comes along, a completely multipurpose and visually striking idea, and Naval Architect Lyle Hess's bulwark is one of them. He designed it for his Bristol Channel Cutter, a fiberglass cum teak version of the English pilot cutters, in one of which, *Seraffyn*, the Pardey's have sailed the world.

The bulwark can be fitted onto most modern yachts with very little modification, and aside from giving any vessel a tastefully classic look, it can turn an open side deck into a cozy, safe walkway.

The key to the whole arrangement is the Hess-designed cast-bronze stanchion base. There is only one model, hence only one base-to-stem angle (90°), so different deck angles must be accommodated with shims of either wood or hard plastic. The castings can be purchased from the builder in Vancouver, Canada. On the cutter they've put eight per side, spaced about three feet apart.

The bulwark itself can be cut from 1″ teak, ripped to a width of 2¾″ and bullnosed with a 3/8″ bullnose bit; the top of the top piece only, the bottom of the bottom piece only. Since very few pieces of 25′ long teak exist, two starter pieces can be scarfed amidships where the teak can be doubled up for strength, and a hawse pipe installed for a springline to make the whole thing look more intentional. The foreward and aft ends of the bulwark are rounded and fitted with a sturdy 1½″ thick block, which again houses a set of hawse pipes. Three-eighth-inch carriage bolts have been used to fasten the bulwark to the cast bases.

Installation should begin by laying out the stanchion bases and fabricating the shims. Before bolting in place, apply generous amounts of polysulfide between the deck and shim, then the shim and base. Next, laminate the fore and aft lower pieces together using resorcinol glue and bolts, and tie the plank firmly to the stanchion with the help of lines. Now begin at one end to drill and attach the plant to the castings. Use a half-inch spacer between the deck and plank to attain uniformity. You will need the help of a friend throughout the operation to bend and hold the plank in place while you drill and bolt. Next, with the aid of a quarter-inch spacer, put the upper plank in place, gluing and screwing it to the backup plank amidships. Repeat on the opposite side.

One very nice feature of such a bulwark is that it allows one to make do without a genoa track. An endless strop of good wide tape to distribute the pressure can be made fast to the bulwark at any

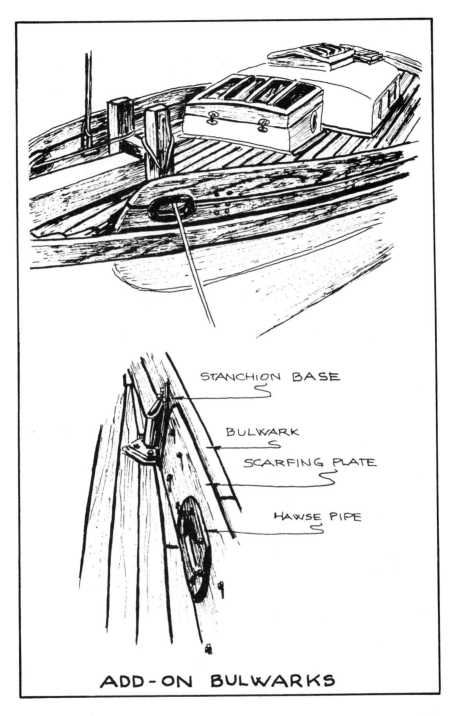

STANCHION BASE

BULWARK

SCARFING PLATE

HAWSE PIPE

ADD-ON BULWARKS

point (see photo) and a block can be shackled to it. Relocating the block requires only a loosening and sliding of the strop.

Whether varnished or oiled, the bulwark will be a feast for the eyes.

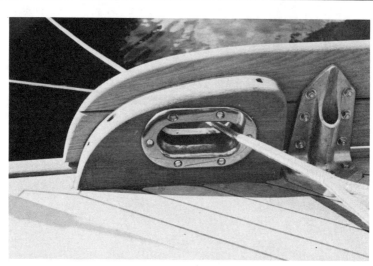

Solid block reinforces the end of the bulwark.

Endless strop replaces genoa track.

THE FINELY FITTED YACHT

Bronze base for bulwark and stanchion.

CAPRAIL STEP

I have always been doomed by my own lack of inventiveness, through which *Warm Rain* has had beautifully varnished caprails, but nothing to protect them from people who insist on doing pirouettes on them in golf shoes. All wood rails should have at least one area for feet, an area that is protected as well as non-slippery. Most marine stores offer a chrome beast with rubber inserts, but this looks about as shippy as snow tires. Some marine antique places have cast bronze plates with molded-in non skid, but finding these is difficult at best, impossible at worst.

I found a nice solution aboard a Philbrooks yacht, as shown in the illustration. They used 1/4" teak stock with thoroughly rounded edges, attached to the caprail with wood screws. The idea seems quite good, although I see little need for such long lengths when a step of about 12", intelligently located at the most often used boarding point, near a stanchion or shroud for hand support, would suffice. Thin brass sheeting, treated with a meat mallet (sigh) as described in "Companionway Non-Skid," can provide very nice footing, physically and visually. Generous amounts of caulking should be used under both to eliminate any possibility of water retention, which will quickly destroy and lift varnish, defeating half the purpose for the step.

Other traditional non-skid procedures, like grooving (who wants to hack away at one's caprail) and woven rope mats (the varnish under these will rot away in no time), are not applicable here. The only other feasible solution, useful especially on yachts with bulwarks, is the installation of a cast bronze oval hawse pipe. These are usually wide enough to house a foot, and have the wonderful advantage of providing a perfect fair lead, as well, for a spring line; it is to be located somewhere on the amidships anyway, where stepping aboard will be facilitated by the beaminess of the vessel.

THE FINELY FITTED YACHT

Narrow teak slats protect varnished caprail and make it less slippery.

CAPRAIL STEP

FOLDING WINCH CHAIR

Most sailboats have few places where one can really relax and fish. Granted, feet can be dangled over the caprail, but then lifelines will still be in the way of reeling arms, and when at anchor, the swinging of the boat will necessitate constant repositioning of the body. The winch chair is a perfect remedy, for it fits into a sheet winch, has a nice padded seat that swivels in any direction, and folds up into a 4″ × 14″ × 10″ space. If desired, a back can be fabricated for true comfort.

If you have Barient winches, you can purchase a gleaming naugahyde version for about $80. All others, make your own and pocket about $50 for a fine dinner.

The first step is to secure the most beat-up and/or the cheapest winch handle that fits your winch. Have a machine shop cut the handle off and weld what's left to a 6″ × 8″ plate. From 3/4″ plywood cut a seat with 2″ radius corners. The overall measurements are up to you, but remember, you're building a seat, not a sofa; 14″ × 10″ will accommodate the average derrière. Bullnose the plywood top and bottom to eliminate slivering. Drill eight holes of 1/4″ diameter in your mounting plate, centre it on the plywood, and using the plate as a template, drill your holes. Countersink them slightly and attach the plywood to the plate with 1/4″ bolts and capnuts. Give the wood a good coat of sealer. For padding the top, 1″ closed cell foam should be used. A tidy canvas slip cover can be made with a zipper in one long side. Don't forget to cut a hole in the centre of the bottom for the winch fitting, and reinforce it with double canvas, then hem it.

If you want the luxury of a hinged back, cut a piece of 1/2″ plywood to 6″ × 14″ with radiused corners. Now from 1″ plywood, cut two 14″ × 1″ strips and screw and glue one each to the back and the seat. See drawing. These will act as bases for the piano hinges and enable the thing to fold and stow flat. Install as long a stainless piano hinge as possible. The canvas cover will begin the same as for the backless version, but the back and seat covers should be sewn together at the hinge (inside) and a common zipper installed underneath, running the length of the hinge. Triangular pieces of doubled-up canvas, having leg measurements of 8″ and 6″ will have to be double stitched onto the seat and back part of the cover to act as a restrainer, preventing backward somersaults.

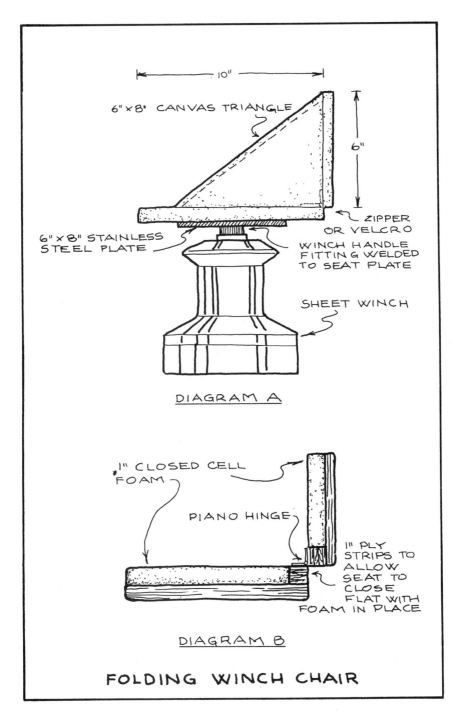

10"

6" x 8' CANVAS TRIANGLE

6"

6" x 8" STAINLESS STEEL PLATE

ZIPPER OR VELCRO

WINCH HANDLE FITTING WELDED TO SEAT PLATE

SHEET WINCH

DIAGRAM A

1" CLOSED CELL FOAM

PIANO HINGE

1" PLY STRIPS TO ALLOW SEAT TO CLOSE FLAT WITH FOAM IN PLACE

DIAGRAM B

FOLDING WINCH CHAIR

EYEBROWS

No other item that can be produced with as little effort as teak eyebrows, brings about as drastic an improvement to your boat's exterior. Whether the deckhouse is fiberglass or painted wood, a single piece of teak requiring no more than one-half hour of annual upkeep, can visually lower and streamline it.

The piece can be milled from 1/2" stock. Anything thinner would be difficult to plug and rather chancy to bend and twist without breakage.

The width need not exceed 1". Length should be measured about 1" from the foremost and aftmost end of the house, if simple cornerless eyebrows are contemplated. The use of a single length is most desirable. Splicing and scarfing are a pain at the best of times, and man hours are better spent looking for a longer piece. The ends should be well rounded and the whole thing radiused on all outside edges with a 3/8" bullnose. This is most vital because, from time to time, eyebrows will be stepped on and slid from, and an unradiused corner will, in most instances, crack and splinter. To assure additional prevention of this, the eyebrow should be installed at least 1" down from the top of the house to be a bit more out of the way of feet.

The next step is to pre-drill and countersink the eyebrow on 10" centres. A dry run should be made. Remove the countersink from the drill bit and, using a pre-drilled hole as a guide, drill the first hole in the cabin side, then put a screw in it and tighten. Gently. This is no place to build up your muscles. Proceed to drill and screw all holes one by one to make sure everything fits and aligns. Back off all screws, remove the eyebrow, then clean both the cabin side and the eyebrow of dust. Lay a fine bead of Dolfinite on the eyebrow and screw it back in place. Again be gentle or you'll cause the thin narrow piece to explode. Remove excess Dolfinite with a sharp stick. Resorcinol glue and plug.

The more ardent will advocate eyebrows that fully circle the cabin. I know; I used to be one of them until I sat down one morning to fabricate my first compound corner. Later that night, with froth of madness on my lips and a piece of wood resembling a shriveled banana in my hand, I decided on straight eyebrows only.

Wanderer IV

Warm Rain

SHORE POWER CORD AND RECEPTACLE

Contrary to what Momma may have told you, running an extension cord into a yacht through a portlight is just not done in better circles. An investment, painful as it is, must be made and the proper shore power cord should be purchased, along with an even more proper shore power receptacle.

Most male receptacles are well made, and waterproof enough when closed, but some I have seen are simple-mindedly fabricated, with the hinges so badly aligned that screwing the lid on can be done only with the help of a sledge hammer. When you are buying the receptable, check it a few times to be sure it functions properly.

Installation should be with the hinge up, so that the natural tendency of the cap will be to fall into a closed position. Even though a rubber gasket is usually supplied with the receptacle, I feel it prudent to run a bead of sealer around the edges after installation. Do not forget to plop a few drops into each bolt hole as well. Do check this seal once every few months, for the receptacle undergoes tremendous forces each time the cord is yanked out.

A note with regard to cord purchase. Be sure you buy complementary hardware. Not all cords fit all receptacles acceptably. Since most are of the twist-lock variety, one should try to buy only those mated perfectly, for poorly fitted ones will require undue force, which, in due time, will cause the prongs to bend and break.

The receptacle should be installed out of the way of feet. I feel a location well aft, as far from normal spray as possible, is preferable to a place in the bow, regardless of the inconvenience this may cause at the home dock.

The female plug should be fitted with a short lanyard that can be run under the hinge pin of the receptacle and tied to hold the plug firmly in place.

When not in use, the cord should be neatly looped and stowed where it won't be bent or nicked by anything heavy or sharp.

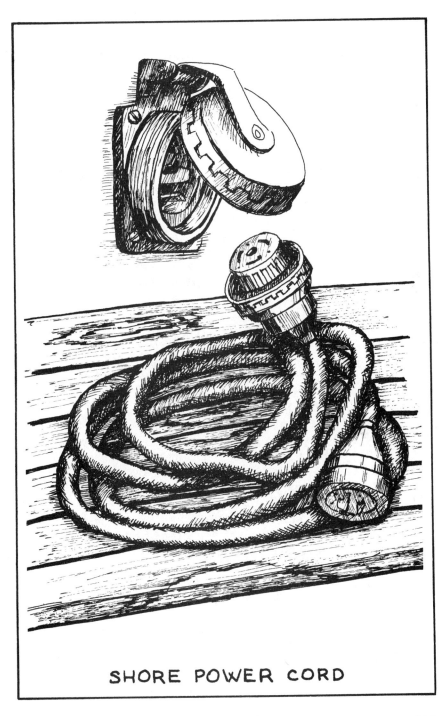

SHORE POWER CORD

SIMPLE SHOWERS

What a wonderfully exhilarating feeling it is to sail into a new anchorage, wash the sea salt and sweat salt from your skin, then sit on deck and just gaze at the sunset. I probably teeter on the brink of insanity as far as cleanliness is concerned, but I just cannot empathize with those people who think that cruising gives them license to stink. Having a shower aboard need not involve hot water tanks and electric pumps and great luxurious shower stalls. Quite the contrary: the simpler the better. The following are but two of the ingenious and extremely inexpensive systems I have found aboard yachts. In almost all cases, preheating water on a stove is step one.

The Cockpit Bucket

The cockpit is of course the most ideal place to hook up a shower. Most have drains, and all are surrounded by materials which will not be hurt or marked by spraying water. Privacy can be gained by lowering the cockpit awning or even more easily by sitting down. If you're a gadget lover, you can rig a nylon curtain (the supple kind like spinnaker cloth are the easiest to stow) by putting a grommet in each of the four upper corners of the curtain and cutting two lengths of plastic battens or poles of bamboo to act as diagonals. Poke their ends through the grommets and suspend them from the boom by means of a lanyard tied at the point of crossover. If you're short of headroom, haul in on the topping lift.

The simplest source of water is of course a bucket; it's very cheap, very easy to fill, and with a slight modification most pleasant to use. The modification involves drilling a hole in the side of a plastic bucket and gluing a threaded flange over it with contact cement. With a male adapter, a plastic valve, the type that's used on a garden hose, can be threaded into the flange. This will enable you to shut the water off while lathering up or looking for the soap. In this way a good shower can be had with as little as two quarts of water. The bucket can be suspended from the boom as well. Installing the spigot on the bottom of the bucket would certainly result in its breaking off after only a few bangings down.

The Spray Tank

Surplus and hardware stores sell portable brass or copper tanks of one or two gallon capacity used commonly to spray insecticides into fruit trees. These are equipped with their own pumps which, with a few strokes, pressurize the tank, and will actually give a very

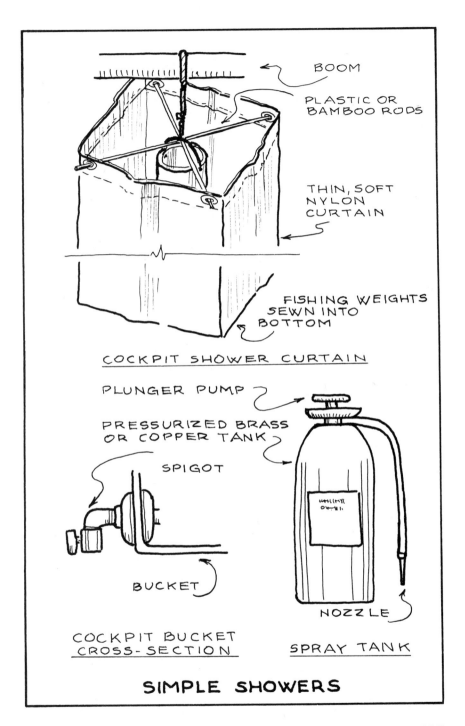

BOOM

PLASTIC OR BAMBOO RODS

THIN, SOFT NYLON CURTAIN

FISHING WEIGHTS SEWN INTO BOTTOM

COCKPIT SHOWER CURTAIN

PLUNGER PUMP

PRESSURIZED BRASS OR COPPER TANK

SPIGOT

BUCKET

COCKPIT BUCKET CROSS-SECTION

NOZZLE

SPRAY TANK

SIMPLE SHOWERS

even and powerful spray. The great advantage of this unit is that it can be filled with water and placed directly on the stove for heating. For greatest water savings, this should be a two person system to free the bather's hands to economize the rinsing.

The Built-In Hand or Electric Pump

If a way can be found to install a shower pan below decks, in or very near to the head, thought may be given to installing a pump (on the head counter if it's a hand pump, and inside a cabinet if it's electric) permanently and equipping it with a flex-hose shower nozzle. The curtain utilized would be similar to the one used in the cockpit, but the grommets could be replaced by snaps which fit into their counterparts on the overhead. The head sink can be filled with warm water from the stove, the free end of the hose from the pump submerged in it, and then the pump can be activated.

Aboard *Warm Rain* we have the most profound shower of them all. The most vital parts are: a tea kettle and Candace. I sit quietly on the cockpit floor while Candace pours warm water over me from the kettle. The spout enables her to refine her aim. The water is guaranteed to be a perfect temperature every time, because she knows full well that when I'm finished, it's her turn.

Oh paradise!

ANTI-CHAFE METALS

Wood is precious stuff. Not only does it drain the pocket initially, but it requires long hours of maintenance; so an attempt should be made to guard and protect it in areas that undergo heavy traffic or wear.

The least demanding and possibly the most visually attractive solution is to use small patches of thin brass sheeting. It can be purchased at most metal salvage or metal fabricator shops, and, since it's mostly sold by weight, a few dollars worth can be made to go a long, long way. It is also a friendly material to use. It can be cut very neatly with tin snips, it can be bent evenly around almost any curve, and it can be held in place by attractive brass tacks.

The most frequent and severe abuse is doled out by ground tackle gear. Both anchor and chain grind and chip away wood mercilessly, so a careful survey should be made around the bow, and all involved areas should be covered with the protective brass. On yachts with bowsprits, the entire area between, and just fore and aft of, the anchor rollers should be so protected. Not only does this part suffer from stray anchor chain, but the swiveled flukes of plow anchors bang and gnaw away at it as well.

As mentioned under other headings, the protective plating is most useful on companionway steps and often stepped-on parts of the caprails. Frequent caprail wear also occurs where fender lines are recklessly hung over the rail. A few small plates and a few harsh words to the crew on the topic of hanging fenders in their designated spots in future, should overcome this problem.

Fairly nasty damage is often caused by dinghies. As they are hauled aboard, the keel strip (brass or aluminum) is often allowed to ride right over the caprail. Since dinghy hauling is more often then not done in the exact same area, a short run (about 8″) of brass sheeting here could add a lot of protection.

Below decks, the weaponry used against wood is much less formidable, usually taking the shape of boating shoes, so only in the few spots where nervous foot tapping occurs (like under chart tables) should protective measures be taken. Two spots that have suffered on *Warm Rain* are the searails on the counters directly outboard of the companionway ladder. It seems that on an excessive heel, anyone going below takes the most vertical route possible by stepping from the companionway on to the counter. Bring on the brass sheeting.

canvas/
sails

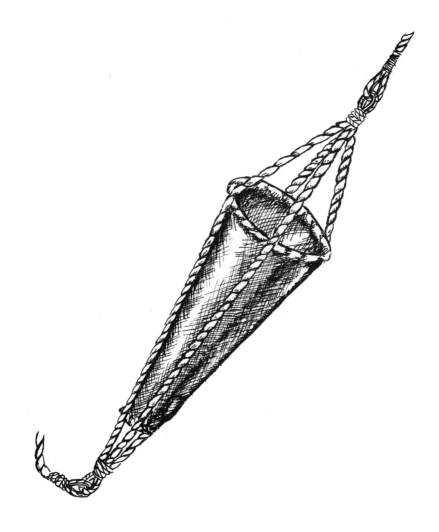

SEWING CANVAS

The equipment you need for sewing with canvas are: tape measure, tailor's chalk, large compass or string and thumbtack, scissors (preferably a bent handled type such as Fiskar's light weight stainless steel, made in Finland, never need sharpening), straight pins, iron, sewing machine with zigzag attachment, size 16 or 18 needle, mercerized heavy duty thread — size 30-40-50, grommets and grommet setter, pencil and string, polyester thread, and a hot knife (a sharpened soldering iron). Following are the basic sewing terms and procedures:

Wrong and Right Side of Material

Simply put, the right side of the fabric is the side you wish exposed, and the wrong side is the one that will not be seen. On most fabrics, this is easily discernible, but on canvas, it doesn't make much difference, unless you are using the very heavy acrylic painted type, as is used for lawn chairs (or beach chairs) and awnings.

Seam

The seam is the point at which you stitch to arrive at the finished size of your product. This is done by placing two pieces of material together, *right* sides together, and stitching on the *wrong* side of the material.

Seam Allowance

This is usually 5/8″ (1/2″ is used in this book's projects) more than the desired finished size of your product. This allows enough material to finish the raw seams in a number of ways, to prevent ravelling.

Hem

This is the finished edge of any fabric that is not enclosed in a finished seam, such as edges of curtains, tablecloths, and in clothing; skirt hems, shirt sleeves, etc. With a hem allowance of any given width, from 1″ to 3″, press the raw edge 1/4″ to 1/2″ to the wrong side of the fabric, then fold to the desired hem length, pin or baste, and stitch.

Seam Finishes

To prevent undue ravelling, there are several finishes for inside seams: a) stitch 1/4″ from the raw edge and pink (with pinking

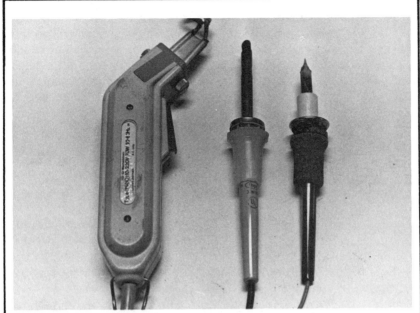

Various hot knives, all cut rapidly and seal edges (as they cut) in synthetic fabrics like acrylic and dacron.

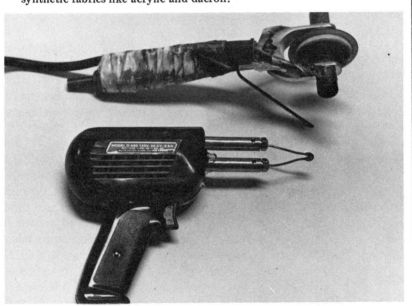

Hot knives. Lower one is soldering gun with sharpened tip.

shears) the raw edge, b) using your zigzag attachment, zigzag your raw edges, being sure the needle enters just inside the raw edge. This can be done to each individual seam edge, or the two seam edges can be held together and zigzag stitched as one, and c) on the wrong side of the material, press the seam open, then stitch through seam allowance and material 1/4" away from the seam on either side. This, of course, will show on the right side of the material, but it looks very nice, especially if another colour thread is used for contrast.

Fastening a Seam — or Back Stitching

If your sewing machine is equipped with a reverse stitch, lower the needle into the fabric about 1/2" from the beginning of the seam. Depress the reverse lever and stitch in reverse until the needle reaches the beginning of the seam. Release the lever and stitch forward. At the end of the stitching line, stitch backward for about 1/2". This secures the thread ends. If your machine does not stitch backward, place the needle 1/2" in from the starting point and stitch forward for 1/2". Leaving the needle in the fabric, lift the presser foot and turn the fabric around on the needle. Lower the presser foot and stitch over the first stitching, continuing to the end. At the end, again pivot the work on the needle and stitch back for 1/2".

Dart

This is a stitched tapering fold in a garment, or any other sewn item, to bring in fullness where not needed. With tailor's chalk, mark on the wrong side of fabric the size and position of your dart. Remember, if you want only 1" darts, fold the material 1/2" (right sides together). Start stitching at the outer edge of the fabric, tapering to a point, then backstitch. If the dart is very large, it can be cut close to the stitching and pressed flat; otherwise, press the dart to one side of the fabric.

Stress Points (Reinforcing)

If you are to be using grommets or heavy duty snaps, the points where these are affixed should be reinforced. To accomplish this, simply cut a square of material 2" larger than your snap or grommet. Place it on the wrong side of the material where the snap or grommet is to be affixed. It can be held there by a basting stitch (either hand or machine). When attaching the snap or grommet, do so through both thicknesses. This will strengthen the stress point. This method can also be used anywhere ties are to be attached at any point in the fabric, such as the edges, corners, etc.

Grommets

This is an eyelet made of metal (preferably brass) used to strength or protect an opening, or to insulate or protect something passed through it. These come in various sizes and must be attached with a grommet setter. They both are available from any fabric shop.

Pin Basting

This is simply placing your two raw edges together (right sides) and pinning every 4″ or 5″ to prevent the material from slipping when stitching. Place your pins perpendicular to your line of stitching. This way you can stitch right over the pins and remove them after the stitching is completed.

More experienced persons will machine baste (temporary stitching), which means placing your two pieces of material under the presser foot and stitching, while holding the raw edges together with your fingers. When doing this, you should use the largest stitch your machine will make (usually six stitches to the inch). This will enable you to pull out the basting threads when the finished seam has been completed. Do not backstitch machine basting. Before removing, clip threads every few inches.

Grommet set left to right: mallet, grommets, setting block, hole cutter and setter; sitting on plastic cutting pad.

Tension

This is probably the most important control on your sewing machine. The best tension for one fabric may not be correct for another. The required tension depends upon the stiffness of the fabric, thickness of the fabric, numbers of layers of fabric being sewn, as well as the type of stitch you are making. It is best to test the stitching on a scrap of fabric you are using, before starting to sew. The location of the top tension adjustment varies on different machines, while the bottom tension is almost always in the bobbin. A perfect straight stitch will have threads locked between the two layers of fabric with no loops on top or bottom (see Diagram A). If the upper thread is too tight, decrease the tension (see Diagram B). If the upper thread is too loose, increase the tension (see Diagram C). Bobbin tension requires adjusting less frequently than the upper thread tension. When adjusting the tension on the bottom case, make *slight* adjustments with a small screwdriver. To decrease the tension, turn the screw counterclockwise; to increase the tension, turn clockwise. But remember, only a quarter of a turn, or 45°, is sufficient.

Here is a good way to check your tension balance: be sure to use polyester thread of the same size on the top and on the bobbin, and a sharp, correctly sized needle for the fabric you are sewing. Begin with a full bobbin. Set the stitch length for about 12 stitches per inch.

Fold a 6" square of fabric in half diagonally, forming a triangle. Make a line of stitching 1/2" in from the fold.
1) If seam is puckered — both tensions are too tight.
2) If the bottom thread lays on the fabric — tighten the upper thread tension, and repeat test.
3) If the top thread lays on the fabric — loosen the upper thread tension, and repeat test.

Grasp the stitching and pull with a snap to make the threads break.
1) If both threads break — tensions are balanced.
2) If neither thread breaks — both tensions are too loose.
3) If upper thread breaks — loosen top tension.
4) If lower thread breaks — tighten top tension.

Both threads do not have to break at the same place, but they should break on the same snap.

Needle, Thread, and Fabric

The size of the needle should conform with the size of the thread, and both should be suitable to the fabric. Here is a good rule

THE FINELY FITTED YACHT

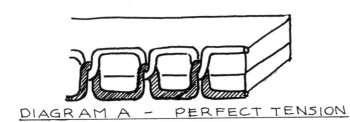

DIAGRAM A - PERFECT TENSION

UPPER THREAD TOO TIGHT

DIAGRAM B - DECREASE TENSION

UPPER THREAD TOO LOOSE

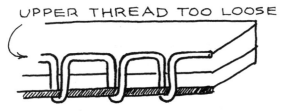

DIAGRAM C - INCREASE TENSION

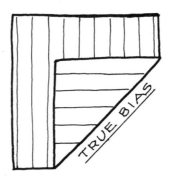

TRUE BIAS

SEWING CANVAS

to remember: the heavier the fabric (e.g. denims and canvas) the larger the needle size (18) and the lower the thread size (30-50, heavy duty); while the sheerer the fabric (silk, tricot) the smaller the needle size (9) and the higher the thread size (80-100). The average sewer rarely uses anything but the medium (thread size 60 and needle size 14) which will sew cotton and cotton blends, shantung, pique, seersucker, velveteen, light weight wool, linen, leather and vinyls.

Casing

A casing is a tunnel to hold either a cord or elastic. If it is to be placed within a circular piece of material, the raw edges of the material should be folded 1/2" toward the wrong side of the material and basted in place. This basting will allow you to pull up and gather any excess fullness when turning your casting hem. When you have turned the hem and adjusted the gathers evenly (remember, your casing hem must be at least 1/4" to 1/2" larger than the material it is to encase), begin stitching, leaving an opening of 2" or 3" to insert your casing material. If you are inserting elastic, fasten a large safety pin on one end of the elastic and use it as a guide to feed the elastic through the casing. Fasten a large safety pin to the other end of the elastic so you will not lose sight of it, and pull it through the entire casing. When the two ends meet, simply sew, and then close your opening by stitching.

A casing on a flat piece of material is very simple. Determine what you want to encase (cording, rope, etc.), the length of the casing area, and the width of the material to be encased. Cut a strip of material the length of the area you are casing, and an inch to two inches wider than the material to be encased. Lay this strip of material on the area where you want your casing, pin baste, and stitch along each side — leaving each end open. Be sure to fasten or back stitch your stitching. You now have a long hollow tunnel into which you can thread your cord, using the large safety pin; or in the case of rope, if it is stiff enough, tape the end with scotch tape and push through by hand.

Casing for Piping

If you are making cushions and wish to put piping around the boxed edges, you will need to make casing out of bias strips. The bias is a line diagonal to the grain of a fabric, i.e. a line at a 45° angle to the selvage. This will enable the fabric to stretch and will make a much smoother tube when sewn over cord. Strips cut out of the lengthwise (warp) or cross grain (woof) of any material, will not stretch and will look bulky when used around corners. (Some of the newer materials will stretch on the cross grain.) See diagram for bias. Bias tape can be bought ready-cut at fabric shops in almost any colour, thus eliminating the need for cutting your own, and if used in a contrasting colour, is very attractive.

Turning Corners

When turning a straight corner, be sure to leave the needle in the fabric, lift the presser foot, and turn the material 90°. Lower the presser foot and continue sewing. Turning round corners is a little more difficult, but can be accomplished by sewing very slowly and easing your fabric around the corner without raising the presser foot.

String and Thumbtack Compass

If you wish to cut out a perfectly round piece of material, a simple compass can be made out of a piece of string, a pencil, and a thumbtack. To make a string compass, cut a piece of string about 5″ longer than the radius of the circle you wish to draw. Tie one end of the string to a pencil near the point. Stretch the string taut and tie a knot at the other end so the section between the pencil and knot is the distance of the radius. Place the canvas on a large flat surface and thumbtack the knot at the centre point of the circle you wish to draw. Holding the pencil perpendicular to the canvas, swing the pencil around lightly to make a circle. Then cut your perfect circle.

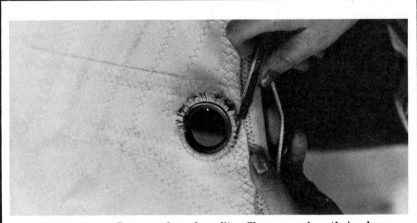

Stitch ripper. Get one of good quality. Cheap ones lose their edges.

COCKPIT CUSHIONS

I'm often accused of having terribly ascetic and Spartan concepts; if this is true, it takes on embodiment in my idea of the proper cockpit cushion. I confess that cushions are mandatory, for no minimally fleshed person can take sitting on a hard teak or fiberglass seat for longer than an hour, all fakirs excluded, but I do not believe in ungodly slabs of foam coated with horrendous naugahyde upon which you sweat in the sun and slither in the rain. Their mammoth size makes them awful to stow and, on deck, they have so much windage that once the wind wedges beneath them, they're overboard in a flash. We have, for some years, used small closed cell pads whose 1″ thickness provides as much cushioning as 4″ of the cheaper stuff.

We made our foam slabs small; 16″ X 12″, but have compensated by making the canvas covers for them in unifying sections. This way, as many as three individual pads can be sewn into one long compartment-like sleeve, providing economical usage under varying requirements. If three people require cushions (usually on the same side), the whole thing can be opened up and each person receives one 1″ thick foam pad. If two need cushions, one flap can be folded under avoiding the last piece flapping in the wind. One person will, of course, receive double thickness, but then that's life. If only a single crew needs a cushion, the thing can be folded into a triple layer and that, let me tell you, is comfort. A very pedestrian ribbon can be sewn on either end, so the cushions can be tied firmly if used as a single seat.

Acrylic or treated canvas for the cover, I feel, is infinitely superior to naugahyde. It has much greater friction, giving security on a heel and it does not become a sweat pad in the sun nor an ice rink in the rain. It will, of course, get soaked, but it dries as fast as any foul weather gear, so that's no argument. The fact that it lets water through is undeniable, but then, closed cell foam doesn't absorb water, so the cover will dry quickly indeed.

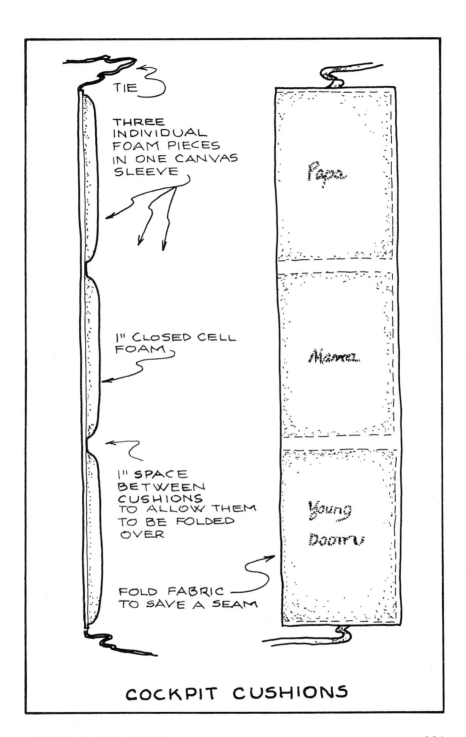

TIE

THREE
INDIVIDUAL
FOAM PIECES
IN ONE CANVAS
SLEEVE

1" CLOSED CELL
FOAM

1" SPACE
BETWEEN
CUSHIONS
TO ALLOW THEM
TO BE FOLDED
OVER

FOLD FABRIC
TO SAVE A SEAM

COCKPIT CUSHIONS

COCKPIT CHART STOWAGE

Charts in the cockpit can be disastrous. When most needed, they fly overboard or end up under hurrying crew's feet, triggering graceless somersaults. But charts abovedecks are often compulsory, and at all times great fun to use, and even the tiniest of cockpits (ours measures 30″ × 42″) will have space for the following clever item.

It is a large canvas pocket that can be snapped or *Velcroed* onto the aft wall of the cockpit. The size of the chart pocket should be 11″ high by 18″ wide. You have to fold a chart in half again to get it in but this can easily be done without permanent creasing. An additional pocket of 2¾″ × 11″ should be added to the outside for stowage of parallel rules, and another 2½″ × 7″ pocket should be sewn for one-handed dividers. If desired, the back portion can be extended to create a flap. Sew three small bits of Velcro onto it (one in, each corner and one in the middle) to help keep your flap shut. The hemming and sewing is identical to previous projects. A piece of Velcro in each top corner, or a snap in the same, should be enough to provide adequate fastening to the cockpit wall.

None of the above is meant to suggest use of this cockpit stowage as an uninterrupted daily procedure, but it would be handy from time to time.

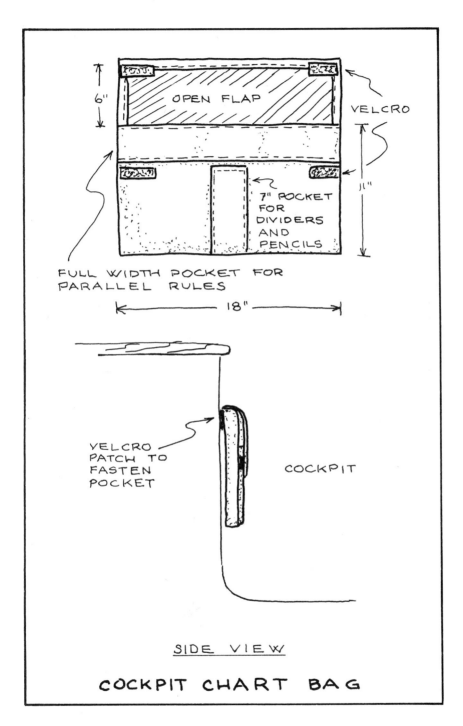

6"

OPEN FLAP

VELCRO

FULL WIDTH POCKET FOR
PARALLEL RULES

7" POCKET
FOR
DIVIDERS
AND
PENCILS

11"

|← 18" →|

VELCRO
PATCH TO
FASTEN
POCKET

COCKPIT

SIDE VIEW

COCKPIT CHART BAG

WINDLASS COVER

Windlasses are very expensive items that should be rinsed of salt water often and protected by a canvas cover whenever possible. Their gears should be kept well-oiled and salt free.

Since most windlasses are a rather ambiguous combination of curves and points and cylinders, two choices are left to the yachtsman. The first is to fabricate a simple drawstring bag which can be pulled over the windlass and tightened. This is a rather pathetic example of ingenuity, but it works.

Those more civilized can undertake designing and fabricating a canvas Chinese puzzle.

For the typical windlass, with a wildcat for chain and a drum for line, two cylinders, with one end of each closed (much like a winch cover), can be made to cover those parts.

If the windlass has no other eccentricities, each side can then be covered with the addition of two more pieces of canvas. These will have to be fitted with a goodly number of darts to allow for the curve of windlass housing, and a hole in each to allow for the wildcat and the drum. First, cut the holes as tight as possible, then continue darting around until you have a proper fit. Cut a slit below the wildcat to allow the cover to be put in place over the chain, as it goes through the deck fitting. Hem the slit as well as the rest of the cover, then sew the two cylinders in place.

Lastly, sew a piece of dacron tape to the bottom of each side of the slit. These will be ties to keep the cover from sailing off into the sunset.

Any windlass will require a cover made up of a rather ambiguous combination of curves and points and cylinders.

WHEEL COVERS

All sorts of these exist with zippers and snaps and flaps and hinges, when all you need are two pieces of canvas and a drawstring in a casing (heavy elastic will do as well).

Cut a circular piece equal in diameter to your wheel plus 1″ seam allowance (1″ instead of 1/2″ because this will be double stitched). Next, cut a piece equal *in length* to the wheel's circumference ($2\pi r = C$) plus 1/2″ seam allowances at each end. Make the width equal to one-third of your wheel's diameter, plus 1″ for the double-stitched seam allowance, plus 2″ for a casing. Fold one long edge under 1/2″, then another 3/4″ for the casing and run two rows of stitching close together. Hem the ends of the casing and the rest of the ends as well. Now, stitch the other side of the straight piece to the edge of the circular piece, with the wrong sides of both pieces out. Use double stitching. Using the safety pin with line or elastic, run same through the casing. Sew the elastic ends together after you've turned the cover right side out, slipped it over the wheel, and established how tight the elastic will have to be to: a) allow the cover to slip over the wheel, and b) pull the cover tight once it's in place.

If you're using a drawstring, cut the line so it's equal to the wheel's circumference plus 10″, and after feeding it through the casing, splice the ends together to prevent them from hiding in the tunnel.

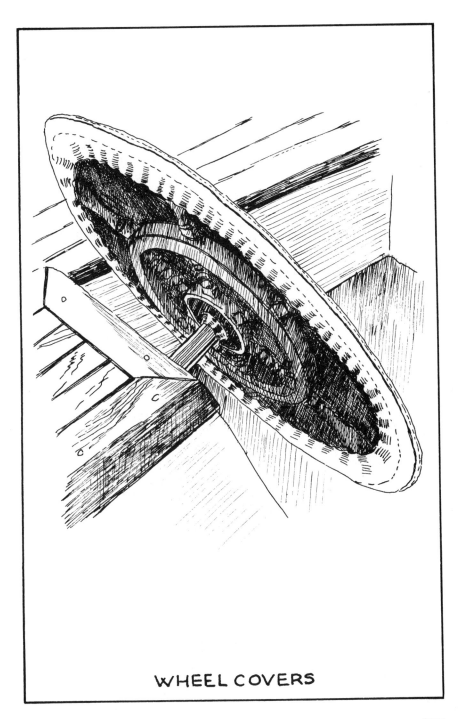

WHEEL COVERS

SEA ANCHORS

Since their highly publicized use by Captain Voss in his circumnavigating dugout canoe, sea anchors have become standard equipment on all yachts engaged in offshore cruising. They are indeed recommended for those venturing even only 15 to 20 miles from the coast, for if forced to run shoreward in a gale, the sea anchor may be the only thing that will save the yacht. Eric Hiscock in *Voyaging Under Sail* recounts when, near the Tonga Islands, a sea anchor, trailed from the stern, slowed them from 5½ to 1½ knots, and enabled them to steer safely a little across the wind, and thus avoid an island and a reef which lay to their lee.

A good sea anchor should be built at least as heavily as the yacht it's trying to slow. The size has been discussed and disagreed upon freely, and although some people carry and use sea anchors with 20″ diameter mouths on seven ton yachts, one has to accept the fact that with resistance of such caliber, tremendous forces will be put upon the yacht's fittings. A 10″ or 12″ opening would seem more reasonable; then, if additional drag is required, warps can be trailed as well. This gives much more flexibility in the amount of drag produced, than the all-or-nothing monster sea anchor.

The most important point of design is the rope framework which must be sewn to the anchor along its entirety. Some sea anchors, whose short bridle extends to the hoop only, are likely to have short life spans as well. The rope hoop can be replaced by a metal one to ensure against collapsing. Use only cotton canvas for the anchor itself, for it has infinitely better chafe resistance than acrylic. The rope should be at least 5/8″ braid. Metal thimbles must be spliced into eyes, uniting bridle and towing line. A streamlined lead weight of at least eight ounces should be sewn into a pocket to keep the anchor from riding along the surface. The tripping line is optional and, indeed, often a hindrance, for it fouls around the sea anchor, rendering it useless.

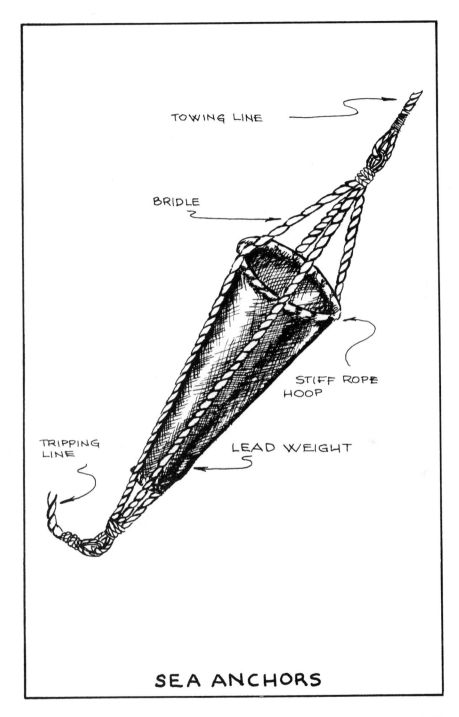

TOWING LINE

BRIDLE

STIFF ROPE
HOOP

TRIPPING
LINE

LEAD WEIGHT

SEA ANCHORS

CANVAS AND SAILS

229

YE OLD CANVAS BUCKET

An absolute necessity on all yachts is the old canvas bucket. No substitutes exist. A tin bucket is a weapon that turns on its master at every step, or steps on its master at every turn, whichever is easiest for it. The jet age plastic buckets are a joke. One needs only to fasten a line on them and heave them overboard while underway at even a pathetic speed of two knots to witness the separation of the stupid wire handle from the stupid plastic pail just in time to wave goodbye to three stupidly spent dollars. A varnished wooden bucket would be charming, but it has even more ferocity than its tin uncle. Hence, the canvas bucket.

It folds yieldingly into the size of a respectable hankie and even on the rampage, it can do little more harm than a wet noodle.

It should be of 10" diameter and 12" height. It should be made of heavy duck canvas so it will stand up when full of water and it must have a stiffening hoop around the rim to keep it from collapsing when being pulled aboard. A piece of canvas 32" X 15" will be required for the sides, and a 12" diameter piece for the bottom. A wooden mast hoop was used in the old days of sailing ships to provide the rim, but those being rather scarce nowadays, one has the option of steaming a piece of 1/4" X 3/4" elm, white oak or ash and monel stapling it into a hoop, or resort to a piece of soft plastic of about the same dimensions that can easily be bent and either glued or through-bolted using a cap nut to eliminate any sharp points. The hoop should then be sewn into the canvas and two grommets installed opposite each other below them.

Half-inch line, carefully halved with a thimble seized onto it will do nicely as a bale. Again half-inch line of at least an 8' length should be used to splice in as a bucket rope. Fit a large knot into the end to protect your handiwork from disappearing into the sea. Some people suggest using a loop around the wrist, but that to me seems a bit drastic, for it can lead to severely bruised limbs or worse — a man overboard. Not even a bucket of your own handiwork is worth that.

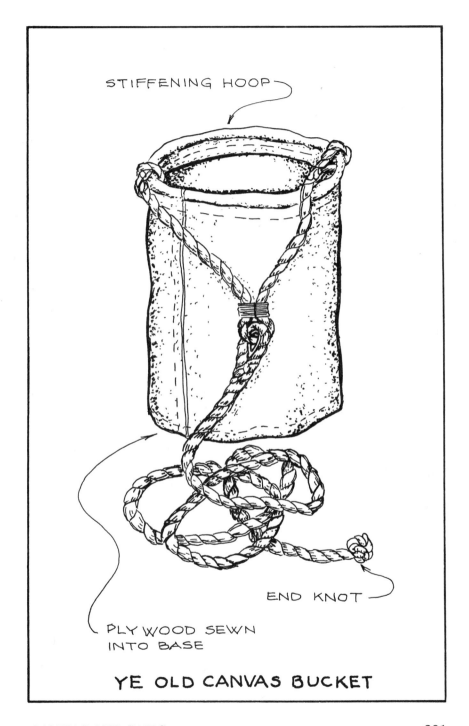

STIFFENING HOOP

PLYWOOD SEWN
INTO BASE

END KNOT

YE OLD CANVAS BUCKET

COMPASS CAP

Compass cards are delicate things, easily damaged by strong sunlight therefore, they should never be exposed unless they are being used. When not in use, a compass cap should be kept over them. Those fortunate enough to have magnificent binnacled, brass shrouds, please flip the page now. The mortals, get out your scissors and sewing kit.

Cut a circular piece of canvas whose diameter is 4″ greater (plus 1/2″ allowance for each seam) than that of your entire compass. At the four points of the compass rose, pinch in your canvas (the sewers call this darting) until you have formed a little dome or cap. Pin and sew these darts. Now, cut two identical rings of canvas whose outside diameter is 1½″ greater than that of your compass ring, and its inside diameter is 1/2″ greater than that of your newly fabricated cap (plus seam allowances). Sew the two rings together. Turn the rings right side out and fit the little cap inside the little ring and sew them together. Cute little beanie, n'est-ce pas? You'll need either Velcro or snaps to attach the cap to the cabin side or compass mount. If your compass is of the vertically mounted variety, three snaps will do, one on top and one on each of the sides. If it's mounted horizontally, use four. Spray with Scotchguard for waterproofing.

Well done, girls. Tomorrow we'll be making tiny underwear for the tiny seacocks.

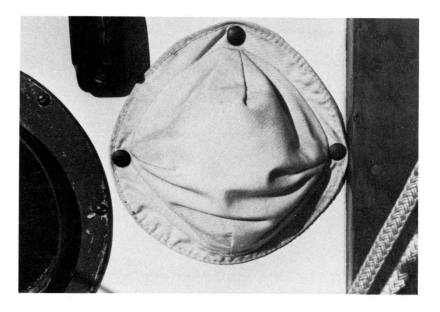

THE FINELY FITTED YACHT

LEE CLOTHS

Any yacht contemplating offshore cruising will have to have its berths fitted with lee cloths, or you might as well just make your bed on the cabin sole (because that's where you're going to spend most of the night anyway); at least then you won't wake up the rest of the crew with your body going thud, thud.

Cotton canvas of moderate weight will work very nicely, although if much voyaging is to be done in the tropics, netting can be substituted to facilitate air circulation.

The cloths should have a finished height of between 14″ and 18″, and an overall length of 20″-25″, with the sides tapering toward the top, again, to facilitate air flow.

Sew the cloth with 1/4″ turned under a 1″ hem, and fit the two top corners with grommets. Install the cloth onto the berth top with screws and finishing washers fitted every 8″ along the bottom edge. Fit the grommets with light lanyards. Lash them to a snap shackle or 1″ piston hank which will, in turn, be snapped into open padeyes screwed to the underdecks.

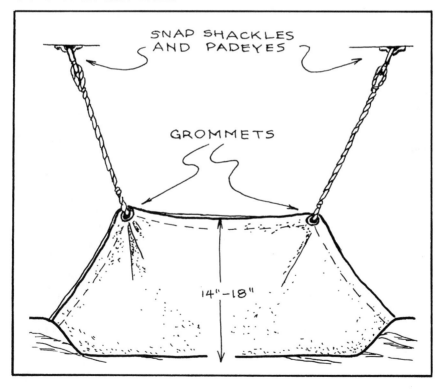

WINCH COVERS

It is recommended that winches be disassembled and greased once a year, and it is suggested that they always be covered when not in use.

The traditional winch covers have a hidden elasticized sleeve inside them, which hold these otherwise leisurely looking little bags in place.

Cut the top circle to the circumference of your winch plus the seam allowance. Cut the side out of a single piece. Make its width the height of your winch (plus seam allowance, plus 1″ for hem), and its length, the circumference of your winch plus two seam allowances of about 1/2″ each. For the little sleeve that lives inside, cut a piece the length of your winch's circumference, plus twice 1/2″ seam allowance, and a width of 3″, plus 1/2″ seam allowance, plus 1½″ for a casing for the elastic.

Begin sewing by stitching the casing. Next, sew the seams of the small sleeve together, then, using the ancient method of the safety pin in the elastic, push the pin in one end of the casing and out the other. Don't cut your elastic to length until you've finished this operation, otherwise — since your elastic will have to be about 6″ shorter than the length of your casing tunnel to function properly — you will forever lose the end of the elastic and end up like a dog chasing its tail. When you've done the threading, gather the casing until its circumference equals that of the narrowest part of your winch, *then* cut the elastic and sew its two ends together, then sew the mouths of the tunnels shut.

Next, sew the seams of the outside full-length sleeve, and hem it. Turn both sleeves wrong side out, set the short one *outside* the long one, then sew them simultaneously to the circular top piece. Now, turn it right side out, slip it over your fist, and give it a little cuddle.

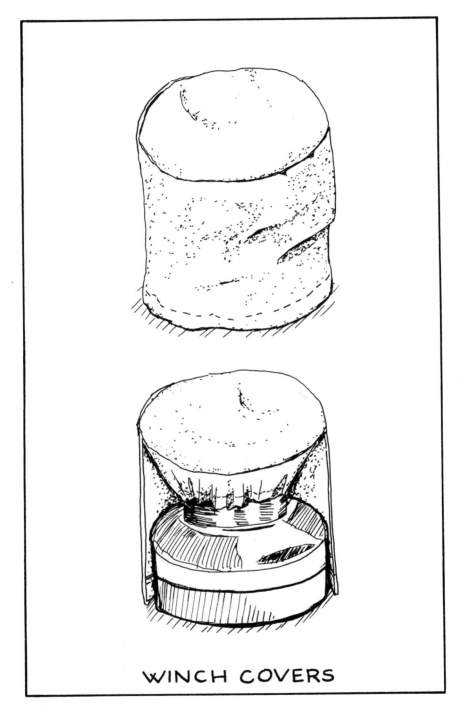

WINCH COVERS

HATCH AND SKYLIGHT COVERS

These are so boringly simple to make that anyone refusing to make them deserves to sand and scrape his woodwork twice a year. They come in very handy over skylights or transparent hatches, both as curtains for privacy, and as screens from the hot sun.

For a hatch with even height sides all around, you will require only one piece for a top, and one long piece to make up all sides. Cut the top to fit snugly, leaving 1/2" seam allowance all around, then cut the sides so they cover the woodwork completely down to the deck, allowing for seams (1/2") plus for an elasticized tunnel along the bottom (2½"). Sew the pieces together, leaving an opening for the elastic (or drawstring if you feel you want more secure control), then insert same, and fit in place.

For a gabled skylight, you will have to make the sides out of four separate pieces: two rectangular ones, and two the same shape as the skylight's ends. Ho hum.

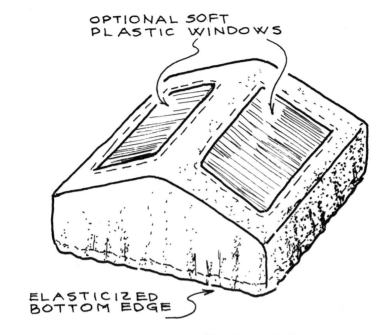

OPTIONAL SOFT
PLASTIC WINDOWS

ELASTICIZED
BOTTOM EDGE

SKYLIGHT COVER

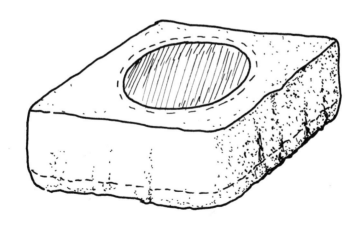

HATCH COVER

HATCH AND SKYLIGHT COVERS

LIFE BELT STOWAGE

Since most man overboard units are comprised of a number of items like strobe lights and sea anchors, a proper quick release stowage place must be made for them. Hooking all the assorted items over life lines and gallows, like so much laundry, is woefully inadequate.

The bag in the illustration contains stowage for all required pieces, and since its front flap can be released by simply pulling on a lanyard, all gear can be plopped quickly overboard.

First, gather up all your items and try fitting them into the open central part of the horseshoe ring. This can probably house the strobe light, dye markers, whistle, sea anchor, and the needed line as well. If this is indeed the case, then a bag can be made from two pieces of canvas.

Cut a piece of canvas as shown, leaving 1/2" for seam allowances, and 2" for hems. Hem all edges. Sew the bottoms of the sides to the sides of the bottom, but leave the front flap unattached. It should be hemmed. Now cut a piece to form the restraining belt. This should have a finished width of 3", and a length that will let it hang over the front flap by about 2". The other end of the belt will be sewn to the edge of the back.

Sew a small brass padeye into the center of the top of the flap 1" from the edge, and sew two similar padeyes, one on each square flap, 1" from its edge. Place grommets to accommodate the eyes, in corresponding spots of the belt, and the front flap.

Lastly, fit a single piece of light lanyard with three pull pins, which you can bend from good stainless wire; put all your gear into the bag, and close the flap and the belt by running the pins through the padeyes. Sew one end of the lanyard to the bag; the other end will be tied to the last pin. Sew and lash the bag (top and bottom) to the lifelines or gallows, close to the helmsman.

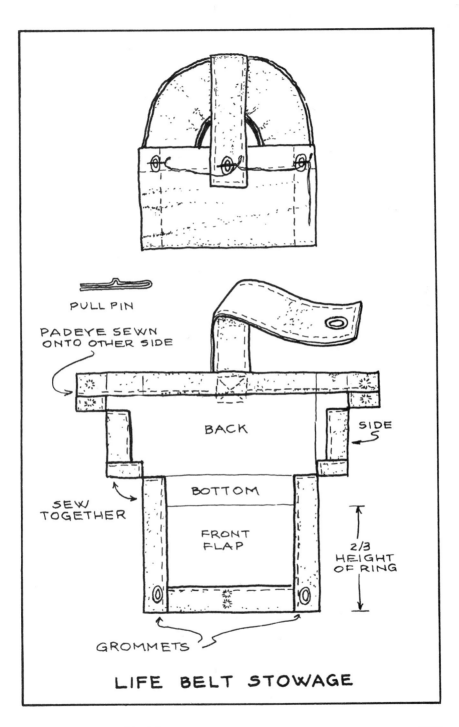

PULL PIN

PADEYE SEWN
ONTO OTHER SIDE

BACK

SIDE

SEW
TOGETHER

BOTTOM

FRONT
FLAP

2/3
HEIGHT
OF RING

GROMMETS

LIFE BELT STOWAGE

CANVAS AND SAILS

WEATHER CLOTHS

These are slabs of canvas strung between the top lifeline and the caprail in the area of the cockpit, traditionally, to keep the crew out of wind and spray, and, more recently, to write the yacht's name upon in horrendously large letters.

They should be so designed, that they run from the stanchion just forward of the cockpit to a stanchion just aft of it. Anything more would just impair visibility, and give precious little in return.

The cloth should be cut to a final size that allows for a 1/2'' to 1'' space between it and the lifelines, stanchions, and caprail. This way it can be pulled taut, otherwise, it will chatter horribly in any sort of blow.

Put a generous hem of 1½'' all around, into which grommets for lacing can be set. Cut and sew your major grommets only to begin with, that is, one grommet for the top and bottom of each stanchion, then lash the weather cloth in place, to see how it sets. Now, mark in location for additional grommets (if any), along the bottom, making sure you don't put one in unless you have a place to fasten it to. If no other guiding factors are present, place a grommet every 8'' along the top and sides.

At this stage, mark out a 6'' × 10'' area over which a pocket of the same size can be sewn. This will be a perfect spot for odds and ends, like sailing gloves and caps and sunglasses. If you plan to stow things there on a semi-permanent basis, sew a flap over it, and secure it with a piece of Velcro.

Lastly, set all your grommets, and lace the weather cloth smartly into place.

For yachts with stern pulpits, a more complex cloth can be made to surround the entire pulpit (see photo).

THE FINELY FITTED YACHT

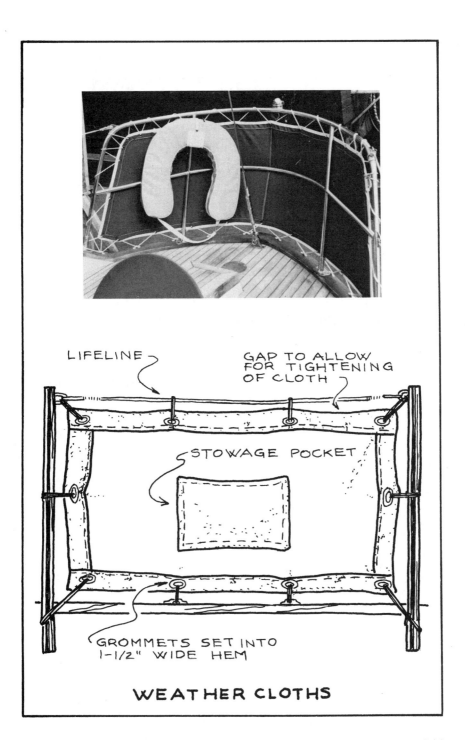

LIFELINE

GAP TO ALLOW
FOR TIGHTENING
OF CLOTH

STOWAGE POCKET

GROMMETS SET INTO
1-1/2" WIDE HEM

WEATHER CLOTHS

DINGHY STRAPS

For dinghys stored upside down, a set of cross straps should be fabricated, as mentioned in the section on dinghy chocks.

The least expensive and most functional material to use is the surplus seatbelt. If you can get it without the buckles, so much the better, for you'll just have to cut them off anyway.

A set of dinghy straps will be made up of two long pieces and two short ones, as shown in diagram. If properly measured and fitted, only a single knot holding the two short pieces together will need to be untied to loosen all the straps to the point where they can be slipped off the dinghy. To be able to accomplish this, the lines (a) and (b) which are fed through the padeyes to connect the long strap to the short one, will have to be of adequate length (between the padeye and the short strap) to allow the long strap to slip back and over the aft corner of the dinghy. This is not nearly as complicated as it sounds, so just go to it and think it out.

At each end of each strap, allow four inches of extra length to be folded back and stitched, leaving a loop for the lines, as in diagram.

Be sure that your two short straps are short enough so that the lanyard, which makes up the single knot atop the dinghy, can be pulled to tighten all the straps firmly. If the straps are so long that they meet — or worse yet, overlap — no matter how ferociously you tug at your lanyard, your straps will still just dangle like soggy spaghetti.

LINE (a)

LINE (b)

STITCHED
LOOP FOR
TIE-DOWN

DINGHY STRAPS

WINDSAILS

In the tropics, some sort of wind funnel system must be installed over a hatch if the belowdecks are to remain habitable. The complicacy of the design depends on one's philosophy of cruising, that is, whether he spends most of his stationary time at anchor or at the dock. If the yacht will be primarily at anchor, a very simple funnel can be made facing permanently toward the bow, since the anchored yacht points predominantly into the wind.

If you prefer being lashed to the land, you'll have to pay in hours invested in fabrication, since you will have to be prepared for the wind coming from any, and all, directions.

Simple

The more aesthetically inclined can attempt to fabricate a six-foot high cowl vent out of canvas, or better yet, spinnaker cloth. The latter is much easier to stow. Those less ambitious can make a square funnel, as in the diagram.

Cut three identical sides (if your hatch is square), with the bottom edges equal to the opening of your hatch, plus 1/2" seam allowances, and 1½" hem allowances. Cut the fourth side to only half height, leaving the top half open for the funnel's mouth. Cut a perfectly boring square piece for the top, with seam allowances on three sides and hem allowance facing the bow. Sew a couple of batten pockets diagonally to the underside of the top (look at any of your sails for proper construction), and cut a couple of discarded battens to fit. Radius the corners very well to keep them from coming through the canvas. Stitch a loop onto the centre of the top to allow for attachment of a halyard, which will be holding the windsail aloft.

Now, stitch all pieces together, attach two snaps in the bottom hem of each side, and screw the reciprocal part onto the outside of your hatch coaming, as close to the deck as possible. The installation of the snaps at such a low point is mandatory, to allow your elasticized mosquito screen (see that section) to be slipped over the top of the coaming. If this is made impossible by your specific coaming arrangement, a permanent screen will have to be sewn into the bottom part of your windsail.

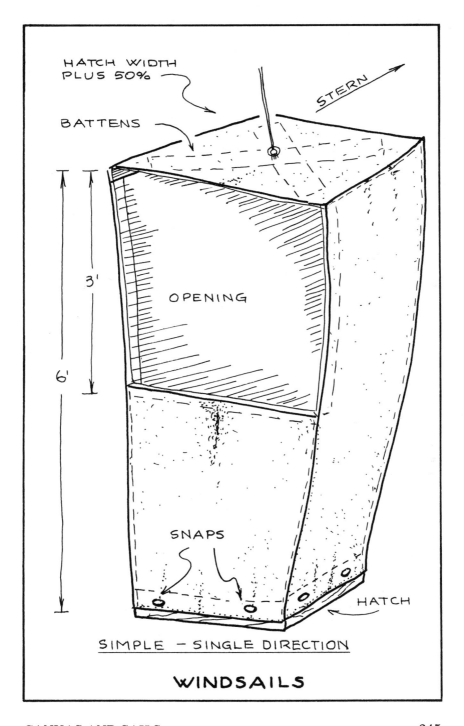

HATCH WIDTH PLUS 50%

STERN

BATTENS

3'

6'

OPENING

SNAPS

HATCH

SIMPLE — SINGLE DIRECTION

WINDSAILS

The More Complex One

Cut four pieces to the shape and size of the half piece in the simple windsail. Stitch these together as above and fit with snaps.

Cut and stitch the square piece for the top with batten pockets, as above, but do not stitch the pockets into place just yet.

Now, measure the diagonal at the tops of the bottom pieces, then measure the diagonal of the square top. Using these measurements, cut two diagonal baffles as in diagram. Add 1″ extra width in one of them for a seam allowance, because this piece will be cut in half and stitched to the centre of each side of the one piece baffle, to form a cross. Hem and stitch these pieces now. Next, stitch the newly sewn cross to the top, then stitch on your batten pockets. Now, let the cross about 10″ into the sides and stitch along the four corners. Use double stitching, for much strain will be experienced by the windsail.

With the bottom of the windsail snapped to the hatch coaming, and its top held aloft by a halyard, it is now ready to funnel air belowdecks, regardless of the wind direction. Oh, the good life!

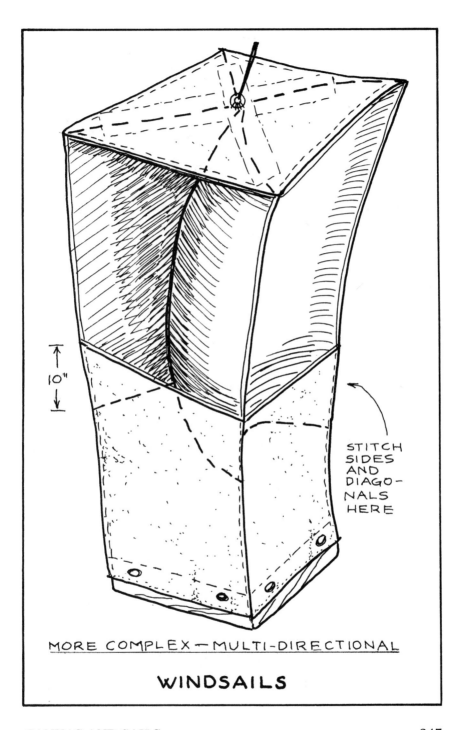

10"

STITCH
SIDES
AND
DIAGO-
NALS
HERE

MORE COMPLEX — MULTI-DIRECTIONAL

WINDSAILS

THE BEST BOSUN'S CHAIR

Dangling 45' high in the air can decidedly be fun, provided the dangling is done from an intelligently designed and conscientiously constructed bosun's chair, and not a pathetic contraption that some deprived individual pilfered from the swing of a neighborhood's playground.

A bosun's chair is called that for a purpose, so one should not settle for a bosun's bench, or bosun's stool, or even a bosun's swing. To be perfectly accurate, it should be called a bosun's *high* chair (about 45'), and as its namesake, it should be fabricated with a back, and sides, and a front, and a part that goes between the legs, so you won't slip out in a careless moment and totally destroy your freshly varnished skylight.

Construction

The chair is basically a double walled canvas sling (not acrylic, because it will chafe through in no time), with a 3/4" piece of plywood in the seat to act as a stiffener. Cut a piece of 3/4" plywood to 10" × 16", radius all corners, and round all edges like you've never done before. Sand to remove all slivers.

Next, cut two identical canvas pieces to a length of 50" and a width of 12". Now, leave the middle 16" at the cut width, and trim the end flaps so they'll form triangles with ends shaped, as in the diagram. Leave 1" all around for double seam allowance. Next, get some heavy dacron scraps from your sailmaker and cut them to two identical pieces, as shown. Now, lay the four pieces together into a four layer sandwich — with the dacron as the bread and the canvas as the baloney — then stitch them all together with two rows of stitches, one 1/4" from the edge, the other 1/2" inside that. Leave one 16" edge of the seat unsewn so you can turn the whole sling rightside out and slip the plywood into place. Now, fold the seam allowances under on these last 16", and double stitch the seam closed.

An additional bit of reinforcement can be had by running a 2" nylon belt (like a seatbelt of a car) between the dacron pieces, from one tip through to the other.

Next, cut and sew two, or four, canvas piggyback pockets onto each side flap, being sure to leave each pocket a goodly belly of 3" extra, so getting hands in and out when aloft will be made possible. A number of small pockets is infinitely superior to one large one, for then standard rigger's tools can have their own special compartments,

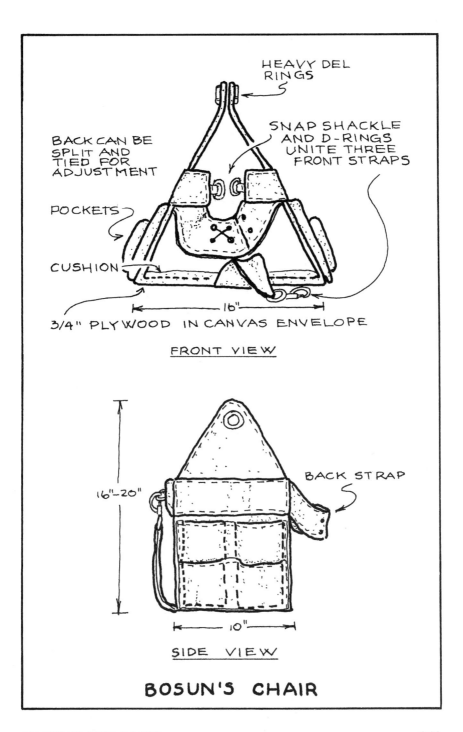

HEAVY DEL RINGS

SNAP SHACKLE AND D-RINGS UNITE THREE FRONT STRAPS

BACK CAN BE SPLIT AND TIED FOR ADJUSTMENT

POCKETS

CUSHION

16"

3/4" PLYWOOD IN CANVAS ENVELOPE

FRONT VIEW

BACK STRAP

16"-20"

10"

SIDE VIEW

BOSUN'S CHAIR

eliminating lengthy nerve-racking searches. Sew the pockets on most carefully, for you'll be going through six layers of fabric.

Now, cut a strip of canvas to a 6″ width and a 50″ length and fold and sew it into a 3″ X 50″ piece, most of which will run clear around the sitter much like a belt. It will be sewn to the outside of both sides of the chair just above the pockets, and will meet in the front, along with a short piece coming up vertically from the bottom of the seat. The vertical piece will consume about 10″ of the belt, while the rest can make up as large a horizontal belt as your corpulence dictates. Make it a comfortable fit, remembering that you'll be getting in and out of it, as well as just sitting in it.

Where the three ends of the belt meet in the front, you can either sew them permanently (and securely) together, or install a "D"-ring in the end of the horizontal belts and a snap shackle in the end of the vertical belt.

Lastly, and most importantly, take the chair to a sailmaker and get him to install a good size Del ring (1″ hole is minimum) into the tip of each side, for the hauling-halyard to run through. This is done on a machine that exerts 2000 lbs. of pressure, so don't try to do it yourself with pliers. May you dangle happily ever after.

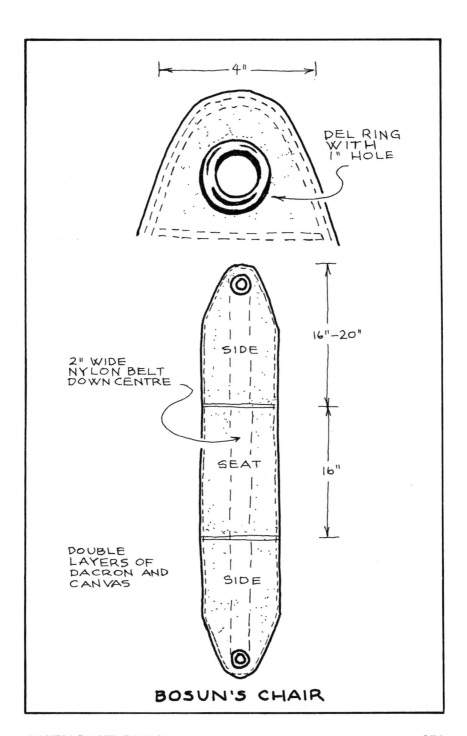

4"

DEL RING
WITH
1" HOLE

16"–20"

2" WIDE
NYLON BELT
DOWN CENTRE

SIDE

SEAT

16"

DOUBLE
LAYERS OF
DACRON AND
CANVAS

SIDE

BOSUN'S CHAIR

WINTER AWNING

Unless one lives in the absolutely perfect climate, that's not too hot and not too cold, not too dry and not too wet, and not too dusty nor too smoggy, one best get the proverbial lead out, along with some needle and thread, and begin sewing an awning. The owner of a yacht with even minimal teakwork — say hatches and caprails — and a painted wood or fiberglass coachhouse, will save himself annual maintenance time of at least one week, by having the yacht covered during the months that it is seldom used. Aside from reducing cosmetic demands, the awning will lengthen the life of the yacht considerably, by keeping rain out of joints and seams. It will also reduce the number of times teak needs to be sanded or cleaned with caustic chemicals, as well as hide paint, gelcoat and metals, from the elements.

Support

To be effective and have a lengthy life, an awning must be kept tight, that is, well supported, and well tied down. The boom is an obvious base for the aft section of the awning. The forward section can be held up by the reaching pole, or even the boat hook. Either can be run from a mast fitting and have its forward end held up by a halyard. This should not be done literally, for then a cutout, collar, etc., will have to be made; instead, the halyard can be tied to a loop sewn into the awning, while the reaching pole can be tied to the bottom of the same line *below* the awning. See diagram. This will, in effect, remove any pull from the awning itself, because the weight of the pole is being borne by the loop.

The outboard edges of the awning will be held up by lifelines, while the front can be supported by the bow pulpit.

Fastenings

As mentioned, the awning must be kept tight, or it will flutter and beat itself to death in a single windstorm. *Warm Rain's* awning did just that, after being left untied in two places. The fluttering acrylic was chaffed through in three spots after a day and a half long storm. Just attaching sandbags to the perimeter of the flaps of the awning is woefully inadequate, for the wind will *lift* the awning's great surface and chafing will begin. The best solution is to have a generous number of tiedowns sewn to the underside of the awning. These can be located anywhere a firm base can be found, e.g. stanchions, boom, pulpits, and rigging. Each tiedown should be sewn

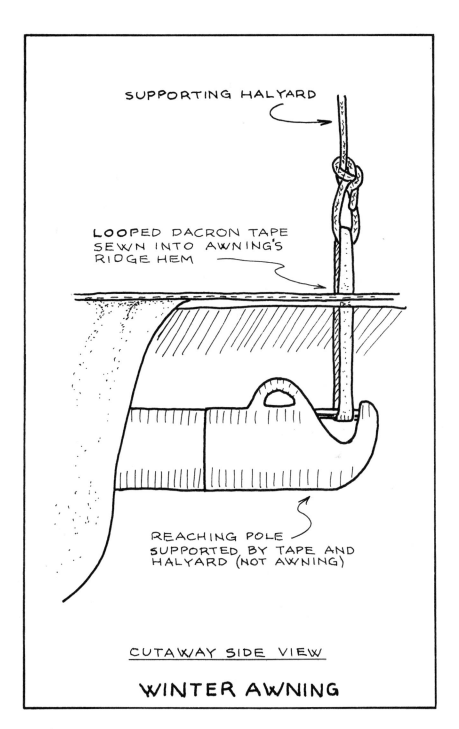

SUPPORTING HALYARD

LOOPED DACRON TAPE
SEWN INTO AWNING'S
RIDGE HEM

REACHING POLE
SUPPORTED BY TAPE AND
HALYARD (NOT AWNING)

CUTAWAY SIDE VIEW

WINTER AWNING

to a sizeable patch to distribute the forces somewhat on the fabric. Don't scrimp. Make the patches as large as possible; you'll have lots of scrap pieces around, so use them. If you're a patch connoisseur, you may consider using heavy dacron instead of canvas or acrylic, for dacron is measurably more chafe resistant than the other two. Any sailmaker will happily inundate you with his scraps.

Chafe Spots

Wherever the awning makes contact with a hard point, a sacrificial chafe patch should be used similar to those used with tiedowns. Again, make the patches large. An awning is usually of a monstrous size, and seldom will it be secured in the same place twice, so a patch should be large enough to allow for any wandering. *Warm Rain's* chafe patches measure 14″ X 14″ over a stanchion top of 1″ diameter. Why not? You can never be sure. Use dacron.

Sectioning

The more utilitarian minded will design his awning in three sections. One section will cover the yacht from the mast to the bow, the next will cover aft from the mast to the rear of the cockpit, and the last piece will cover what's left. In this way, the central piece can double as a sun or rain awning by itself, if so required.

Awning tiedown with large dacron chafe patch.

Joints

Where the three pieces of awning join, an extremely secure, yet quite quickly releasable, attachment should be made. Snaps have no place in a large awning, for they continually corrode and eat away the fabric around themselves. Besides, they usually come apart when you least want them to, and more often than not, they will snap together only after you've dislocated your finger joints three or four times while pressing desperately.

Twist locks in canvas covers are an hilarity. My friend, Gary Storch the sailmaker, told me a story of a two-piece awning held together in such a fashion. From underneath, twist locks look much like snap locks, or at least they did to one fervent crew member, so he grabbed one wing of the awning in each hand, and proceeded to undo the "snaps" with one quick yank; and by God, he did!

Heavy Delrin zippers reinforced with ties, make the most positive joints for, apart from providing an even, noncorrosive attachment, they limit all possibility of spotty joints with large open

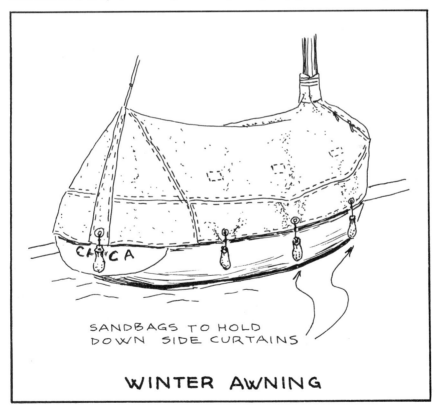

SANDBAGS TO HOLD
DOWN SIDE CURTAINS

WINTER AWNING

spaces between, where water and dirt can enter. The ties should be placed on either side of the zipper (one pair every two feet or so), and the bulk of the fore and aft strain should be taken up by them; the zipper should just more or less keep out the wind. It should be fitted with double pulls, to facilitate closing and opening in both directions.

Since zippers are not waterproof, one should consider having a Velcro-fitted flap hinged from one section of the awning to the other.

Openings

One would appear somewhat tragic standing outside one's beautiful new awning with no way to get in. A short flap about 20" wide, running 20" above the lifelines, zippered on its foreward and aft edges, and hinged along the keel line, would show prudence. To gain entrance, the flap could be rolled up and tied in the open position with a tiedown sewn to the awning just above it.

The location of the opening is, of course, important. One's immediate reaction is to place it so it can be used in conjunction with the lifeline gate, and that's all well and good, unless, of course, the gate is misplaced to begin with — or even worse — nonexistent.

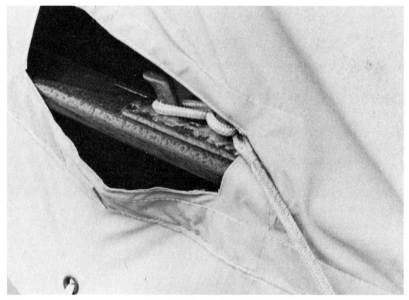

Well reinforced cutout.

THE FINELY FITTED YACHT

In that case, most people would tend to place the opening amidships, especially if the yacht had severely pinched ends, and this would be a mistake. Granted, it is most comfortable to board where the yacht is snuggled to the dock, but once you're in under the awning, doubled over on the side deck, staring at your feet, what will you do? What *will* you do? Waddle — that's what — and that's no fun, especially if you're lugging something heavy, like groceries or an albatross, so *don't* cut the entrance amidships, unless you have a centre cockpit. Then it's okay, but otherwise, cut it somewhere aft, so you can keep your graceless waddling to a minimum.

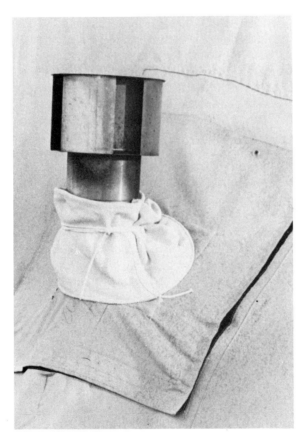

Asbestos collar makes a safe choker to keep chimney-cutout watertight.

If you have a three-hundred-year lease on a dock, and you're not really going anywhere for any length of time, by all means save some money and some labour, and cut an entrance on one side only; if neither of the above, cut two.

Cut Outs

Most well brought up yachts have mooring lines holding them to docks. Areas will have to be cut out of the awning to accommodate them. Like your chafe patches, your cutouts should be big and extremely well reinforced, to allow for chafing. See photo. The finest fitted yacht would probably have its cutout trimmed with a little strip of leather.

Chimney Outlets

In northern climates, awnings do a marvelous job of keeping in heat as well as providing a semiwarm, dry area, to hang umbrellas and galoshes. But to have this warmth in the first place, you need a reliable diesel stove, and diesel stoves have chimneys, which need to stick their noble heads out through the awning. If a standard cutout is made, water will gush in to inundate the deck and house, and the awning will flutter and ripple around the pipe, resulting in pathetic draft. So, a little flap should be fabricated, and held in place with a set of zippers or Velcro, and the centre of the little flap should be fitted (finely) with a little boot made of asbestos. See photo. The diameter of the boot should exceed the diameter of the pipe by 6″, again to allow for slight shifting of the awning.

Flap Hold-Downs

The sides, or flaps, of the awning should be kept from banging around. As mentioned, the awning itself must be secured to the tops of stanchions, etc., with tiedowns, so the securing of the usually short flaps should be no great undertaking. Also, as mentioned, snaps and twist locks should be avoided, as should desperate attempts to elasticise the flap bottoms. Spur-grommets should be set every four feet or so (reinforced with a patch), and made fast with a short line, to either whisker stays or sandbags.

If a bowsprit is present, a single line can be laced through from side to side, below the bowsprit.

The sandbags need not be large, 4″ diameter bags, 8″ high, with a drawstring around the top, should be plenty. A small trick should be used in sewing the bags: instead of cutting out small pieces for say, ten bags, just cut and sew one long tube, 4″ in diameter

THE FINELY FITTED YACHT

Sandbag hold-down.

Collar for shroud outlet.

(remember 1/2″ seam allowances on either side of the piece), with a length of ten times 10½″ (8″ for bag, twice 1/2″ for seam allowance, top and bottom, and 1½″ for the tunnel for the drawstring). When sewn, simply cut the long tube into 10½″ sections, sew in the bottom, and finish the top.

General Design Points

Cutouts in the top of the awning should be as few as possible. The topping lift (and the staysail stay as well on cutters), should be disengaged and stowed against the shrouds.

The mast collar should be generously high, with ample length of tape (about 20″ each), to be wrapped tightly around the collar. The ends of the tape (halving a single 48″ piece is preferable) should be stitched to the top corner of the collar, so an inadvertent funnel won't be created.

Shroud-cutouts should be fitted with hinged flaps, and held in place with Velcro. Make the width of your cutouts at least 3″, to allow for some fore and aft play. Fit the bottoms of the flaps, as well as the piece they adjoin, with grommets and ties, or the weight of the sandbags will pull the flap away.

Slopes

Be sure all surfaces are generously sloped or water will settle in areas and, with the pressure of its weight, either tear the awning, or at least drip through.

Laying-Out and Assembly

Fabricating an awning of this nature takes more time to design than to sew. Remember, you can't just fold bits of cloth every which way and hope they'll fit. They won't. You will have to create a great number of panels, each of them accurately measured and laid out on a diagram. Don't be frightened by all the odd shaped pieces you come up with, just measure and label all sides accurately. Run your fabric fore and aft, to lessen the number of small pieces required. Allow 2″ or more per hem; 3″ if grommets are to be set in them. It would show prudence to cut out and machine bast only the centre section of the awning first, then take it down to the boat, fit it, and mark in all needed adjustments. The centre section is the easiest to make, having the fewest triangles, so it's the best one to practice on.

Some people recommend sewing all the bits and pieces (ties, reinforcements, etc.) onto each small part before incorporating it into a section. This is folly. Indeed, none of the above should be even

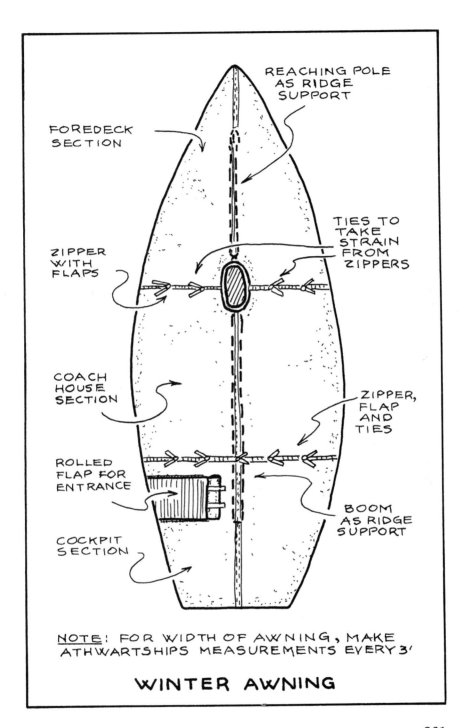

NOTE: FOR WIDTH OF AWNING, MAKE ATHWARTSHIPS MEASUREMENTS EVERY 3'

WINTER AWNING

thought about until *all* sections have been adequately fitted together, for, although I'm first to admit that small pieces are easier to handle and sew onto than large ones, I just cannot conceive what good an easily sewn on chimney collar is going to do three feet aft of the chimney.

The ridge of the awning should be reinforced its full length, for great tension will be put upon it. This can be done by running an 8" wide piece of fabric over (or under) the ridge seam. *Over*, will help waterproof the seam, *under* will act as a chafe patch. Up to you.

Seams should be sewn so the high piece will overlap the low piece, otherwise, you'll be sewing handy little troughs for water and dirt to be caught in.

Flaps (sides) can be sewn on last, since their fit is not nearly as vital as that of the top pieces. This will cut down on the amount of bulk you'll have to handle during fitting.

Dacron tape — not grommets and line — sewn per diagram should be used for all ties.

Good luck.

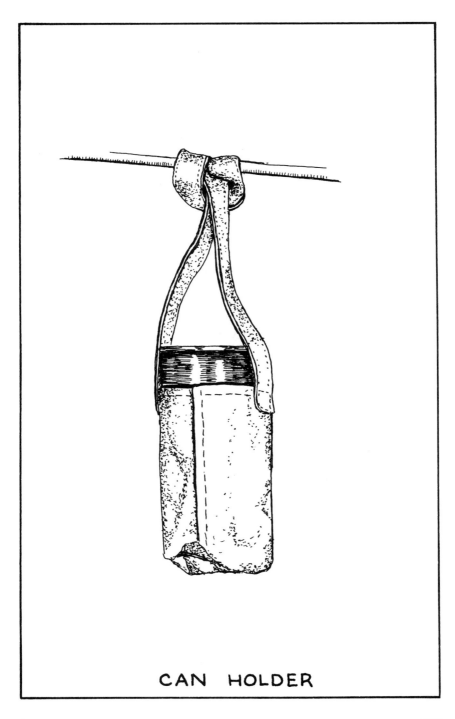

CAN HOLDER

SUN AWNING

The varieties of these have such a great range that I'm almost afraid to begin; but here goes.

Cockpit Only

In temperate climates, where the avoidance of the sun is mandatory only on uncustomarily hot summer days, a small awning fitted just over the cockpit, will be quite adequate. In its simplest form, it could be made up of the dinghy sail slung over the boom and lashed to the lifelines.

A more advanced awning would be a rectangular piece of treated canvas (Vivatex), supported in a similar fashion, except that the boathook could be slung athwartships over the boom, to act as a spreader to give a bit more head room.

Coach House Awning

If the sun is severe enough over a long period to overheat the deck and coach house, an awning, stretching as far forward as the mast, should be fabricated. Side curtains could be bypassed in favour of uninterrupted ventilation.

Full Cover

If you're in such vicious heat that the coach house awning is not enough, you should give thought to either moving to another climate, or constructing an awning that covers the yacht from stem to stern. In such a case, the construction would be very similar to the winter awning, except that the precautions against water leakage could be bypassed.

With all three awnings, rapid rigging and stowing are most important, for if the thing is a monster to use, then sewing it will be a waste of time, because no one will ever bother putting it up anyway.

Construction

Cut your pieces of canvas with allowances for seams (1/2″), and hems (2″), making sure that the edges always fall short of their intended anchoring spot, so they can be pulled taut. Since much windage and strain will be encountered by most of these awnings, the corners should be reinforced with a patch of canvas or dacron before the spur grommets are set in, or dacron tape tiedowns sewn on.

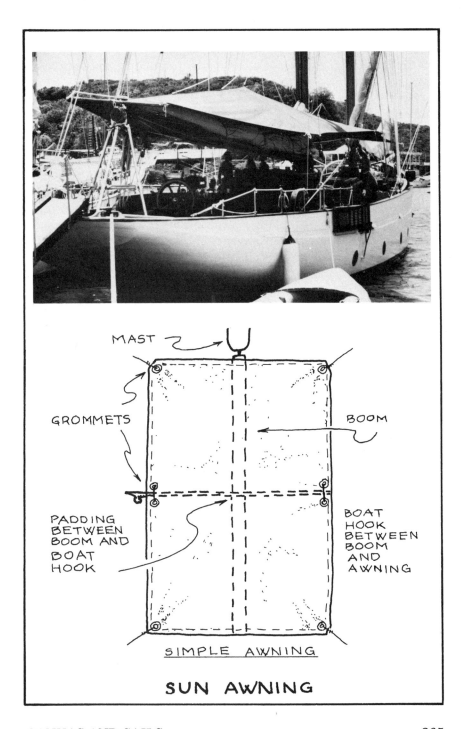

MAST

GROMMETS

BOOM

PADDING
BETWEEN
BOOM AND
BOAT
HOOK

BOAT
HOOK
BETWEEN
BOOM
AND
AWNING

SIMPLE AWNING

SUN AWNING

For added stiffness, a ridge rope can be installed in much the same fashion as the piping in cushions. See "Cushions" section.

If side curtains are required for early morning and late afternoon sun, the best solution may be a single portable flap, about 3′ × 6′, which could be moved from one spot to another depending on the yacht's position.

A most commendable secondary function of sun awnings would be to trap rain water. This can be simply done by reverse rigging most canopies, that is, having a trough down its spine instead of a ridge. To do this, hang the foreward end of the awning from the shrouds (slung *below* the boom), and the aft end, spread by the boat hook, from a lanyard on the backstay. Tilt the awning foreward or aft, as you prefer, then simply place a bucket at the mouth of the trough and call in the bucket brigade. In the tropics (where sun is the longsuit and good drinking water the short), I have seen a 40 gallon water tank filled in 45 minutes during one of their average drizzles.

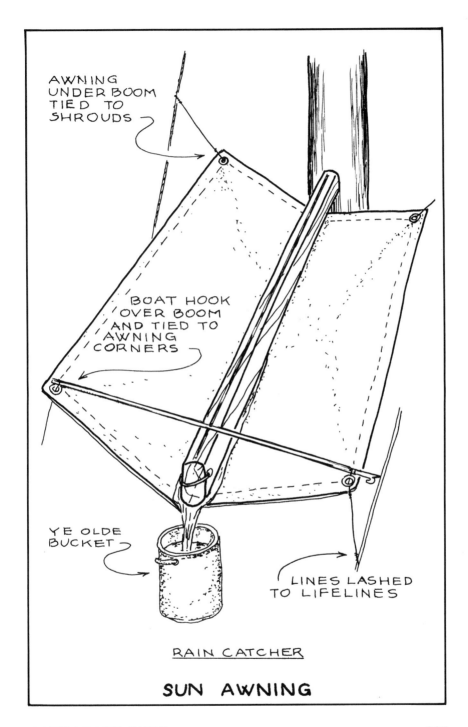

AWNING
UNDER BOOM
TIED TO
SHROUDS

BOAT HOOK
OVER BOOM
AND TIED TO
AWNING
CORNERS

YE OLDE
BUCKET

LINES LASHED
TO LIFELINES

RAIN CATCHER

SUN AWNING

SAIL CARE

Intricate adjustments are made to the amount and type of resins. Coating and impregnation procedures are complex. Weave constructions become more specialized. And the cost of sails continually goes up, making it easy to understand why, whether you race or cruise, keeping your sails in top shape is all-important.

Racing Sails

For all of you lunatic fringe sailboat racers (and I'd include myself in that category), your main interest is to keep your sails fast, recognizing that the "racing life" of the sail is probably substantially shorter than the sail's structural life. That fundamental axiom applies to all racing sails — unresinated, resinated, soft or firm. Here's what you do to keep them in shape.

Don't use your best racing sails when you don't have to. Any sail has a limit to its racing life, and since sails aren't cheap, daysailing or practicing boat handling with your newest, hottest rags is a fast way to make them slow. You might even want to use one suit of sails for major regattas and another for less important events or club racing.

Store your sails dry. Racers can dry their working sails on a lawn or on their boat if there isn't too much wind. It is especially important for resin-coated fabrics to be dried thoroughly, as they tend to soften up a bit and can develop reduced stretch resistance if they remain wet. If you sail in salt water, it's especially important to keep sails dry. Salt draws the moisture out of the air and tends to keep sails damp.

The amount of sunlight a sail receives when drying can be more detrimental for big boats than small boats. This is because the ultra-violet degradation that can break a sail down, though the process takes quite a while, is more critical on big boats that must sustain higher wind loads.

However, sunlight *can* affect nylon spinnakers, which are very sensitive to ultra-violet light due to their light-weight construction. A three-quarter-ounce spinnaker fabric can lose 50 percent of its strength after just two weeks of direct exposure to sunlight.

Always fold or roll your sails. This will keep them smooth and flat and *much* faster especially in light air. Some people prefer to fold their sails on the same crease time after time. Others don't care. I'm in the "don't care" school. It seems to me that if you have many small creases over the sail that will eventually disappear you're better off than having five or six large, semi-permanent creases that can cause resistance to air flow, just as a rough bottom can slow a boat's progress through the water.

Rolling sails has been in vogue for the past four or five years, although rolling very stiff, resin-coated fabrics finished with Condition Yarn Temper or Duroperm has been around for even longer. There is no doubt that rolling keeps sails smooth. I have never felt any particular need to roll mainsails, but I'm convinced it helps keep jibs fast. The best way to roll a jib is to start from the head and roll to the foot. That will keep the head of the sail in the center of the rolled tube when you're finished and the luff wire — if you have one — will stay in the tube better as well. The luff wire can actually act as a coil inside the tube which makes the rolled sail stiffer and easier to transport. If you have a jib with hanks, roll from the head straight down the luff. When you're ready to hoist, all the hanks will be at the front of the tube, ready to snap to the headstay.

If your spinnaker has a fairly stiff finish, keep it folded as well. Many wrinkles can eventually break down some of the newer spinnaker fabrics. To roll a stiff-finished chute material, join the clew and then the rest of the sail laterally, rolling it from the head down to finish the package. That way, the luff tapes won't crinkle as badly either, which at times can cause the luff itself to shrink.

Don't worry about dirt or blood on sails unless the stain can easily be rinsed off with water or truly bothers your aesthetic sensitivity. Dirt doesn't slow sails down, but washing highly-resinated sails can make them softer and cause them to lose their shape.

Never let your sail luff unnecessarily. Sheet them in just enough to keep them quiet, reducing the vibration and shaking that strains cloth and also loosens shackles, tangles sheets and pushes battens out of mainsails. Obviously, it's important to take sails down at the dock, but you can also lower your mainsail between races and sail around on the jib.

Cruising Sails

It isn't crucial to have wrinkle-free cruising sails, so it's okay to leave them stuffed in their bags for a week or so. It's also okay to leave them wet for short periods of time, although if you're planning on storing your sails for long periods, it's important they be dried thoroughly to prevent mildew. Mildew won't grow on synthetic fibres and will not affect their strength, but it can grow on the dirt that gets on sails and it can develop into an unsightly mess.

Unlike racing sails, washing cruising sails will not damage them. In fact, while removing salt and dirt, washing your sails will make them softer and easier to handle. Use warm water and a mild detergent. Probably the easiest technique is to lay the sail flat on an asphalt driveway or lawn and scrub it with a long-handled brush. Be sure to rinse the sail thoroughly and dry it in the shade if possible.

A good cover is essential for the cruising sail. Ultra-violet radiation over a prolonged period can seriously weaken your sail fabric and a sail that is left in the sun, especially in the tropics, can lose a serious amount of strength after less than a year. Acrylic fabrics, although expensive, make the best covers because they are absolutely insensitive to ultra-violet rays and because they won't fade.

Make sure your sails are furled securely before leaving your boat for any length of time. Sails can become completely destroyed in a squall or a storm because a portion of the sail was left loose and started flapping. That goes for roller-furling headsails as well. Make sure the sails are furled smoothly and the furling lines are secure.

It's extremely worthwhile to have your sails checked periodically by your sailmaker. He'll be able to repair small rips or weak seams before they become a problem and he'll wash and fold them properly.

Basically, a small amount of time spent caring for your sails can, in the end, make you race fast or cruise efficiently. Fortunately, there are no mysteries in sail care — only a little common sense.

Stain Removal

Any of the suggestions below will help you on new stains. If you're serious about cleaning a stain, do it soon. Waiting will probably make the job impossible.

Blood Stains

Scrub the stain with a concentrated mixture of dry detergent and warm water. Make the mixture as thick and pasty as possible and apply it to the stained area with a brush. Let the mixture stand on the stain for about 15 to 30 minutes to let the detergent work, and then rinse with warm water. If the stain is still there (and at least some of it probably will be) you can bleach the stained area with something like Clorox and warm water and then re-rinse. Bleach nylon only at room temperature and then rinse thoroughly.

Oil, Tar and Wax

Oily, black stains are extremely tought to remove from sails, but try the following: first, scrape off the excess gook with a spatula. Do not heat the stain because it will drive the stain deeper into the fabric. Place some drycleaning fluid on a soft, absorbent cloth and then place the sail stain side down on the cloth. Next, pour some more fluid on the sail so it will soak through the cloth and carry the stain out onto the absorbent cloth. Sail cloth is so tight that this method will probably take a while. Squeezing the fluid through the sail with another absorbent pad will help. Also, coated sail cloth (most three-quarter-ounce spinnaker cloth, Duroperm or CYT) won't allow fluids to soak through, so you'll have to blot from one side. After you've done what you can, soak the stain in warm water with a laundry pretreatment product, rinse, scrub with a mild detergent and rinse again.

Mildew

Mildew won't affect the strength of your sail, but it's best to remove any stain soon or you'll have it for a long time. Wash the stain in hot, sudsy water (with some bleach added), then rinse and dry. Moisten the stain with lemon juice and salt and let it dry in the sun. Rinse in warm water.

Rust

Soak the stain in oxalic acid for 15 to 30 minutes and then rinse thoroughly. You can get oxalic acid powder at a drug store. Use manufacturer's recommendations about the amount of water to cut it with.

Things To Avoid

Dacron polyester is essentially unharmed by any normal chemical commonly used around boats — including battery acid, acetone, gasoline, etc. Some solvents will tend to soften the resins (especially resins used in coating rather than impregnation), but the resin will reharden after the solvent evaporates.

Nylon, on the other hand, is sensitive to some acids and bleaches, especially in warm solutions. Since spinnakers (which are almost universally made from nylon) tend to get very tight and relatively weak, you should keep them away from acids and bleaches. When removing stains (such as mildew stains) on spinnakers, make sure you are using a room temperature bleach solution, and make sure you rinse the sail thoroughly after cleaning.

SAIL CLOTH

A key ingredient of sail design is in the cloth, where myriad combinations of weaves and finishes can interact at a microscopic level to create the perfect sail.

Fortunately, your sailmaker has given the problem of sail cloth selection a lot of thought and has probably chosen well from the staggering array of available fabrics which have been developed out of the infinite variety of weaves and finishes.

In most cases, it is wise to rely on his recommendation since his choice is based on a deep understanding of fabrics as well as first hand experience with sails suited for your boat and the conditions you will be sailing in. But sometimes there is a choice among several materials or finishes, each of which might be satisfactory for your sail. Understanding what tradeoffs are involved will help you assist your sailmaker in choosing the right cloth for your sailing aspirations. At the very least, it's important to understand the theories a sailmaker employs in selecting cloth.

One simple tradeoff, for instance, and the one people are most used to dealing with, is whether to opt for "soft" or "firm" material. This is an overly simplified way of classifying cloth since "soft" cloth for one maker may mean "firm" cloth for another, just as a big breeze to a Long Island Sound sailor may seem pretty insignificant to a native of San Francisco Bay.

When it comes to designing your sail, a sailmaker is aided primarily by knowing what boat you sail, where you sail it and what the average wind and sea conditions are. In addition, he has to know or at least be familiar with, how your mast and rig behave. These pieces of information help him to decide how to design the sail's shape and size, and, just as important, they help him choose the right cloth.

Many people underestimate or ignore the importance of sail cloth on sail performance, though more and more people are coming to realize that in addition to affecting the feel or handling properties of a sail, sail cloth can also influence shape, performance and the longevity of a sail just as strongly as the sail design and construction. Sailmakers have realized this as long as sails have been made, and as a result, they spend a lot of time analyzing available fabrics to determine what will work best.

For instance, a 505, Cal-20 and Finn mainsail might all be roughly the same size, but each will have different characteristics which would lead your sailmaker to choose widely different fabrics for each sail. Before looking into the choices your sailmaker might make, let's look at what goes into the various fabrics he would be choosing from.

First, sail cloth is made by interlacing continuous strands of filaments called yarns. Weaving these groups of filaments in various ways allows each interlaced yarn to spread out or compact as it moves in and out in the weave. This also makes the resulting fabric pliant and non-porous. For instance, in spinnaker cloth, the filaments are spread out to minimize porosity in spite of the loose packing of the yarns. The number of yarns per inch in the weave are kept to a minimum to save weight. In mainsail and jib fabrics, the filaments move in such a way as to allow the yarns to deform and brace the weave to provide maximum resistance to stretch.

Yarn for sail cloth is almost exclusively either nylon or polyester. Polyester is sold under many trade names by various fabric producers, but Du Pont's Dacron is by far the most common polyester yarn used in sail cloth. The individual properties of nylon and Dacron determine what fabrics they are used in. Nylon, because it is very strong and light weight for its size and bulk, is best for spinnaker materials.

Nylon's relative stretchiness isn't a factor in spinnakers. Dacron, which is denser and less stretchy, although weaker (stretch resistance and strength have nothing in common) than nylon, is extremely well-suited for working sail fabrics, where stretch resistance rather than ultimate strength is the major factor. In addition, both nylon and Dacron shrink with heat. This shrinkage is extremely important — even crucial — in finishing modern, tightly-packed fabrics. For nylon materials, this shrinkage isn't terribly important. For Dacron materials, however, where maximum tightness is important in reducing bias stretch (stretch along a line diagonal to the warp and fill yarns; warp yarns run parallel to the cloth panel and fill yarns run perpendicular to the panel). Any amount of tight packing produced on a loom would be insufficient to provide the fibre packing density that a combination of tight weaving and shrinking with heat can produce. Even the tightest fabrics produced on the most powerful looms can be tightened anywhere from 10 to 20 percent through heat shrinkage.

Nylon or Dacron yarns used for sail cloth are available in certain specific sizes. Because of this, and because there is an infinite number of spacings that can be chosen for the warp yarns and fill yarns, describing fabric by weight only is sort of like describing a boat by weight only. If someone told you he had a 5,000-pound boat, you

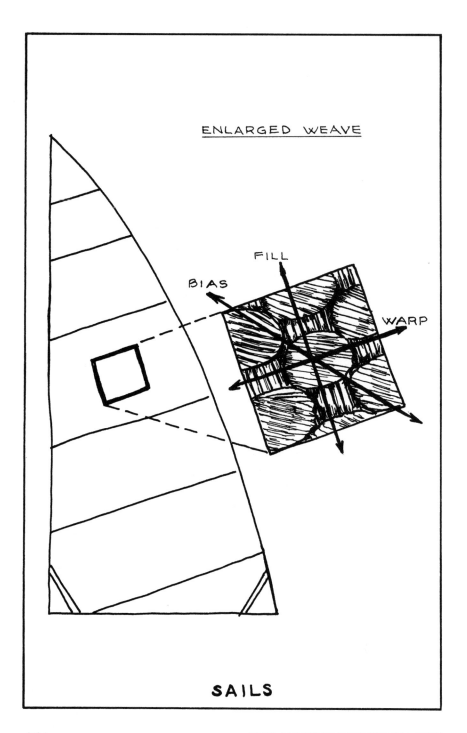

ENLARGED WEAVE

FILL

BIAS

WARP

SAILS

THE FINELY FITTED YACHT

would know as much about his boat as you would about a fabric you were told weighs five ounces. The term "five ounces" refers to the weight of a piece of fabric 36″ X 28½″, a sailmaker's yard — at least in the U.S. Elsewhere, sail cloth weight refers to ounces for a square yard, or in the metric system, to grams per square meter.

For any weight and type of cloth, it is the stretch properties of the particular fabric which determine how a sail made from it will be shaped and how that shape will change with changes in wind velocity, sheet tension, mast bend, stay sag, and other factors. As one example, a sail made out of a material that stretches very little along the leech and quite a bit on a line between the clew and the middle of the sail will tend to develop a deep draft aft with increasing wind loads. If that's the case, the correct balances of stretch and stretch resistance have not been considered and the sail will not perform properly. For instance, another case where balances must be carefully weighed is in high-aspect and low-aspect mainsails. Because there are high leech loads on high-aspect mains, stretch resistance in the fill yarns is extremely important. In low-aspect mainsails, fill stretch resistance is not as important, but controlling the bias stretch, which affects the large center area of the sail, becomes more important. For most genoas, it's important to minimize the bias stretch and to carefully balance the stretch in the warp and fill yarns. Stretch properties, and how they are used effectively, have many variations.

Sailmakers generally measure the stretch properties of sail cloth by pulling on it and recording the stretch in various directions. What is more interesting is how those properties get into the cloth in the first place and why.

Stretch properties depend primarily on two things — weave and finish. The weave builds inherent stretch properties into the cloth by placing certain sized yarns and a certain yarn spacing in both the warp and fill. Two basic categories of weave are mainsail weaves and genoa weaves.

Mainsail weaves tend to have larger fill threads to withstand the higher leech loads they are subjected to. Genoa fabrics are designed for maximum stretch resistance in the bias direction. In these fabrics, fill and warp stretch are balanced to allow the stretch between the leech and the mid-sections of the sail to work together to prevent or delay the sail from becoming too full or the draft from moving aft as wind pressure builds.

After weaving, a sail cloth must be finished so its final properties are precisely tailored to the requirements the particular sail is

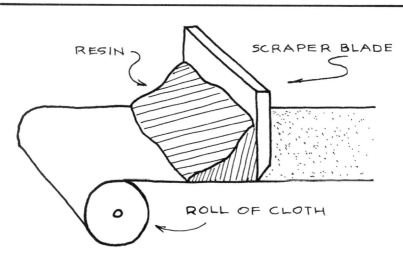

RESIN

SCRAPER BLADE

ROLL OF CLOTH

RESIN LIES UN TOP OF SAIL CLOTH
MAKING IT STIFFER AND MORE STRETCH
RESISTANT.

RESIN COATING

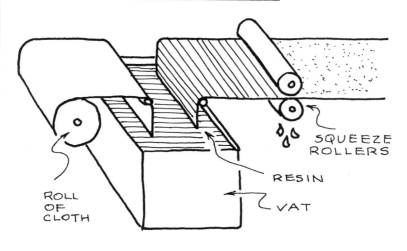

SQUEEZE
ROLLERS

RESIN

ROLL
OF
CLOTH

VAT

RESIN SOAKS INTO SAIL CLOTH
MAKING IT SOFTER AND MORE PLIABLE.
PURPOSE IS TO CONTROL STRETCH.

RESIN IMPREGNATING

SAILS

THE FINELY FITTED YACHT

destined for. Due to the wide range of possible finishes, the end use is vitally important. A one-design boat might need a firm finish to lock in the shape while a cruising sailor might desire a fairly soft finish for ease of handling. A tightly-woven fabric can be made soft (but relatively stretchy), hard and difficult to handle with extremely low stretch, or anywhere in between the two. The process requires taking the fabric as it comes off the loom and cleaning, shrinking, crushing and otherwise treating the cloth.

Beyond simply making the cloth stretchier or softer, the details of the stretch properties can be changed in finishing. For instance, the relative amounts of stretch in various directions can be adjusted to make the fabric work better for a certain application. This is an area that almost borders on alchemy and is very important in producing highly engineered, long-lasting sail cloth.

The two most important areas of finishing are shrinking the fabric with heat and applying resin to it. Dacron shrinks approximately 10 to 20 percent by panel length with heat. Shrinking an already tightly woven fabric causes additional tightening or jamming of the yarn intersections in the fabric and stabilizes the inherently unstable lattice structure of the weave. Shrinkage with heat combined with tight weaving builds power and resiliency into fabrics and gives them the guts to stand up to repeated luff tension, sheet trimming, wind loading and other factors.

Resins can also be used to further stabilize the fabric's structure. Currently, there are two types of resin applications in common use — impregnation, where the resin is put *into* the fabric, and coating, where the resin is applied to the surface of the fabric.

For sail cloth, the most widespread of these two methods is impregnation. In this process, the cloth is first passed through a solution containing a structural bonding resin, then squeezed to give uniform penetration, and finally dried at a closely regulated temperature. This process physically places the bonding agents into the fabric and between the filaments and yarn intersections where it ties the structure together from the inside. Resin curing is then carried out at high temperature and pressure, providing extraordinary internal bonding. A carefully resin-impregnated fabric will show no surface resin at all, even at a microscopic level. The additional resistance to stretch is built *into* the fabric. By playing around with the amount and type of resin that gets put into the fabric, many degrees of stretch resistance can be obtained.

When extremely high degrees of stretch resistance are required, Dacron fabrics are usually coated — one side only — with a very

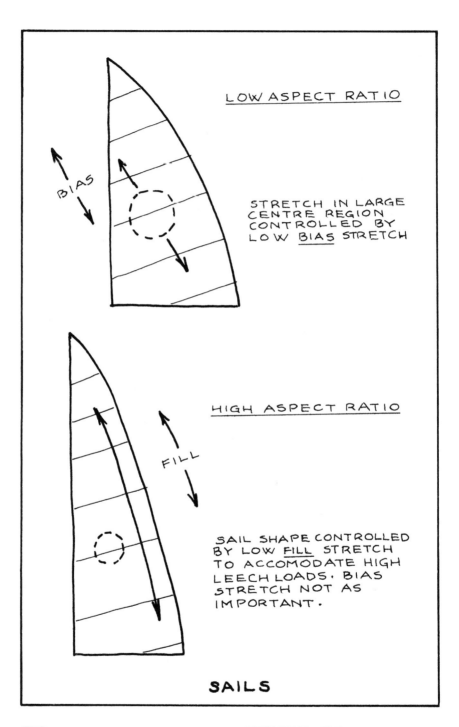

LOW ASPECT RATIO

STRETCH IN LARGE
CENTRE REGION
CONTROLLED BY
LOW BIAS STRETCH

HIGH ASPECT RATIO

SAIL SHAPE CONTROLLED
BY LOW FILL STRETCH
TO ACCOMODATE HIGH
LEECH LOADS. BIAS
STRETCH NOT AS
IMPORTANT.

SAILS

tough, very low stretch, resin. Dacron fabrics of this type are marketed under various names by various manufacturers (Condition Yarn Temper or Duroperm are just two) and are extremely crisp to the touch. They might be tough to get down a hatch, impossible to bag unless folded, and, generally, difficult to handle on a boat. However, they have extraordinary shape-holding capability. Sails built out of these fabrics hold their designed shape over a very large wind range and can eliminate the necessity to have special sails for various wind conditions.

In many cases, proper attention to the choice of fabric stretch properties (that is, the balance between fill, bias and warp stretch inherent in a particular weave) will allow you to avoid crispy, hard-to-handle fabrics with little or no reduction in sail performance. However, there are also many applications where a high degree of stretch resistance (even with increased handling problems) is very important. For instance, in most one-designs, the only way to get a jib to perform efficiently over the widest range of conditions is to use fabric that has been heavily impregnated or coated. On offshore racing boats as well, headsail materials, especially for lighter, full-sized genoas which must hold their shape over huge changes in wind loads, must be resinated to some degree. Remember, however, that resinated fabrics do not have to be ultra crisp. They can be very soft — almost indistinguishable from resin-free fabrics — and still have significantly reduced stretchiness. Your sailmaker knows best what the tradeoffs are for your boat and for your sailing, so if you want a sail that's easy to handle and don't care about ultimate shape holding, or if you don't care about handling as long as you're fast, he can probably make a recommendation on the best fabric to use.

A great deal has been said about the lasting properties of resinated fabrics, and the subject of resin in sail cloth is a controversial one. First of all, it is important to realize that resination is not black and white. The point is that there exists an infinite range of possibilities.

All fabrics, unresinated and resinated alike, become stretchier and softer for use. However, any good, tightly-woven, resinated fabric will never become softer or stretchier than an unresinated fabric of comparable weave that has been used — or abused — equally.

Modern resinated fabrics, even though they will eventually lose some of their resistance to stretch, have extraordinary lasting qualities. This is due largely to the fact that the resin actually prevents the stretching and inter-fiber movement that causes fabrics

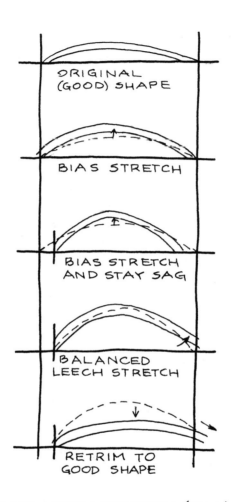

ORIGINAL (GOOD) SHAPE

BIAS STRETCH

BIAS STRETCH AND STAY SAG

BALANCED LEECH STRETCH

RETRIM TO GOOD SHAPE

BALANCING LEECH STRETCH (FILL) AND BIAS STRETCH IN GENOA FABRICS INCREASES THE USEFUL RANGE OF THE SAIL. SHOWN ABOVE IS A SEQUENCE OF STRETCH AND ADJUSTMENT IN A TYPICAL GENOA AS WIND STRENGTH CHANGES.

SAILS

THE FINELY FITTED YACHT

to break down. In addition, modern fabrics have resin stretch properties and fabric stretch properties arranged so the two complement and reinforce one another. This is tricky to do, but results in maximum ruggedness and shape-holding, combined with an excellent life span. My personal experience has been that, except on the very highest racing level where people tend to be a little superstitious, a sail built out of properly resinated fabric will stay fast for at least one or one-and-a-half seasons of hard racing — as long as the sail isn't severely abused.

The other side of the coin is that really excellent sails can be made out of extremely soft fabrics as long as the greater stretchiness of the fabric is understood and allowances are made by the sailmaker. These sails will be long-lasting, easy to handle, simple to store, and, generally, a joy to have around. If you're cruising, they're a must. If you race, there are lots of applications where soft sails will work fine. If you race seriously, you might have some sails you wish were softer to the touch, but you'll be thankful for their range because you won't have to keep changing them when the wind changes, and your boat will go faster.

Now, let's get back to our choice of fabrics for three boats — Finn, 505 and Cal-20.

The main differences between a Finn main and a 505 main are as follows: the 505 main sits on a mast that is stiffened by spreaders and deck level support and is therefore not very "bendy". Also, with a trapeze, the 505 becomes overpowered only in a very strong breeze. Even then, it can plane to windward by cracking off a bit and by allowing the sails to keep generating full power. A Finn, on the other hand, has no mast bend control at all and extremely limited stability. Therefore, the main must respond to mast bend and depower the boat simultaneously as the main sheet is trimmed in response to increasing wind strength.

The 505 main, then, needs to be able to maintain its shape over a very broad range of wind strength with relatively little mast bending taking place which would tend to flatten the sail. In this application, an extremely stiff fabric would be in order — with enough fill stretch resistance to keep the leech clean and controlled. Generally, a 4.5- to 5-ounce weight fabric with a "square" construction (equal weight yarns in warp and fill) might be necessary, giving good bias and fill stretch resistance, finished with either a super-stiff coating (like Duroperm or Condition Yarn Temper) or a firm impregnated resin. Actually, either fabric finish could be chosen, the final choice depending on how the sailmaker chose to design the sail.

For the Finn, a reasonable fill stretch would be desirable, but too stiff a fill would prevent the leech from opening enough to allow the sail to depower. However, in this case, a great deal of bias stretch and resilience is required to allow the sail to keep up with the mast bend and not over-flatten the sail. Of course, too much bias stretch would cause the sail to become fuller, so in this case, with sharply limited stability and a limited control of mast bend, choosing exactly the right balance of bias and fill stretch is critical if the sail is to allow the boat to be sailed effectively in a broad range of conditions. To obtain the correct amount of bias stretch, a lighter, softer fabric (say 4-ounce) is required, which, in addition, would have heavier fill yarns to resist the leech loads.

For the Cal-20, with its larger, overlapping jib, the main would tend to be trimmed tighter than a 505 main and would probably require stretch resistance on the fill. In addition, the larger jib tends to "pre-bend" the air in front of the main and reduce the pressure differentials which cause the sail to get fuller. That, combined with the desire on the part of many Cal-20 owners to have an easily handled sail, would lead a sailmaker to choose a softer fabric with less bias stretch resistance.

These hypothetical choices are not necessarily gospel however, since different sail designs and different sailing techniques can require different sail fabrics. It is your sailmaker's job to combine your boat's characteristics and your sailing needs to come up with a fabric choice and a sail design that will work best for you.

Jim Linville is the president of Dimension Sail Cloth in Putnam, Conn., a former world Tempest champion and an active one-design and offshore competitor.

tools

ACCESSORIES

The Dovetail Jig

It is difficult to ascertain why a dovetail joint carries such prestige, and why it evokes memories of the great days of fine craftsmanship — perhaps it reminds one of the times when joints such as these were done by hand, one dovetail at a time.

Romantic reminiscences aside, the dovetail is still an extremely functional joint, virtually unequalled in strength and practicality, especially for interior work. On the exterior of a yacht, the somewhat delicate dovetail could become a victim of weathering, especially if the wood is not varnished conscientiously.

The jig in the photo enables one to prepare an average joint (God only knows what that is) in about the same time as most other methods of joining would require. The only tool needed is a 3/8″ chuck electric drill motor. This should be of good quality, as the jig must be used at high revolutions (about 3,000) to perform the cleanest cuts with the fewest tear outs.

The jig comes with grid, bit assembly, guide handle (with depth stop) and, most happily, detailed illustrated instructions. It is obtainable for about $25 from the Princeton Company.

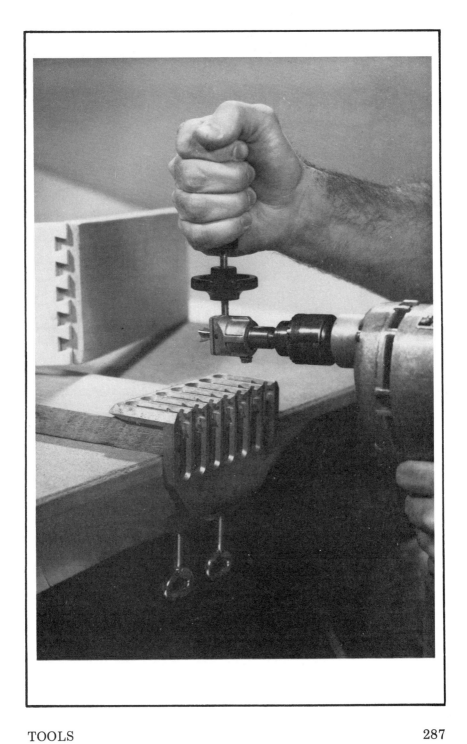

Centre Doweling Jig

Doweling is probably the best way to join boards, edge to edge. Using a tongue and groove joint is acceptable, but when working with expensive hardwoods, one does not want to waste even 1/2″ for a lap joint. Doweling is a rapid operation that leaves the full widths of the boards intact. The only equipment needed is a drill motor and a jig (see photo) which costs about $20.

The jig clamps boards from 7/16″ to 2-1/8″ in thickness, and its automatic self centring yields accurate centre drilling even on round stock. The drill guide is hardened, and the guide holes are drilled and reamed for extreme accuracy. Drill bit sizes accommodated are 1/4″, 5/16″, 3/8″, 7/16″ and 1/2″. If you're contemplating cabinet work of any quantity, you may as well fork over the $20 and get it over with.

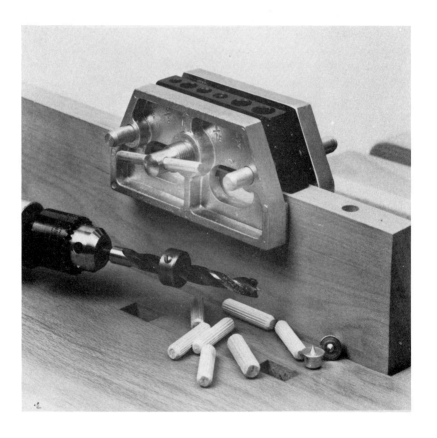

THE FINELY FITTED YACHT

Doweling Jig Clamps

Using dowels on right angle joints will save a great amount of time, because it eliminates the plugging of externally drilled holes. The doweling clamps shown make drilling of doweling holes simple and accurate. The clamps position the pieces and align the holes. The guides supplied are for 1/4″, 5/16″ and 3/8″ drill bits, and should be enough for most occasions.

The freestanding clamp (without the holes) remains stationary, while the guide clamp (with the holes) can be slid along as the drilling requires. The jig (as apparently most things nowadays) costs about $20, and again, if major cabinet work is anticipated, the investment can be well justified.

CHISELS AND KNIVES

Chisels

A good chisel should be well balanced, and designed for the work required. Delicate arcs cannot be cut with a 1″ wide blade and, conversely, attempting to chisel away a large mass with a 1/4″ sliver-picker is proof of lunacy.

I do not for a minute suggest that a different chisel be purchased for each line cut; indeed, a handful (small hand) of well thought out ones like 1/4″, 1/2″, 3/4″ and 1″, will do for all projects in this book. There are various things to examine when purchasing chisels and the following section will elaborate on these.

Generally

The bevel edge cabinet maker's chisels and square edge framing chisels are used for all general forming work and are usually struck with a mallet.

Mortise chisels are narrow chisels with thick heavy blades and a very broad bevel angle which serves to break waste when the chisel is employed to cut deep, square holes (mortises). These chisels are also meant to be struck strongly.

Conversely, chisels not designed to be struck are paring chisels. These are usually longer and more delicate and are always kept shaving-sharp, as they are moved solely by hand pressure.

Using any chisel requires a knack, one easily acquired, but nonetheless a knack. Practice makes perfect. However, here are a few hints: first, mark out your work carefully and accurately using a solid square of the right size for easy handling. Second, always begin work inside your marked lines and cut into the waste wood. Third, rough out the whole cut, pare away the waste carefully, and then pare carefully down to the mark for your final finish trimming. Using these basic rules, you'll have a nice clean-sided, flat-bottomed hole when you are finished.

Blade Stems

Basically, two types of blade stems exist, the socket and the hooped.

(a) Socket. The handle fits into a socket that is actually cast as part of the blade. These tools are designed for heavy malleting. This type of handle will retain a firm joint for a long time.

(b) Hooped. Here the end of the blade fits *into* the wood handle which is reinforced and kept from splitting by a metal hoop.

Normally, these are for lighter work, and are sometimes equipped with a leather stock-washer between the handle and the shoulder of the blade, to avoid unnecessarily "shocking" penetrations into the wood.

Handles

The modern composition handles seem to work very well although the connoisseur may prefer wooden ones. The best handles are made from rather rare boxwood. Ash is second best. Any wood handled chisel required to do heavy work should be equipped with a steel hoop at the free end to keep the handle from being mulched. An alternative is leather tipping.

Knives

A retractable bladed razor knife is a must for all workshops. It can cut insulation, sharpen pencils, and make very fine line markings on wood. The retractable blade is beautiful for stowing and eliminating nicks in the searching hand.

A refined cousin of this is a wooden handled European model, with a sheath over the blade. It can be sharpened instead of being replaced. It runs the entire length of the handle and can be gradually pulled out as the edge is ground.

Care

All chisels and knives should be sheathed when stored, to preserve the edge. Very simple inexpensive sheaths can be fabricated from cardboard and duct-tape. Make them and use them.

Lastly. A chisel is not an axe, a prying tool, screwdriver or wire cutter. It should be used with care. Cut to a small depth at a time, clear away rubble, then cut deeper.

Stones

Never use a stone without using ample oil. By carrying away the metal chips and bits of stone which have been ground off, the oil keeps the stone from clogging. If a stone becomes clogged with debris, put some oil on it and rub briskly with a rough cloth.

Washita is the most rapid cutting of the four grades of natural stones (Soft Arkansas, Hard Arkansas and Black-hard Arkansas being the others), and will produce the fastest edge. Soft Arkansas is the best general purpose stone and will produce a very sharp edge. Hard Arkansas is the best all-round stone for the final polishing of an already sharp tool. Black-hard Arkansas is the ultimate finishing stone. It's very slow cutting, but will produce an absolutely razor edge (for perfectionists).

India and Crystolon stones are man-made. India doesn't cut as fast as Crystolon. Fine India is roughly equivalent to Natural Washita, and therefore is a preliminary final honing stone. Crystolon is most useful when an edge is very dull or has been chipped and you need speed more than a sharp edge.

What to Buy

It's a good idea to have at least one very fast cutting stone to remove a lot of metal when you nick a blade or try to salvage a badly worn edge. Coarse Crystolon or Coarse India are best.

Next, you may have never gotten your tools as sharp as you can and should. The very sharpest edge works best, and once you've achieved it, occasional honing on a Hard or Black-hard Arkansas or stropping will maintain the edge; however, if the steel you are using is not the first quality, all the honing in the world won't help as the edge will crumble.

Lastly, you can skip a grade as you move up. In other words, you can move from a Washita to a Hard Arkansas as you are honing. A single stone with two different surfaces back to back is the best basic unit.

Honing Guide

Chisel and plane blades must have accurate bevels to work at their best. This can be hard to ensure when holding a blade by hand. A honing guide guarantees accurate bevels. There are a number of tools available to do this. The bevel you put on the blade is determined by how far back on the guide you hold the blade. The jaws of the guide are screwed tight to hold the blade in position, and then the guide is run along the stone on its roller. The usual angle is $25°$.

MARKING TOOLS

Accurate, well made tools which help you lay out your stock are invaluable. These tools are a delight to hold in your hand, to look at and, most important, to use. Excellent marking tools are not a luxury; they will help you avoid mistakes. Remember, measure twice and cut once.

Cutting Gauge

This is especially useful for scoring across the grain. A super sharp blade cuts cleanly without tearing. Solid brass strips inlaid in the rubbing face will make for long wear. It is adjustable with a thumb screw.

Double Slide Marking Gauge

This is a particularly useful tool. Both sides have a hardened steel pin for general marking, and top and bottom adjust independently with two steel thumb screws. The scales are usually fitted into the slide on both sides, allowing easy reading of the distance of the pin from the rubbing block. It can easily be used for mortising layout also.

Folding Rules

Folding rules fold neatly to fit into your pocket. They should be tough and close grained. Most are marked in inches (1/8″ graduations on one side and 1/16″ on the other).

Sliding Bevel

This is essential for marking off odd angles, dovetail work, and framing. It should have brass fittings to protect the ends against damage and a solid brass locking lever to allow adjustment.

Scratch Awl

A scratch awl is particularly good for light marking of layout. A very sharp point will scratch a super fine mark on the wood surface.

Calipers and Dividers

Inside calipers are designed for transferring or measuring interior dimensions, and outside calipers for transferring or measuring outside dimensions very accurately. Dividers are used for scribing arcs and circles, and can also be used to mark off absolutely straight or curved parallel lines. The bow springs and threaded spool mechanism ensures sensitive adjustment and that the settings will not change when transferring dimensions or marking out.

FILES

Filing is one of man's oldest arts. A good file or rasp used properly should cut cleanly and smoothly. The teeth should not "catch" the wood fibres. The right file does the work you want to do better and usually faster.

Files are formed by raising a continuous tooth evenly across the file. There are two basic kinds of files: single cut and double cut. The teeth in single cut files run in one direction only, but run in two directions on the double cut files. (The latter will cut quicker and more coarsely.)

Rasps differ from files in that the teeth are formed individually and are not connected to one another. Files will cut smoother than rasps, but when used on wood, will work much slower and are susceptible to clogging.

In order of ascending smoothness of cut, files are graded: Coarse, Bastard Cut, Second Cut, and Smooth. Rasps are graded in ascending order: Wood Rasp, Cabinet Rasp Bastard, Cabinet Rasp Second Cut, and Cabinet Rasp Smooth. In general, a longer file or rasp will have somewhat coarser teeth than a shorter one.

Your stock should be held firmly in a vise or clamp. For general filing, the stock should be at about elbow height. If the work requires heavier filing, it should be lower, and if that is finer, it should be near eye level.

In general, the file or rasp at the handle end should be held in your hand with your thumb along the top edge. The other end of the file or rasp should be grasped with the thumb and forefinger of your other hand.

PLANES

Until 30 or 40 years ago, a craftsman could literally get hundreds of different types of planes.

In this day of power-driven tools, we are apt to forget how important hand planes are for fine woodworking. Each plane has its own special purpose — work which it can do more easily and accurately than any other. Not only can you usually do more careful (and better) work with a hand plane, but also — often because of power tool set-up time — you can work faster. For example, the scrub plane can rough out stock very rapidly.

Skill at hand planing is one of the most important abilities of any craftsman. Experience with hand planes will help you understand exactly what a power tool is doing when you use it for a particular job (an important and subtle appreciation if one is to achieve consistently good results with power tools). Also, a hand plane is a far more forgiving tool. Careful work sacrificed for speed can ruin more otherwise good work than anything else.

Here are a few hints about using any plane. First, keep the blade as sharp as possible. The Bench Oilstones and the Honing Guide are excellent for this purpose. Second, generally plane *with* the grain. (Look at the side of the stock and you can easily see which way the grain runs.) If you don't work with the grain, you run the danger of "catching the grain," lifting chips of wood and producing a rough surface.

When planing end grain, push the plane one way to the middle of the board only; then repeat this process going in the other direction. This prevents splitting the board at the edge.

Sharpening Plane Irons

There are two steps to putting a proper edge on any plane iron: grinding (i.e. shaping) the edge, and honing. Grinding may be required when the edge has developed a nick, whenever the edge has become "thick" due to frequent honing, or if the bevel has become rounded due to rocking on the oilstone.

When grinding, a good natural grindstone used with water is best. Thus, there is no danger of drawing the temper out of the edge by excessive heat buildup. The shape of the edge for a bench plane when used for rough, course work can be rounded slightly by 1/64" to 1/32". For more general work, a square edge with the sharpness just rounded off the corners is preferred. For jointing, the entire edge must be dead square.

Wooden Body Planes

In Colonial days the standard plane used by cabinet makers and carpenters alike had a wood body. A fully equipped workshop might have as many as 30 or 40 — one for every shape needed. A wood block wedged in the body of the plane was used to hold the steel cutting blade in place. In North America, we gradually have grown accustomed to using the "Stanley-type" steel body plane, as the knurled knob blade adjuster was easier to use than the wood wedge.

However, there is no real substitute for the wood-bodied plane. Although not now best for casual carpenters, a wood plane will produce better results on important pieces. The wood sole will not mar the work surface, and the wood-to-wood contact between the sole and the stock lets the plane slide easier than with a steel-bodied plane. Also, because a wooden plane is lighter than a comparable steel plane (superior planing is accomplished by pushing a sharp blade *through* the wood, *not into it*), it is less fatiguing to use.

The Use of Bench Planes

Of all the bench planes, the Jack is usually the first to be used — for the preliminary cleaning up and squaring of stock and the accurate truing of short edges. For truing long edges, the Jointer (Trying) Plane must be used. The Smooth Plane is used for final smoothing on flat surfaces of any roughness after a Jack Plane has been used and after gluing.

The most common fault when using bench planes is "dipping". For accurate results, it is critical to avoid this. Just pay attention to the following two simple rules:

— At the beginning of each stroke, put slightly more pressure on the front of the plane.

— At the end of the stroke, keep slightly more pressure on the back of the plane.

HAND SAWS

The difference between an adequate saw and the best lies in the balance of the tool, the ruggedness and comfort of the handle, the quality of the steel (plus the accuracy and sharpness of the teeth), and, in general, ease of use.

There are many different types of saws — both as to size and design. As usual, each will perform its own special function best. For example, you can crosscut a board with a Rip Saw, but it will work much slower and will produce a very rough finish. In contrast to a Rip Saw where the teeth are set and filed to cut with their points, Crosscut Saw teeth are filed to cut with their edges and shaped with no hook to prevent snagging on wood fibers. Select the proper saw for each job and you will do better work.

CLAMPING TOOLS

Woodworking is made unnecessarily difficult when you are not able to hold or clamp your work in the proper position — quickly, easily, and accurately — with no movement of the stock.

Every workshop should have a number of clamps with different functions, as each does its job better than any other can.

Usually, when using any portable clamp, place a wood pad between the clamp and the wood surface. Always wipe up excess glue right away and apply pressure gradually. Clamps can exert tremendous force, so apply only enough to get the job done. Check squareness and alignment as you draw up.

Now, a word or two about how to select your clamps. There is an old saying in woodworking that you can never have enough clamps. While certainly not literally true, the saying has a certain ring of truth to it because most woodworkers never think about what clamps they need until the last minute — often just before gluing up. At that point it's really too late, and they find themselves trying as best they can to make do. At the very least, the result is a lot of aggravation. At worst, it means out of square frames, buckled panels, or glue set before final assembly can be completed and aligned.

Don't ignore the needs of your shop for proper clamps. Think about what you really had to have (but didn't) during the past year. You should have on hand at least three of each size or type of the clamps that you do decide to maintain. Also, in general, stock longer or larger clamps than short ones — although the very small ones are terrific for work on smaller pieces where the larger, heavier clamps would simply overwhelm the workpiece.

Miter Clamp

Here is an interesting "one evening" project that will provide you with an uncomplicated clamping jig with many advantages for mitering. It is adjustable to any size frame; it applies uniform pressure to all four joints simultaneously; it leaves joints visible so you can be sure they are *straight and tight*; it is light and easy to handle, minimizing the danger of damage to frames; and it eliminates the necessity of buying a clamp for each joint.

This practical jig overcomes the disadvantages of most other "miter clamps" which hold work of very limited size range, and apply little, if any, pressure to the joint itself.

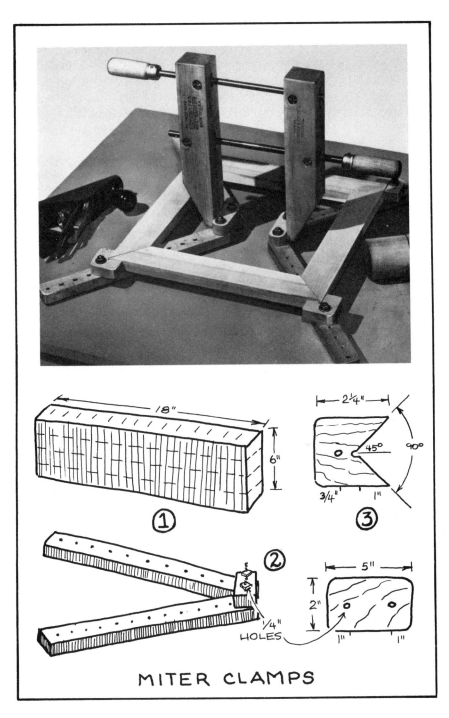

① 18" 6"

② ¼" HOLES

③ 2¼" 45° 90° ¾" 1"

5" 2" 1" 1"

MITER CLAMPS

Legs

(Four required.) Use straight, clear hardwood strips 1″ × 1¾″ × 18″ long, or as much longer as you wish, for the jobs intended. To make the legs, take a piece of 2″ × 6″ (1¾″ × 5½″), stand it on edge, mark its centre line down its spine, then very carefully mark 1″ intervals along the line and drill 1/4″ holes as marked through the entire width. Accuracy is important. Now rip the wood into four 1¾″ × 1″ pieces.

Counterbore all holes on the underside of each leg to accommodate the flat-head machine screw to be used in the assembly of the clamp. This will permit the clamp to lie flat on the bench.

Swivel Bars

(Two required.) Use the same 1″ × 1¾″ hardwood cut 5″ long. Locate centres 1″ in from each end, and drill 1/4″ diameter holes. Round the ends for neat appearance.

Corner Blocks

(Four required.) Make these from the same hardwood stock, cut 2¼″ long. Mark for two 1/4″ diameter holes, with one of them being 1″ in from the end so it will be centred at the bottom of the right-angle "V". This will provide relief for the corners of the frame being clamped so that it will draw up properly, without crushing any sharp corners on the frame. Cut perfect 90° recesses into each block.

Assembly

You will need eight 1/4″ × 2¼″ flat-head machine screws, with nuts or wing-nuts to fit. Assemble the swivel bars onto the legs as illustrated. The corner blocks are assembled into each of the legs at positions determined by the size of the frame to be mitered. Make certain that the corner blocks are assembled at the same relative position in each leg.

Clamping

With both pairs of legs placed on the bench so that the swivel bars are on top, the four corner blocks can be roughly positioned to fit the frame. The swivel bars should be parallel to each other, and separated by some convenient distance. Pressure is applied by drawing the swivel bars together by means of a Handscrew. On very large frames, the swivel bars may be a considerable distance apart, in which case a bar clamp can be used.

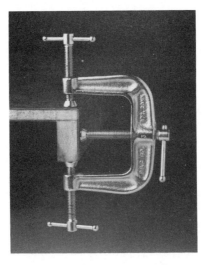

Three-way edging clamp provides "right-angle" pressure to the edge, or side, of work.

LIST OF SUPPLIERS

CATALOGS

Spyglass
2415 Mariner Square Drive
Alameda, CA 94501

> *The* Spyglass *catalogue is actually a very beautifully produced reference volume, edited by a most gracious gentleman by the name of Dick Moore. The contents depart from standard catalogue fare with many articles and outfitting tips, aside from the few hundred pages of all marine gear imaginable.*

Thomas Foulkes
Landsdown Road, Leytonstone
London, England, E11 3HB

> *This has been the bible of cruising boat outfitters for many years. The catalogues normally run about 200 pages and cost about $10, but are well worth the price.*

Lands' End Catalog
2317 N. Elston
Chicago, IL 60614

Mariners Catalog
National Fisherman and International
Marine Publishing Co.
Camden, ME

James Bliss Co.
Dedham, MA 02026

Manhattan Marine
116 Chambers Street
New York, NY 10007

Jay Stuart Haft
8925 N. Tennyson Dr.
Milwaukee, WI 53217

THE FINELY FITTED YACHT

SPARS

Le Fiel
Mast and rigging, aluminum
13700 Firestone Blvd.
Santa Fe Springs, CA 90670

Shepperd Woodworks
Wood spars
21020 70th West
Edmonds, WA 98020

Super Spar
Masts, aluminum
7231 Rosecrans Ave.
Paramount, CA 90723

Forespar
Spars and fittings
3140 Pullman St.
Costa Mesa, CA 92627

Metal Mast Marine
Aluminum spars and related fittings
P.O. Box 471
Putnam, CT 06260

Sparcraft
Masts and assorted hardware
P.O. Box 925, 770 W. 17th St.
Costa Mesa, CA 92627

Forespar, Inc.
Rigging and spinnaker poles
3140 Pullman St.
Costa Mesa, CA 92626

WOOD

American Forest Products
All hardwoods and marine plywood
14103 Park Place
Cerritos, CA 90701

American Hardwood
1900 E. 15th St.
Los Angeles, CA 90021

Rogers Woodworking
Custom marine woodwork
874 W. 18th St.
Costa Mesa, CA 92627

Albano Marine Woodwork
Custom wood parts
% Wave Traders
1702 Bridgeway
Sausalito, CA 94965

H & L Woodwork
2965 E. Harcourt St.
Compton, CA 90221

The Harbor Sales Co.
Marine plywoods
1401 Russell St.
Baltimore, MD 21230

Penberthy
5800 S. Boyle Ave.
Los Angeles, CA 90058

RIGGING

Forespar
3140 Pullman St.
Costa Mesa, CA 92627

Hood Industries Rigging
951 Newhall St.
Costa Mesa, CA 92627

Ronstan (Alexander Roberts)
Running rigging
1851 Langley Ave.
Irvine, CA 92705

Universal Wire Products, Inc.
Rigging
222 Universal Drive
North Haven, CT 06473

DECK HARDWARE

American Precision Marine
Deck hardware
1260 Montauk Highway E.
Patachoque, NY 11772

Barient
Winches, etc.
936 Bransten Road
San Carlos, CA 94070

Barlow Winches
Alexander Roberts Co.
1851 Langley Ave.
Irvine, CA 92705

Clamcleat
Sneve-Nysether Co.
Box 1201
Everett, WA 98206

Gibb
Winches, turnbuckles, hardware, Hasler vang gear
82 Border St.
Cohasset, MD 02025

Harken
Blocks
1251 E. Wisconsin Ave.
Pewaukee, WI 53072

Hye
Deck gear
1075 Shell Blvd., #12
Foster City, CA 94404

Johnson Yacht Hardware
Lifeline hardware
Main Street
Middle Haddam, CT 06456

Lewmar Marine Yacht Hardware
Winches and rigging hardware
892 W. 18th St.
Costa Mesa, CA 92627

Merriman Holbrook
Complete line of deck hardware including winches
301 River St.
Grand River, OH 44045

Navtec Inc.
Rigging hardware
P.O. Box 277, Maynard Industrial Park
Maynard, MA 01754

Nicro-Fico
Complete line of hardware for running rigging
2065 N. Ave 140th
San Leandro, CA 94577

Ronstan (Alexander Roberts)
1851 Langley Ave.
Irvine, CA 92705

Schaeffer Marine
Complete line of deck and running rigging hardware
Industrial Park
New Bedford, MA 02745

Wilcox-Crittendon
Complete line of marine hardware
Middletown, CT 06457

GENERAL HARDWARE

Harding Machine Marine Parts
Individual custom hardware
1733 Monrovia Ave., Suite N
Costa Mesa, CA 92627

Harris Marine
Individual custom hardware
1281 Logan
Costa Mesa, CA 92626

Vic Berry
Best fuel and water tanks in the whole world
760 Newton Way
Costa Mesa, CA 92627

R.C. Plath Co.
Bronze hardware and anchor windlasses
337 N.E. 10th Ave.
Portland, OR 97232

Caseco
All types stainless steel fasteners
1215 S. State College Blvd.
Fullerton, CA 92631

Moritz Foundry
Windlass and other beautiful bronze cast marine hardware
133 Industrial Way
Costa Mesa, CA 92627

Beckson Manufacturing
Pumps, vents, hatches, etc.
Box 3336
Bridgeport, CT 06605

Danforth
Anchors, compasses, instruments
500 Riverside Industrial Parkway
Portland, ME 04013

Mariner Yacht Hardware
Blocks, deck hardware
1714 Seventeenth
Santa Monica, CA 90404

Nicro-Fico
Complete line of hardware for running rigging
2065 W. Ave 140th
San Leandro, CA 94577

PYHI
ABS plastic portlights and vents
1647 N. Avalon Blvd.
Wilmington, CA 90744

Rostand, Inc.
Ecclesiastical brass and marine hardware
Milford, CT 06460

Seagull Marine
Avon, Whale pumps, CQR anchors and Simpson Lawrence
Windlass and British hardware
1851 McGaw Ave.
Irvine, CA 92705

Wilcox-Crittendon
Complete line of marine hardware
Middleton, CT 06457

Yacht Specialties Co., Inc.
Wheel steering
15 5 E. St. Gertrude Place
Santa Ana, CA 92705

Bomar Company
Hatches
1021 E. State St.
Westport, CT 06880

ELECTRONICS

Dawn Electronics Corp.
Knotmeter and taffrail log
P.O. Box 91736
Los Angeles, CA 90009

Davis Instruments
Navigation supplies
857 Thornton St.
San Leandro, CA 94577

Fisheries Supply
Everything
Pier 55
Seattle, WA 98101

Kenyon Marine
Navigation instruments, hardware
New Whitfield St.
Guilford, CT 06437

Ray Jefferson
Radios, electronics, instruments
Main & Cotton St.
Philadelphia, PA 19127

Signet Scientific Comp.
Yacht instruments
129 E. Tujunga Ave., P.O. Box 6489
Burbank, CA 91510

Telcor Instruments Inc.
Yacht instruments
17785 Sky Park Circle, Box CC
Irvine, CA 92664

VDO Instruments
Knotmeters
116 Victor
Detroit, MI 48203

GENERAL

Ferro Corp.
All fiberglass materials
18811 Fiberglass Road
Huntington Beach, CA 92648

Detco Grove
Two part polysulfide caulking for teak decks
3452 East Foothill Blvd.
Pasadena, CA 91107

Larwyck Development
Windvanes
17330 Raymer St.
Northridge, CA

Dickinson Marine
Diesel stoves and heaters
#103 4241 21st Ave. West
Seattle, WA 98199

Marine Vane Gears
Windvanes
Cowes, Isle of Wight
England

Alco Mining
Lead ballast casting
16908 S. Broadway
Gardena, CA

Norcold Inc.
Refrigerators
11121 Weddington
North Hollywood, CA 91601

Norton Products
Holding plate refrigeration systems
173-M Monrovia Ave.
Costa Mesa, CA 92627

Thalco Uniglas Co.
Fiberglass
1212 McGaw Ave.
Santa Ana, CA 92705

Boat Transit
Boat hauling cross-country
P.O. Box 1403
Newport Beach, CA 92663

Fatsco
Beautiful solid fuel ship's stoves
251 N. Fair Ave.
Benton Harbor, MI

Lavender Fasteners
All stainless steel fasteners
884 W. 18th St.
Costa Mesa, CA 92627

Southwest Instruments
Navigation aids, marine supplies, books and everything you can dream of
235 W. 7th St.
San Pedro, CA

Aquadron/Acme
First aid kits
1113 Johnston Building
Charlotte, NC 28281

Atlantis
Foul weather gear
Waitsfield, VT 05673

Canor Plarex
Foul weather gear
4200 23rd Ave. W.
Seattle, WA 98199

Aonolite
Reinforced fiberglass foam
425 Maple Ave.
Carpentersville, IL 60110

Doris Hammond
Canvas bags
260 Kearny St.
San Francisco, CA 94108

Edson
Steering equipment
480 E. Industrial Park Road
New Bedford, MA 02745

Guest
Yacht lights
17 Culbro Drive
West Hartford, CT 06110

Interlux Paints
Marine finishes
220 S. Linden Ave.
So. San Francisco, CA 94080

A.B. Optimus
Stoves and lanterns
P.O. Box 907, 1251 Beach Blvd.
La Habra, CA 90631

Paul Luke Inc.
Stoves and cabin heater
East Boothbay, ME 04544

Sailrite Kits
Sail and awning kits
2010 Lincoln Blvd.
Venice, CA 90291

Samson Cordage Works
Dacron and nylon braided line
470 Atlantic Ave.
Boston, MA 02210

Z-Spar Koppers Co. Inc.
Marine finishes
1900 Koppers Building
Pittsburgh, PA 15219

Woolsey Marine Ind.
Marine finishes and winches
201 E. 42nd St.
New York, NY 10017

TOOLS

The following companies have some of the most beautiful tools imaginable. Their catalogues alone are a feast for the craftsman's eyes.

Brookstone
127 Vose Farm Road
Peterborough, NH 03458

Garrett Wade
302 Fifth Avenue
New York, NY 10001

Leichtung
701 Beta Dr. #17
Cleveland, OH 44143

Adjustable Clamp Co.
417 N. Ashland Ave.
Chicago, IL 60622

The Princeton Co.
P.O. Box 276
Princeton, MA

WOODWORKINGS

H&L Marine Woodworking Inc.
2965 E. Harcourt St.
Compton, CA 90221

H&L is the major North American source of prefabricated teak or mahogany wood workings. Their range spans from the simplest flag pole, through items like towel racks, doors, drawers, magazine racks, book racks, etc. They will also custom fabricate hatches, cockpit grates and swimsteps to your specifications. Their work is usually of very good quality and their prices are most reasonable. A number of ideas in this volume were taken from their products.

GLOSSARY OF TERMS

— A —

Acetone — A very combustible, fast evaporating, fluid used for cleaning surfaces. The only thing that will dissolve and clean polyester resin.

Arbour — An attachment used with a drill motor; supports hole saws of different sizes. Usually has a drill bit inserted through its center.

— B —

Back-Up Plates — Reinforcing plates, usually steel or brass, used when bolting through vulnerable material such as wood or fiberglass.

Bedlog — A set of raised tracks upon which the main hatch slides.

Bevel — The act of cutting to a taper.

Bevel Square — An adjustable tool which, with two arms and a wingnut, can be used to duplicate or record angles.

Bolt Rope — Roping around the edge of a sail or awning, needed to distribute the strain on the cloth.

Bull-Nose — (A) to round off a sharp edge; (B) a concave bladed router bit used to round off a sharp edge; (C) the rounded edge itself.

Butt Connector — A metal press fitting that unites two wires end to end without complex splicing.

— C —

Cap Nut — A finishing nut with one side sealed off.

Carriage Bolt — A smooth-headed bolt with squared shoulders to keep it from turning.

THE FINELY FITTED YACHT

Center Punch — A pointed tool for making marks on wood or metal.

Cleat Stock — Square cross-sectioned strips of wood used to join perpendicularly uniting pieces of plywood.

Countersink — To set the head of a screw or bolt below the surface; tool used for this purpose.

— D —

Deck Beams — Athwartship beams that support the deck.

Dolfinite — A very oily bedding compound best used on fiberglass to wood, or wood to wood joints.

Dovetailing — A very positive method of corner joints for wood, using intermeshing wedge shapes for each piece as fasteners.

Dovetail Saw — A very stiff-bladed hand saw with a well reinforced blade for very accurate cutting.

Dowels — Wood turnings used as a common attachment, usually to join boards edge to edge.

— E —

Elbow Catch — A spring loaded catch for cabinet doors, usually hidden and accessible through a finger hole.

Epoxy Glue and Resin — A high strength synthetic adhesive that will stick anything to anything.

Eye — A closed loop, in wire-rope or line.

— F —

Feather — To even two adjoining levels into each other.

Flare — To widen or ream the end of a pipe for coupling purposes.

Flathead — A bevel-shouldered screw.

Gelcoat — A very hard outer coating (usually color pigmented) of a fiberglass boat.

Grommet — A brass eye sewn or pressed into canvas work.

– H –

Hack Saw — A very fine tooth bladed saw (the blade is removable) made for metal cutting.

Hatch Coaming — Built up buffer around the inside of a hatch opening to keep out water intruding under the hatch.

Hole Saws — Circular, heavy walled saw blades of infinite diameters used in conjunction with a drill motor to cut holes.

Hose Barb — A tapered fitting, with terraced ridges that allow a hose to slip on but not off.

Hose Clamp — An adjustable stainless steel ring used to fasten hoses to fittings.

Hose Ties — Plastic ties with a barbed tongue and eye used to fasten hoses to bulkheads, sole, etc.

– I –

Inboard — Toward the centreline.

– K –

Key Hole Saw — A very narrow bladed hand saw with one end of the blade unsupported, used for hole or curve cutting.

– M –

Machine Screw — A fine threaded, slot headed fastener made to be used with a tapped hole.

Mat — An unwoven fiberglass material made up of randomly layered short fibres.

Miter Box — A wood or metal frame which is used with a hand saw to cut material at a given angle.

Miter Gauge — The sliding fitting on a table or band saw against which the piece of wood is laid to assure a straight cut. The gauge itself is adjustable to any angle required.

Molding — Trimming pieces of wood or plastic that hide joints or mistakes or both.

— O —

Oval Head — A screw with a head of that shape.

— P —

Pad Eye — A through bolted deck fitting to accommodate blocks, lines, etc.

Pet Cock — A small 90° turn off-on valve ideal for fuel switch.

Plastic Resin Glue — A powder base, mixed with water, that forms a very strong, water-resistant glue.

Plug — A tight fitting wood dowel used to fill screw-head holes.

Polysulfide — An unbelievably effective, totally waterproof sealing-bedding compound.

— R —

Rabbet — A groove cut in a plank.

Resorcinol Glue — A two-part, completely waterproof, glue.

— S —

Scribe — To reproduce the curve of a surface onto another surface by using a compass with pencil.

GLOSSARY   317

Sheet Metal Screw — Coarse treaded, self-tapping screw.

Shrink Tubes — Plastic tubing slipped over wire splices then shrunk by heat to seal the splice.

Silicone Seal — A quick drying non-hardening sealing compound.

Swedge — Method of attaching, by pressure, fittings onto a wire rope.

— T —

Thimble — A round or heart-shaped metal–eye chafe protector, around which rope can be seized.

— V —

Vented Loop — A bronze fitting with a valve that prevents siphoning of water into appliances below the waterline.